The Rise and Fall of James Busby

The Rise and Fall of James Busby

His Majesty's British Resident in New Zealand

PAUL MOON

BLOOMSBURY ACADEMIC
LONDON · NEW YORK · OXFORD · NEW DELHI · SYDNEY

BLOOMSBURY ACADEMIC
Bloomsbury Publishing Plc
50 Bedford Square, London, WC1B 3DP, UK
1385 Broadway, New York, NY 10018, USA

BLOOMSBURY, BLOOMSBURY ACADEMIC and the Diana logo are trademarks of
Bloomsbury Publishing Plc

First published in Great Britain 2020

Copyright © Paul Moon, 2020

Paul Moon has asserted his right under the Copyright, Designs and Patents Act,
1988, to be identified as Author of this work.

Cover design by Tjaša Krivec
Cover image: Busby, James 1800–1871 (© Burton Bros, photographer/Hocken Collections)

All rights reserved. No part of this publication may be reproduced or transmitted
in any form or by any means, electronic or mechanical, including photocopying,
recording, or any information storage or retrieval system, without prior permission
in writing from the publishers.

Bloomsbury Publishing Plc does not have any control over, or responsibility for, any
third-party websites referred to or in this book. All internet addresses given in this book
were correct at the time of going to press. The author and publisher regret any
inconvenience caused if addresses have changed or sites have ceased to exist,
but can accept no responsibility for any such changes.

Every effort has been made to trace copyright holders and to obtain their permissions
for the use of copyright material. The publisher apologizes for any errors or omissions
and would be grateful if notified of any corrections that should be incorporated in
future reprints or editions of this book.

A catalogue record for this book is available from the British Library.

Library of Congress Cataloging-in-Publication Data
Names: Moon, Paul, author.
Title: The rise and fall of James Busby : His Majesty's British Resident in
New Zealand / Paul Moon.
Other titles: His Majesty's British Resident in New Zealand
Description: London ; New York : Bloomsbury Academic, 2020. | Includes bibliographical
references and index.
Identifiers: LCCN 2020019738 (print) | LCCN 2020019739 (ebook) |
ISBN 9781350116641 (hb) | ISBN 9781350116658 (pb) | ISBN 9781350116665 (ePDF) |
ISBN 9781350116672 (eBook)
Subjects: LCSH: Busby, James, 1801-1871. | Colonial administrators—Great Britain—
Biography | Colonial administrators–New Zealand—Biography. | New Zealand—Politics and
government—19th century. | Diplomats—Great Britain–Biography | Maori (New Zealand
people)—Government relations--19th century. | Treaty of Waitangi (1840 February 6) |
Declaration of Independence of the United Tribes of New Zealand (1835)
Classification: LCC DU422.B8 M66 2020 (print) | LCC DU422.B8 (ebook) |
DDC 993.01092 [B]--dc23
LC record available at https://lccn.loc.gov/2020019738
LC ebook record available at https://lccn.loc.gov/2020019739

ISBN: HB: 978-1-3501-1664-1
       PB: 978-1-3501-1665-8
       ePDF: 978-1-3501-1666-5
       eBook: 978-1-3501-1667-2

Typeset by RefineCatch Limited, Bungay, Suffolk

To find out more about our authors and books visit www.bloomsbury.com
and sign up for our newsletters.

Contents

Preface   vii
A Note on Conventions   xi
Acknowledgements   xiii

1   The Ambitions of the Father   1
2   The Tenacity of the Son   15
3   'I am to Take Charge'   33
4   Cardinal Virtues   55
5   Convergence   83
6   Landed   107
7   Trouble at Home   133
8   Independence   159
9   Visitors and Schemers   179
10 The Rattlesnake   205
11 'Your Functions will Cease'   227
12 'Satan Rules'   243
13 The Ink-blotter   265
14 Colossal   283
15 Everlasting   303

Bibliography   321
Index   341

Preface

Once an idea enters the historical bloodstream and begins to circulate, it can be very difficult to remove. This is particularly so when it comes to people's reputations, and is certainly borne out in the case of James Busby. With no counsel to defend him, he has suffered at the hands of generations of historians whose representations of the man have been largely unfavourable. Admittedly, even while he was alive, his reputation was sometimes smeared by his superiors, and ridiculed by those he represented. But it is in death that the disparaging depiction of his character and abilities was embalmed. In 1898, the politician and sometime historian, William Pember Reeves, portrayed Busby's career as Resident as 'a prolonged burlesque', and then warming to this condemnatory theme, alleged it was 'a farce without laughter, played by a dull actor in serious earnest', who was 'small-minded' and 'caustic'.[1]

From this point, the contagion began to spread, and by the later twentieth century, Busby's reputation as someone who was vain, inept, petulant and prickly was entombed in the historiography of the period. In Keith Sinclair's view, he was a 'pompous young man', who 'found himself cast as the central figure in a solemn farce'.[2] Peter Adams denounced Busby as a 'small-minded man when it came to his own prestige and the trappings of his newly acquired position', who quarrelled 'over the size and lavishness of his house', and who confirmed the prejudices of others through his 'pedantry and pomposity',[3] while Claudia Orange unflatteringly depicted Busby as a 'pernickety and troublesome character when his personal interests were affected'.[4] From such a confluence of condemnatory assessments spanning more than a century, Busby's character has stood little chance of a fair hearing.

Unwittingly, such criticisms have simply ended up echoing the sorts of chauvinism that surfaced when Busby served as Resident in New Zealand. And although the archival material from the period sometimes seems to support such views, so much of that material is the product of those who

---

[1] W. P. Reeves, *The Long White Cloud: Ao Tea Roa* (London: Horace Marshall & Son, 1898), 158–9.
[2] K. Sinclair, *A History of New Zealand* (Auckland: Penguin, 1988), 51.
[3] P. Adams, *Fatal Necessity: British Intervention in New Zealand, 1830–1847* (Auckland: Auckland University Press, 1977), 41.
[4] C. Orange, *The Treaty of Waitangi* (Wellington: Allen and Unwin, 1987), 14.

bore some animus towards Busby. Beneath the thick sediment of official correspondence from the era that has contributed to this characterization lies a bedrock of prejudice: the prejudice of establishment versus outsider; of ruling-class versus working-class; of military versus civilian; of English versus Scot; of experienced versus novice; of Church of England versus Church of Scotland; and many other forms of rivalry that riddled the relationships Busby endured with others, and that shaped subsequent representations of him.

Surveying the quarries of evidence from which aspects of Busby's life can be excavated requires analysis, but it also demands insight. Summing up his life in a few pithy and sometimes poisonous phrases might accord with other purposes, but it does not allow either the detailed relief of his character to be examined, or a coherent explanation for his views and decisions. In brushing off the detritus that has accumulated around Busby's reputation since the nineteenth century, the evidence explored here in relation to his life reveals a very different person from that rendered by his contemporaries, and later by some historians. His intellectual abilities were far greater than have been conceded, his resolve to innovate rather than merely to go through the motions of whatever role he held led to unexpected advances in the posts he was given, and while committed to particular ideas, he was seldom stubbornly doctrinaire in their pursuit. When flexibility was required, he could bend with the best of them.

Of course, there were shortcomings too. His naturally dour personality did not endear him to others, and sometimes inadvertently gave the impression of aloofness. He had few close associates, and fewer friends, and his overly earnest approach to the challenges so often strewn in front of him sometimes gave others the sense that he was too earnest, too rigid, and in many ways an unlikeable individual. Yet his enduring legacy, particularly in New Zealand, is the greatest testimony to his remarkably idiosyncratic approach to circumstances. He is also a person without comparison in New Zealand history. No other individual occupied the role of Resident, no other played a vital part in the drafting of two of the country's founding documents in the era, and no other British representative was required to establish peace and order in the country without any means of enforcing his rule. To this extent, any account of Busby's life must avoid merely positioning him as a point in the continuum of British imperial expansion in the South Pacific, and explore his life on its own terms.

While any account of James Busby will necessarily encompass histories of colonies, empire, and indigenous peoples, as well as the geographies, economies, and cultures of many territories, this work is foremost a biography of an individual rather than a colonial history, in which individuals tend to feature more as mere moving parts in a great imperial apparatus. In addition, it is a biography written as much as possible from the perspective of the

PREFACE

subject. Standing on an outcrop overlooking the past, it is easy to trace the inevitability of events, and judge those involved accordingly. However, no individual is granted such omniscience over their own life and destiny, and so it is with this account of Busby, in which events unfold in front of him in the way he experienced them, rather than with the benefit of a historian's hindsight.

Unavoidably, the documentary record trailing Busby's life is uneven, and there are times when his voice falls silent. Potentially vital records relating to his parents' relationship and their movement around eastern Scotland at the end of the eighteenth century perished during a church fire at St Mary's Whitekirk and Tyninghame Parish Church in 1914. Other family documents from this period have simply disappeared, including material dealing with the family's financial situation, and the education the Busby children received.

One of the most important sources of information on Busby's life up until his thirties was the collection of correspondence between himself and his parents and siblings. In these letters, valuable insights into his thoughts on a range of issues were revealed. Surprisingly, for the scale of this archive, his previous biographer, the journalist Eric Ramsden, made only scant use of them, preferring to rush through this period of Busby's earlier life in order to focus more on his later career as Resident in New Zealand. The State Library of New South Wales holds the copy of this correspondence on microfilm, but on enquiring about access to it, I was told that the microfilm reel was 'affected by the acid syndrome and was withdrawn from the State Library Collection'. Hoping that a set of the correspondence still lay somewhere in the Library's archives, I sought further details, and discovered that the original letters had been in the possession of the family at the time when the (now irreparably damaged) microfilm was made. The Library had made many requests to make a new microfilm of the Busby family papers but was unable to obtain the cooperation of the owner before his death in 1998. The owner who lent the papers to the Library for copying back in 1964 was Tom Merewether Heath, and he had passed away by this time. In 2005, other family members were contacted but they did not know the whereabouts of the original papers. They were contacted again in 2018 to see if the papers had been located, but evidently, it looks as though they are now lost.

Fortuitously, a transcript of much of this correspondence was produced by Augusta Busby (who died in 1962), and while it is the single most important collection about the family, it suffers from editing decisions which in some sections render the record incomplete. However, it remains a substantial repository of the family's life, mainly through the letters between its members. One of the major bodies of correspondence that is absent from this collection, though, is the exchanges between James and his wife, Agnes. They could potentially have offered some more insight into James's personal life, but the couple's exchanges seem to have ended up as one of those piles of papers that a descendant decided was not worth the effort of storing, and so was dispensed with.

Other mishaps have also diminished the body of primary sources on Busby's life. Letters to his brother pertaining to a critical period when he was battling authorities in New South Wales were lost when the brig *Wellington*, which was transporting them, was taken over by the convicts on the vessel. And we can only speculate as to how important James's contacts with some of his friends and associates in New South Wales and Britain were. In very few instances, this correspondence has survived, but largely, they are presumably now permanently missing, with only allusions to them in other sources hinting at their existence.

When the Residency imploded in 1840, much of the official documentation relating to the preceding seven years of James's tenure was passed on to the colony's new government, and most likely entered the protection of the Colonial Secretary, Willoughby Shortland. They were hardly a priority for the fledgling regime of Lieutenant-Governor William Hobson, and this bundle of letters was shuffled through the bureaucracy of successive administrations with little thought to its value, surfacing only as late as 1913, when a reference to them appeared in Department of Internal Affairs records. This reference mentioned that the letters had been stored in the Police basement in Johnson Street in Wellington, and had survived a fire in part of the building.[5] By 1946, they were back in the care of National Archives, but somewhere along this 106-year route, much of the material was lost.[6] Biographies are exercises in recovery – reassembling the subject's life from the surviving fragment of eclectic bodies of evidence. Although unavoidably incomplete, it is from this corpus that a more intimate and nuanced impression of Busby emerges.

---

[5] Author's notes for James Busby, Inward Records, 1832–1939, Inward Records 8156, ANZ.
[6] P. Parkinson, *Preserved in the Archives of the Colony: The English Drafts of the Treaty of Waitangi* (Wellington: New Zealand Association of Comparative Law, 2006), 15.

A Note on Conventions

For most of this work, James Busby is referred to by his Christian name. This is to help single him out from the many other Busbys – siblings, parents, children, and more distant relatives – who could potentially crowd the narrative and obscure the subject if they were referred to solely by their surname. Another convention applied here relates to the spelling of Māori words. Macrons are used, in keeping with current orthography, while the orthography of quoted material is reproduced in its original form.

Acknowledgements

I owe a great deal to the staff at the following institutions: Auckland University of Technology Library; Auckland Public Library; Auckland War Memorial Museum Library; University of Auckland Library; State Library, New South Wales; Hocken Collections, University of Otago Library; University of Canterbury Library; National Library, Wellington, Alexander Turnbull Library; Te Ara Poutama, Faculty of Māori Development, Auckland University of Technology; St Mary's Parish Church, Whitekirk and Tyninghame; National Library of Scotland; Central Library, Edinburgh; National Archives, United Kingdom; Cambridge University Library; Alnwick Library, Northumberland; University of Edinburgh Library; British Library; Residents' Services, London Borough of Lambeth; Haddington Library, Scotland; New South Wales State Archives; Woodhorn Museum, Ashington. Particular thanks are due to all the staff at Bloomsbury Publishing.

Personal gratitude goes to Lisa Airy, Professor Rob Allen, Dr Lloyd Carpenter, Ali Clarke, Professor Peter Cleave, Martin Collett, Dr Melissa Derby, Dr Ned Fletcher, Debra Hill, Maddie Holder, Dan Hutchins, Lilianna Kalinowska, Professor Pare Keiha, Paula Legel, Professor Ged Martin, Katherine Pawley, Leanne Radojkovich, Donal Raethel, David Rankin, Hanita Ritchie, Elwyn Sheehan, Helen Smith, Professor Russell Stone, Dr Thomas Torrance, Dr Ron Trubuhovich, David Walden, Rosie Wallace, Ernie White, Matthew Wright, and Milica Zjajic-Moon.

1

The Ambitions of the Father

Geoffrey Chaucer knew it. While there was always some jostling for position within social groupings in medieval England, in general, the possibility for upward mobility from one class to another was severely limited (whereas downward movement, as in every age, was comparatively easier). As Chaucer's parson summed up the country's social structure at the time, 'God ordained that some folk should be higher in estate and in degree, and some folk more low, and that each should be served in his estate and in his degree'.[1] By the 1700s, however, although Britain's class system still maintained much of its rigidity, it was beginning to buckle in places under the weight of the nation's nascent industrialization. Whereas in earlier eras, marrying judiciously or a career in the Church were among the few ways of inching one's way up the social hierarchy, opportunities for swift advancement broadened dramatically in the eighteenth century. Radical improvements to transport, the emergence of new institutions of finance and commerce, a long-running revolution in technology, and a stable parliamentary democracy (albeit encompassing a narrow franchise)[2] meant that upward mobility could increasingly be propelled by personal ambition rather than privilege of birth.

One of Scotland's greatest eighteenth-century intellectuals, the economist Adam Smith, wrote a manifesto of sorts for this emerging group. Rather than mimicking the traits of aristocrats, he proposed that the ambitious members of the middle class had to possess 'more important virtues':

> he must acquire superior knowledge in his profession, and superior industry in the exercise of it. He must be patient in labour, resolute in danger, and

---

[1] G. Chaucer, *The Canterbury Tales*, G. J. Davis, trans. (Bridgeport, CT: Insignia Publishing, 2016), 415.
[2] D. C. North and B. R. Weingast, 'Constitutions and Commitment: The Evolution of Institutions Governing Public Choice in Seventeenth-Century England', *The Journal of Economic History* 49, no. 4 (1989): 803–32.

firm in distress. These talents he must bring into public view . . . by the severe and unrelenting application with which he pursues them.[3]

This was no theoretical prescription for a newly minted middle class which was fumbling its way through the world, and seeking some intellectual guidance on how it should act. Instead, as an Edinburgh resident, Smith was confronted everywhere by unbridled energy of this social group that was extending its influence demographically, culturally, and economically throughout the city. And by the end of the eighteenth century, Edinburgh's prominence as one of the centres of Enlightenment Europe (from which it acquired its appellation 'the Modern Athens')[4] was being matched by its growing commercial prowess.[5]

Stretches of Edinburgh's Thistle Street are still little changed from their appearance in the late 1760s, at the onset of this epoch of rapid commercial and cultural expansion. Tenements in this part of the New Town were constructed – based on plans by the architect James Craig – 'as plainer artisan dwellings and workshops'.[6] And it was in Thistle Street (which runs parallel to the nationally counterbalancing Rose Street) that James Busby was born on 7 February 1802. (He was christened the following day at nearby St Cuthbert's Church.)[7] Thistle Street may have been regarded as 'narrow and inferior',[8] but it lay in a part of the city that was separated from the decrepitude, stench, disease, and violence for which the old town, with its dark, congested, labyrinthine alleys, was notorious.[9]

However, whatever favourable circumstances had led the Busbys to live in this relatively desirable part of the city did not last for long, and by the time James was two years old, his family had shifted to North Richmond Street.[10] At the beginning of the nineteenth century, this was not the stunted cul-de-

---

[3] A. Smith, *The Theory of Moral Sentiments* (London: Henry Bohn, 1853), 76–7.
[4] *The Edinburgh Magazine and Literary Miscellany* (Edinburgh: Archibald Constable and Co., 1825), 337.
[5] R. A. Houston, 'Literacy, Education and the Culture of Print in Enlightenment Edinburgh', *History: The Journal of the Historical Association* 78, no. 254 (1993): 373–92.
[6] Historical Environment Scotland, 'Statement of Special Interest', 41–5 (odd nos.) Thistle Street, LB43357; D. Campbell, *Edinburgh: A Cultural And Literary History* (Oxford: Signal Books, 2003), 83.
[7] National Records of Scotland, Old Parish Registers, Births, 685/2 120 518, St Cuthbert's, 139; E. Ramsden, *Busby of Waitangi: H. M.'s Resident at New Zealand, 1833–40* (Wellington: A. H. & A. W. Reed, 1942), 27; G. Martin, 'James Busby and the Treaty of Waitangi', *British Review of New Zealand Studies* 5 (1992): 13.
[8] H. Arnot, *The History of Edinburgh from the Earliest Accounts to the Year 1780* (Edinburgh: Thomas Turnbull, 1816), 547.
[9] *Report on the Condition of the Poorer Classes of Edinburgh* (Edinburgh: Edmonston and Douglas, 1868), 11–12.
[10] *Edinburgh and Leith Directory, from July 1804 to July 1805* (Edinburgh: Denovan and Co., 1804), 69.

sac that it is now, nor the sooty stone-walled slum that it had become in the late Victorian era. Instead, it was a middling neighbourhood on the southern outskirts of the city,[11] built in an area that just two decades earlier had been pastoral land.[12] It was the sort of place that accommodated the country's growing merchant and professional classes. Its members were not gentry (even if they had pretensions in that direction), but neither were they drawn from working-class factory fodder,[13] and were distinct from what Defoe called the 'meer [sic] labouring people who depend upon their hands'.[14] James's parents fell into this category, and as recent arrivals in the city, were part of its rapidly expanding population. In 1801, the city had 82,560 residents. Ten years later, this figure had reached 102,987 – an increase of almost 25 per cent.[15] Such growth was not unusual for British cities during the Industrial Revolution, but what distinguished Edinburgh's population surge at this time was that it was not due to demand for factory workers. Rather, it was establishing itself a centre of commerce and learning. The Royal Bank of Scotland had been founded there in 1727, and in the eighteenth century, the city's university produced the geologist James Hutton, the philosophers and historians David Hume, John Mill, and Adam Smith, and the biographer James Boswell. Interest in the sciences in particular existed throughout Edinburgh at a popular as well as academic level, and towards the end of the eighteenth century attracted widespread public attention, with audiences drawn to lectures on the latest research and findings of local scholars.[16]

The Busbys were one of thousands of families who had moved to Edinburgh from the late eighteenth century for the opportunities it offered, both in employment and, to a lesser degree, social mobility. James's father, John (born in 1765),[17] was among the 'private gentlemen, merchants, traders &c.' who constituted the burgeoning middle class in the city at this time.[18] He was

---

[11] *Plan of the City of Edinburgh*, 1807, EMS.s.59A, National Library of Scotland [NLS].
[12] *To the right honourable Thomas Elder of Forneth, Lord Provost of the city of Edinburgh, this plan of the city including all the latest improvements is . . . dedicated by . . . Thomas Brown & Jas. Watson, 1793*, EMS.b.2.56, NLS.
[13] L. Davidoff and C. Hall, *Family Fortunes: Men and Women of the English Middle Class, 1780–1850* (London: Hutchinson, 1987), 21; L. Leneman, '"No Unsuitable Match": Defining Rank in Eighteenth and Early Nineteenth-Century Scotland,' *Journal of Social History* 33, no. 3 (2000): 678.
[14] D. Defoe, cited in A. Briggs, 'The Language of "Class" in Early Nineteenth-Century England', in *Essays in Labour History*, eds. A. Briggs and J. Saville (London: Palgrave Macmillan, 1967), 44.
[15] J. Anderson, *A History of Edinburgh from the Earliest Period to the Completion of the Half Century 1850* (Edinburgh: A. Fullerton & Co., 1856), 607.
[16] S. Schaffer, 'Natural Philosophy and Public Spectacle in the Eighteenth Century', *History of Science* 21, no. 1 (1983): 1–43; J. B. Morrell, 'The University of Edinburgh in the Late Eighteenth Century: Its Scientific Eminence and Academic Structure', *Isis* 62, no. 2 (1971): 158–71; A. Toynbee, *Lectures on the Industrial Revolution in England* (London: Rivingtons, 1884), 84.
[17] *Sydney Morning Herald*, 18 May 1857, 1.
[18] *Edinburgh and Leith Directory, from July 1804 to July 1805*, front matter.

from the small Northumberland town of Alnwick, and was the eldest son of George Busby, who had risen from being a coalminer to a coal master, and who had been born in Stamford[19] – a village about eight kilometres north of Alnwick. George's wife, Margaret, came from the nearby village of Dunstan, and the family's fate and fortunes – such as they were – had been tied up with coal for at least two generations.[20]

Like his father, John Busby started his working life in the mines, and also like his father, graduated to another role – in this case, as a mineral surveyor and civil engineer.[21] However, while such august positions might have conveyed the impression that their possessor was highly trained, it is likely that John had little more than a rudimentary primary-school education. Self-ordained job titles such as these were both common and accepted in the late eighteenth century, and provided that their holder was capable of demonstrating his worth in practice, then over time, reputation could easily trump education.[22] In many ways, John was typical of that emerging group of Britons at this time who, while still far from wealthy, were gradually breaking loose from the ties to the land-owning classes that had bound previous generations to servitude and economic hardship.[23] Moving from rural Northumberland became necessary if he was to find employment in his new profession, and so in 1797 or 1798, he made the decision to head north to seek benefits from Scotland's thriving economy.[24]

It was in Scotland where the Busbys also underwent another shift – this one in their denominational allegiance, from the Church of England to the Church of Scotland. The former was Anglican, and the latter Presbyterian (with its adherence to Reformation principles such as predestination, by which 'some men . . . are predestinated [sic] unto everlasting life' as the Presbyterians' confession of faith put it.[25] A successful life in this world – where piety was entwined with profit – could be interpreted as a sign of God's favour, heralding salvation in the world to come.[26]

---

[19] *The Northumberland Poll Book* (Alnwick: W. Davison, 1826), 178.

[20] T. S. Ashton and J. Sykes, *The Coal Industry of the Eighteenth Century* (Manchester: Manchester University Press, 1929), 134, 227

[21] *Inverness Courier*, 11 July 1822.

[22] See T. D. Ford and H. S. Torrens, 'A Farey Story: The Pioneer Geologist John Farey (1766–1826)', *Geology Today* 17, no. 2 (2001), 59.

[23] E. P. Thompson, 'Eighteenth-century English Society: Class Struggle without Class?', *Social History* 3, no. 2 (1978): 133–65.

[24] B. Harris and C. McKean, *The Scottish Town in the Age of Enlightenment, 1740 – 1820* (Edinburgh: Edinburgh University Press, 2014), chap. 2.

[25] Extract from the Westminster Confession of Faith, in W. Fisk, *Discourse on Predestination and Election* (Springfield: A. G. Tannatt, 1831), 15.

[26] J. Sanchez-Burks, 'Protestant Relational Ideology and (in)Attention to Relational Cues in Work Settings', *Journal of Personality and Social Psychology* 83, no. 4 (2002): 920–1.

However, the Busbys' initial engagement with the firmly Protestant Church of Scotland seems not to have occurred out of passionate doctrinal conviction, but unusually, neither was it merely one of custom or convenience, as might be expected. The denominational transfer took place when John Busby married Sarah Kennedy in 1798 at Whitekirk. This was a Church of Scotland church in Tyninghame, East Lothian, about forty kilometres east of Edinburgh.[27] But what brought the thirty-three-year-old John and his fiancée to this remote location to marry, and in a denomination with which he had no prior association? The church was on the estate of Thomas Hamilton, the ninth Earl of Haddington, and it is probable that Haddington's association with John commenced around this time. John had been contracted to undertake geological surveys at Salisbury Crags in Holyrood Park (roughly two kilometres east of Edinburgh Castle) which Haddington claimed ownership of.[28] It is possible that John secured this work through Sarah, who may have previously been employed on Haddington's estate.[29] Less likely is the explanation that Sarah's connection with the Kennedys of Culzean Castle[30] (being the only daughter of James Kennedy, who was supposedly attached to the family of the Earls of Cassilis and Marquesses of Ailsa),[31] bestowed vaguely aristocratic credentials on her, which she subsequently used as a means of introducing her and her husband to Haddington. But whatever the reason, Haddington took on the role of the Busby family's friend, and later patron.

There is another possible reason that had a bearing on the Busbys' involvement in this very small and comparatively remote church during the period of their marriage and the birth of their first son. While John and Sarah were married at Whitekirk in 1798, the church's baptismal records show that their first child – George – was born on 18 December 1797 (and baptised on 7 January 1798).[32] A sympathetic lord of the manor, with sway over the local parish, would certainly have been beneficial to the Busbys at this time. Cases of illegitimacy – known as 'ante-nuptial uncleanliness' – were routinely investigated by Church authorities for births occurring within nine months of

---

[27] Although there is no surviving record of the marriage either in the Scottish or English parish archives. An alternative marriage date of 1789 (possibly a typographical error) was proposed, without any reference, in a 1996 publication, but similarly, there is no surviving record of a marriage at that time either in the Scottish or English parish archives. For the unsourced marriage date of 1789, see M. Busby, *The Busby Family* (Wellington, 1995), 3. The wedding was officiated by the Reverend William Campbell.
[28] *The Scottish Jurist, Containing Reports of Cases*, vol. 2, Edinburgh, 1830, 441–5.
[29] Martin, 'James Busby and the Treaty of Waitangi', 15.
[30] *The Genealogical History of Pioneer Families of Australia*, ed. P. C. Mowle (Sydney: John Sands, 1939), 32.
[31] *Bulletins of State Intelligence &c.* (London: London Gazette, 1847), 3; Martin, 'James Busby and the Treaty of Waitangi', 13.
[32] Old Parish Registers, Births 709/ 50 204, Haddington, January 1798, 197.

marriage. As George's appearance in the world preceded his parents' marriage, there was no question as to his status, and their crime. The Church had its own disciplinary courts, empowered by statute as well as Church law, to investigate and punish offenders, with the most severe sanction being excommunication and imprisonment.[33] The absence of any investigation whatsoever into the Busbys' illegitimate birth, together with the probability that the family was housed by the Earl of Haddington in Tyninghame (until around 1800, when they moved to Edinburgh) points to the possibility that their patron shielded them from the tentacles of Church authorities, keeping the young family tucked away in some small, secluded settlement in the remote expanses of flat farmland that stretched over East Lothian.

George's baptismal record, in addition to potentially incriminating his parents at the time, is the first surviving contemporaneous record of the Busbys living in Scotland. And within a few years, with their respectability restored (or at least, their moral misdemeanour sufficiently concealed), they settled in Edinburgh and eventually had six sons and two daughters, of whom James was the second. He was preceded by George (1797–1870), and followed by Catherine (1804–1872), John (1806–1884), Margaret (1808–1813), Alexander (1808–1873), William (1812–1812), and another William (1813–1887).

To support this growing brood, John was forced to find work where he could. He advertised in newspapers that he was available for 'Boring and Serching [sic] for Coal limestone, freestone, sandstone and marle', and listed the names of sixteen previous clients who were prepared to recommend his services.[34] Years later, when presenting his credentials to an official in New South Wales, he provided an inventory of his accomplishments as an engineer, including designing and installing a water system for Leith Fort, as well as projects involving Telford's Caledonian Canal, and public works at Stirling Castle and on Loch Ryan.[35] He unblushingly wrote how '[p]erhaps without impropriety, I may remark that . . . I have been more than once considered not unworthy of being associated with such men as Jessop, Rennie, Telford, and Stevenson'.[36] As impressive as these appointments may have appeared, though, John's exact role in them may not have been as illustrious as he

---

[33] L. Leneman and R. Mitchison, 'Scottish Illegitimacy Ratios in the Early Modern Period', *The Economic History Review* 40, no. 1 (1987), 41, 60.

[34] Newspaper advertisement, *c.* 1798, cited in A. D. M. Busby, *Busby Family Records [BFR]* 1 (Sydney, 1994), 42.

[35] *Historical Records of Australia [HRA]* 1, vol. 11, ed. F. Watson (Canberra: The Library Committee of the Commonwealth Parliament, 1917), 912.

[36] J. Busby to Colonial Secretary, 26 April 1834, in New South Wales Legislative Council, *Votes and Proceedings of the Legislative Council* 1 (Sydney: Government Printer, 1852) 6.

implied. The fact that his name did not feature in works published about these projects in this period suggests he was hired perhaps more for his physical abilities than his engineering expertise.[37]

In July 1802 – five months after James's birth – John sailed from Edinburgh to the county of Caithness, in the far north of Scotland, where he was engaged for the next three months by various landowners in the region to bore into the ground to determine its composition and mineral content, and to establish where wells might be dug.[38] In 1805, after just a year in their North Richmond Street home, John hauled his family to a cottage in Moray Street (now known as Spey Street).[39] This was about a kilometre to the east of Edinburgh, and was surrounded by horticultural land.[40] The eight years they spent there was to be the longest period the family spent in one house while in Britain. However, while Sarah and the children remained in Edinburgh, John continued to travel for work around Scotland and occasionally further. The following year, for example, he and his brother, Daniel, took on a mineral-surveying job in the fishing village of Dundrum, around fifty kilometres south of Belfast – a 'tiny, impoverished place . . . backward and remote' that was part of the estate of the Marquess of Downshire.[41]

Around 1807, James commenced his schooling. His family's financial circumstances (enhanced by John's recent employment in Ireland) enabled him to attend for more than a few years, which was often the limit for poorer families. And being in Edinburgh, the comparative scarcity of factory jobs both removed the quantity of demand for unskilled workers, and heightened the need for sufficient education if a pupil was to enter the main alternative of a profession.[42] Once a pupil in Edinburgh's schools could 'read with ease some of the most simple English Authors and the Bible', they would graduate to secondary education, which had an emphasis on 'classical learning'. It was into this academically uncertain environment that James was thrust, and from which he emerged aged thirteen highly literate and ready to enter Edinburgh University.[43]

---

[37] T. Telford and J. Rickman, *Life of Thomas Telford, Civil Engineer* (London: J. and L. G. Hansard and Sons, 1838); R. W. Jardine, 'James Jardine and the Edinburgh Water Company', *Transactions of the Newcomen Society* 64, no. 1 (1992): 121–30.
[38] J. Henderson, *General View of the Agriculture of the County of Caithness* (London: B. McMillan, 1815), 83–104.
[39] *The Post-Office Annual Directory* (Edinburgh: Abernethy & Walker, 1810), 39.
[40] *The Stranger's Guide, being a Plan of Edinburgh & Leith exhibiting all the streets principal buildings & late improvements*, Edinburgh, 1805, EMGB.s.25(15), NLS.
[41] W. A. Maguire, *The Downshire Estates in Ireland, 1801–1845* (Oxford: Clarendon Press, 1972), 78–9.
[42] R. D. Anderson, 'School Attendance in Nineteenth-Century Scotland: A Reply', *Economic History Review* 38, no. 2 (May 1985: 282–3.
[43] Records show he commenced Edinburgh University in 1816; see *Historical Alumni* (Edinburgh: University of Edinburgh, 2018), n.p.

Although he was making his name primarily as a mineral surveyor, in 1808 John was prepared to branch out into whatever area he felt he could profitably turn his skills to, including ship-salvaging. On 28 October the previous year, the trading vessel *Earl of Dalkeith* was washed ashore on a stretch of coast near Alnwick[44] (John's home town). He later reported how the ship was submerged in six metres of water, and that a committee of engineers sent by the insurer to assess the situation 'pronounced as hopeless any attempt to save any part of the cargo'. However, John devised a plan to save the cargo. He informed the insurers of this, and made an agreement with them that he would keep three-quarters of the value of everything salvaged. 'I proceeded with the undertaking', he explained, 'which occupied me a whole summer. But after deducting an immense expense for machinery applied before I succeeded in adopting what was at length successful, I saved property which cleared me about £1,000 stg.'[45] The present-day value of this undertaking is around £87,000, making it a particularly lucrative project for around three or four months' work. The same year, John rushed to Ireland, hoping to repeat this success with another shipwreck he had just heard about, but the cargo on that stricken vessel was pigs in cages, and apart from badly decomposed carcasses, there was little of value left to salvage, and the effort was abandoned.[46]

In 1810, John resumed work with his brother, Daniel, for the Marquess of Downshire. They had secured a five-year contract, with John receiving an annual payment of £541. On the basis of their surveying and testing, the brothers reckoned that 200 acres of tidal land in Dundrum could be reclaimed, and that the harbour could be deepened to allow large ships to enter it, which would dramatically boost trade in the region. Such proposals were in keeping with John's role as an engineer, but his ideas soon billowed out into other areas. He recommended that a bathing resort be established in the settlement, and that a major housing programme commence, with the leases paying for the development of public parks. Surprisingly, he was given approval for his grand scheme, and in 1812, a large-scale building programme got under way. As an indication of the grand scale of the undertaking, John and his brother were now employing over eighty staff on the project.[47] This was a very successful enterprise for Dundrum, and initially also for the Busbys, with each brother building a house for himself in Main Street.[48] However, as the houses

---

[44] *Lloyd's List*, no. 4203, 10 November 1807, 178.
[45] J. Busby to T. Brisbane, 13 February 1826, in *Historical Records of New Zealand*, 1, ed. R. McNab (Wellington: Government Printer, 1908), 651.
[46] *BFR* 1, 56.
[47] Maguire, *The Downshire Estates in Ireland*, 79.
[48] These were the Manor House and the Lodge, the latter at 187 Main Street.

were nearing completion, fortune deserted them. The Marquess, acting on advice from his increasingly anxious personal staff, determined that John and Daniel were less than competent at managing the project, and they were 'encouraged' to resign.[49] Just as John was on the cusp of owning his own home, and running a large and profitable business, all that he and his brother had worked for was snatched away from them. The next year, John returned to Ireland with his family.[50] Undeterred by the previous setback, he had purchased a few acres of farmland shortly after arriving in Ireland, and put the eleven-year-old James in charge of it, while he and his brothers continued their formal education at the Royal Belfast Academical Institution.[51]

Amid travelling and working, in this decade, John had also begun to tap into an inventive seam running through him. In 1813, he published a paper on a method he had devised for cleaning out the spaces under water where foundations for bridges and piers needed to be built (he had already deployed this technique at the new vitriol works in Belfast).[52] And shortly afterwards, he received recognition (and ten guineas in prize money)[53] from the Highland Society of Scotland for his inventions. One of John's inventions – a portable water pump – so impressed the Scottish politician Sir John Sinclair that he recommended it as something that may be of use to the British Army. In a letter to the Duke of Wellington in 1822, Sinclair described John as 'ingenious', and praised the utility of his mobile boring device (to which the Duke responded with an acknowledgement, but no further interest).[54]

Yet for all his inventiveness and preparedness to work, regular employment in a fixed location continued to elude John, and opportunities Ireland, which just a few years earlier looked to be so promising, were drying up. After eight years in Ireland, in 1818, the Busbys returned to Edinburgh, moving into 3 Orchardfield Place, another 'affordable' area, about four kilometres to the west of the city.[55] James, however, had not come back to Edinburgh with his

---

[49] G. Wheeler, 'John Lynn – Architect/Contractor/Engineer', in *Lecale Miscellany* 15 (1997): 45–6; A. B. S. Downshire, *Letters of a Great Irish Landlord: A Selection from the Estate Correspondence of the Third Marquess of Downshire, 1809–45* (Belfast: H. M. Stationery Office, 1974), 26, 32.
[50] John Busby is listed in the country on 22 April 1814. See D. G. Lockhart, 'The Land Surveyor In Northern Ireland Before The Coming Of The Ordnance Survey Circa 1840,' *Irish Geography* 11, no. 1 (1978): 107.
[51] *The Act of Incorporation and Bye-Laws of the Belfast Academical Institution, 1810* (Belfast: Royal Belfast Academical Institution, 1815), 3–4.
[52] *The New Monthly Magazine and Universal Register* 1 (London: H. Colburn, 1814), 465–6.
[53] The current equivalent of approximately £1,200.
[54] *Prize Essays and Transactions of the Highland Society of Scotland* 6 (1824): xxxiv, 618–21; J. Sinclair to Duke of Wellington, 2 May 1822, and reply from Duke of Wellington, 7 May 1822, in Papers of the Busby and Kelman Families, 1822–1879, CY Reel 985, ref ML MSS. 183, State Library, New South Wales [SLNSW], 1–8.
[55] *The Post-Office Annual Directory* (1818), 85.

parents. He had left Ireland two years earlier and returned to Edinburgh (possibly boarding with his brother, George, with funds supplied by their father), and had begun studying medicine at university.

Although James was aged only fourteen when he entered university, this was not unusually young for this period, as secondary schooling for most students finished around the same age.[56] There were no entry examinations for Edinburgh's medical school in the early nineteenth century, and students could nominate which lectures they wished to attend.[57] However, James lasted just one year at university, and although the exact reason is unknown, it is possible that the family lacked the financial means to support another child at university[58] (his older brother, George, was also studying medicine at the time).[59]

The next two years did little to satiate James's intellectual thirst, but his curiosity had to be held in abeyance while he took on work with his father on the latter's return from Ireland. This period in James's passage to adulthood was marked by his entry into the world of a wage-earner (albeit a wage that contributed to the family's upkeep). But far from having abandoned any sense of ambition, James used this time to shift and sort through his thoughts. He was able to look to his father's experiences – as someone who had gone from coalminer to professional, and from village to city, and who had built a career and acquired some status in equal measure. However, with no clear career having yet enticed James, he decided to experiment, pursing his budding interest in horticulture to see where it would lead. So with the paltriest of capital that he had managed to scrape together, he travelled to France in 1819 to explore the viticulture industry there, and to produce what he envisaged would be a comprehensive study of his findings.

Although not published until six years later, James's *Treatise on the Culture of the Vine, and the Art of Making Wine*[60] contains several elements that make it possible to assemble both where he spent most of his time in France during 1819, and the efforts he made to unearthing information about his subject. Yet what is most remarkable about his *Treatise* is not James's voracious thirst for information, or the skill with which he organized and presented the material. Rather, it is the self-assuredness of its teenage author that he possessed the ability to acquire insights into viticulture that had hitherto eluded others.

---

[56] L. Patterson, 'Schools and Schooling: 3. Mass Education 1872–Present', in *The Oxford Companion to Scottish History*, ed. M. Lynch (Oxford: Oxford University Press, 2001), 566–9.
[57] R. Anderson, 'The History of Scottish Education pre-1980', in *Scottish Education: Post-Devolution*, eds. T. G. K. Bryce and W. M. Humes (Edinburgh: Edinburgh University Press, 2003), 224.
[58] Martin, 'James Busby and the Treaty of Waitangi', 17.
[59] *Australian Almanac for the Year of Our Lord 1831*, ed. R. Mansfield (Sydney, 1831), 211.
[60] J. Busby, *A Treatise on the Culture of the Vine, and the Art of Making Wine* (Sydney: R. Howe, 1825).

Where did this almost precocious confidence stem from? Undoubtedly, the influence of his father had left a significant imprint on James. There was also a deeply ingrained inquisitiveness and ambition in James's own psychological make-up that contributed to the way he approached adulthood. He noted in his account of his trip to France how he had been 'attentively observing' the country's wine districts, and had made a particular study of the soils, resulting in findings that 'made him doubt very strongly the information he had received, though from the most respectable sources'. Already, his own authority was unashamedly challenging received wisdom on the subject, but he did not dwell too long on any one topic.[61] From the geology of Cadillac – the small village on the banks of the river Garonne, in the southwest of France, where he settled for a few months – James swung his attention to the economics of wine-making in the region, providing detailed calculations on land costs, capital requirements, and the value of production, and then making a comparative study with the value and output of cultivated land in England.[62] His conclusion was that vineyards were the most lucrative use of land, and that they warranted more research and investment. The remainder of his research offered a comprehensive survey of grape varieties, propagation, planting locations, soil composition, and various other aspects of viticulture. Not all the material he gathered was his own, and he frequently acknowledged the works of the French scientist Jean-Antoine Chaptal (1756–1832), whose own books on the topic appeared only in French at this time, suggesting that James had acquired some facility with that language.[63] And as for his expertise, the works on viticulture which James eventually published (some based on his first visit to France) earned him the endorsement of the famous contemporary viticulturist Nicholas Herbemont, who described him as 'a man of sense' and his observations 'worthy of utmost confidence'.[64]

If, as Heraclitus asserted, character is destiny, then the extent to which James plunged himself so deeply into a topic of which he would have had little prior knowledge, and in a foreign country which he had not previously visited, points to a character that was supremely confident, curious, and courageous. His exploration of France's wine industry made him an expert on the topic while still in his teenage years, and even if he had ever experienced some sliver of doubt about his abilities before departing, they had been banished by his return to Scotland.

---

[61] Ibid., xix–xx.
[62] Ibid., xxi–xxvi.
[63] Ibid., 40.
[64] N. Herbemont, in *Pioneering American Wine: The Writings of Nicholas Herbemont, Master Viticulturist*, ed. D. S. Shields (Atlanta, GA: University of Georgia Press, 2009), 232–3.

At the same time, the detailed soil analyses James included as part of his research are suggestive of a close working relationship with his father. On his return to Edinburgh in 1820, with his older brother, George, ensconced at university, James now took on the mantle of a de facto eldest son, working with his father in some ways more as a partner than as an employee. While James had been in France, John had taken on work locally, this time on the fourteen acres of land bordering Inverleith Row that had been set aside for Edinburgh's newly relocated Botanical Gardens.[65] James returned to working with his father and to both sharing and acquiring new horticultural knowledge as he assisted with the great relocation of plants to the new site from their former home around three kilometres away in Hopetoun Crescent, off Leith Walk. However, as in the other work he later claimed involvement in, John's role in the gardens' relocation was likely confined to manual labour rather than the engineering methods that had been devised specifically for this project.[66]

From 1820 to 1822, the Busbys lived in Castlebarns,[67] (now the eastern end of Morrison Street), which, like their earlier few residences, was on the periphery of the city: this time, in a row of recently built housing that backed on to fields, about two kilometres away from North Richmond Street. The more affordable locations dotted around the outskirts of Edinburgh where John and his family lived, coupled with the intermittent nature of his employment, suggest a picture of a family that was neither prosperous nor poor. With the haggard beggars, weather-beaten street merchants, drunkards, vagrants, the impoverished elderly, and the even more impoverished sick, there were reminders everywhere of how porous the Edinburgh's social boundaries could be for those families who found their fortunes fading. The ambitious middle classes could not afford to avert their gaze from this stratum of squalor that was visible in society, but at the same time, they had to try to fix their focus on opportunities for social and financial betterment. Where you lived in Edinburgh mattered to a considerable extent in this era when it came to upward social mobility,[68] and the Busbys' pattern of moving, but never to a location that signalled an elevation in their status, signifies an element of social stagnation setting in. For a family that aspired to better themselves, there was difficulty in 'maintaining "respectable" standards in the old

---

[65] *HRA* 1, vol. 11, 885; J. H. Balfour, *Guide to the Royal Botanic Garden, Edinburgh* (Edinburgh: Edmonston & Douglas, 1873), 5.
[66] W. McNab, 'On Preparing Large Trees Intended to be Transplanted', *The Quarterly Journal of Agriculture* 2 (1831): 823–9.
[67] J. Grant, *Cassells Old and New in Edinburgh* 2 (London: Cassel, Petter, Galpin & Co., 1882), 215; *The Post-Office Annual Directory* (1820), 89; D. Wilson, *Memorials of Edinburgh in the Olden Time* 1 (Edinburgh: A & C Black, 1891), 179.
[68] R. Q. Gray, 'Styles of Life, the "Labour Aristocracy" and Class Relations in Later Nineteenth Century Edinburgh', *International Review of Social History* 18, no. 3 (1973): 430–1.

tenements, with their social mixture, gregarious street (or court or close) life and lack of privacy'.[69]

At some time in 1822, James moved out of the family home, and into Edinburgh's old town, taking up lodgings at 95 Grassmarket – just 200 metres from Edinburgh Castle. He remained there for around a year, suggesting that he was earning enough money to support himself. His occupation was listed as haberdasher,[70] but he seems to have had little affection for the role, and by 1823 had abandoned both the job and his room in Grassmarket, and returned to living with his family.

For all their shuffling from one part of Edinburgh to another, after two decades, there was little to show for it in terms of improved status, wealth, or careers. Nor were John's employment prospects cause for hope that the family's circumstances would improve at any time in the foreseeable future. For someone who was perennially ambitious, such conditions were increasingly untenable. Edinburgh had started out promising to fulfil the family's aspirations. Now, with John in his mid-fifties and possibly feeling past his prime, and with James frustrated with his lack of a career, it was thwarting them. And while on the one hand the Busbys may have typified those families who were mired in this middling group, on the other hand they were also in a separate sub-group which was on the outer of Edinburgh society: John was an Englishman in Scotland, and one who metaphorically still had coal-dust under his fingernails; he was Church of Scotland through a conscious (and possibly convenient) act of affiliation rather than by birth; and although he had a profession, it was one practised more in the outdoors than in the office, with his constant travelling for work giving a faint impression of vagrancy – of someone struggling to maintain a foothold in his preferred city of residence. Given all these circumstances, it would have been evident to John that the opportunities for advancement in the city were slender and narrowing as he got older.

Despite his age, though, John's ambition was not yet dampened – far from it, as subsequent events demonstrated. At some point in the early 1820s, a new and radical idea germinated in his mind. With his hopes for his family having struck largely barren ground in Edinburgh, with the prospect of a gentrified retirement receding ever further into the future, and with Sarah's asthma making life in Scotland increasingly difficult for her health,[71] the idea of a new start in a colony (with none of the calcified class structures that had

---

[69] J. Symington, 'The Working Man's Home', in *Happy Homes for Working Men and How to Get Them*, ed. J. Begg (London: Cassel, Petter, Galpin & Co., 1866), 162.
[70] *The Post-Office Annual Directory* (1822), 89.
[71] Sarah's asthma was reported on by some of her descendants. See *BFR* 1, 58.

hindered the family in Britain) took root. It was an idea that was part opportunity, part antidote, and one that was nourished by the convergence of various circumstances in the family. John and Sarah's eldest child, George, was on the cusp of graduating from university as a doctor, while James had returned from France, brimming with ideas about viticulture, but with no outlet for them in Scotland's cold, 'pensive and dripping'[72] weather (or as Edinburgh-born Robert Louis Stevenson more bluntly recalled it, 'one of the vilest climates under heaven').[73] For James, simply staying put would compromise his ambition. Emigration was looking like an increasingly viable solution, and by late 1822, the Busbys were fastening their hopes and destiny to the farthest colony in the Empire: New South Wales.

---

[72] J. Thomson, 'Winter', in J. Thomson, *The Seasons: A Poem* (New York: Clark, Austin & Co., [1736] 1854), 127.

[73] R. L. Stevenson, *Edinburgh: Picturesque Notes* (New York: Macmillan, 1896), 2.

2

The Tenacity of the Son

What image did New South Wales conjure up in the minds of migrants from Scotland in the 1820s: burgeoning field of enterprise or colonial chaos?[1] Of course, all would-be migrants hoped for the former – immigration was, after all, as much an act of faith as of fact. Yet for most, their one-way journey to the antipodes tended to rely on the slimmest of information about their destination. There was a handful of works published on the colony that gave some impression of its social and geographical dimensions,[2] and there was also the more common knowledge that New South Wales had been for decades a dumping ground for Britain's surplus convicts.[3] By the 1820s, the notoriety of the colony was well established. It was said to be a place of 'pernicious vice',[4] where 'every means and opportunity was sought for the indulgence of the wildest depravity'.[5] Such statements were exaggerations, with many of those deported having committed only the most minor of offences,[6] but reputation and rumour often trumped truth, and the stain of being known as 'miserable' and 'wretched' remained long after New South

---

[1] As examples of this range of views, see *The Annual Register, or a View of the History, Politics, and Literature of the Year 1823* (London: Baldwin, Craddock, and Joy, 1824), 71–80; J. Oxley, *Journal of Two Expeditions into the Interior of New South Wales* (London: John Murray, 1820).
[2] As examples, see D. Collins, *An Account of the English Colony in New South Wales: With Remarks on the Dispositions, Customs, Manners, &c. of the Native Inhabitants of that Country* (London: T. Cadell, 1804); G. Barrington, *A History of New South Wales: Including Botany Bay, Port Jackson, Parramatta, Sydney, and all its Dependencies* (London: M. Jones, 1802); W. C. Wentworth, *A Statistical, Historical, and Political Description of the Colony of New South Wales* (London: G. and W. B. Whittaker, 1824).
[3] R. V. Jackson, 'Jeremy Bentham and the New South Wales Convicts', *International Journal of Social Economics* 25, nos. 2/3/4 (1998): 370–9.
[4] G. Barrington, *A Sequel to Barrington's Voyage to New South Wales* (London: C. Lowndes, 1800), 34.
[5] T. Reid, *Two Voyages to New South Wales and Van Diemen's Land* (London: Longman, Hurst, Rees, Orme, and Brown, 1822), xi.
[6] I. Donnachie, 'The Convicts of 1830: Scottish Criminals Transported to New South Wales', *The Scottish Historical Review* 65, no. 179 (1986): 34–47.

Wales had ceased to exist primarily as a penal settlement.[7] What was in less dispute, though, was the harshness of the environment, which during the 1790s had driven the colony's residents to the brink of starvation for several years.[8]

On the face of it, then, there could have been few less desirable locations in the Empire for a British family to emigrate to. However, since 1810, New South Wales had been under the firm and resourceful rule of Governor Lachlan Macquarie, who had largely transformed the territory from a despondent penal colony to a thriving society. This was achieved through an increase in non-convict immigration, combined with an ambitious public works and civil reform programme.[9] From a high point in 1818–20 of roughly 2,600 convicts being sent to the colony each year, in the following six years, the figure dropped to approximately 1,600 annually.[10] In contrast, non-convict immigration in the 1820s was on the rise, averaging 650 annually in the first half of the decade, and increasing to almost a thousand a year from 1826 to 1830.[11] The principal reason for this influx, and one which no doubt had a bearing on the Busbys' motive to move to New South Wales, was summed up by a more famous Scottish migrant, the explorer and surveyor Thomas Mitchell, who on arriving in the colony promptly wrote to his brother, stating 'it is a famous country for getting rich'.[12] However, there was a challenging sequence of steps that needed to be taken before the Busbys could secure their passage to New South Wales. It was not that there were restrictions on travel to the colony, but that the family wanted the British government to pay the fares for the journey – with the total cost of their relocation reaching around £240 (the modern equivalent of approximately £14,000).[13]

Their embryonic plan to migrate to New South Wales coincided with the recent release in Britain of three reports on the colony written by a Northumberland-born judge, John Bigge, that were to have a major effect on future immigration to Australia. As a consequence of growing public and official disquiet over the transportation of convicts to New South Wales, the

---

[7] Reid, *Two Voyages to New South Wales*, 258, 307.
[8] I. D. Whyte, *Migration and Society in Britain, 1550–1830* (London: Palgrave Macmillan, 2000), 135.
[9] D. Sylvester, 'Governor Lachlan Macquarie, Sir James Mackintosh and the Scottish Enlightenment', *Journal of Australian Colonial History* 12 (2010): 23–38; M. Steven, 'The Changing Pattern of Commerce in New South Wales, 1810–1821', *Australian Economic History Review* 3, no. 2 (1963): 139–55.
[10] C. Liston, 'Sir Thomas Brisbane', in *The Governors of New South Wales, 1788–2010*, eds. D. Cline and K. Turner (Sydney: The Federation Press, 2009), 137.
[11] C. Wright, *Wellington's Men in Australia: Peninsula War Veterans and the Making of an Empire c. 1820–40* (London: Palgrave Macmillan, 2011), 28.
[12] T. Mitchell, cited in ibid.
[13] The fare per individual is quoted as £30 in Whyte, *Migration and Society in Britain*, 135.

Colonial Office had decided to appoint a Commission of Inquiry to investigate the practice, with Bigge being selected in 1818 by the Secretary of State for War and the Colonies, the third Earl Bathurst (who also doubted the merits of the existing convict transportation system) to head the Inquiry.[14]

In the late eighteenth century, New South Wales had been seen by British officials as little more than a barren expanse of territory[15] suited only for the criminal refuse from the mother country. But as the settler population increased, the Colonial Office was keen to assess the colony's other prospects.[16] Bigge's report had been produced primarily to inform British government policy, and much of its content reflected that orientation. On the issue of free settlers (that is, non-convict migrants to the colony), he stipulated that 'the great advantage that is derived from their introduction depends much more upon their respectability and their means, than it does upon their numbers'[17] (a criterion that would certainly seem to encompass the Busbys).

Bigge also provided the most detailed survey of the colony's demographics. In 1820, New South Wales's total population was estimated at 23,939, of whom 1,307 were free immigrants, and a further 1,495 had been born in the colony. 159 were former convicts who had been fully pardoned, and 962 were prisoners with conditional pardons. 3,255 were free by virtue of having served their sentences and 9,451 remained convicts. 1,422 held tickets of leave, and a staggering 5,668 were children – roughly a quarter of the population in a colony that was primarily an open-air prison. About half of the entire population lived in the wider Sydney area, which was the colony's capital, and half of these were convicts. And as a sign of the insignificance with which Bigge viewed the indigenous population, their numbers were absent from his count.[18]

From 1822, on the advice of Haddington, John and James had been lobbying the Colonial Office (both in person and by letters) to fund the family's fares to the colony, and to arrange offers of employment once they arrived. The correspondence addressed to the Colonial Office from John was probably

---

[14] J. Ritchie, 'Punishment and Profit: The Reports of Commissioner Bigge on the Colonies of New South Wales and Van Diemen's Land, 1822–1823; their Origins, Nature and Significance', (PhD thesis, Australian National University, 1969), 1–5.
[15] D. Allen, *Early Georgian, Being Extracts from the Journal of George Allen, 1800–1877* (Sydney: Angus and Robertson, 1958), 32.
[16] Ritchie, 'Punishment and Profit', 2–3.
[17] J. T. Bigge, *Report of the Commissioner of Inquiry into the State of the Colony of New South Wales* (London: House of Commons, 1822), 155.
[18] Bigge's mention of Aborigines was largely incidental in his reports. See G. Blyton, 'Rum and Corn Pipes: The Introduction of Alcohol and Tobacco into Aboriginal Populations of the Hunter Region of Central Eastern New South Wales, Australia, in the First Half of the 19th Century', *AlterNative: An International Journal of Indigenous Peoples* 9, no. 4 (2013): 299.

from the pen of James, and was written in a very stylized, formal tone, as though trying to portray the family as educated and sound, rather than improvising and erratic. One such letter, addressed to Bathurst in 1822, gives a flavour of the confidence and officiousness of these dispatches. 'Your Memorialist having of late turned his attention to the state of the Colony of New South Wales, conceiving that there is an extensive field for his exertions, in a country of such vast extent and variety of geological structures', it began assiduously, 'begs to offer to His Majesty's Government his services in the various departments of the profession in which he has engaged for the last twenty years.' It went on to hint at the possibility that John might assist in discovering 'vast sources of wealth' through his expertise in mineral surveying, and that he could prevent floods and assist in dealing with droughts.

The prospects of individual settlers venturing to the colonies was not something that Bathurst would normally consider, and so the Busbys' correspondence was diverted to the Under-Secretary for the Colonial Office, Robert Wilmot-Horton. Wilmot-Horton saw some potential use in New South Wales for someone with John's skills, and so arranged for him to meet Bigge on 19 June.[19] Bigge agreed in principle to offer John a position, but John baulked at the issue of income, and made an audacious counter-offer, which included free passage for the family to New South Wales, an annual salary of 200 guineas, the guarantee of five years' employment with the colonial government (for which he would only work three and a half months each year), a house large enough for his family, and grants of land to himself and his sons.[20]

There was no immediate response from Bigge, and so John (with James's literary assistance) crafted another 'memorial' to the Colonial Office, in January 1823, this time advising that the family would be accompanied on any migration to New South Wales by a nephew and niece, making it a group of ten settlers in all. Aware, perhaps, of how officials might construe such a large party as being something of a liability, this second memorial detailed the calibre of the family, and the potential advantages its members would offer in the colony.[21]

John had based himself in London for months, believing that proximity to the decision-makers in government would help his cause. However, with little apparent movement on the issue from officials, he returned to Edinburgh to replenish the family's finances (or at the very least to stop them being drained

---

[19] Colonial Department to J. Busby, 18 June 1822, in Papers of the Busby and Kelman Families, 1822–1879, CY Reel 985, ref ML MSS. 1183, 9–12.
[20] John Busby to R. Wilmot-Horton, 26 July 1822, in *BFR* 1, 60–1.
[21] John Busby, 1823, in *BFR* 1, 62–3.

further by being away). However, he persisted with his barrage of correspondence to anyone in government he felt could aid his objectives. The trouble with this approach was not just that being at a distance of over 500 kilometres from London slowed the pace of communication and diminished the effectiveness of lobbying in person; it was that it left the entire future of the family dependent on a prolonged exchange of letters with the Colonial Office.

A scornful depiction of that department, written just over a decade later, gives a good impression of what the family was up against. Sardonically personified as 'Mr Mothercountry', the Colonial Office was said to be run by anonymous officials who wielded power over the Empire as well as their hapless overlords in government. Trying to establish precisely who was responsible for various decisions was nearly impossible, 'for here we get . . . involved in the clouds of official mystery. . . . We know not the name, the history, or the functions of the individual, into the narrow limits of whose person we find the mother-country shrunk.' However, the relative anonymity of these officials in no way implied that they were ill suited to their task: 'Long experience has made him thoroughly conversant with every detail of his business; and long habit has made his business the main, perhaps . . . the sole source of his interest and enjoyment. . . . No pile of despatches, with their multifarious enclosures, no red-taped heap of colonial grievances or squabbles, can scare his practised eye.' The problem for the Busbys was that their contact with the Colonial Office was mainly in the form of written submissions, and such was the constitution of the department that obtaining a fair hearing in this way was regarded as unlikely.[22] Grappling for some certainty in such a bureaucratic fog through means of letter-writing alone was not going to achieve much, and fearing that the momentum of migrating was being lost, in 1823 the family dipped once again into the shallowing pool of its finances and dispatched James (now twenty-one) to London to lobby directly on the family's behalf for a paid fare to New South Wales.

London in the 1820s was the largest and richest city in the world.[23] The capital of the world's greatest empire was brimming with 'ships, towers, domes, theatres, and temples . . . all bright and glittering',[24] and had a population of more than one million – over seven times that of Edinburgh.[25] Yet

---

[22] C. Buller, in E. G. Wakefield, *A View of the Art of Colonization, with Present Reference to the British Empire* (London: Parker, 1849), 285–90.
[23] J. Landers, *Death and the Metropolis: Studies in the Demographic History of London, 1670–1830* (Cambridge: Cambridge University Press, 1993), 180.
[24] W. Wordsworth, 'Composed upon Westminster Bridge, September 3, 1802', in *The Complete Poetical Works of William Wordsworth*, ed. H. Reed (Philadelphia: Troutman & Hayes, 1848), 191.
[25] G. Arvaston and T. Butler, 'Metamorphoses, Transformation and European Cities', *Ethnologia Europaea* 34, no. 2 (2004): 5.

James took an instant dislike to it. Maybe the reason was that he was not in London for its sights or splendour, but for something far more serious. It was as though in travelling to London to find a means of funding his parents' and siblings' passage to Australia, he had taken the entire burden of his family's fate on his shoulders. And he also was also labouring under a sense of mounting anxiety. What capital they had accumulated for forging a fresh future in New South Wales was gradually diminishing with every week that James remained unsuccessful in his goal. The sense of ambition which he had been brought up with, together with his capacity for work, which he had exhibited since his teenage years, was now being a complemented by a new trait that he was starting to reveal: tenacity.

James initially targeted as the object of his campaign Edward Barnard, who had been promoted to First Assistant Clerk of the Colonial Office in January 1822. Barnard was the official who was best informed about the state of New South Wales, and accordingly had to contend with a steady flow of would-be migrants enquiring about the colony and submitting their applications to settle there. He had a reputation for efficiency, and for exerting some influence over Bathurst.[26]

On 29 March 1823, Wilmot-Horton finally acceded to the prolonged pleas and requests from the Busbys that had come via Barnard, and informed John that he would be appointed as a civil engineer in the colony, with an annual income of £200. It was a three-year contract that would require John to work for 200 days per year. And better still, at the conclusion of his employment by the government, he would be allotted a parcel of land. After months of official procrastination, suddenly there was an apparent sense of urgency. Wilmot-Horton informed John (in whose name James was negotiating) that he was to depart 'forthwith' on any vessel sailing from London to Sydney. The immediate future quickly seemed to be taking shape for the family, but there was one impediment to imminent departure: John was advised by the Colonial Office that if his children wished to travel with him, the sons would require £500 (over twice John's promised annual salary) in capital. Provided they managed this, they would be regarded as 'settlers', which would entitle them to a grant of land, plus the right to avail themselves of convict labour to develop it.[27]

This was a significant obstacle. Just as all the pieces of the opportunity seemed to be slotting into place, the precondition of £500 capital for James and his brother to accompany their parents to New South Wales brought the

---

[26] Ritchie, 'Punishment and Profit', 26–7; Z. Laidlaw, *Colonial Connections, 1815–1845: Patronage, the Information Revolution, and Colonial Government* (Manchester: Manchester University Press, 2005), 132.

[27] R. Wilmot-Horton to J. Busby, 29 March 1823, in *HRA* 1, vol. 11, 106–7.

family's plans to a standstill. From the promise of an imminent departure, the Busbys now felt stranded in Britain – James in London, and the rest of the members in Edinburgh. It was a sort of limbo that risked descending into purgatory. The family had already vacated its house in Edinburgh in anticipation of an imminent departure. Now they were squeezed into small lodgings, waiting for circumstances to take a turn for the better.[28] To exacerbate their situation, the Busbys were caught in a complex tangle of loans and debts to various family members and associates, which had left them even more out of pocket. In one letter, James mentioned that his brother George was almost in tears at the damage such dealings might inflict on their father's reputation.[29] And it was not just reputations at stake. Seventeen days later, James again wrote to George, trying to encourage him not to give up hope of graduating from medical school, despite the family's increasingly dire financial circumstances.[30] James returned briefly to Scotland, and then headed back to London to launch a fresh offensive in his family's campaign to become government-supported migrants to New South Wales.

The family's money worries were certainly at the forefront of James's mind at this time. In mid-June 1823, he committed £105 of the funds set aside for their planned migration on a speculative venture. He purchased (on credit) a range of Sheffield cutlery with the intention of acting as an agent for the products when he eventually arrived in Sydney. Despite the large sum involved, James was seemingly relaxed about his acquisition. 'Whether it will do much for me, I cannot tell, but it can do no harm', he wrote casually to George, before concluding in a more hopeful tone that '[i]t promises well'.[31] Apart from this faint prospect of future profit, though, there was little to be optimistic about. On 23 June, James returned to his accommodation at 3 Jewin Street, Cripplegate, in London (where he and has father had lodged during their previous stay in the capital). The following day, he visited the Colonial Office and discovered that Edward Barnard, who had been the family's main point of contact, had moved from his previous role in the department.[32] His replacement – a Mr Bailey – was unfamiliar with the details of the Busbys' application, and unconcerned with their predicament. Bailey 'told me', an exasperated James wrote, 'that no allowances could possibly be made for the

---

[28] J. Busby to G. Busby, 12 August 1823, in Letters from James Busby to his Brother George Busby 1823–1830, Auckland Institute and Museum Library, MS46, folder, 2, 6.
[29] James Busby, 25 June 1823, in *BFR* 1, 63.
[30] Ibid., 63.
[31] James Busby to G. Busby, June 1823, in *BFR* 1, 64.
[32] Busby seems to have been mistaken about Barnard having 'retired' as he was still in the employ of the Colonial Office at this time. See L. M. Penson, 'The Origin of the Crown Agency Office', *The English Historical Review* 40, no. 158 (April 1925): 205.

family'. James was in no mood to accept 'no' for an answer, though. With the rest of his family huddled in temporary accommodation in Scotland, he needed to find a way out of the stalemate as soon as possible. He managed to track down Barnard in another office, and waited outside – patiently but resolutely – for three hours until the official deigned to call this visitor to his room. Once there, Busby explained the economic benefits of his family being given an assisted passage to New South Wales. Barnard turned out to be more accommodating to Busby's pleas than Bailey had been, but only slightly. He explained that there were doubts about how long John's services might be required in the colony, and that the family needed £1,000 of capital to emigrate. This was the crux of the problem. James told George how he could not assure Barnard that the family would have such funds available, 'as I still had some heavy debts due to me in this country, and I was uncertain whether I should be able to recover in time'.[33]

Sensing that James would not be easily dissuaded about his family's chances of going to New South Wales, Barnard suggested to him that he write a letter to Bathurst, which Barnard would take the responsibility of delivering personally. This caught James slightly off guard, because he and his father had already spelt out the family's intentions very clearly to the Colonial Office. Barnard's offer hinted that the family's previous pleas had not been given much attention. Perhaps though, James speculated, the Colonial Office simply wanted more specifics. He told Barnard of his plans to start a wine-making enterprise in the colony, and asked whether the Governor was likely to award him a grant of land in New South Wales to accomplish this. The answer (which James underlined in his letter to George) was a resolute 'no'.[34]

James was then sent by Barnard to the Navy Office, five kilometres away in Seething Lane. The purpose of this visit was to advise staff there that the Colonial Office had ordered a passage for the Busbys and to find out when the next ship was due to sail to New South Wales. At the Navy Office, there was more disappointment for James. He was told that all berths on the vessels scheduled to leave for the colony were fully booked, and that the Colonial Office should have sent a formal request for the Busbys, which it had not done. James went back to the Colonial Office, informing staff there of what he had been told by the Navy Office, and received confirmation that the matter would be resolved straight away. It was not. The following day, James returned to the Navy Office, and was once again told that it had received no instructing letter from the Colonial Office, as was required.

James was sent back to the Colonial Office, and from there to the Home Department, where he was advised that the earliest chance of securing berths

---

[33] James Busby to G. Busby, 26 June 1823, in *BFR* 1, 64–5.
[34] Ibid., 65.

to New South Wales would be in April the following year, meaning that the family would have to delay their plans for a new life in the colony for another ten months. This was deeply worrying news, and led to James making ever more frantic efforts to organize transport to New South Wales. Again, he found himself rushing through the congested lanes and across the busy streets of central London trying to make some progress.

Back at Downing Street, he met Bailey and proposed that the Colonial Office pay for the family's passage in a private ship. Bailey considered the idea and replied that he would discuss it with Barnard. The following day, James met with Barnard directly and 'represented very strongly the hardship of our situation'. He told the official that he could arrange a cheap fare with a ship departing from Leith, and that his family was prepared to 'submit to a great deal of inconvenience rather than be detained'. Barnard voiced doubts about the idea, but promised to raise it with Bathurst.[35]

In the midst of the scramble between various branches of the Government, James was scouring London (including its outskirts) for more affordable accommodation, but could find none that was cheaper than his present room.[36] The only pause in the otherwise frantic clambering through the mysterious channels of officialdom occurred on Sundays, when James's attention switched from the temporal to the spiritual. On the Sabbath, he attended the Caledonian Church at Hatton Garden, where the preacher in residence was Reverend Edward Irving. Irving – a fellow Scot – had acquired a large following for his flamboyant preaching style, with the essayist William Hazlitt observing that '[y]ou can scarcely move along for the coronet-coaches that besiege the entrance to the Caledonian Chapel in Hatton Garden; and when, after a prodigious squeeze, you get in [you only] . . . have standing room'.[37] James wrote how Irving was 'doing wonders', and that 'there is nothing left for us Scotsmen to do but burst with pride'.[38]

But as Monday followed Sunday, James reverted to type: as the increasingly despairing young man on whose actions his entire family's future hinged. In what almost amounted to an ambush, he decided to capture the attention of Barnard when he was out of the office. He waited around close to the entrance of the Colonial Office, and when he saw his target exiting the building, followed him, catching up with the official at the corner of the street. But as soon as James started talking to him, Barnard walked off, finding refuge in a nearby hotel. Astonishingly, James would not give up on his prey. He waited

---

[35] Ibid., 65–6; J. Busby to John Busby, 26 June 1823, in Letters from James Busby to his Father John Busby 1823–1834, Auckland Institute and Museum Library, MS46, folder, 3, 1.
[36] James Busby to G. Busby, 26 June 1823, in *BFR* 1, 66.
[37] W. Hazlitt, in *The Literary Chronicle*, 2 August 1823, 482.
[38] J. Busby to G. Busby, 26 June 1823, in *BFR* 1, 66.

outside until Barnard left the hotel, and again accosted him, this time pleading his case even more forcefully until Barnard finally relented, reassuring James that he would attend to the matter.[39]

On 13 July, James had yet another meeting with Barnard, whose patience now seemed to be wearing thin. 'He was in such a hurry I could scarcely get him spoken to', James noted. He then resorted to the pen, and in a long letter to Barnard, reiterated the frustrations of the family, before mentioning that the Colonial Office might soon be receiving a message from Haddington, which would 'tell him in the strongest terms of the situation of the family, press upon him the loss of time, and that his kindness if not followed up will be ruinous'. But James went further in his letter, issuing a veiled threat. He mentioned that he had been in contact with the Earl's son, Lord Binning, who was the Member of Parliament for Rochester, and who had some influence not only on account of his standing as a politician, but also because of his close relationship with George Canning, who was at this time Secretary of State for Foreign Affairs.[40] James injudiciously warned that Binning 'may impute the neglect, or rather oversight, for not ordering a passage for us . . . to different gentlemen having management of the Navy Office', but immediately applied some balm to this inflammatory suggestion with advice to Barnard that 'my father would accede to the cheapest arrangement that could be made . . . and that instead of the regular cabin provision he would be content to receive in a private ship the same rations . . . as would be served on a transport'.[41]

James could have stopped at this point, content in the knowledge that he had made his plea, and had applied some leverage which he hoped would advance his cause. But instead of breezing through the salient details, he plodded on, producing a long-winded epistle that laboriously repeated several points he had raised earlier with officials. Eventually, he alighted on the topic on which he considered himself an expert: viticulture. He provided in excruciating detail his vision for the establishment of a wine industry in New South Wales, including estimates of the economic viability of the industry. And throughout this meandering letter, James made sure to pepper the text with reference to several minor members of the aristocracy and other notables, hoping that their names would both impress and carry some influence with Barnard.[42] James's confident tone when addressing officials,

---

[39] J. Busby to G. Busby, 12 July 1823, in Letters from James Busby to his Brother George Busby 1823–1830, Auckland Institute and Museum Library, MS46, folder, 2, 2.
[40] *The Asiatic Journal and Monthly Register for British India and its Dependencies* 23 (London: Kingsbury, Parbury, & Allen, 1822), 384.
[41] Summary by James Busby of James Busby to E. Barnard, 12 July 1823, in *BFR* 1, 66.
[42] Among the names mentioned were Lieutenant-General Sir John Hope, Robert Dundas, the 2nd Viscount Melville, Sir John Sinclair, Sir Robert Grant, and Lord Balgray.

though, belied the acute financial vulnerability the family was in. He reported dispiritedly to his brother about the hardships he anticipated lay ahead even if they managed to reach New South Wales.[43] Meanwhile, James's funds were 'nearly exhausted', causing him to borrow from associates in London, with an assurance that his father would very soon reimburse them.[44]

A few days later, there was suddenly cause for optimism. 'I have great hopes', James jubilantly announced to his father, 'that if we get Melville [Edinburgh-born Privy Counsellor Henry Dundas, the 2nd Viscount Melville][45] to interfere we shall have money advanced to us for our passage . . . in which case our best plan is to get a steerage passage in the *Triton* . . . and in such a large ship . . . we have every chance of being comfortable'. That same day, James went to the Transport Office at Deptford, where he met with a Captain Young – 'a most friendly man' – who unfortunately told him clearly that 'not one ship in ten could accommodate . . . [the] family'.[46] There was never any thought, though, that they would travel separately to the colony. Apart from George, who planned to join them once he had graduated, the Busbys moved together like a familial solar system, with all the individual members orbiting dutifully around a central ambition.

James was frustrated with Barnard's lack of assistance over this matter, criticizing him for suffering from 'the insolence of office'. And to compound James's problems, he was now resorting to borrowing more money and buying food on credit wherever he could. He had been unable to find any work in London to support him, and had recently fallen very sick. The miseries were mounting up as he desperately sought a passage for the family to New South Wales.[47] Weeks later, there was still no respite from the rejections. James had been to visit Melville's secretary to see if the Viscount would be prepared to represent the family to Wilmot-Horton, but was effectively brushed aside. His tenacity was by now being tested to its limits, but despite the personal privations and ongoing frustrations with officialdom, James kept up with his campaigning.

In the previous few weeks, James had made contact with the agent of a private shipping company, and even the representative of a convict ship, but both options proved to be too expensive.[48] So with what by now must have

---

[43] James Busby to G. Busby, 12 July 1823, in *BFR* 1, 67.
[44] Ibid.
[45] J. Foster, *Members of Parliament, Scotland*, 2nd edn. (London: Hazell, Watson and Viney, 1882), 112.
[46] J. Busby to John Busby, 16 July 1823, in Letters from James Busby to his Father John Busby 1823–1834, Auckland Institute and Museum Library, MS46, folder, 3, 5; James Busby to G. Busby, 12 July 1823, in *BFR* 1, 67.
[47] Ibid., 68.
[48] M. Nix, 'The Australian Company of Edinburgh and Leith, Part One: A Mode of Business', *The Great Circle* 27, no. 2 (2005): 21; J. Busby to John Busby, 2 July 1823, in Letters from James Busby to his Father John Busby 1823–1834, Auckland Institute and Museum Library, MS46, folder, 3, 3.

felt like monotonous regularity, he returned to lobbying government officials. On 12 August, he went to the Admiralty, which provided him with no assistance, and so he walked to the Colonial Office, deliberately arriving unannounced in an attempt to secure a meeting with Wilmot-Horton. However, Wilmot-Horton was away, so James returned the following day to put his well-rehearsed case again to any official who would listen.

This protracted drama continued until 15 August 1823, when notice was given by Wilmot-Horton (at the direction of Bathurst) in a letter addressed to John Busby[49] (which James immediately opened). In it, Wilmot-Horton advised that a role of mineral surveyor and civil engineer had been created for John in Sydney – a position that would probably involve management of coalmines in the area, and in supplying Sydney with water – and that the family would travel to the colony by a ship that was due to depart Leith at the beginning of September.[50] More details followed, including mention of a personal recommendation from Bigge for John's services in New South Wales, and the specifics of his terms of employment. Once again, it seemed that fortune was favouring the persistent. A position of some rank – and a government position at that – had been created for John, and there were opportunities for James and George (when the latter completed medical school) to find employment as well. It helped that the recommendation for John to go to Sydney had come from none other than Bigge, who saw the need for someone with John's particular expertise in the colony.[51]

There was just one small wrinkle in the scheme left to iron out: James urgently needed to get back to Leith, in Scotland, so that he could depart with the rest of the family. He was completely without money by this stage, and had possibly even foregone some meals in an effort to make whatever funds he had left stretch to another few days. He then received a letter from his father, advising him that all passengers had to be on board the ship and ready to depart by 26 August – just over a week away. John had deposited £5 into a bank so that James could draw on this to pay for the fare back to Edinburgh, but had neglected to say which bank the money had been deposited into. James frantically raced around London until he found the institution where the funds had been lodged and was able to return by coach to Leith.[52]

---

[49] R. Wilmot-Horton to J. Busby, 15 August 1823, in Papers of the Busby and Kelman Families, 1822–1879, CY Reel 985, ref ML MSS. 1183, 35.
[50] This had previously been hinted to John in R. Wilmot-Horton to J. Busby, 29 March 1823, in *HRA* 1, vol. 11, 107.
[51] Ibid.
[52] J. Busby to G. Busby, 22 August 1823, in Letters from James Busby to his Brother George Busby 1823–1830, Auckland Institute and Museum Library, MS46, folder, 2, 7.

THE TENACITY OF THE SON

In spite of the delays, the financial hardship, and the enormous uncertainty over their future, the Busby family held tight to the belief that they functioned best – or perhaps could only function – as a single unit, no matter how unwieldy. Such an unusually close bond may have originated partly from the Busbys being a family of the suitcase. For more than two decades, they had shifted houses, cities, and even countries, as often as possible together. Not being rooted to one place, this quasi-nomadic clan consequently had few established wider social networks, and even fewer long-term, intimate ones. So when it came to looking to someone for support, turning to each other was all they knew. And now they were on the brink of the boldest shift of their lives – with the few remaining possessions that they had not sold packed in preparation for their departure.

One thing that had not yet been bundled away, however, was John's disputatious impulse. As the family waited for word that their ship was ready to be boarded, he dispatched a parting demand to Bathurst over the handling of the costs relating to their journey. Colonial Office staff had been partially in error in this matter, and agreed to cover the additional cost John insisted be paid.[53]

With the departure date was set for 7 September 1823,[54] the Busbys loaded themselves and their luggage onto carts and made their way along the five-kilometre route to the recently completed dockyard at Leith. For most of the family this would be the final time they would see Scotland. The weather was overcast, with the temperature struggling to reach ten degrees Celsius for much of the day.[55] High tide was at three o'clock that afternoon, and with thickening cloud cover above, it was a chilly, damp scene that the Busbys faced as they boarded the 405-ton *Triton*, and settled themselves into three adjoining starboard cabins for their voyage to Port Jackson, in Sydney.[56] Their furniture had been stowed away the previous day, along with two dairy cows, two pigs, two goats, a crate of chickens, some seeds for their planned garden, some cases of wine, preserved fruits, and some tree and plant cuttings (which were accidentally doused with seawater, and died soon after). The Busbys had joined forty-nine other passengers and twenty-four crew for the journey, and at four that afternoon, the *Triton* weighed anchor and headed north. There were seven of the family in total on the ship: John and Sarah, and their children James, John, Catherine, Alexander, and William.[57]

---

[53] John Busby to Bathurst, 3 September 1823, in in Papers of the Busby and Kelman Families, 1822–1879, CY Reel 985, ref ML MSS. 1183, 47–8.
[54] *Hobart Town Gazette [HTG]*, 23 January 1824, 2.
[55] *Blackwood's Edinburgh Magazine* 14 (London: William Blackwood, 1823), 616.
[56] R. Brown jr, passage on ship Triton, in Papers of the Busby and Kelman Families, 1822–1879, CY Reel 985, ref ML MSS. 1183, 17–18.
[57] *HTG*, 23 January 1824, 2.

A few days into the voyage, the *Triton* was hit by a ferocious storm off in Pentland Firth, about five kilometres north of John o' Groats. After the vicious winds and lashing rain had subsided, one passenger wrote how during the height of the storm, 'we were scarcely able to keep our beds, self and bedfellow rolling alternately upon each other. . . . It was no uncommon thing to see those on the lee side sprawling on the floor covered with pea soup, salt beef and a variety of other eatables while those on the weather side would be precipitated over the tables to share in the sufferings of their fellow passengers on the leeward side.'[58] So violent and prolonged had this bad weather been that the first Sunday church service on the ship was not held until 28 September. In an account of the voyage on the *Triton* made by George Augustus Robinson[59] (a London builder and lay preacher who eventually became Chief Protector of Aborigines in the Port Philip district),[60] the services were depicted as being much like those conducted any other Sunday on a British ship in this period, and it conformed to the usual Anglican format. The difference, however, was that this vessel's passenger list was made up almost exclusively of Scots, and their Puritan tendencies surprised Robinson. That afternoon he decided to play a few religious tunes on his flute, but was requested to cease as most of the other passengers disliked any music on the Sabbath.

James occupied his considerable spare time giving lessons to his younger brothers, and keeping a detailed record of the trip, as well as maintaining his correspondence with George. James's letters made mention of things like food flying through the air and landing on people, together with broken crockery in every direction during the sudden onset of a 'hurricane', his mother falling 'into a dreadful state of alarm' when a window broke during a storm, and his ideas for establishing an importing business when he reached Sydney.[61]

Occasionally, he made transparent certain feelings and views that were usually shielded by his outward demeanour. In one of his few personal comments on religion, for example, he described as a 'really gratifying sight' the crew and passengers of the ship attending the Sunday prayers and sermon. And on his relationship with his older brother, whom he was clearly missing by this time, he had moments of untypical candour. Three months

---

[58] George Augustus Robinson papers, Mitchell Library, ref A7022.
[59] Ibid.; N. J. B. Plomley, *An Immigrant of 1824* (Hobart: Tasmanian Historical Research Centre, 1973).
[60] B. Buchan and M. Heath, 'Savagery and Civilization: From Terra Nullius to the "Tide of History"', *Ethnicities* 6, no. 1 (2006): 18.
[61] James Busby to G. Busby, 26 September 1823, in Letters from James Busby to his Brother George Busby 1823–1830, Auckland Institute and Museum Library, MS46, folder, 2, 9.

after departing Leith, he wrote to George saying 'I fear my former letters have disappointed you. I confess there was a barrenness in them', and then added even more candidly that he was writing 'to the brother of my heart'.[62] Such deeply felt affection helps to explain the family's inclination to remain together, rather than splinter off as the children reached maturity.

The dreary, lilting routine of life on the ship was occasionally punctuated by alarming episodes of drama that potentially jeopardized the lives of all on board. On 9 October, two days before the *Triton* reached Tenerife, the crew caught sight of 'a very suspicious-looking brig'. The captain raised the ship's colours to show its national affiliation, but almost immediately, the mysterious vessel 'hoisted the black flag and fired two guns, crowding all sail after us'. However, for some reason, the brig did not approach any closer, and eventually sailed out of sight, with the crew and passengers of the *Triton* none the wiser as to its identity. The following evening, there was yet another suspicious encounter, which James relayed in a letter to George: 'an Englishman in a boat with four Spaniards came alongside from a man-o-war cutter anchored close by us. He endeavoured to appear Spanish, but he was evidently an Englishman. . . . He pointed to a fine-looking ship near us and told us he had brought her in.' The next day, though, an officer from another vessel informed the *Triton*'s captain that the cutter was a Spanish privateer, and potentially a threat.[63]

The *Triton* reached Tenerife on 11 October, but fears at the port over a rumoured contagious fever meant that the passengers and crew were quarantined, and so were prohibited from going on shore. Meanwhile, fevered European politics were capturing James's attention. In April 1823, France had invaded Spain (which exercised dominion over Tenerife), complicating an already tricky situation that had ensnared several European powers in the contest between absolute monarchists and constitutionalists that was boiling over in Spain.[64] James described how there 'are violent Constitutionalists here', and that the previous day, a Russian vessel, 'supposed to be on a voyage of discovery, came into touch for refreshments, but as soon as she showed her colours, they fired on her from the ports, and all the military were drawn out'. There were also two French ships which, according to James, intended to bomb the port. As the *Triton* was potentially in the line of fire, its captain summoned help, and within a few hours, James described witnessing 'one of the grandest sights possible – a 74 gun [Royal Navy] ship come to anchor close by us'.[65]

---

[62] James Busby to G. Busby, 28 September 1823; 11 October 1823, in *BFR* 1, 83–4.
[63] James Busby to G. Busby, 11 October 1823, in *BFR* 1, 84.
[64] A. Nicolle, 'Ouvrard and the French Expedition in Spain in 1823', *The Journal of Modern History* 17, no. 3 (September 1945): 193–6.
[65] James Busby to G. Busby, 11 October 1823, in *BFR* 1, 84.

After a two-day stay, the *Triton* was provisioned and ready to depart to its next port of call: South Africa. James continued to give daily lessons to his younger siblings during the voyage, but was far from satisfied with the results. Ten-year-old William, he complained, was 'as idle as ever', and John, aged seventeen, was 'very dull at the mathematics'. James was finding other aspects of the journey more enjoyable, though. There were 'two excellent singers on board' as well as a guitarist and a string trio, providing plenty of musical entertainment for the passengers.

It was on this leg of the voyage, though, that the Busbys faced one of the most terrifying episodes of the journey. At four in the afternoon on 29 October, while the *Triton* was more than a hundred kilometres off the coast of Sierra Leone, one of the crew saw a sail to the south, and over the next few hours, it continued to bear down on the ship. There is a sense of growing disquiet in James's account of the situation. The ship 'showed no colours, though ours were displayed a considerable time', and although this mysterious vessel was downwind, it was gaining on the *Triton*. By sunset, the ship had got much closer after hours of tacking, and as it passed near the *Triton*, it 'fired a shot, the ball of which wheered [sic] close under our stern'. This large ship was close enough now for James to see that all its portholes were open, suggesting that it was preparing to fire on the *Triton*. It was now about ten in the evening, and on the captain's orders, the crew and many of the male passengers scurried into action, loading muskets and preparing to be attacked. For the next hour and a half, as all the men on board lay still, anticipating an imminent strike, the only sound heard on board was the creaking of the ship's rigging and the lapping of waves on its hull. The terror James and the others of his family felt was without precedent in their lives. Then, just before midnight, the approaching ship fired a shot that landed in the ocean just to the rear of the *Triton*. In response, the captain hoisted English colours and waited as both vessels passed each other. There was no communication from the crew of the hostile vessel, and it soon sailed away. 'What she was and what her intention was we left to conjecture', Robinson recorded. 'Although we lost sight of her we were not without some apprehension of another visit of a more formidable nature than the first.'[66] After discussing the incident with captains from other vessels once he arrived in Cape Town, James concluded that it was most likely a pirate ship that had fired on them, and that their escape was more a case of fortunate circumstances than anything else.[67]

The tension of this episode was followed by many more mundane weeks at sea, with the food on offer not presenting itself as much to look forward to

---

[66] George Augustus Robinson papers, Mitchell Library, ref A7022.
[67] James Busby to G. Busby, 6 December 1823, in *BFR* 1, 85.

during these stretches of tedium. Each mess of six adults had a daily allowance of bread, coffee, sugar, rum, flour, raisins, and butter. And five times a week, they received around two and a half kilos of beef, or whatever other meat was available. Fish, potatoes, pickled cabbage, oatmeal, rice, and tea were sometimes added to this spartan menu when available. It was hardly a diet to maintain the health of those on board, and towards the end of October, several of the crew and passengers began developing boils 'occasioned by the saltness [sic] of the provisions'. The 'prickly' heat only made things worse, and soon the majority of those on the ship were experiencing the discomfort brought about by boils and infections. And to make matters worse, rats were discovered in the bedding of two passengers who had become sick, resulting in the captain ordering that all their linen and blankets be thrown overboard.

Of course, such privations and discomfort were to be expected, but for the Busbys, there had not been any preceding experience that was as challenging or as long as this voyage had been so far. The ordeals were not yet over, though. On 22 November, a group of passengers got drunk, and soon descended to fighting and throwing around furniture. It was described as 'a disturbance . . . not to be equalled by any Irish row that ever occurred in the neighbourhood of St Giles and the most serious one that occurred on board of this ship during the voyage'.[68] Several of those involved in the fighting suffered injuries as they continued to brawl, while the Busbys (among those others who had remained sober) were forced to hide until the melee died down.

So it was with anticipation and relief that the Busbys stepped on shore once the *Triton* had docked at Table Bay in Cape Town on 6 December – the first time they had stood on land in twelve weeks.[69] James was one of those who decided to use this stop to spend time exploring the area, and in particular, visiting vineyards in the vicinity – a subject that had dominated his interests since his trip to France. Cape Town provided him with the first example of the industry in operation outside Europe. Once on shore, James, Catherine, and some others went by horseback to Constantia to explore one of the oldest vineyards in the southern hemisphere. Overawed, James later depicted it as 'a perfect paradise', and regarded the information he acquired during the visit as 'more pleasure than instruction'.[70] Even the prospect of several more weeks confined in the *Triton* could not rein in James's anticipation of the day when he set foot in New South Wales and began to preparations for establishing his own vineyard. The specifics of how this would materialize had yet to be determined, but this in no way diminished his conviction that his future lay in this field.

---

[68] George Augustus Robinson papers, Mitchell Library, ref A7022.
[69] *The Cape Town Gazette, and African Recorder*, 13 December 1823, 1.
[70] James Busby to G. Busby, 6 December 1823, in *BFR* 1, 86.

Five days after arriving in Cape Town, the *Triton* departed for the last leg of its voyage: ten thousand kilometres to the Australian colonies. The winds were generally favourable, allowing the ship to make good progress, but the journey was accompanied by an increased frequency of storms, which gradually battered the *Triton*, leaving it with damaged sails and fittings. And as the Busbys and others were to discover, many of the belongings stored in the hull had been tossed around and in some cases damaged by the violent weather that pummelled the ship as it battled its way through the Indian Ocean.

But the destination was getting closer. On 18 January 1824, the *Triton* changed its course, turning northeast in the direction of Tasmania. The following day, it dropped anchor around thirty kilometres from Hobart, near Bruny Island, and waited for a pilot to board to guide the vessel to Tasmania's capital, where it docked on 20 January at around six in the evening.[71] New South Wales was now tantalizingly close. After months of confinement in a ship, not only a return to land, but arrival in the new and probably permanent home for the family was just a matter of weeks away. James recalled that his mother, who had been beleaguered by bad health for much of the journey, was now feeling better, and that he and the rest of the family were 'in excellent spirits' as they anticipated the final brief stint of the voyage to Sydney. 'The scenery on both sides of the river is enchanting', James wrote when entering Hobart. And excited by the imminent conclusion of the voyage, he added that 'our hopes are raised by is appearance'.[72]

On reaching Hobart, John could not help but launch himself immediately into work. He visited local farms, acquired assistants, and surveyed the extent and quality of coal deposits in the area. He then produced a report on his findings for the Governor.[73] There is no evidence he was paid for his services, or even that he sought any remuneration. More likely, it was a case of John hankering to do something to exercise his mind after many months where he had few opportunities to do so. With John's brief report completed, and the rest of the family impatient to reach their destination, the Busbys boarded the *Triton* for the final time on 19 February, and sailed north towards Sydney, arriving at Port Jackson five days later,[74] almost half a year after departing Leith. The vessel had been like a metaphorical chrysalis, out of which the family would emerge in Sydney, ready for their plans to unfurl.

---

[71] *HTG*, 23 January 1824, 2.
[72] James Busby to G. Busby, 20 January 1824, in *BFR* 1, 86. Also see James Busby records, Mitchell and Dixson Libraries manuscript collection, 1823, MLMSS 1668.
[73] *HTG*, 20 February 1824, 2.
[74] *The Sydney Gazette and New South Wales Advertiser [SGNSWA]*, 26 February 1824, 2.

3

'I am to Take Charge'

New South Wales in 1824 was in the process of transforming from an outpost of penitence into a nursery of enterprise. However, despite the fledgling nature of the civil society that was emerging (ironically with the assistance of convict labour) from the penal settlement, the Busbys had no intention to take baby steps in their first foray into the colony. The months they had spent confined in their cramped quarters on the *Triton* gave them time to fine-tune their intention for their lives in New South Wales, but it also turned their desire for success into a pent-up force, just waiting for the opportunity to be unleashed. So on setting foot in Sydney, the Busbys were fully primed for the next and dramatically different phase in their lives.

Even as the *Triton* inched its way into the harbour, the passengers on the vessel would have begun to absorb some sense of the scale and appearance of the town. There were stone cottages interspersed with larger buildings (some of them three storeys high) dotted seemingly at random on acres of cleared land. On the approach to Sydney, some of the terrain – from the coast to the hinterland – was still heavily draped in native flora, while on the more developed areas, the skyline was punctuated with windmills.

Once they had disembarked, this most recent crop of settlers could also not help but notice that this was still very much a penal colony. In many places where land was being cleared, where rocks were being hewn for construction, where roads were being laid, or any other sort of work where manpower was required, the Governor had allowed for convict labour to be used.[1] One effect of this was the ready supply of what amounted to practically free labour – a feature of the colony that immediately gave it an economic advantage.[2]

Three weeks after he arrived in Sydney, James's tone was already that of someone who had ascended into a new social class. Gone were the hurried

---

[1] G. Karskens, 'Defiance, Deference and Diligence: Three Views of Convicts in New South Wales Road Gangs', *The Australian Journal of Historical Archaeology* 4 (1986): 17–28.
[2] P. M. Cunningham, *Two Years in New South Wales* 1 (London: H. Colburn, 1827), 6.

moves from one lot of rented rooms to the next. Gone was the cold, confined life of urban Edinburgh, and apparently gone too were the financial difficulties that had been persistent enough to force the family from Britain. Now the Busbys were in a more pleasant, lofty, and refined sort of society. 'We have been for the last 10 days in a house which my father has taken in the Environs of Sydney, and in which after we get settled I have no doubt we shall feel exceedingly comfortable' was James's satisfied assessment of the family's first days in the colony. Even more important to him, though, was the easy access he and the family had to the highest echelons of the colony's society – something that would have been unthinkable in Britain. 'Our reception from the Governor and others from whom we had expectations of friendship have in no way disappointed the hopes we had formed,' he wrote, still slightly taken aback by how quickly he had entered the orbit of Sydney's great and good. 'Capt. Piper, the Naval Officer, in particular has shown a very great degree of kindness and attention,' while James's several conversations with the Governor about his viticulture plans were apparently very well received. On the day of the Busbys' arrival, the Governor, Sir Thomas Brisbane, was in Sydney, conducting business for a few hours before planning to return to Parramatta (around twenty kilometres away) later that afternoon.[3] John Busby managed to secure a quick appointment with Brisbane where he presented his credentials. John's salary had been back-dated to a month before he had arrived in the colony,[4] and so the family could now look forward to a relatively secure income for the next three years – a level of certainty they had never previously experienced. James also had discussions with Brisbane about his wish to secure a grant of land as soon as possible. The Governor told him that he 'must not be in a hurry', but instead should act judiciously, while 'flattering' James, and informing him that he 'would be happy to give . . . [James] every assistance' in his viticulture venture.[5]

The following morning, Piper took James and John to meet another Sydney notable, Major Frederick Goulburn, New South Wales's Colonial Secretary, who gave the new arrivals a warm welcome, and then spent a long time in discussion with John about the various possibilities for engineering projects in the colony. James was particularly impressed that Goulborn 'seemed to possess more information on the subject of the vine than most people I have talked to'.[6] By May, John had received a 2,000-acre grant of land on the Hunter

---

[3] *SGNSWA*, 26 February 1824, 2.
[4] Report by the Board on the Claims of Mr Busby, 8 June 1826, in *HRA* 1, vol. 12, 548.
[5] J. Busby to W. Kelman, 19 March 1824, in Papers of the Busby and Kelman Families, 1822–1879, CY Reel 985, ref ML MSS. 1183, 67–8.
[6] Ibid.

River (known at the time as the Coal River).[7] It was not to be a permanent plot for the family's agricultural plans because of its indifferent soils and awkward terrain, but it was a start at least.[8]

Yet, no matter how promising the path ahead appeared, twists of circumstances had a habit of interrupting the destiny that the family had mapped out for themselves. Unknown to the Busbys, on 25 February, the day after they had arrived in Sydney, 2,000 kilometres to the southeast, the brig *Elizabeth Henrietta* had been forced aground on Ruapuke Island, around fifteen kilometres off the southernmost part of New Zealand's South Island. In early April, news of the ship's fate reached Sydney. A recovery expedition was sent, but returned to Sydney on 3 June, claiming that the *Elizabeth Henrietta* was 'irreclaimable'.[9] All that remained was for the hull to be burned and for the iron on the vessel to be salvaged.[10] There was probably only one person in the continent who could offer hope for an alternative to scrapping the ship. John Busby convinced Brisbane that he was capable of salvaging the vessel, based on his previous experience, and was granted permission to attempt it. 'We are all in the bustle of preparation,'[11] James wrote excitedly to William Kelman (a friend who had travelled to Hobart on the *Triton* with the Busbys), clearly welcoming the prospect of his father achieving (in James's eyes) another famous triumph for the family.

John departed Sydney for southern New Zealand on 29 June, and with a team of six men and ten weeks' worth of provisions, to set to work on the recovery operation. Just four weeks later, the *Elizabeth Henrietta* was once again afloat, but it was a further ten weeks until the cutter *Mermaid* – the ship that was to transport them back to Sydney – was due to arrive at Ruapuke. John later recorded in his report on the salvage how he and the other men with him 'were reduced to lengthen out our scanty provisions with the addition of shell fish, and fern root' as they waited for their transport back to New South Wales. Of more concern than the near starvation he was enduring, though, was the inevitable anxiety of his family back home. He had been absent for eight months, with no communication with them at all during that time, leaving them in a state of 'extreme distress'.[12]

---

[7] *The Oriental Herald, and Colonial Review* 3 (London: J. M. Richardson, 1824), 441.
[8] Abstracts from orders for grants and town allotments, State Archives, New South Wales, 2/1928; COD67.
[9] *Historical Records of New Zealand South Prior to 1840*, ed. R. O. Carrick (Dunedin: Otago Daily Times, 1903), 63; R. McNab, *Murihiku: A History of the South Island of New Zealand and the Islands Adjacent and Lying to the South, from 1642 to 1835* (Wellington: Whitcombe and Tombs, 1909), 264–5; *HTG*, 4 June 1824, 2.
[10] *SGNSWA*, 10 June 1824, 2.
[11] J. Busby to W. Kelman, 22 June 1824, in Papers of the Busby and Kelman Families, 1822–1879, CY Reel 985, ref ML MSS. 1183, 71.
[12] J. Busby, in McNab, *Murihiku*, 266–7.

John's own distress on returning to Sydney was compounded by local officials having second thoughts about whether even to pay him, and if so, how much. So began one of his lengthy and often fervent campaigns to receive the remuneration he felt he was due. It was not until February 1826, and after much correspondence and personal protestations, that the Governor relented to John's demands, and paid him £300 for his salvage of the brig.[13] This was a more than satisfactory outcome, both for the colony's government, which otherwise faced the loss of a vessel, and on balance for John, who eventually received more than a year's salary for his efforts.

John's eight-month absence from the family so soon after they had arrived in New South Wales had put James in the unanticipated role of de facto head of the family. James's dilemma was that he had planned to establish a vineyard and then a winery, and in the three years it would take for his vines to fruit, he would presumably be able to rely on the support of his father. However, with John gone, and his fate increasingly uncertain after months without contact, James decided that he would have to earn a living for the family in addition to establishing a vineyard. Of course, John had been absent from the family many times before, but that was back in Britain, where correspondence was possible, and where the destinations were known – unlike a remote island of a little-known territory that still had a reputation at this time as being inhabited by 'hostile savages'.[14] Now, in addition to John's unknown fate, the family had to contend with an unfamiliar country. Most of the accents would have been recognizable – Irish, English, and a few Scots – but the arid landscape, the incessant heat, and the unusual composition of the society (a military-run penal colony evolving into a civilian settlement) were all dimensions of New South Wales that were alien to the twenty-two-year-old James and his family. But circumstances drove James to look at ways of supporting his mother and siblings if worst came to the worst with his father.

Reflecting on this possibility, and the nature of the new rural existence that the family was entering into, James wrote that '[t]he solitude necessary to such a life is what we must all learn to submit to or we shall do little good in this part of the world'. Part of this sense of solitude derived from the fact that he had just taken up a 2,000–acre grant of land adjacent to that of his father's. It was now possible, he boasted, to ride for over eleven kilometres in a straight line through the family's land – a stark counterpoint to the crowded, compact existence the family had been accustomed to in Edinburgh.[15]

---

[13] R. Darling to Bathurst, 4 March 1826, in *HRA* 1, vol. 12, 203.
[14] J. L. Nicholas, *Narrative of a Voyage to New Zealand* 1 (London: Hughes and Baynes, 1817), 42.
[15] J. Busby to W. Kelman, 22 June 1824, in Papers of the Busby and Kelman Families, 1822–1879, CY Reel 985, ref ML MSS. 1183, 71–2.

And the nature of the family was changing in other ways too. Kelman had written to James asking him whether he had noticed the 'attachment' he had formed to James's sister, Catherine. 'It certainly did not escape my notice,' James responded, sounding more like Catherine's father than her brother. He explained how he felt disappointed that the letter was the first intimation he had received from Kelman of his interest in Catherine, but deliberating in the place of his father, he wrote (seemingly almost as much for posterity as for the moment) 'I shall become very far from a barrier to your union which in consequence of reciprocal attachment, the high opinion my father formed of your principles makes it a gratification to grant his consent.' Only one circumstance troubled him, though: the idea that, once married, Catherine would have to leave New South Wales and live with Kelman in Tasmania. Their mother, Sarah, had an exceptionally close bond with Catherine. 'I fear it will be difficult to reconcile my mother to part with her only daughter in a way that might make her reasonably despair of ever seeing her again, and her delicate state of health might cause it to prey still more deeply upon her spirits,' James cautioned his future brother-in-law. The solution he prescribed for Kelman was one that would not unduly upset the Busbys' family unity, even if the intrusion of a marriage was inevitable: '[it] makes me still more anxious', he told Kelman, 'to convince you of the superior prospects of this country', in reference to where James and John had acquired grants of land. James followed this with a list of the earnings of people he knew, in the hope that this would add weight to his plea for Kelman to leave Tasmania.[16]

In the meantime, months without news of John had placed an almost unbearable strain on the Busbys. The youngest member of the family, William, described how during the latter months of their father's absence, he and his siblings 'anxiously scanned the ships as they sailed up the harbour in case the vessel may be from New Zealand and carry news; but there was none', and that Sarah was 'so sorely tried' by the stress of it all.[17] It was not until January 1825 that news of John finally arrived, which flooded the family with relief. A ship docked at Sydney with the announcement that the members of the salvage team were all safe, 'and that the active Mr Busby' had succeeded in salvaging the *Elizabeth Henrietta*.[18] In early March, John's accomplishments were being trumpeted in Sydney in the local press. Despite the almost overwhelming scale of the salvage effort, John 'was not to be intimidated', the *Sydney Gazette and New South Wales Advertiser* noted. 'With the aid of only six men, in the space of 26 days, Mr Busby completed his Herculean

---

[16] Ibid., 72.
[17] W. Busby to J. Spinner, n.d., in *BFR* 1, 94.
[18] *SGNSWA*, 20 January 1825, 2.

task. The crew were out of provisions, and had been living for some time upon almost nothing – in which privations Mr Busby participated.' And as a parting thought, the journalist expressed the hope that the colonial government 'will not fail, most liberally, to reward Mr Busby for all his toil and ability'.[19]

At the time of his father's expedition to New Zealand, James had had little if any contact with Māori, even though there were Māori who had been visiting Sydney since the first decade of the nineteenth century.[20] So it is highly likely that the first insights he acquired into the indigenous inhabitants of New Zealand were from his father's account of his time in the country. What remains harder to know, though, is the extent to which James – who had by now acquired some knowledge of the world – took his father's colourful anecdotes of his adventure as being entirely accurate. John was clearly something of a raconteur, and judging just by the quantity of material that was handed down in the family about the events that relate to his salvaging of the *Elizabeth Henrietta*, the episode was a significant feature in his repertoire.

Always on the lookout for commercial opportunities, when the salvage work was complete, John had decided to acquire a cargo of flax from a nearby Māori community, which he hoped to take back to Sydney to sell. Accompanied by two sailors, he gingerly approached a group of Māori, and with the best of intentions, walked up to their chief (who was seated) and stroked his head. Unknown to John, though, the heads of chiefs were regarded as extremely tapu (sacred), and touching them was absolutely prohibited.[21] There was 'consternation and fury' within the community at this desecration, but because of the gravity of the offence, the guilty men were not immediately killed. Instead, their fate was to be determined by the community's tohunga (a uniquely distinguished person who was part leader, part priest). After long deliberations, a verdict was given. John and the two sailors with him were brought in front of the community, stripped of their clothes, and the fires were prepared for these captives to be cooked and then eaten. However, at the final moment before the prisoners were to be killed, John happened to wipe the perspiration from his forehead and removed his wig in the process. Those Māori present were initially shocked at this 'miracle', and fled from John. Gradually, though, some of them ventured out from the concealment of the forest and tentatively crept toward him, 'expressing their desire to see the miracle performed once again'. He was now regarded as a deity by this group

---

[19] *SGNSWA*, 3 March 1825, 2.
[20] H. Petrie, *Chiefs of Industry: Māori Tribal Enterprise in Early Colonial New Zealand* (Auckland: Auckland University Press, 2013), 28–73.
[21] R. Taylor, *Te Ika a Maui, or New Zealand and its Inhabitants* (London: Wertheim and Macintosh, 1855), 55; W. Brown, *New Zealand and its Aborigines* (London: J. and D. A. Darling, 1851), 9–14.

of Māori for apparently being able to scalp himself, and despite some hesitation, they eventually consented to let him and the two sailors leave.[22]

How much, if any, of this account is true is impossible to determine. The central events may have had some basis in fact, but it is worthwhile noting William's recollection of these stories from his father, in which he commented that 'I have hardly paper and ink enough to describe to you the number of romantic experiences which my father has been relating to us since his return.'[23]

In a way, the postscript to John's venture in New Zealand is more significant than the undertaking itself. The reason for this is that it revealed an increasingly polarized domestic political situation in New South Wales, which had repercussions for the Busbys. The first sign of this was a cooling of a relations between the Busbys and Brisbane. After returning to Sydney, John spent a year battling with the colonial authorities – and the now less cooperative Governor – to be paid for the salvage work he had performed in New Zealand. (It was not until Brisbane's replacement arrived that John finally received some remuneration for his efforts.)[24] There were already indications of this deterioration in relations in December 1824 (while John was still 'missing' in New Zealand). James had complained to Kelman in a letter that he remained 'idle' because of delays in decisions being made by Brisbane: 'I am not much indebted to the Governor, I assure you; had I no other friend than him, I would long since have given up hope of doing anything . . . [he] has behaved ill.'[25] The reason that the once affable Brisbane had become so remote was to do with a rift that had opened up between himself and Goulburn. As Brisbane perceived James in particular as having fallen in with the Goulburn 'faction', the favour he had formerly bestowed on him quickly evaporated.[26] The Busbys were simply unfortunate to get bogged down inadvertently in the swamp of colonial politics.

Among the profusion of recommendations that Bigge had managed to squeeze into his reports about New South Wales was one that an agricultural training project be established for youths aged fifteen to twenty in the colony, 'in which they should be taught the cultivation and fencing of land, and more especially, the management of sheep and cattle'. This training farm would be operated by staff 'who possessed a competent knowledge of agriculture', and which in addition to educating those present, would aim to achieve 'the

---

[22] A. D. M. Busby, in *BFR* 1, 92–3.
[23] W. Busby to J. Spinner, n.d., in *BFR* 1, 94.
[24] R. Darling to Bathurst, 4 March 1826, in *Historical Records of New Zealand* 1, 656–7.
[25] J. Busby to W. Kelman, 20 December 1824, in Papers of the Busby and Kelman Families, 1822–1879, CY Reel 985, ref ML MSS. 1183, 107–8.
[26] J. E. O'Hagan, 'Sir Thomas Brisbane, FRS, Founder of Organized Science in Australia', *Journal of the Royal Historical Society of Queensland* 6, no. 3 (1961): 603.

effectual separation of as many children as possible from their parents in the lower classes of the inhabitants, and early instruction in those habits by which their future exertions may be rendered profitable'.[27] Bigge believed that the poor habits of convict parents had been visited on their sons – a situation that (among many others) needed rectification if the colony was to prosper. This proposal came to fruition in the form of a farm for orphans, under the overall supervision of the Reverend Thomas Reddall, who was responsible for devising much of the colony's education regime from 1820.[28] Reddall was a member of an interim committee that had been formed by Brisbane to oversee orphan schools, and in August 1824,[29] Goulburn arranged for he and James to meet, with a view to James instructing the youths at the Male Orphan School on cultivating vines for grape production. (James was sufficiently impressed by Goulburn that he dedicated his 1832 book about New South Wales to him).[30] The school was located in Cabramatta – around thirty kilometres southwest of Sydney – on a 12,300-acre block of land.[31] James immediately travelled to the site, and, satisfied with what he saw, accepted the offer of a position at the orphanage the following month.

James saw the role in grand terms. He later explained that ran the orphan school along the principles 'similar to that of *M. Fellenberg*, in Switzerland'[32] – a philosophical approach that emphasized 'a pure moral atmosphere', in which the school leader worked to 'control whatever evil passions the pupil may naturally possess'. The idea was that such an institution not become 'a reformatory or penitentiary', but a place where the natural abilities of each pupil were emphasized.[33] James Busby as Australia's first pedagogue? Not quite, but he did believe he could improve rather than just maintain the organization he had been put in charge of. It also suggests that James was keen to depict himself as someone who, despite not completing a university education, was nonetheless widely read. Inadequacy might be too strong a word to append to such behaviour, but there were to be many other episodes in his life where he laboured to give an impression of himself as someone

---

[27] Bigge, *Report of the Commission of Inquiry on the State of Agriculture and Trade in the Colony of New South Wales*, 74–5; A. Barcan, *Two Centuries of Education in New South Wales* (Sydney: New South Wales University Press, 1988), 26.

[28] *The Asiatic Journal and Monthly Register for British India and its Dependencies* 12 (1821): 610.

[29] *Reports from the Committees* 7 (London: House of Commons, 1831), 73.

[30] J. Busby, *Authentic Information Relative to New South Wales and New Zealand* (London: Joseph Cross, 1832), iii.

[31] W. H. Wells, *A Geographical Dictionary; or Gazetteer of the Australian Colonies* (Sydney: W. and F. Ford, 1848), 366; *The Public General Statutes of New South Wales, 1824–1837* (Sydney: T. Richards, 1861), 44.

[32] J. Busby, in *Reports from the Committees* 7, 73.

[33] W. Chambers, *A Tour in Switzerland, in 1841* (Edinburgh: W. & R. Chambers, 1842), 40.

learned, and who was easily the match of those around him, despite them being better educated or more experienced.

This role was a sudden ascent in responsibility for the perpetually ambitious James. In December 1824, he outlined to Kelman the scope of the position: 'I am to take charge of the farm and to employ the young men in cultivation and cultivating the vine, and I am to have for my trouble one-third of the whole increases and produce.' Naturally, this revenue would not be achieved immediately, but the prospects were obvious to James. 'There are 400 head of cattle and a flock of sheep, and I think there will be from 70 to 100 acres under crop.'[34] It was a scale of operation he was eager to manage. At the age of twenty-two, he was now in charge of all the teaching staff, labourers, and servants at the orphanage, as well as managing its budget and shaping its syllabus. Within months of commencing this demanding role, he had extended the range of topics he taught from viticulture to agriculture more generally, and by June 1825, there were around 500 head of cattle on the school's farm, and almost 300 breeding ewes, as well as additional land constantly being planted with crops.[35]

James plunged all his energies into his new position. He did not just apply a specific philosophy to the institution, he also expanded its operation to the point where it generated an unexpected profit, by supplying livestock and vine cuttings to local farmers.[36] Yet far from being daunted by the increased workload that came with his extended responsibilities, James seemed to be invigorated by it. And throughout this busy and stressful period in his life, he worked on completing his 270-page book, *A Treatise on the Culture of the Vine*. Five months earlier, the publisher had sought subscriptions for the book through heavy advertising in the colony's newspapers, but interest was slight.[37] Just a month before publication, a mere ninety copies had been ordered. 'I am only printing 300 copies in all, and 50 clear to give away to friends in the colony and at home,' was how James saw the work's reach.[38] (An anonymous reviewer, writing in the *New South Wales Magazine*, rancorously assessed the work as '[a] dry and elaborate compilation', which James had allegedly partly plagiarized).[39]

---

[34] J. Busby to W. Kelman, 20 December 1824, in Papers of the Busby and Kelman Families, 1822–1879, CY Reel 985, ref ML MSS. 1183, 107–8.
[35] Busby was meticulous in his record-keeping for the school, including correspondence with staff, budgets, and plantings. See Letters and miscellaneous papers relating to James Busby and his management of the Male Orphan School Farm, 1825–1826, SRNSW 4/402.3.
[36] B. Bubacz, 'The Female and Male Orphan Schools in New South Wales, 1801–1850' (PhD thesis, University of Sydney, 2007), 259–60.
[37] *The Australian*, 9 December 1824, 4.
[38] J. Busby to W. Kelman, 23 March 1825, in *BFR* 1, 96.
[39] 'Mr Busby's Publications', *The New South Wales Magazine*, 1, no. 2 (September 1833): 94–5.

By this time, though, James was midway through drafting a comprehensive report about the orphan school and its farm, at Brisbane's request. James provided a detailed survey of the land, buildings, and other facilities, and rather than just summarizing the state of the school at that time, devised an elaborate business case for its expansion. Having examined the soils in different areas of the farm (no doubt drawing on the skills in this area that he had acquired from working with his father), he reported to Brisbane that around 2,900 acres would be put to best use as horticultural land, a further 3,610 acres would be good to run sheep on, 2,974 acres was too wet or otherwise unsuitable for any use, and the 2,816 acres remaining was covered in scrub or forest and also deemed to be of little practicable value.[40]

James's report worked its way through the channels of the colony's government, and ended up in the hands of the portentously named archdeacon Thomas Hobbes Scott – an Oxford-born cleric who had been appointed as a member of New South Wales's Legislative Council in 1824 after initially arriving in the colony in 1819 as Bigge's secretary. Although he was possibly unaware of it, there was some denominational politics that had resulted in Busby's report being sent to Scott.

In 1823, Brisbane mentioned that 'toleration was the glory of the Church of England', and so Presbyterians in the colony were free to worship as they chose. The Reverend John Lang, a local Scottish Presbyterian minister, took umbrage at what he saw as the condescending tone of Brisbane's statement, and sent a forthright letter to the Governor, reminding him that such toleration 'was not the glory of the Church of England, but of the British Constitution', and that 'Scotsmen were not, therefore, reduced to the necessity of receiving toleration as a boon from the Church of England'. Infuriated by this response, Brisbane removed his name, and that of all members of his family, from the list of subscribers who were contributing to the building of a Presbyterian church in Sydney.

Brisbane had over-reacted, and when news of his response reached London, Bathurst instructed the Governor to contribute one-third of the cost of constructing the church, plus commit the colonial government to paying an annual salary of £300 for its minister. Brisbane was sincere in his regret for his earlier hasty decisions, and undertook additional efforts to repair relations between his administration and the local Presbyterian community.[41] One of the further impediments in this process of reconciliation was Archdeacon Scott, whose alleged maxim when it came to the role of the Church of

---

[40] Letters and miscellaneous papers relating to James Busby and his management of the Male Orphan School Farm, 1825–1826.
[41] J. D. Lang, *An Historical Account of New South Wales, Both as Penal Settlement and as a British Colony* 2 (London: A. J. Valpy, 1834), 257–8.

Scotland in New South Wales was 'Let Episcopacy reign alone in the Australian colonies; and let no Presbyterian dog be permitted to bark within her ample domain.'[42] Brisbane had been made painfully aware of Bathurst's disdain for such stances, and anxious to avoid again inflaming Presbyterian passions and incurring the ire of London, he endeavoured to look for any opportunity he could – however small – to bridge this denominational divide. Accordingly, James was instructed to send his report to Scott, as part of Brisbane's effort at rapprochement with Scottish Presbyterians. Having then met James, and digested the findings and recommendations in his report, Scott (perhaps more dutifully than sincerely) wrote to Bathurst, expressing favour with James's findings.

For James, however, what mattered was that he had received such high-level recognition for his efforts, and in response, he ploughed ahead with new plans for the orphan school. The subsequent expansion of the farm was both rapid and substantial, but also slightly out of proportion for the purpose of merely educating the students at the school in agricultural techniques. It was almost as though James's focus on training these teenagers had been diverted to a vision of a sprawling agricultural enterprise – the limits of which were still known only in his imagination. By mid-1825, he had planted a vineyard, an orchard, and vegetable gardens. The scope of these undertakings was such that it was well beyond the capacity of the twenty-three students at the school to manage in between their other studies, and so James submitted a request in February 1826 to the committee overseeing the farm for twenty convict labourers to help with the maintenance and enlargement of this agricultural enterprise.[43]

James was now aged twenty-three, and finding himself attempting to issue orders to men who were often much older, who had spent years being brutalized as convicts in the colony, and who were offering their labour solely in the hope of having their sentences reduced.[44] Not only at the time did James fail to appreciate fully the circumstances of these men, but even after he had left the colony, his opinion of its convict labourers remained disparaging. He criticized their 'indolent and depraved habits', and the fact that so few of them had 'industry and steadiness enough to continue their labour from day to day, with the view of accumulating their earnings, in order to better their condition in life'. Instead, his view was that most of the convicts in New South Wales spent 'the greater part of their time . . . in sloth and dissipation', and if

---

[42] Ibid., 259.
[43] Letters and miscellaneous papers relating to James Busby and his management of the Male Orphan School Farm, 1825–1826.
[44] J. B. Hirst, *Freedom on the Fatal Shore: Australia's First Colony* (Melbourne: Schwartz Publishing, 2008), 99–100.

they did manage to work solidly for a short time, it was only so that they could afford to 'plunge the deeper in debauchery during the remainder'.[45]

However, despite the challenging circumstances of the 'indolent' convict labourers hampering his schemes, the climate, and the governing committee of the school exercising too much financial prudence for his liking, James's accomplishment in this desolate outpost of Sydney in just eighteen months was impressive by any measure. Among the successes of the farm were increased sheep and wheat production, the harvesting of five and a half tons of potatoes, a quarter of a ton of wool, the establishment of the vineyard, a flourishing animal husbandry programme, hundreds of additional acres of land being made ready for cultivation, and the construction of fences, huts, and storage buildings throughout the farm.[46]

But while James was taking centre stage in what looked to be a dazzling economic and managerial performance, behind the scenes, personnel changes were taking place that heralded the end of this run of success. In the space of a few months, the three men who comprised the committee responsible for overseeing the school and farm – Reddall, Goldburn, and Dr Henry Grattan Douglass[47] – withdrew their membership, and Brisbane was recalled.[48]

Brisbane's successor was the punctilious Lieutenant-General Ralph Darling, whom James made a point of meeting at the earliest opportunity. Darling was interested in James's work at the farm, and even enquired if he was pleased with his present salary. It was a positive start to dealings with the new Governor, and gave cause for James to reflect on how badly the relationship had deteriorated with Brisbane. 'It is only now', he wrote bitterly, 'that we are acquainted with the full extent of Sir Thomas Brisbane's villainous usage.'[49]

With the committee that had appointed him eviscerated, and uncertainties about the new Governor's intentions, the solid foundations supporting James's relatively secure position at the orphan school were looking shakier by 1826. Outside of his family there were few allies on whom he could call for a favour or support. In August 1826, a series of meetings was convened by his employer, at which James was able to put his case for the financial viability of

---

[45] Busby, *Authentic Information Relative to New South Wales*, 3–4.
[46] Bubacz, 'The Female and Male Orphan Schools in New South Wales', 261; B. J. Bridges, 'The Sydney Orphan Schools, 1800–1830' (MEd. thesis, University of Sydney, 1973), 284–5.
[47] Wentworth, *A Statistical, Historical, and Political Description of the Colony of New South Wales* 2, 311; Colonial Secretary Index, State Records New South Wales, 15 January 1823 (Reel 6040; 4/403), 112.
[48] C. Sheehan, '"I Have the Honour to Remain your Humble Servant"', *Queensland History Journal* 21, no. 12 (February 2013): 835; C. Liston, 'New South Wales Under Governor Brisbane, 1821–1825' (PhD thesis, University of Sydney, 1980), 457.
[49] J. Busby to W. Kelman, 11 January 1825, in *BFR* 1, 98.

the school farm during his tenure in charge of it. More details were requested, and duly supplied by James, but there were no encouraging signs that his position was secure.

Meanwhile, more problems hit the school. The following month, James was about to move into his new house on the school grounds when almost eighty of the pupils were struck with ophthalmia neonatorum – a highly contagious eye infection. 'My house was made a hospital,' he remarked to a friend, and just as the eye infection looked to be under control, there was a bout of what James identified as 'the itch', which delayed further his move to his new dwelling.[50] To this frustration was added the persistent questioning he was getting from his employers, together with a suggestion that the way his income was determined might be altered by the government. He was advised that the shares he held in the farm would be done away with, and that his salary might be reduced, despite the farm making a profit. James discussed his position first with the Archdeacon who was in charge of the committee, and then with the colony's Attorney General. They both tried to allay his concerns, but fell short of giving him the written confirmation he sought that his role at the school was secure.[51]

It was becoming clear that the authorities considered the expenses associated with James's agricultural schemes at the school to be too great, and after two years of fervent devotion to his role, he was informed by the Clergy and School Lands Corporation (the closest thing the colony had to an education ministry at the time) that his services would soon be surplus to requirements.[52]

Early in December, James finally had his fate confirmed. It was the committee's financial illiteracy, he believed, that was partly responsible for its decision to terminate his employment: 'The immense expenditure of the Orphan Schools, which no one took the trouble to analyse, paralysed them,' he wrote shortly after being given notice.[53] With no immediate prospects of work ahead of him, James ruminated over what he should do next. He considered taking his claim against his former employers all the way to Bathurst at the Colonial Office, but while privately he conceded that going to London for this purpose would take too long,[54] he was still prepared to be combative when

---

[50] J. Busby, 1 September 1826, in *BFR* 1, 109.
[51] Ibid., 111.
[52] *Documents on the Establishment of Education in New South Wales 1789–1880*, ed. D. C. Griffiths (Melbourne: Australian Council for Educational Research, 1957), 32–48; B. H. Fletcher, 'Christianity and Free Society in New South Wales 1788–1840', *Journal of the Royal Australian Historical Society* 86, no. 2 (2000): 93–113.
[53] J. Busby to G. Busby, 8 December 1826, in *BFR* 1, 119.
[54] J. Busby to G. Busby, 14 October 1826, in *BFR* 1, 113.

defending his rights. He told George that he mood was one of obstinacy, and in a moment of hyperbole announced that 'it may be requisite to proceed before the Lord Chancellor of England before they can dispossess me or deprive me of it [his claim]'.[55] However, two months later, he had changed his mind. 'I have already reconciled myself to lose everything,' he wrote despondently to his older brother after realizing that he had signed his employment agreement without paying sufficient attention to its provisions, and had trusted the verbal assurances his employers had given him (although he later claimed that when he sought clarification for ambiguities he had come across, 'offence was taken and no explanation as given').[56]

In September 1826, James took his concerns about the nature of his employment and the ambiguities of his contract to the solicitor-general, John Stephen. Stephen concluded that the state had an obligation to make a payment to James for having terminated his contract.[57] However, the parties were nowhere near agreeing to what that payment should be. With complete disregard for his prospects for future employment by the state, James dug his heels in. He refused to concede anything in the protracted and clumsy attempts at negotiations that followed, and was doggedly determined to do what he believed to be right rather than what was expedient. But by pursuing his cause in such an uncompromising fashion, he revealed a significant blind spot in his professional life: an inability to anticipate the longer-term consequences of his obstinacy.

As the dispute over James's contract dragged on, inevitably, the colony's new Governor was drawn into it. In Darling, James was confronted by a very different kind of colonial leader from the sort Brisbane had been. One nineteenth-century source described him as 'a clever but narrow-minded officer . . . who was so thoroughly imbued with the spirit of military routine that he was a most unsuitable person to preside over a civil administration'. He had acquired a reputation as 'a mere official formalist, a man of system and routine, a strict and severe disciplinarian',[58] and was dissatisfied with the manner in which the dispute involving the termination of James's employment was playing out. As far as Darling was concerned, James was demanding payment from the Corporation in a matter 'in which they had no beneficial interest' because James's appointment predated the formation of the Corporation.[59]

---

[55] J. Busby to G. Busby, 8 December 1826, in *BFR* 1, 119.
[56] J. Busby to G. Busby, 10 February 1827, in *BFR* 1, 121.
[57] Bubacz, 'The Female and Male Orphan Schools in New South Wales', 262.
[58] D. Blair, *The History of Australasia: From the First Dawn of Discovery in the Southern Ocean to the Establishment of Self-Government in the Various Colonies* (Glasgow: McGready, Thomson & Niven, 1878), 333.
[59] R. Darling, 31 March 1828, in *HRA* 1, vol. 14, 96.

It was not just the loss of wages which James was claiming for, though. He was also asserting a right to a percentage of the value of the farm's produce, 'at a very high Rate', according to Darling. The matter could have ended up lengthy litigation, which would have been costly to all those involved, but fortunately the parties to the dispute had enough good sense – at Darling's firm recommendation – to submit to the decision of a small committee of arbitrators. Legal principles would guide their deliberations, but with this being an extra-judicial process, a degree of natural justice could also be applied. The arbitrators eventually decided broadly in James's favour, and although they reduced his claim, he was still awarded £1,033,[60] which was over twice his father's annual salary. The lesson that was reinforced for James from this drawn-out episode was that when it came to asserting one's rights, stubbornness evidently paid dividends. Yet he rejected this settlement and so the grievance continued to fester.

In the meantime, James had moved back to his parents' house in Liverpool Street, in the centre of Sydney.[61] His career as a school superintendent and farm manager – both of which roles he regarded himself as having excelled in – had drawn to a close. He was deflated but not defeated, and knew that if enough pressure of the right sort was applied to the relevant officials, some opportunity would eventually emerge. So while fighting the Commission, James had simultaneously been courting senior officials in the colony's administration, including Darling, with a view to being given a government post. One of the officials with whom James discussed his prospects was Lieutenant Colonel Henry Dumaresq, who had recently been appointed to the colonial government, and who was 'immediately granted a place on the peak of the social heap'.[62] James described him slightly disparagingly as one of those people who 'flatters a little', but nonetheless, he regarded him as a useful contact.[63]

In January 1827, as James was finalizing a note to the school committee on the matter of arbitration, he received a letter from Dumaresq, notifying him that the Governor wished to see him immediately. James went promptly to Dumaresq's office, where he was given news that the Governor had a position in mind for him. The only fly in the ointment was James's obduracy when it came to accepting a settlement over his long-standing employment dispute. Darling's view was that while this grievance remained unresolved, James could not take up the position he had envisaged for him.[64]

---

[60] Ibid., 100.
[61] *SGNSWA*, 23 December 1826, 3.
[62] M. C. Connor, 'The Politics of Grievance: Society and Political Controversies in New South Wales, 1819–1827' (PhD thesis, University of Tasmania, 2002), 122; *SGNSWA*, 12 December 1825, 2.
[63] J. Busby to G. Busby, 8 December 1826, in *BFR* 1, 119.
[64] Ibid., 119–120.

Darling recommended that James visit the Archdeacon to resolve the matter once and for all, which he duly did. However, despite the offer of a government job now being within reach, astonishingly James was not only unprepared to compromise on his stance regarding the money which he still felt he was owed, but announced that he was happy for the issue to go to court. The Archdeacon, who was also under pressure from the Governor to settle the dispute, approached John Busby to see if he could exercise any influence over his son. The response from John was hardly encouraging. As James later wrote, '[m]y father said that he always would advise me not to contend with Power, that he himself had several such contests and though successful it would have been much better for him to have turned his back upon them'. Conciliation looked hopeless in the face of such intransigence. James hoped for the issue to go to court not just for the sake of his claim, but to make the reputation of his employers 'stink', as he put it.[65] This was precisely the situation that Darling was so eager to avoid.

Towards the end of February, James was invited to a dinner at Government House, where the Archdeacon was also in attendance. Despite the intensification of the dispute between them and the impending court case, the encounter was remarkable for its civility. 'We drank wine together and chatted together,' James recalled, 'but of course, not a word of business'.[66] Afterwards, the Archdeacon suggested to James that both parties stick to arbitration instead of litigation, which James reluctantly agreed to, and a final settlement was reached within a month. James was genuinely surprised by this dramatic turn of events. 'Three weeks ago this was the last result I would have expected for there was really ill-blood between the Archdeacon and me,' he wrote.[67]

Now that the blockage to James's employment with the colonial government had been removed, events suddenly flowed quickly. 'The same day,' James wrote, with underlining for emphasis, 'the Governor sent for me and I was gazetted Collector of the Internal Revenue and a Member of the Land Board . . . at the salary of £400 for the one and £100 for the other appointment.'[68] The office of Collector of Internal Revenue was instituted in April 1827, with the primary purpose of collecting and accounting for revenue from land sales or rent, and then forwarding these funds to the office of the Colonial Secretary.[69]

---

[65] Ibid., 122.
[66] J. Busby to G. Busby, 29 June 1827, in *BFR* 1, 125.
[67] Ibid., 125.
[68] *The Asiatic Journal and Monthly Register for British India and its Dependencies*, 24 (1827): 780; *The Monitor*, 6 April 1827, 1; J. Busby to G. Busby, 29 June 1827, in *BFR* 1, 127.
[69] B. H. Fletcher, 'Administrative Reform in New South Wales Under Governor Darling', *Australian Journal of Public Administration* 38, no. 3 (1979), 257; T. Callaghan, *Acts and Ordinances of the Governor and Council of New South Wales* 1 (Sydney: William John Row, 1844), 553–4.

The Land Board was another of Darling's administrative initiatives, by which settlers would have to verify that they had the requisite capital to develop any land they received a grant for.[70]

James was thrilled at his appointments, and took particular pride in the fact that his role at the Land Board would entitle him to prefix his name with 'the Honourable'. 'What would the Grass Market say to this?' he asked George rhetorically. (The Grass Market was an old and popular market square in the centre of Edinburgh.) He also noted that he was now defined as 'Esquire', and that he had 'an authorised station in society'.[71] The hankering for status that seemed to have receded to a simmer in James's mind in recent years was now again fully on the boil.

The fact that the Governor was prepared to entrust the responsibilities of these two offices to James (albeit temporarily) is a sign of how highly he regarded his administrative abilities. From James's perspective, instead of dealing with orphans and hiring convicts in a remote school farm, he would now be working for the colonial government, in the centre of Sydney, and in an office. This held out the promise of the sort of class ascent that had been one of the defining desires of the family for decades. In addition, by working directly for the government, Busby would be part of the apparatus of the colony's administration, rather than bickering with it from the outside, as he had recently been forced to do.

Darling's motives in appointing James went beyond his strategy for administrative reform. With James occupying a position in the colonial administration, the Governor hoped this new employee would be more inclined to terminate the legal action he was still threatening against the Commission (thus avoiding any public embarrassment for the government), and would also enable senior officials to keep a closer eye on him. Despite James's reputation for being stubborn and occasionally quarrelsome, Darling had faith that he would not be foolish enough to bite the hand that fed him. Furthermore, the position would only be a temporary appointment. The Governor had a relative in mind to fill the post once that person arrived from England, and so James would hopefully occupy the role just long enough to allow the claims he had against the Commission to be settled, with the constraints of working for the government preventing him from becoming too outspoken about his negotiations for recovering money he still felt was owed to him, despite a settlement of sorts having already been reached through arbitration.

James launched himself into these new roles with his customary vigour. As the positions had just been created, he had to organize everything from the

---

[70] B. H. Fletcher, *Colonial Australia Before 1850* (Melbourne: Nelson, 1976), 77.
[71] J. Busby to G. Busby, 29 June 1827, in *BFR* 1, 125.

ground up, and within a few months, was already considering hiring two clerks to assist him. He usually began work at ten in the morning, undertaking his revenue-collecting role until around three in the afternoon. He would then start work on the Land Board business, which would often last until late in the evening. This latter posting he described as 'not the most pleasant employment owing to the character of the president . . . overbearing, obstinate. . . . He and I are tolerably good friends, as I make it a point to give him his own way.'[72]

Apart from such minor personality differences, though, and the considerable workload he faced, James thrived under the pressure of his roles – particularly at the Land Board. Indeed, he depicted the sheer quantity of work he was required to get through almost as a mark of accomplishment in itself. 'I give you an idea of the extent of my correspondence', he boasted to George, 'when I tell you that from the Colonial Secretary's Office alone I have received this day letter No. 100. I have . . . bills in my possession to the amount of £50,000; my last month's collection £3,359. To keep a cash book and manage the correspondence will be all I am able [to do]. . . . I myself have written upwards of 50 letters [today] requiring some consideration.'[73]

James was required to deliberate on the circumstances of each application before him, and the nature of the prose he adopted in his reports on the applications would have made for tiresome reading by the already overworked Colonial Secretary, Alexander Macleay, to whom they were addressed.[74] In one typical piece of faux-judicial writing, James responded to a claim submitted by a settler in an especially turgid manner:

> On the question of allowing Rations to Mr Cowper's fifth child, who was born in the Colony, I would feel more difficulty, as, however reasonable it is to suppose that the Rations for his family should include any addition, which should be made to that family by birth, it is still a question open to dispute and subject in my opinion to be settled rather by the Rule, which Custom may have established in such cases, than by the authority of any more defined principle.[75]

Not only was such verbosity the norm for much of James's official writing, but there is also a haughty air in his reports, in which the long-winded and slightly pompous nature of the 'judgment' outweighs the often routine issue under consideration.

---

[72] Ibid., 127.
[73] J. Busby to G. Busby, 22 July 1827, in *BFR* 1, 129.
[74] H. Golder, *Politics, Patronage, and Public Works: The Administration of New South Wales, Volume One: 1842–1900* (Sydney: University of New South Wales Press, 2005), 35.
[75] J. Busby to Colonial Secretary Macleay, 22 September 1827, in *HRA* 1, vol. 13, 759.

Indeed, James occasionally let slip his personal pretentions in his reports. 'I would have considered it desirable still further to elucidate the subject by Queries on two particular points', he pontificated in one instance, 'not so much because the Evidence produced has been insufficient to enable me to come to a satisfactory conclusion, as because, in a Judicial Enquiry like the present, it is particularly desirable that the most direct Evidence, which is procurable on every point, should be obtained.'[76] From minor clerical employee to a dispenser of justice in the manner of a judge is how James had elevated the perception of his role in his mind, and he subsequently attempted to imply this through the tone of his prose. He may have been driven simply by an unrealistic estimation of the need for there to be a legal flavour to his reporting, but it is also possible that he saw this legal tone as a way of impressing on others his expertise and intelligence. However, applicants were frustrated by his wordy magisterial meditations on issues, while those with legal training were easily able to detect the presence of a poseur in their midst.

The rest of the Busbys were progressing in various ways in the colony. George, who had completed his medical studies in Edinburgh, was elevated to the prestigious post of Assistant Surgeon on the Civil Establishment in 1827. In addition to working for the colonial administration (and later also running a private medical practice), he began to build up substantial land holdings in the colony.[77]

Alexander Busby had begun working for his father as an assistant (for £100 per annum) in the various civil engineering projects that were underway in the colony at the time.[78] Alexander's specialist knowledge in engineering expanded, and he became an expert in his own right, eventually being elected as a Fellow of the Geological Society of London.[79] As for Catherine, her fate was tied to that of Kelman, whom she had met on the *Triton* and had shortly afterwards become engaged to. They were married three years later at St James Church, Sydney.[80] Kelman eventually established his own vineyard (after gaining experience working for James) and became a successful winemaker.[81] And of course, the family patriarch – John – remained in demand

---

[76] Ibid., 760.
[77] *SGNSWA*, 5 January 1827, 1; D. S. Macmillan, *Wealth and Progress: Studies in Australian Business History* (Sydney: Angus and Robertson, 1967), 32; *Statistical Register of New South Wales for the Year 1861* (Sydney: Registrar General's Office, 1862), 90; *SGNSWA*, 11 February 1826, 1.
[78] J. Maclehose, *The Picture of Sydney: And Strangers' Guide in New South Wales for 1838* (Sydney: J. Spilsbury, 1838), 166.
[79] *The Australian*, 30 September 1826, 3.
[80] *The Monitor*, 17 February 1827, 8.
[81] A. Lambourne, *The Treaty-Makers of New Zealand: Heralding the Birth of a Nation* (Lewes: Benton-Guy Publishing, 1988), 54 and 72; J. McIntyre, *First Vintage: Wine in Colonial New South Wales* (Sydney: UNSW Press, 2012), 66.

for his services, and was renowned (begrudgingly by some) for his great feat of supplying water to Sydney, as well as for discovering significant seams of coal in the colony.[82]

But with the family becoming established, respected, and reasonably well known within Sydney, it was perhaps inevitable that there would be detractors. When the *Sydney Monitor*, for example, derisively referred to James as 'a young man . . . formerly a linen-draper of Edinburgh',[83] the message that he was a person with a position and pretensions in the colony above his station was clear. Obviously stung by this barb, James wrote to his brother, unsuccessfully trying to downplay the effect of the comments on him. 'It is well this did not come out sooner,' he wrote dismissively; 'I think my character is too well established for it to injure me now.'[84] The labelling of James as a former 'linen-draper of Edinburgh' was a reference to his work in a haberdashery in Edinburgh in 1822[85] – a fact that curiously (even suspiciously) had made its way to the colony and surfaced in the press five years later.

However hard James took this slight, it was a threat to his reputation more than to his livelihood. The latter was jeopardized, though, with the imminent arrival in Sydney of Darling's relative, who had been promised James's role of Collector of Internal Revenue. James had always known that his tenure in the job was limited, but since he had taken on the position, he had shaped it in his own image, and in turn had allowed his public persona to be defined by it. In December 1828, he tried to convince Darling to employ him elsewhere, but the Governor was adamant that there was no money spare to take any additional staff at this stage.[86]

At the same time, James's correspondence offers a small glimpse into his personal life. On 21 December 1828, he visited the Reverend Richard Hill, who had been a chaplain in the colony for a decade.[87] Hill had recently been ill, and James went to see how his wife was faring as the cleric convalesced. The topic of the conversation turned to James's future, with Mrs Hill asking 'jocularly' when he was going to settle down and marry. James was slightly irritated by the question, and brushed it off, as he had perhaps become used to doing by now, being a single male of marrying age (he was about five

---

[82] *A Concise History of Australian Settlement and Progress* (Sydney: Sydney Morning Herald, 1888), 59; *Report of the Commission to Inquire into the Supply of Water to Sydney and Suburbs* (Sydney: Thomas Richards, 1869), 96; B. H. Fletcher, *Ralph Darling: A Governor Maligned* (Oxford: Oxford University Press, 1984), 162.
[83] *The Sydney Monitor*, 21 August 1830, 2.
[84] James Busby to George Busby, 22 August 1830, James Busby Papers, ML MSS 1668.
[85] *The Post-Office Annual Directory* (Edinburgh: Postmaster-General of Scotland, 1822), 89.
[86] J. Busby to G. Busby, 21 December 1828, in *BFR* 1, 148.
[87] C. M. H. Clark, *A History of Australia: New South Wales and Van Diemen's Land, 1822–1838* (Melbourne: Melbourne University Press, 1962), 238.

weeks short of his twenty-seventh birthday). Just how tetchy James was on the subject, though, is revealed in a letter he wrote to George about this episode: 'at last she [Mrs Hill] said, joking aside, she had heard I really was going to be married, and when I pressed her to know the name of the victim, who should you suppose it to be? But <u>Miss James</u>! I have not spoken to the girl this three months, and I have once or twice <u>been absolutely rude to them</u>; for I could not but observe that the old lady made <u>a dead set</u> at me.' James was aware of how swiftly such a rumour could travel through Sydney's small, gossip-ridden population, and he identified the mother of the woman to whom he was supposedly betrothed as the author of this lie. 'I have not lived 30 years a bachelor to <u>finish</u> by marrying her daughter,' he went on, ensuring that there was no ambiguity in George's mind about the notion. 'I told Mrs Hill I had never thought of such a thing for the moment, and that I had as much intention of marrying Miss James as I had of marrying her [Mrs Hill].'[88] Outside his immediate family and the demands of his mercurial career, James had shown little inclination to engage in social activity with either gender. There was certainly nothing in his letters even to suggest that his attention was ever on anything other than visions of his future success.

In addition to being loveless at this time, James was also largely humourless. His younger brother, John, recounted an episode to George, in which he took advantage of the fact that Sydney was full of the news of the engagement of James to 'Dolly' James. John mischievously wrote 'Mrs James James-Busby' on a piece of paper and placed it on James's desk. The prank achieved its purpose, and when James found out, John wrote how 'the resultant explosion near took my head off'.[89]

It was not that James was antisocial, but more that he was fixated on his career. Despite having been squeezed out of one job with the colonial government (he was still working for the Land Board), his mind was not idle. He exploited the increase in free time now available to him by reviewing his life in New South Wales to date. Several features appeared clearly in his mind, like mountaintops protruding above the clouds: there was his mother's health, which was erratic, and generally fragile; there was his father's career, which was steady and busy; there was his older brother's role as surgeon, which was obviously beneficial to George personally, but which also conferred some status on the family as a whole; there was Catherine, who had married Kelman and who had recently given birth to their first child. But above all, the highest peak in this mountain range of memories was undoubtedly the treatment James had received at the hands of the colonial government – first in the

---

[88] J. Busby to G. Busby, 21 December 1828, in *BFR* 1, 148.
[89] John Busby (jnr) to G. Busby, 21 December 1828, in *BFR* 1, 149–150.

termination of his position at the orphan school, and second in the failure (as he saw it) of the Governor to give him a suitable replacement appointment with his temporary position as collector of the Internal Revenue coming to an end. These twin injustices weighed on him. He was on the verge of turning twenty-seven, but believed that he was still far from fulfilling his potential.

4

Cardinal Virtues

The Busbys' sometimes bumpy ascent in Sydney's social circles was not just a matter to be commented on scornfully by the press, or observed largely with indifference by most of the colony's population, for whom survival rather than status was a priority. It was something that the family itself could not help but be aware of, and for some of them, this rise in rank was a source of deeply felt pride, even if their financial position had not quite yet caught up. John in particular believed that the moment had arrived when he had fulfilled his ambition to become part of the landed gentry and decided to express this by having a house built for the family – in the prevailing Regency style – that would mirror to visitors and passers-by how he saw himself, proclaim prosperity and taste, and even demand a degree of deference.

If newspaper reports were anything to go by, the family could easily afford it. At the end of 1828, the entire family's income was paraded in the press, mainly as an attempt to humiliate them. The Busbys 'receive, of the public money, annually, about £1,600' was the revelation that was published.[1] The impression left was that the family's success was due to government largesse, and although it was an exaggeration, the slur stuck. In reality, the situation for the Busbys was far from gilded, and when it came to building their house, it was left to James to fret about funding for the project. It was not quite a folly, but the cost of constructing a grand house was still just beyond the Busbys' means.

At the start of 1829, James was still juggling loans and trying to ensure that the family could afford items such basic items as saddles. 'I don't know whether it will be prudent under present circumstances', he told George, sharing his anxieties about the family's finances, 'to do anything more in the matter [of a new house]'.[2] And although it was no consolation, the Busbys

---

[1] *SGNSWA*, 5 December 1828, 2.
[2] J. Busby to G. Busby, 3 January 1829, in *BFR* 1, 153.

were not the only ones facing budgetary challenges. The onset of an economic depression in the colony in 1829 had almost put a halt to house-building in Sydney,[3] and the 'distress' that the sudden hardship caused was 'inconceivable', according to James. New ideas were called for. John floated the idea of converting the ground floor of the planned family home into office space that might be leased as an interim remedy for their money shortage. James even considered converting the proposed stables for their new house into temporary accommodation for the family.[4]

Possibly because of the financial strain that was now confronting the Busbys, for the first time James revealed cracks opening up in the family's once indubitable unity. What is most remarkable about this is that it took so long for it to happen in the first place. Of the children living with the parents, only William was not yet in his twenties. James was twenty-six, John junior twenty-two, and Alex twenty. Even Catherine (twenty-four), who was married, had moved in with the family. Only George (now thirty-two) was living away from home. And it was George that James confided in regarding how badly the situation within the family had deteriorated. He rightly stressed how he had always put the family's interests above his own, and how it was who had also managed most of the family's financial and employment affairs. Now, though, his pent-up frustration at dealing with his father's stubborn and capricious personality boiled over: 'My father seems in everything . . . where something disagreeable or troublesome is to be done, to be under John's (junior) influence more than mine, and I confess I don't care how soon our interests and our councils are separated.' James had managed thus far to rein in some of his father's instinctive volatility, but he was not prepared to struggle on a second front with what he saw as his younger brother's irritating intrusion in the way that the family functioned. He claimed that since John had begun working for a living, he had begun to 'act more selfishly, and to make his measures the more disagreeable'. Catherine's presence had maintained a veneer of peace at home, but as she was there only temporarily to help their mother, James was afraid that the situation would implode once she left. In uncharacteristically harsh language, he wrote that the sooner he and his brother 'cease to be members of the same family the better it will be for ourselves and all connected with us'. As far as James was concerned, his father was ultimately responsible for this family friction, accusing him of acting 'covertly and by stealth'.[5] His father managed to rub salt into this wound by

---

[3] D. N. Jeans, 'Town Planning in New South Wales, 1829–1842', *Journal of the Royal Australian Planning Institute* 3, no. 6 (1965): 191.
[4] J. Busby to G. Busby, 3 January 1829, in *BFR* 1, 153.
[5] J. Busby to G. Busby, 25 January 1829, in *BFR* 1, 160–1.

accusing James of being responsible for inflicting the current financial crisis on the family through his extravagant lifestyle.[6]

The construction of the grand residence for the family (a purpose that was looking increasingly forlorn given James's desire to cease living with his parents, and Catherine's imminent return to her husband, who was finishing a house of his own) was the latest issue that was exasperating James. His father had somehow managed to set aside £300 for the cost of the building, but James estimated that an additional £700 would be needed, and without this extra amount, it would be 'madness to attempt anything'. Writing to George in March 1829, James described his father's circumstances as being in such a precarious state that he was determined to sell off all his possessions to free himself from any association with John. 'Whether I shall have anything left', he said fatefully, 'I think extremely doubtful'. So bad were the family's finances that many of the creditors for their household purchasers had not been paid for up to nine months. The more James ruminated over the situation, the more rancorous he became. 'I cannot so far overcome my scorn of him' was how he summarized his feelings.

As well as being angry, James was also miserable. Life at home with his family was 'very unpleasant', and to illustrate the point, he explained how 'breakfast and dinner pass without an average of ten words more than what are absolutely necessary, and after that everyone gets out of the way as fast as he can'.[7]

The effects of this schism on James were demoralizing, especially considering how tightly bound to each other the members of the family had previously been. Writing to George had become a sort of confessional for him, and in this period of despair, he opened up about how the collapse of the family was impairing his ability to function anywhere near his normal self. 'I find myself almost incompetent for business and for anything but going to sleep. I feel a degree of faintness that almost unfits me for exercise'[8] was his worrying admission. Of course, he could simply have packed up and left to live elsewhere in Sydney, but his innate sense of responsibility to his siblings and parents (particularly his mother, who at times was so ill with asthma that she had trouble walking) still played on his mind. If he was to 'divorce' himself from some of his family, it would be particularly difficult to achieve.

Work was a distraction and to some extent a refuge for James, although he was facing the prospect of losing his cherished role of Collector of the Internal Revenue, which contributed to the problems gnawing at him. He took a

---

[6] J. Busby to G. Busby, 1 February 1829, in A *BFR* 1, 161.
[7] J. Busby to G. Busby, 1 March 1829, in *BFR* 1, 164–5.
[8] J. Busby to G. Busby, 3 March 1829, in *BFR* 1, 166.

position on the Board of the Commissary General and the Commissary of Accounts, but it was only a month-long appointment, after which he would be back in the same position as he was beforehand. There is a depiction of James at this time written by his younger sibling, John, which almost descends to caricature at moments, but which nonetheless offers another perspective of his beleaguered brother:

> He [James] has just stumped off to his office, growling like a bear with a sore head. Really, I think he grows more pompous every day. I cannot resist jibing at him – which he takes in ill part. He is a sad dog . . . Also, he has now a great blister on his shoulder from bathing too long in the hot sun . . . As to his money troubles I fancy they are either not as bad as he makes out, or he has spent more than he has told us . . . With any other young man, I might suspect he had been visiting the Female Factory, but not Hamish! [James's nickname in the family].[9]

There is a stark contrast here between James's pained feelings over his falling out with others in the family, and John's more jocular impression of the situation. But beneath the jovial patina of John's letter are a few jabs directed at his brother. James's extreme frugality, his physical delicateness, and his apparent reticence with women were all thrown into this note. The two brothers were temperamentally worlds apart.

James's apparent lack of romantic interest would have been a noticeable issue in the family. At a time when the average age of marriage was around twenty-one,[10] James, who was now twenty-seven, would have been seen by many as advancing into a state of permanent bachelorhood. If John's account is anything to go by, James was almost like Dickens's character Thomas Gradgrind: '[a] man of realities. A man of facts and calculations. A man who proceeds upon the principle that two and two are four, and nothing over, and who is not to be talked into allowing for anything over . . . ready to weigh and measure any parcel of human nature, and tell you exactly what it comes to'.[11] However, it was not that James was averse to the idea of romance or marriage, but that he was possibly slightly too fussy. One instance that illustrates this occurred in May 1829, shortly after the arrival in Sydney of three sisters from England.[12] James's assessments of them were terse and unsparing. 'The eldest is a very ladylike young woman, and half a dozen years ago I have no

---

[9] J. Busby (jnr) to G. Busby, c. 15 March 1829, in *BFR* 1, 169.
[10] T. McKeown and R. G. Record, 'Reasons for the Decline of Mortality in England and Wales during the Nineteenth Century', *Population Studies* 16, no. 2 (1962): 73.
[11] C. Dickens, *Hard Times* (London: Bradbury and Evans, 1854), 14.
[12] *SGNSWA*, 16 May 1829, 2.

doubt had considerable attraction, but her beauty is something on the wane. It is a pity that she is much too old.' When it came to the next daughter, she was judged by James to be 'much too young', to which he added, '[s]he is not tall, but rather stout, still pretty, but more girlish in her appearance than she doubtless would have been in this climate for the last three years'. On the third of the sisters, he had no comment at all.[13] And as no woman to date had met his exacting standards, he was more than satisfied to continue living the single life, unencumbered by an additional family member – especially when some of the current ones were already the source of so much discontent.

James was also preoccupied more with his professional future than his personal one. Any week now, he was expecting to hear that the replacement for his position of Collector of the Internal Revenue had arrived, whereupon his salary would drop by more than half.[14] At the end of July, he was suspended by the Governor in anticipation of his replacement arriving. Darling was effusive in his praise for James and in his regret that there was no other position available that he could offer him.[15]

James was not happy about this development, but neither was he bristling with a desire for vengeance, as he had been when previous jobs came to an end. Instead, he was distracted by a new plan he was formulating. He wrote of his hope that with the Governor's 'recommendation and representation of the services I have performed, I think that I could influence at Home to get a permanent employment [sic]'. James had come up with the idea creating for New South Wales the role of Guardian or Protector of Slaves, based on the model that operated in the West Indies. This was a position that was emancipationist, or at the very least was intended to ameliorate the condition of slaves, with the Guardian or Protector additionally serving as their legal representative.[16] He saw himself exercising 'a moral superintendence of the convicts in road parties and gangs [and] . . . penal settlements, and to suggest improvements in their discipline and treatment'. It was not a new idea, and James only seemed to have thought of pursuing such a role in the previous few weeks. One of the benefits of such a role is that it would afford James a job where no other presently existed for him, and 'it would not be descending in rank' as he put it. Status was still just as important to him as income.[17]

In mid-October, an official called James to a meeting to discuss his proposed trip to London. The advice could not have been clearer. 'He most

---

[13] J. Busby to G. Busby, 12 May 1829, in *BFR* 1, 184.
[14] *The Sydney Monitor*, 18 July 1829, 3.
[15] J. Busby to G. Busby, 26 July 1829, in *BFR* 1, 192.
[16] C. Q. Spence, 'Ameliorating Empire: Slavery and Protection in the British Colonies, 1783–1865' (PhD thesis, Harvard University, 2014), 4–5.
[17] J. Busby to G. Busby, 26 July 1829, in *BFR* 1, 192.

strongly advises me not to think of going Home for an appointment', James noted afterwards.[18] This only left James's work on the Land Board, which enabled him to survive financially, but not to prosper. He considered taking up positions (even temporary ones) on other boards, and possibly securing another senior role with the government. But as the rejections kept coming, he devised yet another possible role for himself, which would entail nothing less than a reform of the colony's entire land legislation. Despite having no formal legal training, he assembled a range of ideas – most of them dramatic in scale and poorly conceived in consequence – which would radically reshape not only the allocation of land to settlers but also the role of the government in the management of the colony's territory.[19]

James accompanied his proposal with a suggestion that he travel to London to have his application to manage the reforms contained in his scheme approved by the Secretary of State for War and the Colonies, Sir George Murray – an undertaking which he estimated would cost around £300. There was little official support in New South Wales for the proposal,[20] but James persisted with his intention to go to London to convince the Colonial Office of the necessity of his proposed land reform plans. He arranged a meeting with Darling to discuss the matter, but on his way to Darling's office, he fell off his horse and badly bruised his leg. He bandaged up his injury, and arrived at the meeting almost two hours late. Despite the delay, he was cordially received by Darling, who listened attentively to the outline of James's scheme, but offered no decision on whether he would support it.[21] (The fall proved to be worse than first thought, and weeks later, James complained that '[t]here is still a considerable weakness in the joint of my knee; and I am nearly convinced that all the time of my accident one of my ribs was broken. There is still very considerable pain.)[22]

In the pursuit of a new post, James had not entirely abandoned his family, however, and in particular George (in whom he confided the most) remained a beloved sibling. In an effort to 'help' his brother find a wife, in November 1829, James rather clumsily tried to encourage George to take an interest in the twenty-three-year-old Mary Marsden, the second-eldest daughter of the Parramatta parson, the Reverend Samuel Marsden. And in his characteristically helpful way, James devised a pretext for his physician brother to spend time with Mary. George was stationed as a surgeon in Bathurst at this time, which

---

[18] J. Busby to G. Busby, 12 October 1829, in *BFR* 1, 195.
[19] J. Busby, 'Observations on the Alienation of Lands from the Crown in the Colony of New South Wales', Sydney, 25 October 1829, in Busby, *Authentic Information Relative to New South Wales*, 45.
[20] J. Busby to G. Busby, 19 October, 1 November 1829, in *BFR* 1, 196–9.
[21] J. Busby to G. Busby, 30 November 1829, in *BFR* 1, 203–4.
[22] J. Busby to G. Busby, 12 December 1829, in *BFR* 1, 207.

was still a relatively small and isolated settlement, about 200 kilometres northwest of Sydney. 'I am heartily glad Mary Marsden is coming to Bathurst,' James announced to his brother, 'and I hope you will still find her enough invalided to require some attention from you for a little time.' It was clear that the attention James envisaged went beyond the medical sort. 'I hope that if you like her appearance you will not allow the prejudice which you have against the Marsdens to have any influence. I believe she is an excellent girl. I believe among her friends her good nature is proverbial, and no less an authority than Harrington used to say she would make the best wife of any girl he knew in the Colony.'[23] The question that hangs in the air in this statement for any biographer is why James did not see himself as a potential spouse for Mary, especially given the many admirable attributes she supposedly possessed. Possibly he did not find her personally attractive, or his mind was set on returning to England temporarily in the next year, and so he was not ready to settle down with a wife and potentially a child as well.

As the end of the year neared, James was informed that there would be no official support at all for him to go to England. As his options for professional advancement diminished, signs of the ensuing strain started to show. '[R]ecent occurrences have made me extremely sensitive,' he conceded to George in January 1830. He then went on to explain how, among some of his social associates (rather than friends), he had detected 'a dryness of manner' towards them, and that he was regarded as a 'mercenary individual with whom a particular acquaintance was not to be desired'. He identified one person 'who has several times been in town without coming near me, and has made no reply to two letters I have written him'. Yet a few days later, James was apologizing to George in another letter for being too hasty in judging these same people.[24] His normally judicious, level-headed disposition seemed to be deserting him for periods, and in its place, he was exhibiting a degree of nervousness and unease in connection with those around him.

His irritability and slightly anti-social tendency at this time could well have been exacerbated by the cold sores that had recently spread all over his mouth – triggered, he said, by too much exposure to Sydney's harsh summer sun. The remedy that had been prescribed was a 'blue pill', which brought about a severe reaction in James. At the end of January, he became suddenly ill, and was confined to bed for the day. He felt as though all his energy had been drained, and by the afternoon, his entire body was so sore that he could not touch any part of it without experiencing pain.[25]

---

[23] J. Busby to G. Busby, 30 November 1829, in *BFR* 1, 204.
[24] J. Busby to G. Busby, 11 and 17 January 1830, in *BFR* 1, 212.
[25] W. Frazer, *Elements of Materia Medica* (Dublin: Fannin & Co., 1851), 119–21; J. Busby to G. Busby, 25 January 1830, in *BFR* 1, 215.

As James recovered the following month, he began exhibiting more interest in romantic matters. There was a woman he was attracted to, but he never revealed her name in any of his correspondence, probably out of a sense of what he regarded as gentlemanly discretion. For whatever reason, though, this budding romance did not blossom, and in its wake, he shared with George his views on relationships: 'A young fellow would say it does not promise much when one has first to endeavour to make himself in love with the girl, and then endeavour to make the girl in love with him; but we old fellows (we are both on the wrong side of 30) judge better, and for my own part I question whether I shall ever fall in love without an effort.'[26]

With his affections unrequited, James's attention reverted to more immediate matters of concern. In early February 1830, he 'achingly came to the resolution' that without Murray's consent, his prospects for a government job in New South Wales were slim.[27] And while he ruminated on how to tackle the problem of getting official backing for his planned trip to the Colonial Office in London, he had to contend with issues around the construction of the family home, and his father's financial recklessness. 'At the same time as he is saving farthings,' James observed, 'he is throwing away pounds in the most foolish way you can imagine.'[28]

In mid-June, James was summoned to see the Governor. He was convinced that he was about to be given a new job, and headed to the meeting with great expectations. However, as soon as he walked into Darling's small, dark office, all hope for good news disappeared. 'I found the Governor in a very different temper to what I had been accustomed to see him in,' he recalled, 'and to my astonishment he began in an angry or rather vexed tone to berate me about the way we have of late conducted business at the Land Board.' What followed was a tirade from Darling, accusing James of incompetence, neglect, and disobeying direct orders. To his credit, but also with some shame, James acknowledged that he had been remiss in the execution of some of his duties, in particular his failure to comply with some of the specifics of the regulations covering land transactions. Then, in an abrupt departure from this rebuke, Darling asked that James undertake a consolidation of the numerous regulations that had piled up in the apparatus of the colony's government over decades. James was momentarily bewildered by this about-turn – from censure to commendation in a few seconds – but he was quickly aware of the fact that it was an opportunity for additional employment[29] in an environment where alternative prospects were looking increasingly thin on the ground.

---

[26] J. Busby to G. Busby, 29 March 1830, in *BFR* 1, 224.
[27] Fletcher, 'Administrative Reform in New South Wales under Governor Darling', 246–62.
[28] J. Busby to G. Busby, 10 and 22 March 1830, in *BFR* 1, 222–3.
[29] J. Busby to G. Busby, 20 June 1830, in *BFR* 1, 239.

At the same time, James had just about completed his new book on viticulture, and was preparing for its release. The criticism he had endured for the excessive detail of his previous volume still bothered him, and so for this work, he emphasized right from the title that this would be a 'Manual of Plain Directions'.[30] He considered whether he should advertise the book in the *Monitor*. The newspaper had a high circulation, but James was concerned that 'ill-natured criticism' in the paper 'might do mischief'.[31] However, he did eventually publish a small advertisement, deciding not to succumb to the fear of a bad review.[32]

A Manual of Plain Directions for Planting and Cultivating Vineyards was published on 29 June 1830 (James commented, as an aside, that there was a three-week delay in getting the book published because a New Zealand missionary, William Yate, was having a religious book in the Tongan language printed),[33] and although the title and content of his book advanced the impression of James as horticulturalist, the dedication that prefaced the work very much cast him as James the social reformer. Into the field of agriculture, he managed to plant a moral principle – expressing that the purpose of this small book (ninety-six pages) was to 'increase the comforts, and promote the morality of the lower classes of the Colony; and more especially, of the native-born youth'. He had observed the 'temperance and contentment of the lowest classes of the people in the Southern Countries of Europe', where wine was a widespread and commonly consumed drink, and compared this with the problems caused by alcohol in other countries. 'How much would it add to the happiness' of the settlers in New South Wales, he asked rhetorically, if their drinking habits emulated those of the peoples of southern Europe? Wine, rather than spirits, he proposed, was the remedy to the scourge of drunkenness in the colony.[34] Drunkenness was indeed a problem in New South Wales, but James's solution – to place an emphasis on wine instead of spirits as the preferred alcohol for the local population – was what could most charitably be described as ambitious. This plea for drinking reform was developed as the book progressed, with instructions on vine cultivation and wine production preceded by a visionary social plea in relation to those born in the colony of settler parents:

---

[30] J. Busby, *A Manual of Plain Directions for Planting and Cultivating Vineyards, and for Making Wine, in New South Wales* (Sydney: R. Mansfield, 1830).

[31] J. Busby to G. Busby, 6 May 1830, in *BFR* 1, 232.

[32] *The Monitor*, 30 June 1830, 1.

[33] J. Busby to G. Busby, 16 May 1830, in *BFR* 1, 235; W. Yate, *An Account of New Zealand, and of the Formation and Progress of the Church Missionary Society's Mission in the Northern Island*, 2nd edn (London: R. B. Seeley and W. Burnside, 1835), 280.

[34] Busby, *A Manual of Plain Directions for Planting and Cultivating Vineyards*, v–vi.

it is to them, and their children, that the question is important, whether it shall be 'a land of corn and wine, of cornfields and vineyards', or, whether they shall be content to throw away the blessings within their reach, and either deny themselves the use of fermented liquors altogether – as some of them, very much to their credit, have done . . . – or incurring the risk of acquiring a depraved taste for liquor, which . . . becomes a sort of poison.[35]

Growing grapes to make wine was 'a blessing', in James's mind, and swept up in the current of the theory he was advocating, he went as far as to claim that in some countries, advances in the sciences and arts, the existence of good government, and the general happiness of the populace were attributable in part to the presence of vineyards.[36]

In contrast to the reception of his previous book, *A Manual of Plain Directions for Planting and Cultivating Vineyards* was 'very favourably spoken of'.[37] The *Sydney Gazette* was particularly fulsome in is praise, describing the work as 'a help to the farmer . . . [and] an attempt to improve the morals of the country', and was a publication that 'might be easily understood by the most illiterate of his readers'.[38] Writing for the public was becoming infectious for James, and even as the pages for *A Manual of Plain Directions for Planting and Cultivating Vineyards* were being printed in Sydney, he was mulling over the possibility of a new work: 'a small pamphlet which I mean to publish, containing such information and advice to newly arrived immigrants as will be useful to them in facilitating . . . their business with the . . . Government'. He had already written around twelve pages and was aiming for a total of thirty – a work of modest scale, but one which nevertheless would enable would-be settlers to share the benefits of his knowledge of the bureaucratic workings of the colony.[39] The resulting piece – *Advice to Emigrants Newly Arrived in New South Wales* – was published in the *Sydney Almanac* at the end of the year in its appendices, and with James credited anonymously as 'a Civil Officer of the Government'.[40] The work emphasized the 'cardinal virtues' necessary for the prospective settler, including 'industry', 'frugality', 'prudence', and 'circumspection'[41] – traits that he personally valued. Yet the remainder of this short publication was surprisingly thin when it came to useful information

---

[35] Ibid., 11.
[36] Ibid., 12.
[37] *The Hobart Town Courier*, 7 August 1830, 4.
[38] *SGNSWA*, 17 July 1830, 2.
[39] J. Busby to G. Busby, 29 August 1830, in *BFR* 1, 246.
[40] J. Busby, 'Advice to Emigrants Newly Arrived in New South Wales', in R. Mansfield, *Australian Almanack, for the Year of Our Lord 1831* (Sydney: R. Mansfield, 1830), 253–71.
[41] Ibid., 256.

for new arrivals. A large portion of it was dedicated to describing in the most general terms the agricultural opportunities of the colony, followed by a few scattered facts on the workings of the government. However, James obviously regarded it as a sufficiently worthwhile contribution that he published it as part of a collection of other writings the following year (entitled *Authentic Information Relative to New South Wales and New Zealand*).[42]

To some extent, James's professional work, which involved him writing opinions on a range of government-related issues, had become a personal interest for him, and in publishing his thoughts on these matters for a general readership, he was establishing himself as something of an authority on the colony in Britain. However, despite parading his knowledge in this way, there was still no offer of a position from the Governor or the Colonial Office, which was strengthening further his determination to return to London and resolve directly his future with those who had the power to make the sort of appointment he sought.

In the midst of this uncertain period in his life, James managed to maintain a minimum of social contact with those outside his immediate family. The Busbys were pitched fairly well in Sydney's social hierarchy, although status was fickle, and individuals could rise and fall depending on shifts in their personal circumstances.[43] In most instances, New South Wales's class system was much less dependent on the status one was born into, and more on the rank one had ascended to in the colony. The Busbys were in that loose group of 'notable' residents in New South Wales – notable in that they were employed in various responsible positions by the government, and had direct access to senior officials and even the Governor. Yet James apparently cared little for the social side of Sydney life. For example, in June 1830, he mentioned that he intended to visit Samuel Marsden, but with a real sense of social inertia. 'You will see that Mr Marsden and his daughter have returned from New Zealand,' he told George. 'How Mary [Marsden's daughter] is I have not heard. I shall pay my respects to them on the first opportunity. John, I believe has already been, but not seen Mr Marsden himself. But I know little of his trip, not having asked him about it.'[44]

Two months later, James was just as nonchalant during an evening tea party. The Busbys had hosted four guests, one of whom was Miss Agnes Dow, who had arrived in Sydney with her family the previous month.[45] Although

---

[42] J. Busby, *Authentic Information Relative to New South Wales*, 23–42; N. Bayly, 'James Busby: British Resident in New Zealand, 1833–40' (MA thesis, University of Auckland, 1949), 27.
[43] A. Sharp, *The World, the Flesh and the Devil: The Life and Opinions of Samuel Marsden in England and the Antipodes, 1765–1838* (Auckland: Auckland University Press, 2016), 1–8.
[44] J. Busby to G. Busby, 20 June 1830, in *BFR* 1, 240.
[45] *The Sydney Monitor*, 2 June 1830, 4.

this portentous encounter was later excitedly represented by one historian as the start of James's relationship with the woman whom he would eventually marry.[46] James's comments at the time gave no hint of things to come. His laconic account was limited to a few non-committal lines: 'My father thinks Miss Dow [is aged] 25 or 26, but says my mother was the latter [26] when she married!!!! It went off tolerably well.'[47] James gave no indication that he had any attraction, let alone a lasting interest in Agnes, and in the weeks and then months that followed, he made no further mention of her in his numerous letters to family members.

Instead, James seemed to be focussed more on mounting money problems. Kelman, his financially luckless brother-in-law, now owed him £239, and James was extremely reluctant to lend him any more money, knowing that there was little chance of having it repaid. On the other side of the ledger, James owed the government £153 for cattle he had purchased, and a further £326 to several other individuals. Against this, he had an assortment of hinges, latches, and locks that he estimated had a combined value of no more than £40. This bleak situation was made worse for James by his father accusing him of mismanaging the family's finances. The acrimony between father and son was now worse than ever. 'That I should be reduced to beggary . . . by my own liberality to others I could very well bear,' he told George, 'but I confess to be the subject of reproach for what I have done, I have found unmixed bitterness.'[48]

James's financial predicament made his need for a full-time job that much more pressing. He held out hope for a role in Parramatta which Darling had previously hinted could be given to him, but in the first week of December 1830, James was informed that he would not now be getting the position. Indignant at this rejection, he wrote that 'the Governor has finally passed the Rubicon with me'. From this moment, his resolve to leave New South Wales became unshakeable.[49] After all, what other option was there left for him?

To top off his exasperation at this time, James's vision was beginning to fail him. He spent the middle of December scouring 'every shop in Sydney' for eyeglasses, but in vain. He was suffering from near-sightedness that was bad enough that he could not distinguish a person across the street. He managed to put an order in for some eyeglasses from England, but despaired at the time he would have to wait for them to arrive.[50] This point is revealing in that for the preceding few weeks, James had been resolute in his desire to return

---

[46] Ramsden, *Busby of Waitangi*, 33.
[47] J. Busby to G. Busby, 29 August 1830, in *BFR* 1, 246.
[48] J. Busby to G. Busby, 4 and 5 December 1830, in *BFR* 1, 264.
[49] J. Busby to G. Busby, 5 December 1830, in *BFR* 1, 265.
[50] J. Busby to G. Busby, 19 December 1830, in *BFR* 1, 268.

to London. However, the fact that he placed an order for eyeglasses that would take at least nine months to fill suggests that he was not optimistic about being able to leave the colony and return to Britain. Three weeks later, though, this had all changed. On 4 January, he surprised his family by informing them that he had made arrangements to depart for England in the first week of February.

There was another, more slowly developing situation which had hastened James's decision to sail to London to seek a new position. This was the influence of a new theory on the management and use of land in colonies being peddled by the entrepreneur, land-trader, and colonial theorist Edward Gibbon Wakefield. Wakefield's ideas about making aspects of colonization more systematic were gaining ground at this time, principally through the publication and wide circulation of his *A Letter from Sydney, the Principal Town of Australasia*,[51] which he had completed towards the end of a three-year sentence he was serving in England for abduction.[52]

The essence of his envisaged scheme was that a system could be implemented to enable colonial governments to dispose of surplus or waste lands to settlers at a comparatively low price. Those settlers would then farm it (presumably for a profit), thereby increasing the value of that land.[53] More settlers would arrive, which would not only further increase the value of the land, but also lead to the establishment of a civil and relatively prosperous society. The role of the colonial government in this system would be central, as Wakefield made clear: 'In all new countries the government alone has the power to dispose of waste land . . . [N]obody would cultivate without a title; the government alone can give a secure title; and it is, therefore, impossible to use waste land without the active assistance of government.' Through the government controlling the allocation of land, and thus the flow of settlers into the colony, it would therefore possess the capacity 'to civilize its subjects', as Wakefield saw it.[54]

Wakefield was an aggressive lobbyist, and was also seized – like no other private citizen at this time – by the importance of popularizing his ideas through the press.[55] His determined 'campaigning' in this area culminated in 1831 with

---

[51] E. G. Wakefield, *A Letter from Sydney, the Principal Town of Australasia* (London: Joseph Cross, 1829).
[52] P. Templeton, *A Sort of Conscience: The Wakefields* (Auckland: Auckland University Press, 2002), 117–19.
[53] Wakefield, *A Letter from Sydney*, 173.
[54] Ibid., 168–9.
[55] E. Bohan, *Blest Madman: Fitzgerald of Canterbury* (Christchurch: Canterbury University Press, 1998), 25; W. L. Sachs, *The Transformation of Anglicanism: From State Church to Global Communion* (Cambridge: Cambridge University Press, 2002), 109.

the introduction in New South Wales of what were known as the Ripon Regulations. These were an attempt by the colony's government to enact elements of this systematic land-management scheme,[56] and produced what Wakefield later proudly described as a 'perfect revolution in the most important function of colonial government'.[57]

With the possibility of such a revolution in colonial land policies looming, James made up his mind to return to England and advised Darling of his plans. The response from the Governor was lacking in the 'pleasance of manner' which James had been accustomed to.[58] Darling was irked by James's unilateral and as yet unauthorized decision to depart the colony. Technically, he needed the Governor's approval but had deliberately not sought it. However, in a careful balancing act, he wrote a lengthy memorial to the Colonial Office (which he submitted to Darling to forward to London on his behalf) detailing his reasons for wishing to go to London.

The Governor wrote the accompanying covering letter for James's memorial which left little doubt as to his own feelings on this increasingly bothersome former employee. Darling listed for Murray the various positions James had held in the colony, and interspersed this with some commentary where he felt it necessary. He made it clear, for example, that James should not have been disappointed that he was not granted a permanent position as Collector of the Internal Revenue, as it was spelt out to him from the beginning that it would only be a temporary posting (and indeed, in his private correspondence, James also acknowledged this fact on several occasions).[59] Darling also aired the concern that James was angling for the sort of roles that would give him 'more power than it would be prudent to place in the hands of any Individual', which was a veiled suggestion that the regard with which James held himself, and particularly the impression he held of his own abilities, was unrealistic. The Governor excused the fact that he had not offered James other positions by reference to the restructuring of the colonial administration, from a desire to save money.

Having thus set the general scene, Darling detailed why his relations with James seemed to have broken down in some respects. After one lengthy meeting, the Governor had become frustrated when he asked James for a reply to a question, and the latter said that he would not give an answer there

---

[56] R. C. Mills, *The Colonization of Australia (1829–1842): The Wakefield Experiment in Empire-Building* (London: Sidgwick & Jackson, 1915), 167; D. N. Jeans, 'Territorial Divisions and the Locations of Towns in New South Wales, 1826–1842', *The Australian Geographer* 10, no. 4 (1967): 243–55.
[57] Wakefield, *A View of the Art of Colonization*, 44.
[58] Busby used the Jesuit phrase *suaviter in modo, fortiter in re*. J. Busby to A. Busby, 4 January 1831, in *BFR* 1, 274.
[59] R. Darling to G. Murray, 29 January 1831, in *HRA* 1, vol. 16, 39.

and then, but instead would write a letter to him on the topic. And when the letter did finally arrive from James, it came with 'a short, abrupt note', saying he would never work with one group of officials again because of some procedural issue that had bothered him. Darling told Murray that this episode had placed him 'in a very embarrassing situation'.[60]

Darling's letter was laced with comments that diplomatically but unambiguously rebuked James for his recent actions (while in fairness, also acknowledging the value of some of the work he had previously done for the colony's government). Because the Governor was responsible for presenting James's memorandum to the Colonial Office, his covering letter effectively served as his right of reply to the various claims James had made. James should have anticipated this, but the fact that he stubbornly went ahead in demanding that the Governor send his memorandum to London represents a failure of judgment. It not only put him offside with Darling, but it was also hardly likely to endear him to officials in the Colonial Office.

As for the memorandum itself, it fell short of being the sort of glowing endorsement of his abilities and value that James imagined it to be. While surveying the various ways in which he had served the colonial government, he could not help but mention the disputes he had over the nature of his employment at various posts. And to make things worse, James took a swipe at Darling. He described how the Governor appointed him temporarily as Collector of the Internal Revenue, but that there was supposedly some implicit expectation that after more than two years in the position, it would be made permanent for him. James wrote of 'the most indefatigable exertions' he had made to reform the department, which he believed merited his permanent appointment to the role. James then added that the Governor had not acted with the highest standards of justice and good faith, which again was an imprudent allegation to make to British officials. If anything, it demonstrated again that James lacked the sort of discretion expected of someone seeking high office in a colonial administration anywhere in the Empire.[61]

All this sparring with Darling for a position, and its escalation to the highest level of the Colonial Office, became a source of stress for James. Despite his bullish approach to matters, he was sensible enough to know that the stakes for his career had been elevated dramatically, and he now had to go to London to settle his future, one way or the other. On 17 February 1831, the barque *Forth* sailed to England, with James on board,[62] and reached London on 14 July.[63]

---

[60] Ibid., 39–40.
[61] J. Busby to G Murray, 10 January 1831, in *HRA* 1, vol. 16, 40–4.
[62] *SGNSWA*, 17 February 1831, 3.
[63] *Report from Select Committee on Malt Drawback on Spirits: Together With The Minutes of Evidence, and Appendix of Papers* (London: House of Commons, 1831), 73.

Having previously sailed this tortuously long route, this time James made no record of the day-to-day life on board. He was now travelling alone, and instead of an imagination overflowing with entrepreneurial enthusiasm as it had been on his journey to Sydney, his mind was now mired in thoughts of how he might resuscitate his career. Two issues preoccupied him. The first was a series of proposals he wished to present to the Colonial Office relating to possible posts that could be created to fit his particular abilities. The second was the possibility of further viticultural research in continental Europe. Voyages between New South Wales and England were expensive and lengthy, and so James reasoned that he had to make the most of the short time he had budgeted for staying in the northern hemisphere.

While he was still at sea, his brother John jotted a note to Catherine which gives a clue as to how close the relationship between James and Agnes Dow had grown in recent months. James had remained tight-lipped on the matter, not even confiding his thoughts in George, but John's impish observation shines some light at least on the extent of Agnes's feelings about James:

> I caught pretty Agnes Dow standing by Mrs Macquarie's Wishing Tree in the Public Gardens, looking wistfully up into its branches. Of course I could not miss such an opportunity and mischievously asked her for what she was wishing. But all I got was a most becoming blush, and a ladylike snub for my curiosity. But perhaps the dignified little lady was studying botany![64]

Apart from this vignette, though, James was barely mentioned in the correspondence his siblings sent to each other while he was away. However, Agnes was plainly enamoured with James during this time, and while he was absent, she visited his parents and proudly showed his mother a miniature painting by the artist Richard Read of James that she carried with her.[65] James's mother held the picture in her hand and then said that she would not give it back to Agnes until to following day as a means of ensuring that Agnes returned for another visit.[66] It was a playful gesture, but one that nonetheless indicates the seriousness with which those present regarded the prospects of James's relationship with Agnes.

As the *Forth* neared its destination, James completed an unsolicited report for Wilmot-Horton on emigration to New South Wales. James was promoted to write this work after obtaining a copy of Wilmot-Horton's recently released

---

[64] J. Busby, jnr, to C. Busby, undated, *c.* May 1831; in *BFR* 1, 279.
[65] E. Ramsden, 'James Busby: The Prophet of Australian Viticulture', *Journal and Proceedings of the Royal Australian Historical Society* 26, pt 5 (1940): 373; R. A. J. Neville, 'Printmakers in Colonial Sydney, 1800–1850' (MA thesis, University of Sydney, 1988), 90, 101.
[66] W. Busby to A. Busby, 15 September 1831, in *BFR* 1, 310.

pamphlet *An Inquiry into the Causes and Remedies of Pauperism*, while en route to London.[67] This pamphlet presented several opportunities to James: to study the prose style of the reports Wilmot-Horton wrote (and which he presumably would favour); to learn about an issue that was obviously at the forefront of the official's thoughts; and in combining these, to create a report of his own, which by echoing Wilmot-Horton's views, might further his chances of being favourably received at the Colonial Office.

The essence of Wilmot-Horton's proposed reform was 'to enable parishes to mortgage their poor-rates, for the purpose of providing for their able-bodied paupers, by colonization in the British colonies'. The scheme would draw on emigrants 'only [from] such families as consisted of persons within certain ages, and in a state of health such as to secure the full advantages of their situation, not only to themselves but to the colony to which they were going'.[68] It was an idea that James instantly favoured.[69] His report, which he modestly entitled *A Letter on the Emigration of Mechanics and Labourers to New South Wales*,[70] picked up on Wilmot-Horton's idea for introducing legislation into the House of Commons that would alleviate poverty in Britain by sending some of the country's 'surplus' population to the colonies as labourers. '[N]o other single measure,' James assessed fawningly, 'perhaps no combination of measures, is capable of benefiting these Colonies so extensively as this, if conducted on sound principles and with a due attention to the wants of the Colonies, and to the physical and moral qualities of the *persons* whose emigration it is proposed to encourage'.[71]

What James was proposing in his letter was essentially a system of land distribution that was self-funding (echoing a similar principle in Wakefield's planned scheme of systematic colonization). However, what he hoped would make Wilmot-Horton consider his report seriously was his wide knowledge of the circumstances that prevailed in New South Wales. James provided specifics on the extent of the labour shortage, and its effects on the potential economic growth of the colony. It was not just a case of shipping Britain's

---

[67] R. Wilmot-Horton, *An Inquiry into the Causes and Remedies of Pauperism. Containing Letters to Sir Francis Burdett, Bart. MP Upon Pauperism in Ireland* (London: E. Lloyd, 1831).
[68] R. Wilmot-Horton, cited in J. Busby, *Authentic Information Relative to New South Wales*, appendix 1, i.
[69] J. Busby, *Colonies and Colonization: A Lecture Delivered in the Hall of the Mechanics' Institute, at Auckland, with Especial Reference to New Zealand* (Auckland: Philip Kunst, 1857), 16; S. Macready and J. Robinson, 'Slums and Self-Improvement: The History and Archaeology of the Mechanics Institute, Auckland, and its Chancery Street Neighbourhood. Vol. 2: The Artefacts and Faunal Material', in *Science and Research Internal Report No. 91* (Wellington: Department of Conservation, 1990), 88.
[70] J. Busby, 'A Letter on the Emigration of Mechanics and Labourers to New South Wales', in Busby, *Authentic Information Relative to New South Wales*, 1–21.
[71] Busby, *A Letter on the Emigration of Mechanics and Labourers to New South Wales*, 1.

poor there, though. There was the considerable cost of transport, along with the need to accommodate and feed these emigrants on arrival. And not just any labourers would do. James identified the acute demand for men (and they were all men, in his report) who possessed the sort of skills needed in the colony. Yet even trained labourers were not, alone, a remedy for the shortage of skilled workers in New South Wales. James's personal experience of employing people at the Orphan School influenced considerably his view on this matter. The combination of high wages for skilled labourers and low living costs meant that many of them suffered from 'indolent and depraved habits'.[72] From a purely economic perspective, overall, the scheme to distribute some of Britain's (skilled) poor to New South Wales looked promising, as far as James saw it.

Yet for all its insight and analysis, James's report was more diagnosis than prescription. His proposals amounted to a fine-tuning of ideas that were already in circulation, including Wilmot-Horton's. In reference to the anticipated inflow of emigrants to New South Wales from Britain, James pessimistically concluded that 'unless they can make up their minds to live as isolated beings, without the pale of society, they are constrained, by a moral compulsion, to assimilate their conduct and habits to those of their neighbours'. Even if emigration began to occur on a mass scale, James was hardly confident that moral degradation would be avoided. He observed that when it came to emigrants from Britain arriving in New South Wales,

> so great is the alteration of their circumstances, and so entirely are they released from all former restraints of an outward character, – so powerful is the contagion of bad example, where little else is witnessed, and where good moral conduct is not necessary to worldly prosperity, or public estimation, – that unless persons are chosen of fixed moral and religious principles, it is much to be feared, that the majority would yield to the current of dishonesty and dissipation, rather than endeavour to stem it against so many discouragements.[73]

James's trip to London was a fishing expedition, in which he was hoping to land a suitable role for himself. And to aid his quest, he decided to dangle extra bait in a bid to entice officials in the Colonial Office. *A Letter on the Emigration of Mechanics and Labourers to New South Wales* demonstrated his knowledge of the colony, and indicated that his mind was attuned to the social and economic concerns of the day. It also revealed a practical approach

---

[72] Ibid., 2–4.
[73] Ibid., 21.

to the challenges thrown up by emigration to New South Wales. Here was a man who proposed ideas based on experience, rather than as an armchair analyst. However, the *Letter* was lacking in a clear solution to some of the problems it identified, and less still did it make a case for a specific position to be created (for James) to manage the situation. He may have talked himself into the role of an expert on New South Wales, but he simultaneously talked himself out of an appointment there with the indeterminate conclusion of his *Letter*.

The other piece of bait that James relied on to lure officials to take an interest in him was much more likely to succeed. James presented his *A Brief Memoir Relative to the Islands of New Zealand* to the Colonial Office for consideration in June 1831 – the same month as his *Letter*. The *Memoir* was not just more detailed and explicit, but was also more ambitious for James's career. He had obviously laboured considerably on it while sailing to England because its wording is more carefully considered than some of his other writings, and there is great force in many of its passages. He opened by stating that relations between New South Wales and New Zealand were among the most important issues facing the British government, and went on to detail the extent of trade between the two territories to emphasize the point. He conceded early on that there was the issue of the 'ferocious character of the natives' to take into account, but that good commercial relations with some Māori communities had been established in the mid-1820s, which 'demonstrated the practicability of maintaining the trade', and as a result, commerce between New Zealand and New South Wales had been 'thrown open, without restraint, to the enterprize [sic] of private individuals, and it appears, in its increase, to have exceeded the most sanguine expectations which could have been entertained respecting it'.[74]

The issue of trading prospects as a basis for formal British intervention in New Zealand had been frequently brought up with the Colonial Office by various parties since the early 1820s, but there was simply no official appetite for it.[75] It was the jurisdictional considerations coming to the fore at this time that officials were slightly more interested in. Bigge had suggested in 1823 that a commission be established to try offences committed by British subjects in the region, including New Zealand.[76] There was already legislation in place (passed in 1817) which allowed for the punishment of murder and

---

[74] J. Busby, 'A Brief Memoir Relative to the Islands of New Zealand', (London, 1831), in Busby, *Authentic Information Relative to New South Wales*, 57–8.
[75] As an example, see H. Goulburn to R. Sugden, 25 April 1821, in *Historical Records of New Zealand* 1, ed. R. McNab, 532.
[76] J. T. Bigge, *Report of the Commissioner of Inquiry into the State of the Colony of New South Wales*, 60.

manslaughter by the master or crew of any British ship,[77] but it was virtually impossible to police and tended to be honoured more in the breach than the observance.

James, like Bigge, saw the connection between growing trade with New Zealand and the obligation to ensure that the barest minimum of moral rectitude be displayed by Britons directly involved in this commerce with Māori.[78] With similar certitude, James then began to deliberate on New Zealand's indigenous population:

> they are remarkable for a vigour of mind, and a *forecast*, which distinguishes them, perhaps, from all other savages, who have made so little advance in the arts of civilized life . . . As members of a community they are chiefly remarkable for the ferocity with which they engage in the perpetual wars that the different tribes wage with each other; – for that contempt of human life, which is the natural result of a warfare that aims at the extermination or captivity of the hostile tribe; – and, for the revolting practice of eating the flesh of the enemies they have slain, and even of their own slaves, when pressed by hunger.[79]

Following from this, he outlined the basis of Māori social structure as he understood it, and discussed the ways Māori managed trade, before moving to his first important observation about the effect New Zealand was having in New South Wales. According to James, some Māori were effectively acting as hosts for former and escaped convicts. If this trend continued, he predicted that 'the evil will, undoubtedly, increase also', despite the stringent searches made of all vessels leaving Sydney, and the fines imposed on any captain caught illegally carrying convicts.[80] New Zealand could no longer simply be ignored by the British government, as had largely been the case up to this time.[81]

James was proposing a major shift in British colonial policy. Instead of officials persisting with their preference for avoiding further colonial entanglements, he

---

[77] 57 George III. c. 53. – An Act for the more effectual Punishment of Murders and Manslaughters committed in Places not within His Majesty's Dominions [27 June 1817], in *A Collection of Statutes Connected with the General Administration of the Law* 6, ed. W. D. Evans (London: Thomas Blenkarm, 1836), 279.

[78] K. Shawcross, 'Maoris of the Bay of Islands, 1769–1840' (MA thesis, University of Auckland, 1967), 170; P. Moon, *A Savage Country: The Untold Story of New Zealand in the 1820s* (Auckland: Penguin, 2012), 36–7.

[79] Busby, 'A Brief Memoir Relative to the Islands of New Zealand', 61.

[80] Ibid., 61.

[81] E. O'Brien, *The Foundation of Australia, 1786–1800* (London: Sheed & Ward, 1937), 62; J. M. Ward, *Colonial Self-Government: The British Experience, 1759–1856* (London: Palgrave Macmillan, 1976), 108.

was urging that they consider the economic benefits that would flow from a more formal level of engagement in New Zealand. There was also a moral good that he believed would arise from such intervention. A greater official presence in the territory would afford opportunities for 'civilizing, and converting to Christianity, one of the most interesting races of people which British enterprize [sic] has yet discovered in any quarter of the globe'.[82]

Having tried to make the prospects of successful official involvement as enticing as possible, James began to lay out the features of that intervention, as he envisaged it. '[S]ome connection should be formed with the [Māori] chiefs', he recommended, in order that the hand of British justice would be able to reach out from its sleeve in Sydney and stretch to British subjects who were presently seeking sanctuary from the law in New Zealand. In the case of the increasingly lucrative trade between New South Wales and New Zealand, he suggested that 'it has become extremely doubtful whether that trade can any longer be safely pursued, without some treaty with the native chiefs'.[83] And if this threat to trade was not enough to nudge officials from their fear of further involvement, James evoked one of Britain's great historic rivals: the French. '[I]n their late voyages of discovery to the South Seas,' he warned, 'the French directed much of their attention to the Islands of New Zealand . . . and apprehensions are very generally entertained that they will be ultimately taken possession of by that power'. The Russians, James claimed in an slightly alarmist manner, could similarly be interested in New Zealand, as it offered them a useful location for refitting their ships en route to America (a claim that was not troubled by its own geographical improbability). For Britain, however, seizing sovereignty of New Zealand was not the immediate answer, partly because of the expense that would be incurred in such a move, and the risk that it might excite other powers to take a more strategic interest in the region. James's compromise suggestion was one that also heralded his own intention to insinuate himself into New Zealand's administration: 'in my opinion . . . it would be possible for the British Government, at little or no expense, to secure . . . the delivering up of runaway convicts, who might seek shelter on the coasts of New Zealand, and the protection and encouragement of the valuable trade which is already established'. This plan would only work, though, if missionary support was offered. James mentioned Marsden in this *Memoir* as being the harbinger of some still-vague system of pan-tribal government:

> A number of the chiefs of the Northern Island, to whom Mr Marsden recommended that they should make an end of their wars by electing

---

[82] Busby, 'A Brief Memoir Relative to the Islands of New Zealand', 62–3.
[83] Ibid., 64

among themselves a king, to whom the whole should yield obedience, unanimously answered, that no chief of an independent tribe would ever be brought to acknowledge the authority of another chief, unless he and his tribe were first reduced to slavery. But they as unanimously agreed, that 'if King George would send them a king', they would joyfully submit to *his* authority.[84]

This was possibly the genesis of James's plan to install himself as a form of administrator-cum-leader:

Under these circumstances, it appears to me, that if an authorized agent or resident were established by the British Government . . . and invested with the authority of a magistrate over his own countrymen, he would be able to enter into a separate treaty with each chief, or a general treaty with the whole, having for its basis the reciprocal security of British subjects and the natives of New Zealand in their commercial intercourse.[85]

The extent of the authority this agent would exercise over Māori would be limited to whatever powers Māori were willing to concede. The agent would exercise 'persuasion and advice' rather than direct rule in the country, which James was convinced would lead Māori to 'abandon the ferocious character of the savage and the cannibal, for the principles of a milder religion, and the habits of a more civilized people'.[86] The role James had in mind would be one of a Resident, loosely along the lines of the Residency system that was already operating in other parts of the Empire.[87]

The *Memoir* made a compelling case in part because of its more detailed study of the issues affecting New Zealand, and because it offered an inexpensive and elegant solution to a 'problem' which officials in the Colonial Office were not otherwise likely to have been aware existed to this degree. The idea of Britain having a formal presence in New Zealand was not new, and James's proposal on the matter followed one very recently made by Darling to the Colonial Office, in which the Governor recommended the appointment of 'a person in the character of Resident, which appears in accordance with the wishes of the Natives, so as to assure them of the desire of His Majesty's

---

[84] Ibid., 68.
[85] Ibid.
[86] Ibid.
[87] M. H. Fisher, 'Indirect Rule in the British Empire: The Foundations of the Residency System in India (1764–1858)', *Modern Asian Studies* 18, no. 3 (1984): 393–428; C. W. Newbury, 'Patrons, Clients, and Empire: The Subordination of Indigenous Hierarchies in Asia and Africa', *Journal of World History* 11, no. 2 (2000): 228–9.

Government to afford them protection and to tranquillize the minds of the Settlers'. James's hope was that once such an authority took root in the country, British influence could be 'extended and improved to our advantage'.[88] Marsden was of a similar view, suggesting to Darling that some sort of 'legal check' was put on convicts who had escaped from New South Wales to New Zealand, where they were currently effectively free to 'commit every crime'.[89]

From late 1830, Marsden became one of the main voices outside of government lobbying for an official British presence in New Zealand. In April 1831, he relayed to Dandeson Coates (the Secretary of the Church Missionary Society, under whose organization Marsden had been appointed to New South Wales) his views on the territory, lamenting the fact that there were 'many Europeans now in New Zealand whose conduct is most scandalous'. Marsden had met twice with Darling at the beginning of the month, had sent the Governor a letter, and planned to meet him again the following week. He could not have done more to press home his point about the plight of New Zealand at the present time. His principal recommendation was that 'a vessel commanded by a naval officer should visit the different places [in New Zealand] to which the Europeans resort, in order to check the conduct of the masters and crews who visit these islands', and that 'a Resident should be stationed in New Zealand, with proper authority to notice the misconduct of the Europeans and to whom the natives can appeal for redress'. He followed this with a warning that '[i]f no measures are taken the New Zealanders [that is, Māori] will redress their own wrongs and take life for life'.[90] Marsden was sufficiently confident that his pleas to Darling were falling on fertile ground that he wrote to a colleague a week later, convinced that 'the Governor will point out the necessity of a Resident being appointed to New Zealand to whom the natives may appeal for redress for acts of cruelty, etc., done upon them by the Europeans'. If something along these lines was not done, the parson prophesied that 'all commercial connection must cease between New Zealand and this Colony [and] [t]he natives will most assuredly revenge their own wrongs unless some protection is afforded them'.[91]

The feeling that 'something had to be done' about New Zealand had intermittently surfaced in New South Wales almost since the beginning of the century. However, specifics on *what* should be done were generally absent, and among most officials and politicians, there was neither the money nor the

---

[88] R. Darling to G. Murray, 13 April 1832, in *HRA* 1, vol. 16, 237–41.
[89] S. Marsden to R. Darling, 2 August 1830, in *Report From Committee on Secondary Punishments* (London: House of Commons, 1831), 130.
[90] S. Marsden to D. Coates, 18 April 1831, in *The Letters and Journals of Samuel Marsden, 1765–1838*, ed. J. R Elder (Dunedin: Coulls Somerville Wilkie Ltd., 1932), 499.
[91] S. Marsden to E. Bickersteth, 25 April 1831, in *The Letters and Journals of Samuel Marsden*, 499.

will for such intervention. What helped shift this situation slightly, though, was a particularly disturbing event in New Zealand that made it harder for colonial authorities to continue to avert their gaze from the territory.[92] In February 1831, several statements were provided to Sydney authorities from sailors who had been to New Zealand on the brig *Elizabeth* the previous year. In their testimonies, it was revealed that the ship, under the command of Captain John Stewart, had transported more than 100 Māori troops, led by the Ngati Toa chief Te Rauparaha, to the South Island, in return for a cargo of flax. Stewart's complicity in the gruesome events that ensued prevented him from later pleading ignorance. Te Rauparaha told the captain that the location he wished to be taken to was the home of a 'hostile' tribe, which had previously slaughtered several Europeans, for which Te Rauparaha now sought vengeance. Stewart invited the chief of this 'hostile' tribe, along with some members of his community, on board the *Elizabeth*. Eventually, these visitors were taken below deck, where they were tortured and killed by Te Rauparaha, after which his troops pillaged the victims' community. What particularly shocked settlers in New South Wales when they read about this episode in the newspapers were the lurid accounts of torture, cannibalism, and a massacre associated with Stewart's partnership with Te Rauparaha.[93]

Stewart was arrested shortly after returning to Sydney, and charged with murder. William Moore, the New South Wales Crown Solicitor, initially expressed doubts over 'whether any offence has been committed which is cognizable by the Common Law of England',[94] but his reluctance to arrest Stewart, based on a jurisprudential technicality, was overruled by Darling and McLeay.[95] Stewart was brought before the Sydney court in May 1831, but the Crown's case against him collapsed because most of the witnesses had fled New South Wales, and because 'New Zealand tribes, having been engaged in what may be regarded as legitimate warfare according to the usages of their own country, could not, with justice or propriety, be charged with murder, and, therefore, that the Master and crew could not be charged as accessories to murder', as Goderich, the Colonial Secretary, later observed.[96] Goderich's position was correct in law, but nonetheless felt to most concerned like a breach of natural justice.

---

[92] D. M. Loveridge, '"A Knot of a Thousand Difficulties": Britain and New Zealand, 1769–1840', Brief of Evidence before the Waitangi Tribunal, WAI-1040, #A18 (Wellington, 2009), 43.
[93] H. C. Evison, *Te Wai Pounamu: The Greenstone Island, A History of the Southern Maori During the European Colonisation of New Zealand* (Christchurch: Aoraki Press, 1993), 53–4; J. W. Stack, *Kaiapohia: The Story of a Siege* (Christchurch: Whitcombe and Tombs, 1893), 42–4.
[94] W. H. Moore, Legal Opinion, 7 February 1831, in *Historical Records of New Zealand* 2, 588.
[95] Ibid., 589–90.
[96] Goderich to R. Bourke, 31 January 1832, in *HRA* 1, vol. 16, 513.

Darling was one of those frustrated by the outcome of the case, and believed that direct British representation in New Zealand was the first step towards a lasting solution regarding British jurisdiction in territories neighbouring New South Wales. However, as he became embroiled in mounting acrimony over domestic issues that led to his recall from New South Wales in 1831, the previous thoughts he had about installing a Resident in New Zealand to achieve this purpose were discarded while he fought desperately to salvage his career.[97]

When James was called to testify before the House of Commons Select Committee on Secondary Punishments on 27 July 1831 (within two weeks of arriving in London), news of the *Elizabeth* saga had yet to reach London, and so politicians' minds were dwelling on slightly more mundane issues of colonial governance in New South Wales. It was a warm and brilliantly fine day[98] as James entered the rambling assortment of buildings that then made up the Palace of Westminster. On this occasion, he could not have helped but feel gratified and maybe even a little proud that his expertise on New South Wales was sufficiently regarded that it was being sought by Members of Parliament. The committee rooms were above the debating chamber, and for years had proven completely inadequate for their purpose. Rooms were sometimes booked for multiple hearings at the same time, with clerks, politicians, officials, witnesses, and members of the public wrangling their way through the corridors, spilling out of some rooms and into others, with parliamentary staff often hauling piles of paperwork in their wake to wherever there was space to place them. And with it being summer when James appeared, the committee rooms became almost unbearably hot, which added to the overall discomfort of appearing in them.[99] But James made no mention of the shambolic nature of hearings, as this was precisely the sort of situation he hankered after: one of respectability, influence, and a certain degree of prestige.

The Committee chairman opened with questions regarding the role of convict labourers in the colony. James was coy on some points, but generally assessed that the current scheme was not working well, and that convict labour in general was not the economic boon to the colony that people might have imagined. The rest of the questioning then went into minute detail on just about every aspect of convict life in New South Wales, and the relationships between these convicts and free settlers.[100]

---

[97] For details, see R. Darling, *Letter Addressed by Lieut.-Gen. R. Darling, Late Governor of New South Wales, to Joseph Hume, Esq. MP* (London: J. McGowan, 1832).
[98] *Meteorological Journal, Kept by the Assistant Secretary at the Apartments of the Royal Society* (London: Royal Society, 1831), n.p.
[99] H. M. Colvin, *History of the King's Works. Vol. VI: 1782–1851* (London: H. M. Stationery Office, 1973), 525–32.
[100] J. Busby, 25 July 1831, in *Report from Committee on Secondary Punishments* (House of Commons: London, 1831), 73–80.

Such was the interest in James's testimony that he was called back on 5 August, during a 'violent thunder storm', to be questioned further about crime and convicts in the colony. In the intervening week, he had prepared a short paper on aspects of crime and the economy in New South Wales which he presented to the Committee. Part of its purpose was to offer more detail on the topics under review, but it also served to set the record straight regarding some information he had provided during his previous appearance which he realized was not quite accurate. James then presented to the Committee another, more exhaustive document he had written, which itemized the cost of just about all the goods and services in New South Wales. If the Committee wanted to know the cost of firewood, arrowroot, hay, wheat dressing, or sending coals to Newcastle (from Sydney), it was all there in James's report.[101] Crucially, though, the one detail he omitted from all the information he presented to the Select Committee was the very role he was angling for in London: to be the British representative in New Zealand. If he did feel any temptation during the questioning to unveil his ambition, he succeeded in resisting it. After all, it would be the Colonial Office, and not a group of mainly low-ranked politicians, who would make the decision on his proposal, and he was astute enough to know that any indiscretion on his behalf – whether in front of a select committee or anywhere else – could jeopardize his chances for the appointment he sought most of all.

With his appearance before the Select Committee out of the way by the afternoon of 5 August, James spent the next few days penning a long and particularly revealing letter to Alexander, which provides details on his movements and meetings since arriving in London. Once James had secured accommodation in the capital, he had immediately arranged meetings with Goulburn (the former New South Wales Colonial Secretary, whom he had met a day after setting foot in Sydney in 1824, and whom he held in extremely high esteem),[102] and Haddington.[103] Haddington had 'spoken favourably' of James's paper on New Zealand to Lord Howick, the Colonial Secretary, while Goulburn regarded the work as 'of such importance' that he had presented it to Goderich, accompanied by a note of endorsement. James felt very honoured by this degree of support, particularly as he had been explicit with both men that the purpose of his reports was not merely to inform the Colonial Office of the situation in the antipodes, but to 'be employed advantageously for the Public and honourably for myself', as he candidly put it.[104]

---

[101] Ibid., 80–2.
[102] J. Busby to W. Kelman, 19 March 1824, in Papers of the Busby and Kelman Families, 1822–1879, CY Reel 985, ref ML MSS. 1183, 67–8.
[103] See J. Busby to E. Barnard, 12 July 1823, in *BFR* 1, 66.
[104] J. Busby to A. Busby, 10 August 1831, in *BFR* 1, 297.

There was now growing reason for James to feel optimistic about his future. In addition to having Goulburn and Haddington effectively lobbying the Colonial Office on his behalf, he had secured a meeting with Howick, which was particularly encouraging if for nothing else than as an indication of the extent to which the government was finally taking him seriously. James had 'long conversations' with Howick, and relayed how the Colonial Secretary had 'evidently not only read but had <u>studied</u>' his proposals and was 'perfectly familiar' with them. This was a marked contrast to previous encounters with officials who shared neither the patience nor the interest in topics James reported on to read his works thoroughly.[105] Howick was instilling 'something of a new, liberal spirit of enterprise into the colonial office',[106] and James's proposals were in accordance with this mood. The timing could not have been better for him to approach the government with his plans. Howick had showed James the correspondence he had received from Darling, which revealed that not only had some of James's proposals in that correspondence become part of British policy on New South Wales (much to his delight), but that Darling had diligently forwarded all of James's suggestions on to his superiors in the Colonial Office. As a result, James's work was already well known by the time he returned to Downing Street in 1831.

This favourable reception was in marked contrast to the desperate pleading that had characterized James's last trip to the British capital, eight years earlier. It was similarly a different story outside his meetings with officials in London. Whereas in 1823 James had been poor, often hungry, in uncomfortable lodgings, and with barely a single friendly face to turn to, now he was a person of some note. Thanks to a recommendation from Marsden,[107] he was introduced to the MP Sir Fowell Buxton, who was active in the abolitionist movement,[108] and at whose place he shared many meals with the Buxton family. James also met a Mr Mastina, whose brother-in-law was Sir Edward Parry, the Commissioner to the Australian Agricultural Company[109] (through whom James received the introduction). And between official and social engagements, James made a point of showing his gratitude by distributing either bottles of wine or specially bound copies of his book on viticulture to those he met.[110]

---

[105] Ibid.
[106] B. Semmel, *The Rise of Free Trade Imperialism: Classical Political Economy: The Empire of Free Trade and Imperialism, 1750–1850* (Cambridge: Cambridge University Press, 1970), 109.
[107] Sharp, *The World, the Flesh and the Devil*, 730–3.
[108] D. Bruce, *The Life of Sir Thomas Fowell Buxton: Extraordinary Perseverance* (Plymouth: Lexington Books, 2014), 128–30.
[109] W. E. Parry, *In Service of the Company: Letters of Sir Edward Parry, Commissioner to the Australian Agricultural Company* 1 (Canberra: Australian National University, 2005), vi, 331.
[110] J. Busby to A. Busby, 10 August 1831, in *BFR* 1, 298.

Money was far from being in plentiful supply for James, though, and this outward appearance (by his standards, at least) of largesse masked considerable caution over his funds. Before leaving New South Wales he had written to Kelman, asking him for £100 from the money owed to him. However, he had received a reply in the last month from his brother-in-law, written 'in the very kindest terms', but nevertheless refusing the invitation to repay part of the debt to James on the basis that Kelman and Catherine had a growing family and had suffered recent financial losses with their farm.[111] Yet even the normally parsimonious James seems not to have been especially put out by this unpaid debt. The signs coming from the Colonial Office hinted that something may be in the offing career-wise for him, and he regarded his recent appearance before the Select Committee as a minor triumph. In addition, he had enjoyed good company in London over the past several weeks, and was now anticipating the prospect of travelling through Spain and France to assemble material for a new book, with a quick trip to Scotland to be squeezed in beforehand. His financial affairs in New South Wales, along with the slavish bureaucratic routines of his job in Sydney, the chilly relationship with his father, and the various entanglements with the lives of his siblings were in every sense a world away.

---

[111] Ibid.

5

Convergence

As the Colonial Office ruminated over his various proposals,[1] James prepared to leave London, knowing from experience that the wheels of officialdom ground slowly, and that it would be several months before something resembling a decision would emerge. He considered making a fleeting trip to Scotland before going to Spain, but because it was already August, and as he was particularly keen to observe the process of raisin-making in Spain, he needed to rush if he was also going to squeeze in a visit to the country of his birth.[2] Time almost ran out for him, though, and in mid-August 1831, he travelled to Edinburgh for just a week.[3] By the end of the month, he was back at his lodgings at 19 Surrey Street, London, and on 6 September he took a coach to Gravesend, near the mouth of the Thames, where he boarded the *William* which was bound for Cadiz, in southern Spain.

James maintained a diary during the trip, which he later published, along with some supplementary material, as *Journal of a Tour through Some of the Vineyards of Spain and France*.[4] He reached Spain on 26 September, and met, as previously arranged, with a Dr Wilson, whose brother was a wine merchant. Over the next nine days, they travelled extensively through the region, mainly on horseback, visiting orchards, vineyards, garden, cellars, farms, and wineries. James made thorough notes on issues ranging from local hedge plants that might be suitable for use in New South Wales, through to the irrigation of garlic plants, the propagation methods of olive trees, and the use of sulphur in wine-making.[5]

---

[1] Bayly, *James Busby: British Resident in New Zealand*, 18.
[2] J. Busby to A. Busby, 10 August 1831, in *BFR* 1, 298.
[3] Busby did not mention this trip to Edinburgh, but reference to it appears in J. Frew to J. Busby, 13 June 1832, in 'Letters to James Busby, 1830–1866', Auckland Museum, MS46.
[4] J. Busby, *Journal of a Tour through Some of the Vineyards of Spain and France* (Sydney: Stephens and Stoke, 1833). A slight variant of this work was published in Britain the following year. See J. Busby, *Journal of a Recent Visit to the Principal Vineyards of Spain and France* (London: Smith, Elder & Co., 1834).
[5] Busby, *Journal of a Tour Through Some of the Vineyards of Spain and France*, 7–22.

On Thursday 6 October, James continued his exploration alone, as Dr Wilson had returned to his brother's house the previous morning. After about four hours on horseback, he reached the coastal settlement of Bonanza. It had been a slow and arduous journey. 'The road was not made in any place,' he recorded, 'but there were bridges at spots which would be otherwise impassable.' After about five kilometres of this difficult terrain, he gave up on looking at vineyards, and decided to head directly for his destination. On arriving, he captured a brief impression of the area: 'The country was . . . open, and without a single tree or enclosure. I passed several farm steadings, if indeed they are worthy of the name. The buildings were of the most wretched description, and in the worst possible repair . . . Here . . . no farmer lives upon his farm.'[6]

Once at Bonanza, though, James had to put a temporary halt to his movements. He was told by just about everyone he came across that the roads leading out of the town 'were so much infested with robbers, that every person who attempts to travel, unless under . . . protection . . . is sure to be stripped'. There was a system of 'blackmail' (as he described it) whereby a local guide could get a visitor through this dangerous area, but only for an appropriate fee. James had to join a caravan of travellers which consisted of six wagons, a covered cart (transporting James and three friars), several people riding donkeys, and a few travelling by foot. As this motley cavalcade wound its way along the twisted route, slowly its numbers decreased as some of the travellers reached their destinations along the way.

After a week on this journey, James and his remaining fellow travellers were confronted by several men on horseback who were part of a gang run by 'a famous brigand, who has 35 men well mounted and equipped, and levies contributions on all the roads throughout the province'. At the next stop, James and the others had to make a payment to a local resident 'to guarantee travellers against robbers; and 14 dollars having been collected, we saw no more of the party which caused such alarm'.[7]

With few exceptions, the whole stretch of country that James was journeying through was rich as far as soil fertility was concerned, but was 'in the most wretched state of cultivation'. He was surprised to see hardly any fences, walls, or hedges, and just a few people living in 'miserable villages'. Even when the group stopped off at taverns for meals and sleep, James was disappointed with what was provided: 'the inns were of the meanest description; and the fare, which was undoubtedly superior to the daily fare even of those above the rank of a peasant, was such as to indicate the greatest

---

[6] Ibid., 27.
[7] Ibid., 52–107.

poverty'.⁸ At most of the locations he visited, James was able to inspect the horticulture of the region, and often reported on it at length. He also made a point of collecting and labelling small bundles of grape cuttings with a view to planting and propagating them once back in New South Wales.

In late autumn, James sailed from Malaga, in the south of Spain, to Rosas, in the region of Catalonia. From there, he took a coach to Figueras, and then to Perpignan, in the southeast corner of France, proceeding from one vineyard to another, before reaching Paris in the last week of December, having arranged for thousands of grape cuttings to be sent to New South Wales.⁹

Journal of a Tour through Some of the Vineyards of Spain and France is an unusual work. It is partly a travel book, but without much in the way of variety or in-depth descriptions, and partly an instructional volume, but with its informative material dispersed over more than 130 pages. It also contains details on horticulture in the Iberian Peninsula, but much of it is relevant only to that region, while its list of more than 500 grape varieties (some with intricate descriptions) would be more assistance to a botanist than a fledgling colonial viticulturist. Regardless, though, the work was generally well received when it was published.¹⁰

James returned to London in the first week of January 1832. The temperature was near freezing and the metropolis was enveloped in a dense fog.¹¹ Having been on his horticultural 'pilgrimage' through Spain and France,¹² he was keen to ascertain what the Colonial Office had resolved about his reports during his absence. He made an obligatory appointment to visit Goderich, but also began formulating plans to secure a berth on a convict ship that was due to leave for New South Wales in a matter of days. On 6 January, he wrote to the Colonial Office, but pointedly, he never enquired about or even mentioned the proposals he had submitted to them for consideration in July the previous year. Rather, the single focus of his letter was on the comparatively trivial issue of seeking the support of His Majesty's government to establish what he called an 'Experimental Garden' at Sydney, to propagate his vines.¹³

Of course, Goderich was more than astute enough to know that James's letter about grape cuttings was really a transparent effort to nudge the Colonial

---

⁸ Ibid., 28, 34.
⁹ Ibid., 52–107.
¹⁰ J. Mudie, *The Felony of New South Wales: Being a Faithful Picture of the Real Romance of Life in Botany Bay* (London: Whaley & Co., 1837), n.p.
¹¹ *Meteorological Journal, Kept by the Assistant Secretary at the Apartments of the Royal Society* (1832), n.p.
¹² Cited in Mudie, *The Felony of New South Wales*, n.p.
¹³ J. Busby to Goderich, 6 January 1832, in Busby, *Journal of a Tour through Some of the Vineyards of Spain and France*, 109–10.

Secretary to respond to the various proposals James had submitted to him half a year earlier. It turned out, though, that Goderich needed no prompting on the role James coveted most of all. As is so often the case in history, seemingly unrelated occurrences had converged into a particular sequence of events, resulting in changes of great and lasting consequence. While James had been in Europe, the Colonial Office received news of the *Elizabeth* affair. Goderich shared everyone else's disgust at his compatriots' collusion in this evil event. But unlike most others, he was in a position to do something about the challenge of extending jurisdiction to British subjects living in or visiting New Zealand. He had deliberated at length on the matter in a letter to Darling's replacement as Governor of New South Wales, Sir Richard Bourke. Goderich's letter represented the beginning of a sea-change in British views on New Zealand. A committed emancipationist,[14] and inspired by moral concerns as much as political imperatives, Goderich laid out for Bourke's benefit the robust new direction he hoped British policy on the region would take, prompted in part by recent occurrences in the area.[15] In commenting on the reports dealing with the jurisprudential aspects of the *Elizabeth* case, Goderich wrote:

> The unfortunate natives of New Zealand, unless some decisive measure of prevention be adopted, will, I fear, be shortly added to the number of those barbarous tribes, who, in different parts of the Globe, have fallen a sacrifice to their intercourse with civilised men, who bear and disgrace the name of Christians . . . There can be no more sacred duty than that of using every possible method to rescue the natives of the extensive islands from the further evils which impend over them, and to deliver our own country from the disgrace and crime of having either occasioned or tolerated such enormities.[16]

This stance was supported by the Under-Secretary of State for the Colonies, Sir Robert Hay, who wrote a confidential minute to Bourke the same month, indicating that the British government considered it 'very proper' that a Resident be appointed to New Zealand. Hay was disinclined for the Resident to have any troops at his disposal, ostensibly because of a soldier shortage in New South Wales, but more likely because of concerns about the power a

---

[14] W. D. Jones, *'Prosperity' Robinson: The Life of Viscount Goderich, 1782–1859* (New York: St Martin's Press, 1967), 222.
[15] T. E. Williams, 'The Colonial Office in the Thirties', *Australian Historical Studies* 2, no. 7 (1943): 141–60; H. T. Manning, 'The Colonial Policy of the Whig Ministers, 1830–37: I', *Canadian Historical Review* 33, no. 3 (1952), 203–36.
[16] Goderich to R. Bourke, 31 January 1832, in *Report of the Parliamentary Select Committee on Aboriginal Tribes (British Settlements)* (London: House of Commons, 1837), 18–19.

Resident with an armed force would have in a territory where British jurisdiction did not formally apply.[17] Goderich concurred. There would be no soldiers setting foot in New Zealand in the foreseeable future, and the person who was appointed as Resident would necessarily be a civilian rather than a military man (which could be a hint that he had James specifically in mind for the role).[18] The Resident's initial task would be to address the need for greater order among British subjects in New Zealand, and to manage relations with Māori, even if, as Goderich conceded, this could not 'be strictly defended as legal'.[19]

James was unaware at this time of the extent to which the policy for appointing a Resident in New Zealand was being finalized. He had hoped that his letter to Goderich of 6 January about his grape cuttings would have reminded officials about his quest for an appointment, but when he received no response, he decided to meet with Haddington, who advised him to make a more direct approach to the Colonial Office. James wrote to Goderich on 3 February 1832, this time outlining his entire work history since arriving in New South Wales, and then getting to the crux of the issue: his quest for an appointment. Bluffing, he explained that he had embarked on his tour to Spain and France reasonably confident that a position would be on offer to him when he returned to England, based on the verbal assurances he had received from the Colonial Office. He then expressed his surprise that no final decision had yet been reached, before concluding by advising Goderich that if he did not get a prompt offer of 'honourable and permanent employment', he would soon leave England and relinquish all thoughts of ever working for the government again.[20]

Meanwhile, Bourke had independently come to the same conclusion regarding the need for New Zealand to have a Resident. Following advice from his Attorney General, John Kinchela, that a British agent be appointed to the territory with the means to 'suppress Aggression, or to apprehend Offenders or runaway Convicts',[21] he recommended to his Executive Council on 22 December 1831 that 'New Zealand should be placed on a better footing', and that to achieve this, he proposed 'to place a Resident in New Zealand with one of the Colonial Vessels under his orders for the purpose of protecting and promoting Commerce and effecting the apprehension of fugitives'. This Resident would to act to protect Māori 'by every possible means' from maltreatment by Europeans, and would encourage trade.[22] It

---

[17] R. Hay to R Bourke, 21 January 1832, in *HRA* 1, vol. 16, 505.
[18] Goderich to R. Bourke, 31 January 1832, in *HRA* 1, vol. 16, 511.
[19] Ibid., 512.
[20] J. Busby to Goderich, 3 February 1832, in *BFR* 1, 328–30.
[21] J. Kinchela to R. Bourke, 12 December 1831, in *HRA* 1, vol. 16, 485–6.
[22] R. Bourke to Goderich, 23 December 1831, in *HRA* 1, vol. 16, 482–6.

was a proposal conceived in pragmatism, but born with a degree of idealism – as if such an appointment would, of itself, resolve the range of complex challenges in the territory.

However, despite Bourke and Goderich being of one mind on the requirement for a Resident to be appointed to New Zealand, Bourke's dispatch to the Colonial Secretary would not reach London until May, and so ended up having little immediate effect on the final stages of decision-making on this issue in the Colonial Office. Instead, it was another occurrence – completely outside the realm of officials and politicians – that provided that final momentum for policy to be pushed into practice. The event in question was sparked by a minor collision of political motives and denominational jingoism that normally would have subsided, leaving barely a trace, but in this case was inflamed by an otherwise inconsequential Anglican priest temporarily seeing himself as a man of destiny.

The cleric concerned was William Yate, who had established his mission in Waimate North. It was part of an area that was frequented by traders, principally from New South Wales, and so was susceptible to the sort of gossip that was one of the invisible commodities being exchanged in the region at the time. One of the long-standing rumours – of French designs on New Zealand – was enlivened in 1831 with the visit to Northland by the French shop *La Favorite*, commanded by Captain Cyrille Pierre Théodore Laplace. However, far from heralding a seizure of sovereignty, on 2 October the vessel limped into the Bay of Islands, with some of its crew still suffering from the effects of a bout of dysentery.[23] Although the purpose of the voyage was primarily to conduct zoological and hydrographic surveys, and to examine possible trading opportunities,[24] it was wilfully interpreted by many settlers in the region as a threat to British interests in the territory.[25]

The fear among some European settlers of an impending French annexation of New Zealand might have been genuinely felt, but it went hand in hand with a longing for Britain to take a more active role in the territory. The day after *La Favorite* dropped anchor in the Bay of Islands, Yate decided to make an appeal to the King for such intervention. What was novel about Yate's approach was that it came in the form of a petition signed by thirteen local chiefs.[26] These

---

[23] J. Dunmore, *French Explorers in the Pacific: Volume 2, The Nineteenth Century* (Oxford: Oxford University Press, 1969), 250–8.
[24] K. V. Sinclair, *Laplace in New Zealand, 1831* (Waikanae: Heritage Press, 1998), 41.
[25] J. S. Polack, *New Zealand: Being a Narrative of Travels and Adventures During a Residence in that Country between the Years 1831 and 1837* 1 (London: Richard Bentley, 1838), 54–5.
[26] The petition was sent to England on 16 November 1831. N. Ellis, 'Ki to ringa ki nga rakau a te Pakeha? Drawings and Signatures of Moko by Māori in the Early 19th Century', *Journal of the Polynesian Society [JPS]* 123, no. 1 (March 2014): 34.

signatories claimed that it was only Britain 'which is liberal towards us', and that it was from Britain where the missionaries came, who were such a blessing to Māori. Through Yate, the chiefs expressed the fear that 'the tribe of Marian [Marion] is at hand coming to take away our land, therefore we pray thee to become our friend and the guardian of these islands'. And in a further hint that some sort of official British intervention was desired, the petitioners concluded that 'if any of thy people should be troublesome or vicious towards us – for some persons are living here who have run away from ships – we pray thee to be angry with them that they may be obedient, lest the anger of the people of this land fall upon them'.[27]

When Yates's petition reached London, quick exchanges took place between the Secretary of State for War and the Colonies, the Secretary of State for Foreign Affairs, Britain's ambassador in France, and the French Admiralty. It was promptly and easily determined that the French had no such ambitions on New Zealand, of the sort Yate had alleged. But the fact that there had been a flurry of messages between two European powers over this episode brought home to Goderich the necessity of resolving the lingering issue of appointing a Resident to New Zealand. On 18 March, in a wide-ranging dispatch to Bourke, he announced that he would be recommending James for the role. Goderich described him as someone who 'has shewn much intelligence in the information he has given to this Department', and proposed that he receive an annual salary of £500. And on the matter of what sort of force James would have at his command, Goderich tactfully explained the British government's position: 'it will be inexpedient, as well in point of policy as with reference to expence [sic], to detach any Troops to those Islands [New Zealand], at any rate, until they can be more easily spared from other duties, and until the feelings of the New Zealand Chiefs, in regard to their appearance amongst them, can be correctly ascertained'.[28] James received notification of his appointment around 19 or 20 March, and once he got over his initial thrill at the news, there was more waiting until the particulars of the role were clarified.

The specific duties and functions of James's position were fashioned by Hay, the 'very cold' official who controlled outsiders' access to Goderich, and who tended to chisel the detail from the broad outline of ideas that came from his political masters into more precisely sculpted policies.[29] Hay consulted with officials from his own and other departments, and on 26 March he sent a dispatch to Bourke (with a copy almost certainly going to James) containing

---

[27] *The Letters and Journals of Samuel Marsden*, 505.
[28] Goderich to R. Bourke, 18 March 1832, in *HRA* 1, vol. 16, 563.
[29] V. Wallace, *Scottish Presbyterianism and Settler Colonial Politics: Empire of Dissent* (Basingstoke: Palgrave Macmillan, 2018), 122.

a summary of what was expected from the Resident to New Zealand, and from authorities in Sydney.

John Barrow, the Second Secretary to the Admiralty, added his department's view on the Residency, making it explicit that the Admiralty would give no authority to any of its commanders to get involved 'in a territory not belonging to His Majesty, and with the Rulers of which he has no treaty either of alliance or Commerce'. The most that could be hoped for was that British subjects in the territory might be afforded some protection if the need arose and the means were available to assist.[30] This was a signal to Goderich that the Admiralty was not prepared to undertake an interventionist role in New Zealand, beyond purely protective measures, and so James would be unable to rely on a military presence to buttress his Residency.

So much for the Admiralty's preferences. James had some of his own, reflecting quite a different outlook. With his appointment confirmed, it had been necessary for him to remain in London until the details of his posting had been finalized. On 22 May he wrote a brief memorandum, addressed to Goderich, which outlined his expectations when commencing his role. Far from being overawed by the appointment, James was already making demands, some of which were practical, and others that bordered on the preposterous. He requested that he be given a small budget to enable him to offer gifts to the chiefs in New Zealand when he landed. This was probably something that he had learned from Marsden, who was familiar with the way in which gifts were sometimes presented among Māori as a way of honouring the recipient and building relationships.[31]

Equally reasonable was James's request that some provision be made for materials for a house for him to live in when he got to New Zealand.[32] The rest of the memorandum, however, veered into another sphere altogether. James was already assembling in his imagination a heroic self-image which he was believed would befit the role of Resident. He betrayed this in the wording of his opening sentence, where he stated '[a]s the influence which I will possess over the minds of the N. Zealanders will be of an altogether moral character, it is of the highest importance that I should appear among them in circumstances that would command their respect'. And how was this to be achieved? James recommended that he should be given an audience with King William IV prior to leaving London. He believed that Māori, with their 'simple ideas of Majesty', would give James more respect if he could let it be known that he 'had been in the presence of the King'. It was a tenuous argument, and even James

---

[30] J. Barrow to R. Hay, 24 March 1832, in *HRA* 1, vol. 16, 573.
[31] M. Durie, 'Keynote Address: Is there a Distinctive Māori Psychology?', in *The Proceedings of the National Māori Graduates of Psychology Symposium* (Hamilton: Waikato University, 2002), 20.
[32] 'Memo. by Mr. James Busby', in *HRA* 1, vol. 16, 665–6.

must have known so. Yet the grandeur of the position was beginning to beguile him. He even submitted that it was important for his success in New Zealand that he 'should wear a uniform (that of a Consul for instance) as a visible mark of distinction that would be recognised by the English Traders and others upon the Coast'. Not only would such a uniform would be a visible indication to others of James's status, but the notion of being draped in an embroidered tail-coat with standing collar, a plumed hat, breeches, tassels, sashes, and the other paraphernalia that went with the uniform obviously appealed to him aesthetically as well.[33]

James concluded his memorandum with a single brief sentence addressing the overriding purpose of his appointment. On enforcing his authority over escaped convicts and others, he did not even propose a means by which he would accomplish this. On the contrary, he brushed off the matter, dismissing it as something 'probably better left for the consideration of the Governor of New South Wales'.[34] In forwarding this to Bourke (who would be James's superior), the sagacious Hay addressed the issue of the Resident's house, but sidestepped all the other demands James had made.[35]

However, although James's more whimsical requests were politely ignored, the British government was not insensitive to the thorny issue of the Resident's authority in New Zealand. The response was a novel yet ultimately unsatisfactory one: a bill would be introduced to Parliament to address some aspects of British jurisdiction in the region.[36] The proposed statute, popularly known as the 'South Seas Bill', aimed 'to make effectual provision for the seizure, detention, trial and punishment of any such Offenders, either within the said Colony of New South Wales, or within the Islands in which any such Offences may have been committed, or within any adjacent Islands'. This would 'have the power of rendering Mr Busby's Mission effectual to the purposes with which it has been undertaken'.[37]

In tabling the Bill before the House of Commons, Howick highlighted the risks of convicts in territories such as New Zealand, who 'were in the habit of committing great crimes there, often inciting the inhabitants to make war on each other, and assisting them in those wars'.[38] However, the shortcomings with the Bill were immediately evident: surely the colony's Governor already

---

[33] Ibid.
[34] Ibid., 666.
[35] R. Hay to R. Bourke, 14 June 1832, in *HRA* 1, vol. 16, 665.
[36] *A Bill to Authorize the Governor of New South Wales, with the Advice and Consent of the Legislative Council of that Colony, to Make Provision for the Prevention and Punishment of Crimes Committed by His Majesty's Subjects, in Islands Situate in the Southern Or Pacific Ocean, and Not Being Within His Majesty's Dominion*, session 516, vol. 4 (London: House of Commons, 1832), 345–9.
[37] Goderich to R. Bourke, 14 June 1832, in *HRA* 1, vol. 16, 663.
[38] Howick, in *Hansard: House of Commons Debates* 13, 7 June 1832, 505.

had such power to legislate for British subjects in neighbouring territories? Was the Bill's intention to give Britain jurisdiction over territories that would remain outside the Empire, and if so, did the Commons even have the right to legislate for such territories?[39] Howick's response was to clarify that while the New South Wales courts could punish crimes, they had no ability to arrest suspects in New Zealand, 'so that a man may be living at large in that island, and the Government has no power to apprehend him'.[40] The Bill failed to be passed into law, though, and so James's jurisdiction in New Zealand remained practically non-existent.

The citizens of New South Wales learned of the appointment of a Resident to New Zealand in August 1832, with the press immediately making James a target for their vitriol. The *Sydney Monitor* openly attacked him, starting with his appearance before the Select Committee in London the previous year: 'This gentleman after pocketing a deal of the Colonists' money, does all he can (by a testimony the most contradictory nevertheless to itself) to deter transportation to New South Wales.' This was a gross misrepresentation, but as the report continued, it became plain that the object was not accuracy as much as character assassination. James was '[l]ike all men . . . whose minds are a heap of confusion', and as far as this journalist was concerned, it was almost a waste of time 'exposing the absurdities of this religio-politico self-sufficient young man'.[41] The *Australian* was just as snide, describing the reports James had written as coming from his 'flippant, fluent, mis-directed quill', and that while in London, he had managed to 'talk himself into some non-descript berth of £500 a-year at New Zealand'.[42]

Goderich intended to inform Māori about James's appointment. He drafted an announcement written in slightly plainer English so that it might be easier for the missionaries to translate. It expressed a loose set of reciprocal obligations and responsibilities that the British government hoped would resolve the New Zealand problem with as little expenditure and political commitment as possible:

> In order to afford better protection to all classes, both Natives of the Island of New Zealand and British Subjects who may proceed or be already established there . . . the King has sent the Bearer of this letter, James Busby, Esqr., to reside amongst you, as His Majesty's Resident, whose duties will be to investigate all complaints which may be made to him. It

---

[39] These issues were raised by Joseph Hume, Colonel Thomas Davies, and William Burge in ibid., 505.
[40] Howick, in ibid., 506.
[41] *The Sydney Monitor*, 12 September 1832, 2.
[42] *The Australian*, 14 September 1832, 2.

will also be this endeavour to prevent the arrival amongst you of men who have been guilty of Crimes in their Country and who may effect their escape from the place to which they may have been banished, as likewise to apprehend such persons of this Description as may be found at present at large. In return . . . it is confidentially expected by His Majesty that, on your part, you will render to the Resident that assistance and support which are calculated to promote the object of his appointment, and to extend to your Country all the benefits which it is capable of receiving from its friendship and alliance with Great Britain.[43]

During this period – when news of the establishment of the Residency, and of James's testimony before the Select Committee began circulating through New South Wales – James was still on his way back to the colony. At the start of June he had boarded the barque *Planter* at Portsmouth, along with 200 male convicts who were being sent to New South Wales to serve their sentences. Once on board, there were fears that some of the convicts had cholera, and the *Planter* was quarantined for several days until the ship's doctor was certain that there was no risk. The vessel finally departed on 15 June, and reached Sydney exactly four months later.

It had been twenty months since James had last been in the colony, and as the *Planter* headed for Sydney, he appended a dedication to his book *Journal of a Tour through Some of the Vineyards of Spain and France*. Absence from home and family, combined with a new appointment that foreshadowed further separation from them, potentially for several years, may have stirred feelings of regret in James's heart for how relations with his father had deteriorated in recent years (and possibly some guilt for the rigidity with which he had treated John's financial management). So when it came to prefacing the book, detailing his journey through Spain and France, James chose to make a highly sentimental dedication to his father. He commenced with 'dear and honoured father', and expressed candidly 'how much I owe you as a parent and a friend'. The book was James's opportunity of 'paying you [John] this mark of affection and respect', and concluded with the acknowledgement that 'I have learned . . . that there are higher motives for human conduct than the approbation even of the wise and good'.[44]

There was also another relationship that James now had to put on a more solid footing: that with his fiancée, Agnes. It seems like his betrothal to her occurred shortly before he left for England, and now that he was preparing to move permanently to New Zealand, it was no longer possible for him to

---

[43] Goderich to the Chiefs of New Zealand, 14 June, 1832, in *HRA* 1, vol. 16, 664.
[44] Busby, *Journal of a Tour Through Some of the Vineyards of Spain and France*, iii–iv.

remain a fugitive from matrimony. James and Agnes (the latter once described as 'a very dignified and rather exclusive little Scotch lady, but kindly withal')[45] were married on 1 November 1832, by special licence. The wedding took place at Segenhoe, in Hunter's River, with the ceremony presided over by the Venerable Archdeacon William Broughton.[46] Some aspects of the wedding were curious. Having barely mentioned Agnes in correspondence with his brothers, James was now getting married just two weeks after returning to New South Wales. And in addition to this apparently unusual haste, there was the matter of the special licence being obtained, which enabled the wedding to take place outside a church.[47] One explanation for this is that James could have been sent to New Zealand at any moment, and so needed to get married at the earliest opportunity.[48] Certainly, though, it was no act of unbridled passion. Indeed, when James had returned to New South Wales the previous month, he had spent at least three days planting grape vines before even meeting Agnes.[49] His heart had obviously been on other things. However, a few months later, James was sanguine about his relationship, describing himself and Agnes as being 'as happy as possible'.[50] In January 1833, when he had returned to Sydney, James again mentioned how satisfied he was with married life, and noted that he and Agnes were receiving invitations to attend dinners with the elite of Sydney society (although pressures of work meant that he had to turn most down).[51]

The most immediate of James's concerns at this point was where he was going to live in New Zealand. While still on his honeymoon with Agnes, he received notice from the New South Wales colonial secretary, Alexander McLeay, that he was to submit plans for a residence in New Zealand, along with an estimate of probable costs, for consideration by the government. He promptly wrote to John Verge – the architect who had designed the Busbys' family home – to prepare a design for a house that could be constructed in New South Wales, then disassembled, shipped to New Zealand, and erected on site (as a means of bypassing the exorbitant costs of building a house in New Zealand from local materials and using local tradesmen). Verge designed a dwelling that would be framed in Sydney, with weatherboard for the external cladding, and lath and plaster for the interior walls. Verge's plan focussed on

---

[45] C. Mair, in H. M. Simpson, *The Women of New Zealand* (Auckland: Paul's Book Arcade, 1962), 121.
[46] *SMH*, 12 November 1832, 4.
[47] G. P. Monger, *Marriage Customs of the World: From Henna to Honeymoons* (Santa Barbara: ABC-Clio, 2004), 35.
[48] *BFR* 1, 358.
[49] Ibid., 356; Busby, *Journal of a Tour Through Some of the Vineyards of Spain and France*, 111.
[50] J. Busby to A. Busby, 18 December 1832, in *BFR* 1, 361.
[51] J. Busby to A. Busby, 8 January 1833, in *BFR* 2, 372.

reducing costs wherever possible. He advised James that 'everything will be very plain; the rooms, Stores, and closets may appear numerous, but they are small; and I think you could not dispense with any of those conveniences in a Country like New Zealand'. James forwarded the estimated cost of £592 to McLeay, but also added the suggestion that an additional dwelling be built for the 'constabulary force' that he mistakenly envisaged would accompany him in the territory.[52]

However, James was not content with a weatherboard house, and having conferred with Yate in Sydney (probably around January 1833), he wrote a wide-ranging letter to McLeay, advising him that there was a brick-maker in New Zealand along with suitable labourers who could build the outside walls from brick. The meeting with Yate had assumed extra significance because the Governor had decided to delay approving James's house until he had received advice from the missionary.[53] James meanwhile sought approval from the Governor to have tradesmen accompany him to New Zealand, and began suggesting a raft of changes to the house's design. He then moved onto other topics relating to his Residency, focussing on a particular point of concern he had: clothing for the chiefs. He imagined each Māori leader dressed in 'a full suit of English clothing', including drill trousers, coloured waistcoats, and hats. His thinking behind this was 'to make it an object of ambition with the leading chiefs to wear European Clothes and adopt European habits of cleanliness', through which Māori would acquire an interest in fashion which would 'originate a trade more desirable than the present one for Muskets and Gunpowder' and make them appear as 'gentlemen'.[54]

The colonial government's budget could probably stretch to fit the clothing request, but James's house was regarded as excessively costly, and he was told by McLeay that funds would only be available for a basic timber frame to be constructed in Sydney, with the house being clad in weatherboard and not brick. The colonial secretary also suggested that the carpenter on whichever ship took James to New Zealand would be able to erect the frame on arrival, and that the remainder of the house would be assembled shortly afterwards.[55] James was 'much concerned' with this offer, and attempted to make the issue about more than just his own wants. He described his planned house as 'a question which involves . . . the credit of the British Nation'.[56]

---

[52] A. McLeay to J. Busby, 23 October 1832; J. Busby to A. McLeay, 29 October 1832; J. Verge to J. Busby, 8 November 1832; J. Busby to A. McLeay, 11 January 1833, in HRA 1, vol. 17, 46.
[53] J. Busby to A. Busby, 8 January 1833, in BFR 2, 372.
[54] J. Busby to A. McLeay, 11 January 1833, in HRA 1, vol. 17, 47.
[55] A. McLeay to J. Busby, 16 February 1833, in HRA 1, vol. 17, 48–9.
[56] J. Busby to A. McLeay, 20 February 1833, in HRA 1, vol. 17, 49.

Feeling that he was not getting far in his negotiations with McLeay, James wrote directly to the Colonial Office, ostensibly to air his concerns, but most probably because he knew that a copy of the letter would automatically go to Bourke. James hoped that this would be enough to pressure the Governor into acceding to his demands. The first of the two items on his list was a request that he receive a full salary (as opposed to the regulation half-salary he was on) backdated from the time he had returned to Sydney, in October 1832. Bourke's view was that the full Resident's salary would be available to James when he actually went to New Zealand to take up the role. However, James laid much of the blame for his failure to take up his role in New Zealand any earlier on Bourke, who felt it was pointless to do anything until the fate of the South Seas Bill was known, at which point the extent of the Resident's authority would have been more clearly defined, one way or the other.[57]

Next was the issue of the Resident's house. James rehearsed for Hay in minute detail the earlier discussions that had taken place over the planned dwelling, and suggested that the much smaller plan that Bourke approved 'could not be considered a becoming residence for a Functionary with the title of "British Resident"; That it would ill enable me to shew that hospitality to strangers and others which would be a part of the duty of my Station; And that it was little calculated to command the respect' of the territory's Māori or settler populations.[58]

This was an unwise approach by James. In most instances, he would receive instructions from, and be accountable to, the Governor of New South Wales once he took up his position as Resident. It therefore made little sense to antagonize Bourke on the eve of departing to New Zealand by writing to the Governor's superior in London. It was more unwise still, considering that James's principal concern – the size and construction of the Resident's house – had already been determined by the government, based on a very limited budget. However, James had got the position of Resident in the first place precisely by going over the head of his immediate superiors, and so as far as he was concerned, it was an effective means of leveraging his demands, despite the challenges it might later present in this case in dealing with Bourke.

Three days after receiving a copy of James's letter, Bourke wrote to the Colonial Office in response, advising that as there were no plans for a replacement bill for the failed South Seas Bill to be introduced, the time had come for James to be sent to New Zealand. On 25 February 1833, James intimated to Haddington his disappointment over the failure of the Bill.[59] He

---

[57] R. Hay to R. Bourke, 26 October 1833, in *HRA* 1, vol. 17, 253.
[58] J. Busby to R. Hay, 12 March 1833, in *HRA* 1, vol. 17, 42–5.
[59] J. Busby to Haddington, 25 February 1833, in 'James Busby. Official Letters of Various People, 1833–1870', Auckland Museum, MS46.

had vested his hope in its passage because it would have clarified his jurisdiction and almost certainly would have given him a small force to wield the power that increasingly he was coming to see was crucial for the credibility of the Residency. But there was no changing this circumstance, and when Bourke learned that the twenty-eight-gun corvette HMS *Imogene*[60] was on its way back from Tasmania, he suggested that when it reached Sydney, it could transport James to New Zealand.

As James prepared to depart New South Wales, Bourke finalized a detailed set of instructions for him. They remain important not just because they were the most comprehensive and recent instructions James had received regarding his expected duties as Resident, but also because they were produced by the person to whom he would be immediately answerable (even though they 'demanded the impossible' from the Resident).[61] In addition, they were also a signal to the Colonial Office (which received copies of all such correspondence) of how the Governor intended to manage the Residency in New Zealand.

Bourke commenced with a survey of the background leading up to James's appointment, stressing the several serious violent incidents that had occurred in New Zealand against Māori, mainly perpetrated by the crews of British vessels. He regarded it as a 'sacred duty' that Britain's policy on New Zealand endeavoured by every possible means 'to rescue the natives . . . from the evils to which their intercourse with Europeans had exposed them'. He also said that the policy aimed to protect the more well-meaning British subjects from the 'fatal effects' that might result if the assaults on Māori continued – something that he foresaw eventually 'exciting the natives to revenge their injuries by an indiscriminate slaughter of every British subject within their reach'. This was an ominous view, and required the Resident to be a person with 'an accredited character' whose main duty it would be 'to conciliate the good-will of the native chiefs, and establish upon a permanent basis that good understanding and confidence which it is important to the interests of Great Britain and of this colony [New South Wales] to perpetuate'. Bourke conceded that the Resident would struggle to enforce rules in New Zealand, but argued that 'by the skilful use of those powers which educated man possesses over the wild or half-civilized savage, an influence may be gained by which the authority and strength of the New Zealand chiefs will be arrayed on the side of the Resident for the maintenance of tranquillity throughout the islands'.[62]

---

[60] R. Winfield and D. Lyon, *The Sail and Steam Navy List: All the Ships of the Royal Navy 1815–1889* (London: Chatham, 2004), 114.
[61] Bayly, *James Busby: British Resident in New Zealand*, 36.
[62] R. Bourke, in *Correspondence with the Secretary of State Relative to New Zealand* (London: W. Clowes, 1840), 4–6.

Yate's 1831 petition was then referred to, emphasizing that the chiefs who had signed it had sought British protection, and Bourke reminded James to convey to the chiefs on arriving in New Zealand – 'with as much formality as circumstances may permit' – the message to them from the King which Goderich had sent to the New Zealand chiefs. This message emphasised the King's desire to suppress disorder and maintain peace, as well as the plan for James to remain in New Zealand in order to offer Māori the same sorts of protection and privileges that were available to British subjects in foreign states.[63] Goderich was aware of the sway that the British missionaries held in parts of New Zealand – especially in the Bay of Islands region – and so proposed to James that he elicit their help to gather local chiefs together to explain these aspects of his role. In addition, the missionaries would be able to translate any discussions between James and Māori, which would be crucial for the Residency to function without misunderstanding.[64]

As for the extent of the force James would have at his disposal, the best Bourke could offer was that the captain of the ship that would take him to New Zealand would provide a military presence for a few days after James's arrival, with a less reassuring promise that from time to time, British naval ships would visit New Zealand, largely as a symbolic gesture. Bourke's solution to the capacity of the Resident to exercise some authority (and to ensure his personal safety) was for James to rely on local chiefs, for which they could be remunerated with 'presents of inconsiderable value'. This was one of the most flimsy parts of the Governor's instructions. It was not only an unrealistic means of shoring up the Resident's security, but it was also putting James's fate in the hands of a people whom Bourke had just described as being capable of 'indiscriminate slaughter'. Apart from the obvious issue of the expense and probable inefficacy of a few soldiers being stationed with James, the absence of a standing force would oblige the Resident to rely on diplomacy rather than duress, although Bourke failed to make clear what practical options would be open to James when it came to apprehending any British subjects who had transgressed British law in New Zealand.[65] And if James found this too challenging, his only alternative was to return to New South Wales. This would have represented an unmitigated failure as far as James was concerned, and probably for his superiors in Sydney as well. Consequently, there was no real option for him other than to cooperate with locals in the Bay of Islands – with all the implications for political impotence such an approach entailed.

Bourke, however, foresaw the Resident as accomplishing more than apprehending rogue British subjects in the territory, and executing basic

---

[63] Goderich to the Chiefs of New Zealand, 14 June, 1832, in *HRA* 1, vol. 16, 663–4.
[64] *Correspondence with the Secretary of State Relative to New Zealand*, 5.
[65] Ibid., 4–5.

diplomatic functions. In one of the more ambitious aspects of the instructions, the Governor anticipated that through James's intervention and mediation, 'the evils of intestine war between rival chiefs, or hostile tribes, may be avoided, and their differences peaceably and permanently composed'. This was a hopeful expectation, but Bourke advanced it even further, culminating with the suggestion that through James's counselling and encouragement of Māori, they might propose that 'a settled form of government' be established in part of New Zealand, which would encompass some jurisprudential system, along with a rudimentary court. Practicality, not formality, was the driving principle behind this recommendation.[66] The immediate purpose of this regime would be to encourage commerce (particularly the trade in flax) and to bring to an end the trade in shrunken heads (moko mokai). The Resident was thus to fulfil a trusteeship role, exercising a duty of care through cooperation with Māori and settlers, as opposed to imposing colonial rule arbitrarily and by force. These instructions were the closest to a job description that the Resident had. As for the means of implementing the instructions, he would rely on a combination of guidance from the Governor and his own intuition and ability when liaising with a broad spectrum of people in the territory.[67]

Looking back on the British Empire, it is easy to picture it at its apex later in the century, with its flag-waving, its red-coated parades, and the general reverie in Britannia's beneficent ruling of the waves, with Britons congratulating themselves on having spread the blessings of the mother country to the indigenous populations of the Empire. Yet at the time of James's appointment as Resident, the British Empire was not only much less self-confident, but its approach to managing territories in its embrace was often more makeshift in nature and inept in execution. Britain's policy on New Zealand in 1832 and into 1833 epitomized this approach in many ways. The instructions devised for the Residency were a chaotic concoction of humanitarian impulses, political pragmatism, fiscal strictures, and even plain improvisation. It was hardly a recipe for successful intervention in a territory outside the Empire, and accordingly placed a much greater stress on the appointee to make the best of this convoluted approach to the territory. William felt, with some hesitation, that James was the right person for the job. 'I can only hope that the natives of New Zealand appreciate what he is determined to do for them, and not misunderstand his efforts and give way to their natural appetites', he told George at the end of December 1832.[68] For his part, it appeared to more than his siblings by late 1832 that James was able to accomplish the task of acting

---

[66] Ibid., 5–6.
[67] Ibid.
[68] W. Busby to G. Busby, 20 December 1832, in *BFR* 1, 361–2.

as a Resident, even if the instructions on which the role was based fell short of allowing him to achieve anything without the cooperation or consent of disparate groups in New Zealand.

Possibly James's biggest initial challenge when taking up the position would be to galvanize his reputation among settlers and Māori. In the absence of any clear legal authority, and without a military presence to enforce his decisions, he would be heavily dependent on the perception of his authority, and his ability to command respect from the local population. For this reason, a renewed series of attacks on his appointment from the Australian press threatened to undermine him even before he reached New Zealand. One newspaper, when mentioning in early January 1833 that the frame for James's house was under construction, noted that it would be built in the St Helena style. This reference to St Helena – where Napoleon was detained for the final five and a half years of his life – was too irresistible for the journalist to skip over, and he finished off his article by mockingly reminding readers that James was 'not an Emperor'.[69] The *Colonial Times* pitched in with its own venomous accusations against James, starting by deprecating his nationality, with mention of 'Scottish beggars', 'toadeaters of every clan', and labelling 'Jamie' as a 'bock again mon' – a reference to Scottish poachers.[70] The newspaper went on to recommend that the people of New South Wales should petition the colonial government against the 'awful visitation', as it described James's return to Sydney before taking up his post in New Zealand.[71] Finishing off this media mob attack was the *Sydney Monitor*, which alleged that '[o]f all the fatteners on the public fund . . . who did the least for their money, and by whom the public were least benefited, was the family of the Busbys'.[72] In addition to whatever personal toll such public barrages inflicted, there was the issue of these freely rendered criticisms making their way (as newspapers did) to the settler communities in New Zealand, where they would erode James's reputation.

By January 1833, some in James's family had growing reservations over his appointment. William wrote to Alexander at this time, discussing the principal character deficiency that just about everyone could see in James: 'I could wish for him that he be if not more oily-tongued at least more tactful . . . I do not mean that James should so oil his skin that he slip through the fingers of his enemy – that he savours of hypocrisy – but I do not think it is necessary for him to sandpaper his skin either, so that his enemies can get a good hold of him'.[73] This had been precisely James's difficulty for most of his adult life.

---

[69] *Launceston Advertiser*, 3 January 1833, 424.
[70] *Cobbett's Political Register*, 75 (London: Bolt Court, 1832), 211.
[71] *Colonial Times*, 6 November 1832, 3.
[72] *The Sydney Monitor*, 18 August 1832, 2.
[73] W. Busby to A. Busby, 13 January 1833, in *BFR* 2, 382.

His myopic determination to do what he thought was right failed to take into consideration the views of others, and the various means by which goals could be achieved. Furthermore, James never seemed to appreciate, let alone learn from, the diplomatic manner in which many other officials around him conducted themselves. Instead, he persisted with his blunt approach to issues and people. William finished off this appraisal of James on a note of concern – fearing that his brother was incapable of modifying his behaviour: 'He is too honest, and I fear too belligerent; if not <u>rash</u>. And I fear he will never realise the reasons for his difficulties – only grumble at the results. Certainly he would have obtained a freer hand in his enterprises had he been less "prickly" and – yes – less <u>upright</u>'. And in a prophetic mode, William warned, '(f)orward he will go, but what a string they will tie to his tail'.[74]

As the moment of his departure for New Zealand drew closer, James busied himself trying to gather intelligence on the situation in the Bay of Islands, where he intended to establish his Residency. On 4 February he wrote to Yate, who had previously mentioned to him that there were around forty escaped convicts 'of the worst character' living in the region. What worried James was a conversation he had recently had with James Clendon, an English trader who had settled at Okiato, in the Bay of Islands, the previous year.[75] Clendon had advised James that since these convicts had discovered he was to be appointed as Resident and would be charged with apprehending them, they had caused great alarm among settlers and ship' crews. Clendon reported that there was every reason to fear 'the most daring and wanton aggression from them in their present state of excitement'. As an example, he relayed how two settlers were rumoured to have communicated with the Governor about the breakdown of order, and as a result, the convicts had threatened to burn down their houses.[76]

Yate offered a similar warning. He replied to James in early February 1833, warning that a group of escaped convicts, together with sailors who had absconded from their ships ('characters of the worst description'), had devised plans to seize a ship and use it to take them somewhere away from even the slightest presence of British authority. So great was this fear that Māori were being employed by some captains to keep guard of their ships while in the Bay of Islands. Yate suggested that the Resident's own safety and security would be at risk from the moment he arrived. The missionary attributed much of the reason for this atmosphere of heightened aggression to 'gross and infamous allusions' made in some of the Australian newspapers, which had

---

[74] Ibid., 382.
[75] B. Gawith, 'James Reddy Clendon, 1800–1872: Trade, Entrepreneurship and Empire' (MA thesis, Massey University, 2005), 42–4, 50–4.
[76] J. Busby to W. Yate, 4 February 1833, in *BFR* 2, 385.

been supplied to those living in the Bay of Islands. 'Such trash as appears weekly here', he cautioned James, 'gives them encouragement to persevere in their evil practices'.[77]

Yate was emerging as an important figure to James as he prepared to assume the role of Resident. He was as well informed as just about any other settler in New Zealand about the nature of Māori society and polity, and was a gifted preacher, translator, and amateur naturalist.[78] Shortly before James was due to leave for New Zealand, Yate supplied him with a list containing the names of twenty-four chiefs, eleven of whom had signed the 1831 Petition. The missionary suggested that presents of clothes, blankets, fabrics, and tobacco be gifted to these chiefs as a way of building up favour with them, and that the ceremony of offering these presents be accompanied with a feast.[79] Not only were such details crucial to James commencing his Residency on a strong footing, but they reveal the extent to which he was searching for support outside of official circles. The Governor's decision not to provide James with even a few constables to prop up his role in New Zealand threatened to make the Residency a still-born institution. James therefore had no option but to search for alternative sources of support and advice, and it was the Church Missionary Society missionaries whom he looked to as a loose, de facto civil service to aid his Residency, at least in its formative stages.

James's hopes for his posting outweighed the obvious potential for failure, but he was still confronted with the absence of any means of effecting his will in New Zealand, with the vagueness over the legality of his jurisdiction in a territory outside Britain's imperial embrace, and with the severe restriction on the amount of funding available. Even securing a rudimentary cottage for himself had been a fraught affair with an unsatisfactory conclusion as far as James was concerned.[80] Consequently he was forced to re-evaluate his entire financial circumstances, which led him to the decision to divest himself from nearly all his assets in New South Wales, in order to allow himself and the Residency the best chance of success in New Zealand.

He had made the extent of his austere financial situation plain in a letter to MacLeay on 20 February: 'I am now under the necessity of selling off all my property (and all I fear will prove insufficient) to satisfy the pecuniary obligations which I have already incurred.' This was James's last-ditch effort to attempt to wrest some more funds from the colonial government. 'I have too much

---

[77] W. Yate to J. Busby, c. 6 February 1833, in *BFR* 2, 385.
[78] *The Early Journals of Henry Williams*, ed. L. M. Rogers (Christchurch: Pegasus Press, 1961), 101.
[79] W. Yate to J. Busby, c. March 1833, in *BFR* 2, 388.
[80] J. Busby to A. MacLeay, 4 February 1833, in *HRA* 1, vol. 17, 48.

reason to fear', he continued, 'that the Salary of my appointment will prove limited enough to enable me to fill my situation with credit. And what I believe to be almost without a precedent in appointments of a similar nature to mine, I have not received, as His Excellency is aware, a single Shilling to provide an outfit for it.' When James had appealed to the Colonial Office for remuneration to cover an earlier debt, he was informed that, if he accepted his present appointment, it would also serve as compensation for all past claims.[81] There was no doubt that James would be operating in New Zealand under a budget that had been pared to the bone. However, although his pleas were not without some basis, he effectively sabotaged them in the eyes of the Governor by referring to grievances that had undermined his relations with local officials since the 1820s. James had hoped that by resurrecting what he saw as outstanding debts due to him for previous services he had provided in New South Wales, he would be in a better negotiating position, but it was a miscalculation, and another example of his sometimes deficient judgment when it came to dealing with his colleagues in government.

That James was exploring all available avenues in an attempt to improve the circumstances of his appointment is a sign of how disaffected he was becoming with immediate prospects of the Residency. Almost as a last resort, on 12 March, he composed a long and very candid letter to Buxton, whom he had met in London two years earlier, expressing doubts about his appointment. He described how the decisions made by his superiors had pre-emptively weakened his position, and he lay the blame for this almost wholly with Bourke. It was a risky argument to make because, as James acknowledged, Buxton held Bourke in very high regard.[82] Nonetheless, James was determined to make his case, and probably judged that at the worst, he had nothing to lose by addressing his concerns to this one-time acquaintance.

James was becoming increasingly frustrated that his professional opinions on certain matters were being ignored by the Governor. At a dinner party with some officials from the colonial government, James had recently discussed his proposals on the jury system in the colony, following an unusual verdict that had been delivered by a Sydney jury. The officials present, some of whom were members of the Executive Council, expressed surprise that James had written a paper on the topic, and were apparently unaware of his recommendations in this area.[83] James implied in his letter to Buxton that Bourke had dismissed his proposals, and that as Governor, he lacked

---

[81] J. Busby to A. MacLeay, 20 February 1833, in *HRA* 1, vol. 17, 49–50.
[82] J. Busby to T. F. Buxton, 12 March 1833, in 'James Busby; Official Letters of Various People, 1833–1870', Auckland Museum, MS46, 3–4.
[83] It was an issue that Bourke raised with the Colonial Office two months after James's departure for New Zealand. R. Bourke to R. Hay, 29 June 1833, in *HRA* 1, vol. 17, 153.

competence. This could be construed as a case of dented pride, but it is revealing (not for the first time) of James's inability both to relinquish his intense sense of grievance over past injustices (real or perceived), and to exercise a sense of proportion in the matters affecting him.

It is telling, in this case, that when James should have been concentrating on the multitude of challenges he faced as he finalized preparations to take on the Resideny, he contacted someone with whom he was not close, to complain about an event in the past that had no bearing on him now, and that could only be interpreted by the recipient of his letter as a case of wounded pride. The exhaustive detail of past promises and betrayals James set forth in this correspondence to Buxton was made worse by the fact that he included a wad of supporting letters and reports to uphold his claims. It was as though he was preparing evidence for some great court case, whereas in reality, he was merely relating an account of a matter that Buxton had no influence over and probably negligible interest in.[84] The fact that James was unable to gauge this reveals that he had learned little in the decade he had spent in New South Wales about the way his fellow officials operated, and even the very limited extent to which individual MPs were capable of influencing colonial affairs. Instead of being adaptable and compromising, James was rigid and unyielding. More concerning still, though, was that at this point in time, James ought to have been fully focussed on the intricacies of his New Zealand assignment. There was no need for him to write hundreds of words defending himself over long-finished disputes which had no chance of re-litigation.

In the remaining weeks before departure, James finally got around to calling in debts and selling off most of his assets, including his land holdings. However, there were problems finding buyers for his cattle,[85] and his debtors generally pleaded poverty and did not pay up. Typical of the latter was the Rev. Thomas Reddall, who had evidently approached James at some point for an advance of cash. Now that James was requiring repayment, the cleric wrote back, mentioning his 'total inability at present to pay the sum', that he was facing 'many difficulties', and that he was 'much crippled in money matters'. Then, after asking for an extension of time before the loan was repaid, Reddall obsequiously congratulated James for his appointment to New Zealand. That afternoon, James dispatched a one-sentence note to Reddall, agreeing to extend the period of the loan to an unspecified time in the future, and signed it 'in haste', indicating just how rushed he was at this moment.[86]

---

[84] B. W. Higman, 'The West India "Interest" in Parliament, 1807–1833', *Australian Historical Studies* 13, no. 49 (1967): 1–19.
[85] J. Busby to W. Kelman, 15 April 1833, in *BFR* 2, 398.
[86] T. Reddall to J. Busby and J. Busby to T. Reddall, 5 February 1833, in 'Letters to James Busby, 1830–1866', Auckland Museum, MS46.

In the midst of the increasingly frantic efforts to dispose of just about everything he possessed to raise funds for his shift to New Zealand, James received a letter from William Hall, an Anglican missionary (and former shipbuilder) based in the Bay of Islands.[87] Seventeen years earlier, Hall had established a small mission station at Waitangi (which translates as 'weeping waters'), around three kilometres across the bay from the main European settlement at Russell. Marsden was initially anxious that the location was too isolated but Hall dismissed these concerns.[88] He described Waitangi as 'the most eligible and beneficial [site] for a settlement',[89] and within four months of settling in Waitangi, he had developed 'an excellent garden full of vegetables, and about two acres of ground cleared for wheat'.[90] He had also constructed a rough house, and allowed a few of his Māori assistants to sleep in it. However, for these occupants, 'the nails in the weatherboards were such a temptation that they could not suffer it to stand, although it was for their own benefit. They pulled it down to the ground and split up every bit of it to get the nails out.'[91] But although the house was demolished, Hall continued to use some of the fifty acres he had purchased at Waitangi for growing crops.[92]

Due to the byzantine personality conflicts among some of those proselytizing in the Bay of Islands, the Church Missionary Society mission in the area experienced changes in fortunes around this time, one unintended product of which was Hall's decision to dispose of his land at Waitangi. On 15 April 1833, just six days before James was due to leave New South Wales, he received a letter from the missionary, who was staying in a cottage in Blacktown, about thirty-five kilometres west of Sydney. The discussions over the transfer of the Waitangi block appear to have occurred over the previous several months, and in the afternoon of 15 April, the envelope containing the deed to the land was delivered to James. In the accompanying letter, Hall advised James that the senior Anglican missionary in New Zealand, Henry Williams, would explain to Māori in the vicinity what was happening to the land at Waitangi, and in doing so, would remind them that the land had shifted out of their possession through a transaction in 1815. Nevertheless, Hall advised James that it would probably be necessary to make some additional payment to local Māori, as a token gesture to affirm his acquisition of the site.

---

[87] R. A. A. Sherrin and J. H. Wallace, *Early History of New Zealand* (Auckland: H. Brett, 1890), 140.
[88] S. Marsden, in *The Letters and Journals of Samuel Marsden*, 224.
[89] T. Kendall, in *Marsden's Lieutenants*, ed. J. R. Elder (Dunedin: Coulls Somerville Wilkie Ltd., 1934), 83.
[90] W. Hall, in *Marsden's Lieutenants*, 123.
[91] Ibid., 129.
[92] M. McLean, *'The Garden of New Zealand': A History of the Waitangi Treaty House and Grounds from Pre-European Times to the Present* (Wellington: Department of Conservation, 1990), 8.

This would not only signal to Māori that James was the owner of the fifty acres at Waitangi, but more immediately, it would enable him to 'remove all the Europeans that may be settled upon it'.[93]

Making payments to Māori to sort out settler squatters was an augury of the type of unusual social and political situation that James was about to enter into, as was the issue of land tenure, to which Hall alerted the Resident in the case of the property at Waitangi. Although Hall had purchased fifty acres there, it was not entirely clear who now owned which parts of it – a situation exacerbated by the absence of surveys, titles, or land registration. Hall explained how ten acres of the site still belonged to the Church Missionary Society, but then seemingly contradicted this assertion by suggesting that it was a nominal purchase, and 'it was never recorded nor did they ever possess it'.[94] The value of the land rested with the way it had been developed by Hall and fellow missionary, Thomas Kendall. Claims to land ownership therefore rested on a chaotic mix of occupation, previous payments and subsequent additional payments to former Māori owners, the testimony of witnesses to purchases, maps by missionaries, statements resembling aspects of land titles, and the absence of any settler or Māori counter-claim.[95] Such a form of confirming ownership lacked the certainty and the precision of British land tenure, but it revealed at least a desire to approximate it. And importantly, it also exposed how Māori and European were accommodating and appropriating each other's cultural tenets to produce a hybridized legal system, which for all its inadequacies and fragility provided a slight degree of assurance and stability.

During the evening of 20 April 1833, James spent some time with Agnes, with neither knowing when they would see each other again. They had planned for her to join him in New Zealand once he had established himself there, and most importantly, when he had a house where they could live. Until then, James planned to rely on the hospitality of local missionaries in the Bay of Islands. At daybreak the following morning, James boarded HMS *Imogene* (with the frame for his house to be transported on the *New Zealander* at a later date),[96] and in a brief note he dispatched to Alexander just as he was departing, he referred to a letter he had received from Sir Edward Parry. Parry argued that the circumstances under which James was to function as Resident in New Zealand were such that 'no one in England could have believed could have occurred'. Such solidarity, though, was of little use to James as HMS *Imogene* sailed from Port Jackson that day on its 2,200-kilometre journey to the Bay of Islands.

---

[93] W. Hall to J. Busby, 15 April 1833, in 'Letters to James Busby, 1830–1866', Auckland Museum, MS46.
[94] Ibid.
[95] J. Polack, *New Zealand* 2, 205–6.
[96] *Sydney Herald*, 22 April 1833, 2.

6

Landed

At the end of 1827, the English artist Augustus Earle arrived at Hokianga from Sydney, and then trudged his way eastwards through forest and scrub towards the Bay of Islands – the main European settlement in the country. In addition to producing a series of watercolours of this overland journey, Earle's accompanying account offered a social and cultural panorama of the region. In the hinterland, he noted how 'every object we saw was of a character that reminded us forcibly of the savage community we were with. Occasionally we met groups of naked men, trotting along under immense loads, and screaming their barbarous songs of recognition; sometimes we beheld an uncouthly carved figure, daubed over with red ochre, and fixed in the ground, to give notice that one side of the road was tabooed.'[1] This was a common European perception of Māori New Zealand in this era – as the antithesis of, and a threat to 'civilization'.[2] James would have been well aware of such depictions of Māori. While the missionaries with whom he discussed New Zealand would have focussed on their heathen character, there were popular books and an array of newspaper articles that tilted to the stereotypical and salacious in their representations of Māori. The image of Māori as 'a cruel, furious and untameable savage',[3] and 'a thoroughly savage people . . . dirty in their habits, and swarm[ing] with vermin'[4] was almost universally held among Europeans in this era.

Yet there were also signs that change was taking place in New Zealand. As Earle reached the Bay of Islands, he was struck by the 'extraordinary contrast'

---

[1] A. Earle, *A Narrative of a Nine Months' Residence in New Zealand in 1827: Together with a Journal of a Residence in Tristan D'Acunha, an Island Situated Between South America and the Cape of Good Hope* (London: Longman, 1832), 36–7.
[2] H. White, *Tropics of Discourse: Essays in Cultural Criticism* (Baltimore: Johns Hopkins University Press, 1978), 151.
[3] Nicholas, *Narrative of a Voyage to New Zealand* 2, 312.
[4] *Description of a View of the Bay of Islands, New Zealand, and the Surrounding Country*, ed. R. Burford (London: G. Nichols, [1838]), 11–12.

from savage interior to something altogether more familiar to him: 'we came suddenly in front of a complete little English village'.[5] Could New Zealand be an English arcadia after all – a southern-hemisphere Britain?[6] The answer to that lay in the future, but this binary perspective – of savage versus civilized, wild versus tamed landscape, Christianity versus paganism, British law versus indigenous anarchy, all of which coagulated into the notion of Māori versus European – was already ingrained in how most settlers saw the country. It is an important point because the way in which recent immigrants (the first European settlement had been established only nineteen years earlier) framed their view of New Zealand in some ways influenced their expectations of the Resident.

Exasperation with the state of things in the Bay of Islands had certainly given cause for many settlers (and a few Māori too) to anticipate the installation of a Resident as the panacea to all the region's ills. The Bay of Island's designation as the '[h]ell-hole of the South Pacific'[7] was no quaint term of endearment. The town of Kororāreka, in particular, had built a reputation over more than a decade for its lawlessness. One traveller wrote of how he encountered Europeans living there 'who are of so doubtful a character that it would be difficult to guess to what order of society they belonged previous to their being transplanted amongst these savages'.[8] Yet the social composition of the Bay of Islands was more variegated than its reputation of 'vice and lawlessness'[9] suggested. One visitor recorded how he came across 'a respectable body of Scotch mechanics settled here, who . . . seem well pleased with the prospects before them', and that these 'hardy sons of Britain' were also involved in 'instructing the wondering savage in various branches of useful art'.[10] There was also a strong regional missionary presence that brought encouragement to some. In 1830, Marsden commented on a Sunday morning in the Bay of Islands, in which there was 'the pleasing sound of the church bell going, the natives assembling together for Divine worship, clean, orderly, and decently dressed, most of them in European clothing'.[11]

One of the toughest groups that James would have to deal with was that rump of Britons for whom New Zealand's lawlessness was the greatest of

---

[5] Ibid., 38.
[6] This idea appeared explicitly in C. Hursthouse, *New Zealand, or Zealandia, the Britain of the South* (London: Edward Stanford, 1857).
[7] E. Ihde, 'Pirates of the Pacific: The Convict Seizure of the "Wellington"', *The Great Circle* 30, no. 1 (2008): 10; R. Wolfe, *Hell-Hole of the Pacific* (Auckland: Penguin, 2005).
[8] Earle, *A Narrative of a Nine Months' Residence in New Zealand*, 51.
[9] E. J. Wakefield, *Adventure in New Zealand from 1839 to 1844, with Some Account of the Beginning of the British Colonization of the Islands* 1 (London: John Murray, 1845), 310.
[10] Earle, *A Narrative of a Nine Months' Residence in New Zealand*, 51–2.
[11] S. Marsden, in *The Letters and Journals of Samuel Marsden*, 463.

blessings. They were known locally as 'beach rangers' because of their scavenging existence, and many had been thrown off whaling ships for behaviour for which 'had they been taken home and tried, they would have been hanged', and were now leading 'mean and miserable' lives on the fringes of local Māori communities. Even worse were the escaped convicts from New South Wales, who were 'idle, unprincipled, and vicious in the extreme, and are much feared in the Bay of Islands; for when by any means they obtain liquor, they prove themselves most dangerous neighbours'.[12]

There were two jurisprudential issues for James to contend with when dealing with such groups. The first of these was the collection of statutes and regulations that had been enacted prior to his appointment as a result of successive colonial administrations in New South Wales trying to exercise control over British subjects in New Zealand. The second issue, which intersected with this, was the status of Māori sovereignty in New Zealand, and how it might accommodate a form of British proto-sovereignty in the territory.

As far back as 1813 (and again the following year), at Marsden's instigation, Governor Lachlan Macquarie had made proclamations that prohibited the masters of ships from committing offences against Māori.[13] The moral case for these proclamations was beyond question, but not so the legal one. The assertion that British subjects had a duty to adhere to British law while in New Zealand was based on the presumption that the sort of sovereignty exercised by New Zealand's indigenous inhabitants was insufficient to meet this need. However, the proclamations went further, asserting the Crown's protective role over Māori.[14] This jurisdictional extension was formalized (at least as far as the British were concerned) by a succession of statutes passed from 1817 to 1828,[15] although they all suffered similarly from the problem of applying a law outside British territory and affecting a people who had given no consent for it.

James's appointment as Resident was a continuation of this trajectory of British jurisdictional creep, which was inching towards continually greater involvement in New Zealand. However, colonial officials were acutely aware that such intervention was not taking place in a vacuum, especially as Māori continued to exercise their own sovereignty throughout the country. This form of sovereignty was an intricate construct, comprising spiritual and temporal

---

[12] Earle, *A Narrative of a Nine Months' Residence in New Zealand*, 52–3.
[13] *Historical Records of New Zealand* 1, 351.
[14] B. Attwood, 'Protection Claims: The British, Maori and Islands of New Zealand, 1800–1840', in *Protection and Empire: A Global History*, eds. L. Benton, A. Clulow, and B. Attwood (Cambridge: Cambridge University Press, 2018), 156.
[15] Referred to in J. Stephen, Memorandum, 18 March 1840, Enclosure 38, in *Correspondence With the Secretary of State Relative to New Zealand* (London: House of Lords, 1840), 69.

notions of authority, history, social structure, and diplomacy, which manifested themselves to differing degrees in whanau (extended family), hapū (sub-tribe), iwi (tribe), and waka (one of several migratory canoes, to which tribes loosely affiliated themselves federally). Of these groups, hapū were the principal sovereign unit. They held rights to territory, and were economically self-sufficient and politically autonomous. With the onset of European settlement, though, slight changes were beginning to occur in this body politic which often simultaneously involved both emulating traits of British authority, and consciously resisting the systems of the colonizer.[16] The arrival of the Resident would be another stage in how traditional hapū appropriated, rejected, or otherwise adjusted to a new form of British presence in the country.

The British understanding of Māori sovereignty in this era generally tended to be dismissive of its particular character. Nicholas's remarks about the state of Māori society, written just sixteen years earlier, were typical of this imperial view, and left little hope for a greater appreciation of the means by which Māori sovereignty was exercised. He rejected New Zealand's inhabitants as being 'inferior', 'a slave to the impulse of . . . [their] will', 'enveloped in the dark clouds of ignorance', and so forth.[17] On the other hand, the British tended to be more adulatory about their own form of sovereignty, and seemingly with good reason, as it prevailed (admittedly in a number of variants) over the world's largest empire. British imperial rule was still very much a work in progress at this time.

Instead of Britain establishing and maintaining full autocratic rule over all its colonies, by the beginning of the nineteenth century, ideas of limited or partial sovereignty in parts of the Empire were gaining greater acceptance in Britain. Jeremy Bentham, for example, had proposed that sovereignty could be reduced to a 'de facto governing power in the community' without a lumbering legal system accompanying it, and could be limited in both its scope and application.[18] James's appointment was confined to promoting commerce and apprehending fugitives,[19] yet the possibility of apprehending British subjects suspected of committing crimes in New Zealand, along with the desire for the

---

[16] P. Cleave, 'Tribal and State-like Political Formations in New Zealand Maori Society, 1750–1900', *JPS* 92, no. 1 (1983): 52–6; N. K. Hopa, 'The Rangatira: Chieftainship in Traditional Maori Society' (BLitt thesis, Oxford University, 1966), 31–8, 61–3; P. McHugh, 'Sovereignty This Century: Māori and the Common Law Constitution', *Victoria University of Wellington Law Review* 31 (2000): 190.
[17] Nicholas, *Narrative of a Voyage to New Zealand* 1, 8–67.
[18] S. D. Carpenter, *Te Wiremu, Te Puhipi, He Whakaputanga me Te Tiriti: Henry Williams, James Busby, A Declaration and the Treaty* (Wellington, Waitangi Tribunal, 2009), 7; A.V. Dicey, *Introduction to the Study of the Law of the Constitution* (London: Macmillan, 1962), 12–19; J. Bentham, *A Fragment on Government* (Oxford: Clarendon Press, 1891), 60–2.
[19] The essence of this role was outlined in R. Bourke to Goderich, 23 December 1831, in *HRA* 1, vol. 16, 483.

Resident to establish some 'settled form of government' in the country,[20] was a strong indication of how colonial officials foresaw Britain's role in New Zealand's future.

However, so much of how Britain's relationship with New Zealand was shaped from this point onwards depended on the individual appointed to the country, and in James's case, he was taking on the Residency practically blindfolded. His knowledge of New Zealand was second-hand, the boundaries of his authority were ill defined, his understanding of Māori culture and society was lamentable, his means of enforcing his will was non-existent, and as always, and his sense of his inerrant rectitude curtailed the possibility that he could succeed largely though diplomacy and compromise at a time when astute statecraft was vital.

After a fortnight at sea, on 5 May 1833, HMS *Imogene* made its way into the Bay of Islands, just as the clouds in the region were darkening and the winds were building up into what turned out to be a violent storm.[21] Torrential rain lashed the region for the next few days, and flooded several parts of the Bay of Islands, blocking off access between some settlements, and forcing the majority of the population to remain indoors. For James, it was crucial that his Residency get off to the best possible start, and so he planned a grand arrival, with a degree of spectacle that befitted a man of his status (and that the resources at his disposal permitted). However, it would take several days to assemble local Māori, and as the rain was relentless, after a brief trip on shore on the morning of 8 May, he decided to return to HMS *Imogene* and receive those who wanted to meet him (and who were prepared to brave the weather to row to the ship).

Along with the lay missionary Thomas Chapman, Henry Williams boarded the ship that afternoon, and remained there until seven in the evening, chatting on a whole range of issues. The next day, James returned to shore, eager to see as much as he could and talk to everybody. Williams took him to see the infant and native girls' schools, and invited him to dinner for the following evening, where he spent several hours discussing his role with those present.

On 9 May, a messenger reached the Bay of Islands announcing that a bout of inter-tribal warfare had recently broken out Hokianga. However, having only just arrived in the country, James would have been very satisfied to discover that as soon as the warring parties were informed that the Resident wanted to meet the region's chiefs, a hasty peace was reached between the combatants.[22] Maybe the perception of James's authority – which was

---

[20] *Correspondence with the Secretary of State Relative to New Zealand* (1840), 5–6.
[21] *The Early Journals of Henry Williams*, 310.
[22] H. Williams, in L. M. Rogers (ed.), *The Early Journals of Henry Williams*, 311.

apparently sufficient to end a battle – would enable him to rule rather than merely liaise.

Over the next few days, James continued the pattern of spending most of his days onshore at the mission station at Paihia before returning to the ship to sleep. On 13 May, Williams cleared out his small study so that James could use it as temporary living quarters. The missionary uncharitably described this as causing him the 'utmost inconvenience', but acknowledged it was necessary as there was nowhere else in the vicinity where they could accommodate 'so great a personage'.[23] Overall, though, the missionary settlement was buoyant at the Resident's arrival. 'We look forward with sanguine expectations', wrote the author of the *Missionary Register*, 'to beneficial consequences to the Natives from Mr Busby's residence among them'.[24] Indeed, such was the initial closeness between James and the Anglicans that it was later popularly, though mistakenly, assumed that his role of 'consul' was one accredited to the missionaries.[25]

After a few brief periods of respite, heavy gales returned to the area on 14 May, and lasted until sunset, delaying James's planned meeting with local chiefs. Still, though, he managed to leave the ship for the day, and spent more time discussing local issues with the missionaries, as well as organizing details for the great meeting with the chiefs, which all concerned hoped would take place very soon. With the weather easing, and his impatience mounting, James's 'official' landing was set for Friday 17 May. At dawn, it seemed that the whole population in the area was busying itself for the welcome. Understandably, interest in James was not confined just to European settlers, as Williams recorded: 'Canoes from Kororarika, Waikari, and Kauakaua, &c, soon made their appearance with the principal men of those districts . . . Each seemed anxious to learn the nature of Mr Busby's commission and whether the Man of War was to remain in the Bay, and if soldiers were to be landed. The various parties very busy in rubbing up their muskets, &c, as it was determined to give the visitors a native salutation.'[26]

It was not an entirely celebratory event, though. Most of the Māori present were happy to honour this guest of status, but at the same time, they were anxious to know the exact intentions of the Resident. They apparently welcomed the prospect of British soldiers preserving peace in the region (a prospect that would not materialize) but 'with their usual fickleness, or perhaps maturer reflection on their present absolute power, which would depart from

---

[23] Ibid., 312.
[24] *The Missionary Register* (London: Church Missionary Society, 1833), 502.
[25] Hursthouse, *New Zealand, or Zealandia, the Britain of the South* 1, 34.
[26] Ibid.

them', they were cautious over the Resident's motives.[27] This was an early indication that James's presence would bring into sharper focus the issue of where the boundaries of authority lay in the country.

At half past ten that morning, the blasts of a seven-gun salute from the HMS *Imogene* reverberated around the bay as James and others headed towards shore for the Resident's official landing at Paihia. Within seconds, there was frantic activity as hundreds of Māori who had gathered for the occasion prepared themselves to perform a welcoming haka (a ceremonial posture dance). Together with the ship's captain and other officers, James landed at eleven, and as a body they advanced slowly – according to Māori protocol – to the assembled warriors, who were now crouched down, primed to erupt into a dramatic performance as soon as word was given. Williams provided a vivid account of the scene from this point. The warriors 'arose with their usual horrid scream, and rushed forward with the utmost impetuosity till within a few paces of our party, when they halted, and after regulating their ranks, with much vociferation set up a *Haka*, brandishing their muskets, and distorting their countenances to the no small astonishment of the strangers'.[28]

This was followed by a succession of speeches, with the chiefs flourishing their oratorical prowess as a way of honouring James. Once this was completed, it was the turn of the British to provide some (more subdued) spectacle. A row of seats was laid out for the dignitaries, in front of which was a table. The letter James brought from Goderich was placed on the table with a degree of theatricality that suggested that it was an object of almost venerable importance. From the cannon salute to the haka and then the speeches, the volume of the occasion had reduced in stages, and now, as James approached the table, there was complete silence. He picked up the envelope, broke the seal, and took out the letter, which he read to the assembled crowd (a translation had been prepared, most likely by Williams, and was read out straight after James had delivered the English version).[29]

James then delivered his own message, which was steeped in Scottish Enlightenment ideas of progress, and the possibility that such progress could be transposed to other parts of the world. The impulse to civilize, and to introduce the blessings of Christianity to New Zealand, was a deeply rooted personal conviction for the Resident, and he made this known as he once again rose to his feet to address the audience at Paihia:

---

[27] Polack, *New Zealand* 2, 219.
[28] H. Williams, in *The Early Journals of Henry Williams*, 313.
[29] *SGNSWA*, 2 July 1833, 2.

At one time, Great Britain differed very little from what New Zealand is now. The people had no large houses, nor good clothing, nor good food. They painted their bodies, and clothed themselves with the skins of wild beasts. Every Chief went to war with his neighbour; and the people perished in the wars of their Chiefs, even as the people of New Zealand do now. But after God had sent His Son into the world to teach mankind that all the tribes of the earth are brethren, and that they ought not to hate and destroy, but to love and do good to one another – and when the people of England learned His words of wisdom – they ceased to go to war with each other, and all the tribes became one people.

The peaceful inhabitants of the country began to build large houses, because there was no enemy to pull them down. They cultivated their land, and had abundance of bread, because no hostile tribe entered into their fields to destroy the fruits of their labours. They increased the numbers of their cattle, because no one came to drive them away. They also became industrious and rich, and had all good things they desired.

Do you, then, O Chiefs and Tribes of New Zealand! desire to become like the people of England? Listen *first* to the word of God, which He has put it into the hearts of His servants, the Missionaries, to come here to teach you. Learn that it is the will of God that you should all love each other as brethren; and when wars shall cease among you, then shall your country flourish. Instead of the roots of the fern, you shall eat bread; because the land shall be tilled without fear, and its fruits shall be eaten in peace. When there is abundance of bread, men shall labour to preserve flax, and timber, and provisions for the ships that come to trade; and the ships which come to trade shall bring clothing, and all other things which you desire. Thus shall you become rich. For there are no riches without labour, and men will not labour unless there is peace, that they may enjoy the fruits of their labour.[30]

Several speeches from the chiefs followed, after which James presented the more prominent among them with gifts of tobacco and blankets. With the formalities concluded, around fifty settlers joined Williams and the Resident for refreshments outside the missionary's house before a feast was provided to the assembled Māori (consisting of beef, potatoes, and stirabout).[31] The

---

[30] J. Busby, 17 May 1833, in *Church Missionary Register* (1834), 265–6.
[31] Stirabout was a meal made from a mixture of flour, sugar, and water. See *Report from the Select Committee of the House of Lords Appointed to Inquire into the Present State of the Islands of New Zealand and the Expediency of Regulating the Settlement of British Subjects Therein: With the Minutes of Evidence Taken before the Committee and an Index Thereto* (London: House of Lords, 1838), 40.

whole event 'passed off very agreeably', as Williams put it in his journal that evening.[32]

The press, however, ridiculed this event. In one of the more egregious examples, a Tasmanian journalist extemporized on what he supposed had happened when James read Goderich's message to the chiefs. 'The letter was duly translated for the savages, who took it all in with wonderful complacency. M. Busby delivered an oration of a twattlish character, which also went down.'[33] James – defenceless, remote, preoccupied, and largely without allies – could do little to rebuke such slurs. His main way of dealing with such attacks was to turn the other cheek and work even harder to make a success of his appointment.

The next week, James was taken by Williams to Waitangi to see the section where he intended to build his house. The location was across the bay from Kororāreka – far enough away from the iniquitous settlement not to be bothered by its inhabitants, but nonetheless close enough that he could be on hand if needed. James then attended a meeting at Kororāreka, convened by the missionaries, at which the most prominent local chiefs were present. After some discussion, followed by a feast, news arrived that the schooner *Prince of Denmark* had sailed into the bay. James was relieved as on the vessel were his stores of clothes, books, papers, and other items. However, unexpectedly for Williams, the ship also had a cargo of missionaries. These included the Rev. John Morgan, an Anglican (who was due in New Zealand at some point),[34] along with five Wesleyan missionaries. There was now a sudden shortage of accommodation in Paihia, and a frustrated Williams began to grumble as he was required to assist the following two days with helping James bring his belongings on shore, and find lodgings for these new arrivals.[35]

Eventually, as the Wesleyans made their way to other missions in the region, the crowds of visitors to Paihia to meet James dispersed, and the area settled back to normal – except that New Zealand now had a British Resident. The Rev. Richard Davis, who feared the 'evil results from European civilisation to the Maori race',[36] was present in the Bay of Islands during James's 'inauguration', and after the crowds had gone and the initial fuss abated, wrote to a colleague that '[t]he arrival of Mr Busby as British Resident has given a different turn to the native mind. The chiefs who frequent the seaport of Kororarika had given out, that when they came to Waimate they meant to treat us roughly. How different has their behaviour been from their threats! Instead

---

[32] H. Williams, in *The Early Journals of Henry Williams*, 314.
[33] *Launceston Advertiser*, 1 August 1833, 3.
[34] P. L. B. Williams, *John Morgan of Otawhao*, Auckland War Memorial Museum Library, MS-721.
[35] H. Williams, in *The Early Journals of Henry Williams*, 315–16.
[36] J. N. Coleman, *A Memoir of the Rev. Richard Davis* (London: James Nisbet and Co.), 1865, vii.

of blustering and abuse, they conducted themselves respectfully.' James's appointment, he was convinced, was 'the Lord's doing, and it is marvellous in our eyes, because we are so unworthy of these most signal mercies'.[37] It was a partial paraphrase of Psalm 118, the preceding verse of which could well have described James's move from New South Wales to New Zealand: 'The stone the builders rejected has become the cornerstone.'[38]

Following the arrival of the *New Zealander* in June, James oversaw the transporting of its cargo of materials for his planned house at Waitangi. Meanwhile, circumstances were about to provide a bigger challenge to him than resolving his living arrangements. Since arriving in New Zealand, he had regularly held meetings with various chiefs, all of whom were curious to see the representative of Britain. One, however, had held back. This was Pōmare (sometimes known as Pōmare II to distinguish him from his uncle). Although he had been born into high rank, it was through aggressive diplomacy and victories in a series of well-chosen military conflicts that Pōmare had seen his status soar by the early 1830s.[39] He regarded it as beneath his dignity to rush to greet the Resident,[40] and waited until he judged that the time was right. In the afternoon of 20 June, trailed by a large entourage that befitted his rank, Pōmare descended to the mission station at Paihia to meet James.[41]

It must have shocked the great chief, then, that the diminutively framed Scot refused to see him. The reason for the Resident's snub was that Pōmare had recently stolen a small vessel from two local traders and had refused to return it until a debt he was owed by them was repaid. It was a miscalculation on James's behalf. While he obviously felt he was doing what was right, and that depriving the chief of an audience with him amounted to some sort of punishment, he did not yet appreciate the nature of Māori diplomacy. To James, his decision to refuse to see Pōmare was a signal of disapproval of the chief's dishonesty. To Pōmare, however, this snub was a direct assault on his mana (prestige). His dominion over the region was extensive, and his political prowess was matched with military mastery that left little room for a pretender to the throne. James was still an anomaly, though. Practically no-one understood precisely the boundaries of his role, nor the consequences if his will was transgressed. But Pōmare, at least, was not inclined to cower before the imagined power of the Resident. Instead, he quietly seethed with anger over the humiliation he had endured, while contemplating what he

---

[37] R. Davis, in Coleman, *A Memoir of the Rev. Richard Davis*, 158.
[38] Psalm 118:22.
[39] Elder, *Marsden's Lieutenants*, 62–4; C. Terry, *New Zealand: Its Advantages and Prospects as a British Colony* (London: T. & W. Boone, 1842), 195, 199–200, 202–4.
[40] Interview with David Rankin, Te Matarahurahu, Auckland, 21 July 2018.
[41] H. Williams, *The Early Journals of Henry Williams*, 320.

should do next to avenge the insult from the Resident and thereby restore some dignity.

It was not just James, though, who was in the firing line. Such a slight demanded a price in excess of one person's life, and it was quite conceivable that Pōmare could attack an entire settlement of Europeans, partly out of revenge, but also as a warning to any other Māori who might feel that the great chief's status could be exposed to such insults. James's paternalistic rebuff of Pōmare exposed the cultural tear that ran throughout New Zealand, and it was up to Williams to attempt to stitch together some sort of peace before a catastrophe struck the Bay of Islands. The missionary sat down with Pōmare and discussed the matter 'until I was hoarse', as he later wrote. He emphasized that he was not interested in the political issues that concerned the Resident, and was not even prepared to discuss the rights or wrongs of Pōmare's seizure of the boat at this time. Rather, Williams pleaded with Pōmare for over three hours on the need to maintain peace in the region.[42] He succeeded, but it was a close-run thing. And all the while, James remained convinced that his rejection of Pōmare represented some sort of diplomatic win – oblivious of how close he had brought the area to calamity. This episode should have been instructive for James. While he increasingly struggled to exert some influence over Māori and settler alike – and repeatedly cited the lack of a supporting military force as the reason for this – most of the missionaries managed to hold substantially more sway over those living in the region, yet were bereft of any means of enforcing their will.[43] The lesson was that tact and persuasion could achieve a great deal if properly deployed.

It was not until nearly the end of June that James could finally surface from the deluge of work he had been inundated with, and write to his family. His correspondence with Alexander at this time is of particular value because it reveals his personal view on aspects of New Zealand, rather than the 'official' perspective he presented to his superiors in Sydney. To the New South Wales Governor, James maintained the semblance of an efficient, tenacious official, battling away in a savage country, but in private, to his brother, he let his shield slip. Firstly, James believed that at the time of his arrival in the Bay of Islands, the situation with respect to the security of settlers and the economic prospects for the region were more dire than anyone across the Tasman Sea had realized. 'I questioned whether any respectable trader could have remained much longer had ... [my] appointment been postponed', he suggested. But on setting foot in the country, in his mind, James had almost single-handedly arrested this descent into anarchy. His secret ingredient, he

---

[42] Ibid.
[43] *Report for the Select Committee of the House of Lords Appointed to Inquire into the Present State of the Islands of New Zealand*, 107.

conceded, was the authority of the name of the King – something that he had identified as early as 1831 as being critical if he was to have any chance of success as a Resident, and which had become imperative once he learned that he would have no standing military support. Quoting Shakespeare's *Richard III*, he noted that 'The King's name is a tower of strength.'[44]

The proof of this claim, according to James, was that within ten days of his arriving, two convicts had fled New Zealand, one of whom had lived openly in the area for the past seven or eight years. It was the fear of the Resident's moral authority, he believed, that was the cause of their departure. He was also convinced that Māori were now almost in awe of his power – to the extent that 'with them, I expect to establish an influence which will give me almost entire authority over the Northern part of the Island'. This was as ambitious as it was unrealistic, but reflected James's true intentions. The delicate steps needed to tread through the country's complex and potentially volatile political terrain in order to fulfil his instructions were of much less interest to him than expanding his power and status in New Zealand. But the leader in him was careful never to subvert the bureaucrat. Copious reports and correspondence continued to be his forte. He raised the idea with Alexander, for example, of introducing a passport system in New Zealand, whereby those settlers wishing to move to the territory would first have to be authorized by the New South Wales administration, and then issued with a travel document by James in order to protect them from accusations of being convicts (accusations that could get them expelled from New Zealand).[45]

But whenever James looked up from his paperwork, the promise of 'great things' seemed to beckon him. He floated the idea of getting the chiefs to work together more closely, 'with the intention by and bye to build them a Parliament House! where they will meet and discuss matters affecting them all'. This was not idle speculation, though. 'I have no fear', he pronounced, with unchecked confidence, 'that I should be able to bring them forward in the formation of Political Institutions as fast as the circumstances of the people will permit.' The end goal was nothing less than 'the foundation of a Government', with James enlisting the sons of chiefs as his personal guard – all of which stretched Bourke's instructions well beyond their intended purpose.[46]

On Sunday 28 July, Agnes left Sydney for the Bay of Islands in the barque *Nereus*, accompanied by Yate, and after a speedy journey reached Rangihoua

---

[44] W. Shakespeare, *Richard III*, act 5, scene 3. Possibly adapted from the 1549 *Book of Common Prayer*.
[45] J. Busby to A. Busby, 22 June 1833, in *BFR* 2, 415–16.
[46] Ibid., 416.

(a missionary settlement eleven kilometres north of Paihia) on 6 August.[47] The vessel also bought supplies for James, including ammunition for a guard he hoped to establish, an official seal for his correspondence, and 800 copies of Goderich's letter (printed in Māori and English) which he had read out on arrival.[48] Agnes's unexpectedly early arrival finally forced James to deal with his housing situation. The couple moved to a two-roomed hut on the Waitangi site which had previously belonged to Dr Adolphus James Ross and his wife. Although the conditions were cramped, the main advantage this arrangement offered was that it enabled the Busby's to supervise the construction of their house.

During this period, James maintained his correspondence with his superiors in New South Wales, furnishing them with an excess of detail on his work and his deliberations on the state of New Zealand. However, he was well aware that his role was supposed to be so much more than one of an information-gatherer. But while he possessed a desire to exert his influence, he lacked the means. It was a degree of powerlessness that that he could not fully come to terms with, and consequently, when the opportunity came to exercise some authority – no matter how insignificant the issue – he took on the role with undue relish. One early example of this took place in July 1833, and involved a dispute between two local settlers, Thomas Maxwell and Gilbert Mair. Maxwell had constructed a house on a portion of land that was owned by Mair. The latter had apparently agreed that Maxwell could use the land for a period of twelve months, but now that this time had expired, there were questions over whether Maxwell could remain on the site, and if not, what would happen to the house he built.

A potentially complicating factor was that the rights over land – as understood in a British sense – had no legal basis in New Zealand. So rather than burrowing deep into the intractable issue of comparative forms of land tenure in different jurisdictions, James deferred to his sense of natural justice. The matter was relatively minor, but symbolically, the fact of settlers turning to him for some sort of judgment in matters of dispute effectively conveyed a perception that he had been vested with a quasi-judicial authority. He was discovering that symbolism was a major form of political currency, and accordingly, he weighed up the issue with all the officiousness he could muster. It may have been a 'scarecrow of a suit',[49] but James was determined

---

[47] H. Williams, in *The Early Journals of Henry Williams*, 326.
[48] A. Brown, Ordnance Storekeeper, Sydney, Details ammunition etc, embarked on the *Nereus* (ship) for service of Busby's establishment in New Zealand, 24 July 1833, Ref R4086252, Archives New Zealand, p. 40.
[49] C. Dickens, *Bleak House* (London: J. M. Dent & Sons, 1930), 4.

to show he was the sole arbiter of justice for other settlers in New Zealand. On the last day of the month, he issued his 'Memorandum'. It was a three-page hand-written document, outlining the main points of the case, and was in James's best legalese. He concluded with an evaluation of the loss each party potentially suffered, and affirmed the validity of the agreement they had originally entered into (even though, technically, the agreement was unenforceable because it was outside British jurisdiction).[50]

James's relentless correspondence continued throughout this period, despite his having had to shift to more uncomfortable quarters. And regardless of some of the setbacks he had suffered in the way his authority was perceived (and disregarded), he was still inclined to see his Residency as representing something of a turning point in New Zealand's recent history. At the beginning of August, the 'inflexible' and 'energetic' Tasmanian lieutenant-governor, George Arthur,[51] had written to James, expressing – almost as a stock standard salutation – his 'great satisfaction' at James's appointment as Resident, and his certain hope that James would be able to 'ameliorate the condition of the Natives'.[52]

However, the real purpose of Arthur's letter surfaced further along in the text. He had dispatched William Kinghorne 'to pursue some convicts who have abandoned and taken away a small vessel'. Arthur sought James's assistance in Kinghorne's mission to apprehend these fugitives.[53] In addition to the crisis of these convicts having taken control of a ship and escaping, the lieutenant-governor was also sensitive to the damage this event could cause to his reputation.[54]

However, James interpreted Arthur's letter primarily as an endorsement of his position from an important regional leader, and he replied immediately. He pointed out that although the calibre of visitors to New Zealand required him to have the sort of power he had sought but was denied, his mere presence had been 'a very salutary check' on some of the excesses that had marred the country's reputation to that time. The future, according to James's forecast, would be even more promising, and with the assistance of some of the missionaries, national social improvement was just around the corner.[55] James had reacted to Arthur's faint flattery with a paean to his Residency, but when

---

[50] J. Busby, 'Memorandum', 31 July 1833, NZMS185 (1), AML.
[51] J. West, *The History of Tasmania* 1 (Launceston: Henry Dowling, 1852), 95.
[52] G. Arthur to J. Busby, 30 July 1833, in 'James Busby: Official Letters of Various People, 1833–1870', Auckland Museum, MS46.
[53] G. Arthur to J. Busby, 9 August 1833, in *BFR* 2, 423.
[54] *The Colonist and Van Diemen's Land Commercial and Agricultural Advertiser*, 6 August 1833, 3.
[55] J. Busby to G. Arthur, 16 August 1833, in 'James Busby: Official Letters of Various People, 1833–1870', Auckland Museum, MS46.

Kinghorne returned to Hobart in September without having captured the 'runaways'.[56] James's limitations were plainly laid open to Arthur.

Four months after he arrived in New Zealand, James's house at Waitangi was beginning to take on its finished form. One of the biggest problems he faced was with 'workmen leaving and the natives stealing their property',[57] which led to construction ceasing altogether at times. But gradually the building was advancing, with the chimney and most of the framing completed by 24 September. James's financial records reveal payments to a myriad of carpenters, labourers, plasters, and other 'workers', as he pushed ahead with the house.[58]

He maintained two sets of financial records. One related to the expenditure incurred in his capacity as Resident, and the other to his personal disbursements. However, in many cases – particularly involving his house – he did not always manage to keep the two from overlapping. What these accounts also reveal is the web of barter as well as cash transactions that James was enmeshed in. In August, for example, he paid two merchants – Mair and William Powditch – twenty-five pounds of gunpowder, which they in turn paid to a local chief, Hone Heke, which in turn satisfied part of a debt Dr Ross owed to the chief in connection with the house that had been built for him. A month later, James paid for the use of the Rosses' house with a draft made in favour of Mair and Powditch, which went to settle part of an earlier land purchase. The currencies included in these and other transactions ranged from cash to credit notes, tools, tobacco, and food, with a loose exchange rate for the bartered goods evidently prevailing in the region.[59]

Half a year into his appointment, James had still not succeeded in winning over most Māori and settlers in the Bay of Islands to the idea that he was due a certain degree of deference which he believed his role demanded. And nor had his performance as Resident convinced the Australian press (which was a significant shaper of public opinion in the colony) that his appointment had been even remotely a worthwhile one. In November, the *Australian* proved a lengthy and jaundiced overview of James's tenure in New Zealand to date. He was depicted as 'an absolute nullity' when it came to his ability to protect individuals in the territory, to which was added the jibe that James was little more than 'a dealer in small wares' – a reference to his attempts a decade earlier to earn a living as a cutlery importer in New South Wales.[60] The

---

[56] W. Moriarty to W. Kinghorne, 30 July 1833, Archives of Tasmania AB563/1/1, 245, 246; 31 Jul 1833, MB2/2/2/1; W. Moriarty to Colonial Secretary, 24 September, in Archives of Tasmania, AB563/1/1, pp. 265–6; *Hobart Town Courier*, 27 September 1833, 3.
[57] H. Williams, in *The Early Journals of Henry Williams*, 331.
[58] J. Busby, 'Classified Account Book', NZMSS 168, APL.
[59] Ibid.; J. Busby, 'Account Book', NZMSS 168, APL.
[60] *The Australian*, 25 November 1833, 2.

argument was also made in the paper that for the £500 that was being spent annually on the Residency, some dividend should be expected: specifically, that the 'savages of New Zealand' should become 'the most friendly and polished set of people on the globe'. After indulging in some more sarcasm and mischief-making along these lines, the article finally struck at the supposedly underlying decision for the policy that was behind James's appointment: 'putting him there . . . was the convenience of getting rid of a troublesome place-hunter'.[61]

Mid-December 1833 was hot – 'Very hot' is how Williams recorded it in his journal on the fifteenth. As the sun languished overhead, there was a sense of listlessness in the Bay. It was the sort of heat that sapped the will to work, and which saw most people seek shade and rest. Everything felt as though it had come to a standstill. Well, just about everything. Williams observed one afternoon that '[n]umbers of English Sailors landed and rolled into the grog shops here'.[62] Drunkenness was practically an everyday occurrence, but this comment suggested that something worse than usual was in store. With up to thirty ships in the Bay during the height of the trading season,[63] the availability of cheap alcohol, a chance to leave the vessels for a short respite on shore, the widespread prostitution in the Bay, and the small settlement bursting at the seams with hundreds of sailors made for a dangerous concoction.[64]

For the sake of public morality, James decided to enter into the midst of this iniquitous gathering and assert the need for sobriety, order, and propriety. According to the family's oral history, one intoxicated sailor responded to these pleas by vomiting on the Resident's boots, which caused the others present to erupt in laughter, and James to leave in disgust at the indignity of the episode. A captain who observed this confrontation tried to round up his sailors and get them to return to the ship, but was met with derision from the men. When he then threatened to leave without them, they laughed even more loudly, knowing that he would be unable to depart without a crew.[65] This was the sort of circumstance where James was expected to display some influence, yet his powerlessness was cruelly exposed.

A neutral press in New South Wales could have reflected on James's first six months as Resident, and appraised his performance on balance as being beneficial to New Zealand. There had been setbacks and challenges, but there

---

[61] Ibid.
[62] H. Williams, in *The Early Journals of Henry Williams*, 354
[63] K. B. Cumberland, 'A Land Despoiled: New Zealand about 1838', *New Zealand Geographer* 6, no. 1 (1950): 25.
[64] E. Markham, *New Zealand or, Recollections of It* (Wellington: R. E. Owen, 1963), 63.
[65] Busby family history in *BFR* 2, 432.

were also small accomplishments. However, the press was anything but neutral, and in January 1834, James received the most waspish piece yet printed about his Residency – once more courtesy of the *Australian*. 'There has been the devil to pay in the Bay of Islands,' it began, before outlining the supposed crisis in the settlement: 'The houses of the British residing there have been burnt to the ground, and the property consumed, having themselves a very narrow escape for their lives.' There was mention of a crew member from a whaler being stabbed, and general anarchy, against which James was dismissed as being 'worse than useless'.[66]

Knowing the damage such articles were inflicting on his reputation, James could not remain tight-lipped any longer. He had tried turning the other cheek, but that had been slapped too often, and now he felt he had to retaliate somehow in order to put an end to this sort of smear. He decided to raise the matter directly with the Colonial Secretary in Sydney in the hope that something could be done about the adverse commentary oozing from the press. James referred to the article in question as containing 'a calumnious attack upon my character, and an imputation of conduct in my present situation which would have rendered me unfit for any employment of trust or responsibility under the Crown'. This was an important point for James. Since he was a teenager, he had been protective of his reputation, and as he ascended in rank, so too did the priority he placed in it increase. Having seen the misfortune that affected the reputation of others, he was conscious that prominence and prestige could be 'lost without deserving'.[67] A month earlier, Edward Waterton, a Sydney Justice of the Peace, had arrived in the Bay of Islands,[68] and James used his presence to formalize his complaint against the press. In an unusual and unnecessary gesture, he swore an affidavit before Waterton, attesting to the 'falsehood of every statement or insinuation' in the offending article.[69]

Such a formal declaration was futile. With no court proceedings initiated, the sworn affidavit carried no greater weight than an ordinary letter. For James, though, his pleadings – replete with his idiosyncratic baroque legalese – were his way of signalling to his superiors both the seriousness with which he regarded the defamatory comments of the Sydney journalists, and his wish that something be done at an official level to dissuade them from vilifying him any more. 'Till the present occasion', he wrote, 'I never felt myself in the situation that the integrity of my character or conduct was called into question.' He felt that the most recent attacks 'entitled' him to some sort of official

---

[66] *The Australian*, 25 October 1833, 2.
[67] Shakespeare, *Othello*, act 2, scene 3.
[68] *Sydney Herald*, 25 November 1833, 2.
[69] J. Busby to Colonial Secretary, 15 January 1834, in *BFR* 2, 451–2.

recourse, 'for the protection to my character as a Public Servant'. Then turning to his defence, James pointed out that he had 'never . . . given the slightest provocation for the repeated attacks which have been made upon me'. They were 'a direct imputation incompatible with right discharge of my station, and which I could not be guilty of without abusing the trust reposed in me by His Majesty's Government, and rendering myself justly liable to be dismissed from His Majesty's service'.[70] Bourke responded to this over-reaction by drafting a short note to MacLeay, suggesting that there was no need for a libel action, and that James should be reassured that there was no threat to his position arising from these newspaper articles.[71]

There was some comfort for James and Agnes, amidst all this invective, when, on 27 January, they were finally able to move into their nearly completed house at Waitangi (along with two servants – Eliza and William Moore).[72] At last they were in their own home, and James felt he was in a better position to command some dignity, on the basis that His Majesty's Resident was no longer jammed in the spare room of a local missionary. Henry Williams, that missionary, was also relieved. As soon as the couple moved out, he wrote in his journal in a slightly surly tone, 'I had the pleasure of again possessing my Study, which had been occupied by them for these many months past.'[73]

In the afternoon of Sunday 9 March 1834, the 26-gun HMS *Alligator* glided into the Bay of Islands. The captain, Robert Lambert,[74] together with some of his officers, came on shore, and spent several hours with the local missionaries. The next day, William Marshall – the ship's surgeon – met with Henry Williams at Paihia, where he was informed of the state of affairs in the region. That evening, James joined Lambert and Williams, and discussed the issue of the boat that Pōmare had seized from a trader several months earlier and was still refusing to return because of a deal that had gone sour between the parties. After listening to some of the exchanges between James and Lambert, Williams finally spoke, urging prudence. He described any attempt to remove the boat from Pōmare by force as 'extremely hazardous', because it would most likely provoke an even stronger reaction from local Māori.[75]

Williams's wise words were acknowledged by James, but the Resident's reputation for being able to wield at least some authority was at risk if he was unable to wrestle the boat away from Pōmare and return it to the trader. The chief was seen by some Europeans as a person whose actions were in

---

[70] Ibid.
[71] R. Bourke to A. Macleay, in *BFR* 2, 452.
[72] Agreement, 1 November 1833, in Auckland Museum Library, MS46, box 4, folder 15., n.p.
[73] H. Williams, in *The Early Journals of Henry Williams*, 359.
[74] W. R. O'Byrne, *A Naval Biographical Dictionary* (London: John Murray, 1849), 627.
[75] H. Williams, in *The Early Journals of Henry Williams*, 362–3.

'the wild spiritedness of a savage independence', and who had 'laughed Mr Busby to scorn'.[76] James now had two choices. He could do nothing, which had been his only option to date, or he could use the *Alligator* as a means of enforcing his authority through the threat of military action. If he chose the latter, there were several difficulties to contend with. Firstly, the *Alligator* was not scheduled to stay in New Zealand for long, and once it departed the Bay of Islands, the time would be ripe for any Māori attacked by the ship to exact revenge on the Resident, and potentially other settlers as well. Secondly, there was no guarantee that the *Alligator* would be able to achieve the objective of returning the captive boat anyway. And thirdly Lambert would have seen a full assault on Pōmare's pa (fortified village) as disproportionate and inflammatory – particularly as the objective was to resolve a fairly minor commercial dispute.

And it was not as though the fault in this matter lay entirely with Pōmare. On the contrary, many of the clashes that occurred between Māori and traders in New Zealand were the result of the dishonesty of the latter. In this instance, it was reported that the trader in question was 'supposed to be a runaway prisoner of the Crown', and that 'the savage [Pōmare] was cheated by this fellow'.[77] If James took the opportunity of the *Alligator*'s presence to blast Pōmare into submission, the perceived injustice could easily exacerbate the situation. His decision, therefore, was to test the waters. He would use the threat of force to see what reaction it produced in the recalcitrant chief, and then act accordingly.

On the morning of 12 March, the *Alligator* weighed anchor and moved closer to the confluence of the Kawakawa and Waikare rivers, where Pōmare's pa was situated on an elevated outcrop that had a commanding view over the southern part of the Bay of Islands. Lambert turned the ship broadside to the pa and prepared for firing, with all the guns loaded with powder and shot, and the ship's howitzer fitted onto a landing boat that could be rowed closer to the target if needed.

With this impressive show of military might in position, the diplomatic offensive agreed to by James was launched. Henry Williams's brother, William, along with Yate, was dispatched to Pōmare's pa, to see whether he would be amenable to some sort of deal to resolve the impasse. The chief was not delivered an ultimatum, but the warship just off shore, bristling with weapons aimed at his settlement, would have been sufficient to indicate to Pōmare what the likely alternative was if he refused to relinquish the seized boat.

---

[76] W. B. Marshall, *A Personal Narrative of Two Visits to New Zealand* (London: James Nisbet, 1836), 21.
[77] *SGNSWA*, 19 April 1834, 2.

James waited with more apprehension than the others. For the first time he had a military force at his disposal, but exerting his will through the use of force was no simple undertaking. Diplomacy had to run its course, and in this, Pōmare was easily equal to the Resident. About half an hour after the two missionaries had entered the pa to discuss James's offer to have the boat returned, two gunshots were heard. This was the salute used when the chief was leaving his pa. A response was imminent, and Marshall recounted what followed when Pōmare reached the ship:

> he [Pōmare] strode with the air of a monarch along the quarter-deck of the frigate, a tall and athletic young man, his eye scarcely deigning a glance at 'the pomp and circumstance of war', which met him there. Being invited below, he hesitated, but it was only for a moment; the next saw him descending into the cabin, with the same undaunted air, by which his previous bearing had been marked, and he remained there in close conference for nearly two hours, at the end of which Mr Busby came on deck, apparently much pleased, and confessedly glad to have discovered that Pomare, who by his manners had prepossessed every one in his favour, was not the aggressor, but the aggrieved.[78]

For the first time, James had been able to hear directly the other side of the case. Pōmare explained how he had been defrauded by the trader, and then proposed that the missionaries come up with a sum that would represent a fair reparation. This was a shrewd manoeuvre. Pōmare had correctly anticipated that the missionaries, in their desire to preserve peace in the region, would not be inclined to short-change him when they came to settling on an amount for restitution. The amount eventually agreed to was £22, and James was left with little option but to consent to the payment. And in a departing gesture that signified to all present who had the upper hand throughout the entire episode, Pōmare insisted that he be saluted as he left the *Alligator*.[79] James had made the right decision, but Pōmare had controlled the circumstances masterfully. As one journalist noted, the chief was prepared to sacrifice his life 'rather than submit to an act of injustice',[80] so there was no realistic alternative to negotiation if the Resident was to save face, and Pōmare knew it.

From the bedlam in Kororāreka, the frequent inter-tribal tumult in the region, the unregulated trade, the lawlessness, and the absence of the sort of authority that many of the missionaries commanded, James still hoped to fashion his Residency in a way that would address some of the troubled

---

[78] Marshall, *A Personal Narrative of Two Visits to New Zealand*, 22.
[79] Ibid., 22–3.
[80] *SGNSWA*, 19 April 1834, 2.

aspects of life in New Zealand. In particular, he was intent on establishing his influence through working with a collection of chiefs, whom he identified as wielding the greatest power in the area. How to achieve this, though? It is clear that James had no blueprint to which he was working. However, as his request for an embroidered uniform, with tassels and plumed hat, and the pomp he attempted to engineer when reading Goderich's message to the chiefs on his arrival in New Zealand both revealed,[81] he did possess a penchant for pageantry and pantomime. It was through such shows of faux-regal authority that he believed some semblance of statehood could be established. If de facto control would eventually evolve into de jure power, then in James's mind, this stage – involving the outward display of the symbols of state power – would precede both.

The origins for one opportunity James seized on in 1834 to brandish an emblem of authority extended back to 1826, when a Sydney ship-building firm purchased land, at Horeke in Hokianga, as part of a scheme to acquire timber from the region. By 1830, upwards of fifty British settlers were based at Horeke, engaged not just in timber milling but also in shipbuilding, with some of the larger vessels constructed there including the *Enterprise*, the *New Zealander*, and the *Sir George Murray*.[82] However, this industry had advanced without much consideration of the legal status of the ships being manufactured there. New Zealand was still beyond British jurisdiction,[83] and this meant that vessels built in the country did not have the same rights as those constructed in British territories when it came to registration, access to ports, and naval protection.[84] The practical implications of this were made clear on 25 November 1830, when the *Sir George Murray* and its cargo was seized by New South Wales Customs 'for a breach of the Navigation Laws in sailing without a Register'.[85] The ship's owner had tried to hoist 'the New Zealand colours at the mast head', but without any official backing whatsoever, it was a hollow gesture.[86] In January 1833, the *New Zealander* was also taken into the custody of authorities at Port Jackson for not being registered, prompting one newspaper to comment that 'there is something very absurd in a law which enables – at all events, does not prevent a British subject from building a ship

---

[81] 'Memo. by Mr. James Busby', in *HRA* 1, vol. 16, 665–6; *SGNSWA*, 2 July 1833, 2.
[82] T. Raine to G. Murray, 3 January 1829, in *Historical Records of New Zealand* 1, 686; Markham, *New Zealand, or Recollections of It*, 93.
[83] This is discussed in J. Stephen, Memorandum, 18 March 1840, Enclosure 38, in *Correspondence With the Secretary of State Relative to New Zealand*, 69.
[84] J. Davey, 'Atlantic Empire, European War and the Naval Expeditions to South America, 1806–1807', in *The Royal Navy and the British Atlantic World, c. 1750–1820*, eds. J. McAleer and C. Petley (London: Palgrave Macmillan, 2016), 166.
[85] *The Australian*, 26 November 1830, 3.
[86] *Sydney Herald*, 22 August 1831, 4.

at New Zealand, with which he may strengthen the commercial marine of a foreign country – perhaps an enemy – but which ship is liable to be seized in New South Wales'.[87]

As James had been about to depart for New Zealand in 1833, he had been alerted to this matter, and saw the possibilities of some sort of confederation of chiefs coalescing for the purposes of authorizing ship registration, and whatever else might require decisions at more than a tribal (and therefore localized) level.[88] His idea to initiate this project unfurled in the form of a 'national' flag, and in the spirit of democracy, James proposed that this new flag would be chosen only after having received two-thirds of the votes from the chiefs attending the selection process. From such a small beginning, he envisaged a more formal confederation of chiefs germinating, leading ultimately to 'an established Government'. Such an ambition allowed no consideration of the traditional political, cultural, and historical structures that shaped relations between chiefs.[89] Instead of modifying those structures to accommodate his pan-tribal vision, James favoured a clean sweep. Existing chiefly powers would not in any way be undermined, but he was confident that tribal differences would be subsumed by the gains to be had by chiefs acting as a single corporate entity.

The first proposed flag design for New Zealand came from Bourke, and was composed of 'four blue horizontal bars on a white field, with a Union Jack in the upper hoist'.[90] However, the absence of red in the design led to it being rejected by some of the local missionaries, as red was a colour used to denote status among chiefs. James relied on Henry Williams's superior knowledge of Māori culture to inform the subsequent design of contenders for the new flag, and the missionary devised three options, which were prepared in New South Wales and delivered to the Resident by the *Alligator* in March 1834.[91] These prospective national flags were flown outside James's still-incomplete house at Waitangi, and on 20 March, a group of around two dozen chiefs and hundreds of whanau assembled to make their selection.

James, with the assistance of the *Alligator*'s crew, did his best to make the process of choosing the flag as imposing a spectacle as possible. '[T]the great body of the chiefs', Marshall recalled, 'assembled in a large oblong-square tent, screened in on one side by canvass, and canopied by different flags; this

---

[87] *SGNSWA*, 17 January 1833, 2.
[88] J. Busby to Colonial Secretary NSW (Col Sec), 13 May 1833, No. 3, 31–2, in Busby Despatches, qMS [345], ATL.
[89] These are discussed in V. O'Malley, 'Manufacturing Chiefly Consent?', *Journal of New Zealand Studies [JNZS]* 10 (2011): 34–5.
[90] F. Cayley, *Flag of Stars* (Adelaide: Rigby, 1966), 137.
[91] *Correspondence with the Secretary of State Relative to New Zealand*, 69.

was divided into two lesser squares by a barricade across the centre, and the Tangata Mauri were called out of the one square into the other, according to their respective ranks, and to the no small discontent of the excluded.'[92] James then addressed the leaders of the local hapū – his embryonic confederation[93] – after which there were speeches from a number of local Māori leaders.[94] Voting then took place (with two chiefs refusing to take part as they were apprehensive that 'under this ceremony lay hid some sinister design'), and when it was finished, the two unsuccessful flags were folded away, while the winner – which had been the New Zealand Anglican mission's existing flag – was 'flung forth to float upon the breeze, alongside the blood-red banner of Old England; and saluted with a discharge of twenty-one guns from HMS *Alligator*, and three hearty cheers from the crowd of Englishmen present'.[95] A selection of missionaries, other settlers, and officers from the *Alligator* then sat down to enjoy a 'cold collation prepared for them' at James's house, while the chiefs and their entourages were served a meal of pork, potatoes, and korori (a thin paste made of flour and water).[96]

Although Marshall conceded that there was a good deal of spectacle around this event, he believed that James had misjudged the diplomatic dimension of the day. He recalled the Resident's promise from the previous year to have all the chiefs visit him and be his friends, and contrasted the conciliatory spirit of that declaration with the lack of seats offered to the chiefs when the country's flag was selected, and the fact that Māori ate at a separate table from James 'and his "pale-faced" guests'.[97]

According to one account, Pōmare arrived late during these proceedings, accompanied by around sixty musket-armed warriors, and he kept his distance, despite invitations to join James and the other chiefs. There was just a vague fear that violence might erupt, and so William Williams walked over to Pōmare to find out what his intentions were, and specifically why he arrived at a peaceful meeting with an armed force. Pōmare reasoned that if the officers from the *Alligator* were armed (albeit with swords), then he and his men should not be without their guns. The underlying grievance that had motivated Pōmare's belated appearance with his troops was that he felt that James should have given him an invitation to attend the meeting before other chiefs had received theirs. With a 'little soothing' from Williams, Pōmare soon

---

[92] Marshall, *A Personal Narrative of Two Visits to New Zealand*, 108.
[93] J. Busby, 'Address to the Chiefs on the Occasion of the Adoption of a Flag, 17 March 1834', in *He Whakaputanga me te Tiriti: The Declaration and the Treaty: The Report on Stage 1 of the Te Paparahi o Te Raki Inquiry*, Wai-1040 (Wellington: Waitangi Tribunal, 2014), 130.
[94] *The Missionary Register* (1835), 310.
[95] Marshall, *A Personal Narrative of Two Visits to New Zealand*, 108–9.
[96] Ibid., 109–10.
[97] Ibid., 110.

became more accommodating, and a relieved Marshall recorded that 'nothing further occurred to interrupt the harmony of the meeting'.[98]

Yate noted after the selection of the new flag that '[v]essels built in New Zealand, carrying these colours, and having a register from the chief of the district where she was built, countersigned by Mr Busby, will be no longer liable to seizure; but will be allowed to trade as other foreign vessels are in every British port'.[99] As far as he was concerned, a major obstacle to New Zealand's industrial development – the inability to register locally built ships – had been overcome.[100] Overall, Bourke was satisfied with James's organization of a flag for New Zealand, and on 29 April 1834 he wrote to the Secretary of State for War and the Colonies, Lord Stanley, expressing the expectation that the British government would henceforth recognize ships registered in the country.[101]

When news of the flag selection eventually reached Britain, Sir John Barrow, Second Secretary of the Admiralty,[102] sent a memo to Hay, advising him of the details about the flag, together with a drawing of it. The Admiral Commanding in Chief on the East Indies Station was thereafter directed 'to give such Orders to the Captains and Commanders of His Majesty's Ships and Vessels employed under his Orders, as he may deem necessary, for giving effect to the wishes of His Majesty's Govt.' with respect to recognition of the flag.[103] These arrangements were sent to Bourke,[104] who was informed that James's flag-selection process had been approved 'in the name of the King'.[105]

James later argued that recognition of the flag by the King constituted an acknowledgment of 'the Sovereignty of the Chiefs of New Zealand in their collective Capacity',[106] although given that there was no apparatus of a unitary sovereign state operating in New Zealand at the time that the flag was chosen, James's claim was more than a little premature. The *Hobart Town Courier* was in no doubt that the Resident had 'little or no power, and is chiefly useful only as an impartial observer of occurrences round him'. It went on to point out that, from a legal perspective, he could not even function as a magistrate, on the basis that there were no firm constitutional arrangements yet in place to

---

[98] Ibid., 111–12.
[99] W. Yate, 20 March 1834, in *The Church Missionary Register* (1834), 553.
[100] *New South Wales Government Gazette*, Sydney, 17 August 1835, 580.
[101] R. Bourke to Stanley, 29 April 1834, in *HRA* 1, vol. 17, 412.
[102] J. Haydn, *The Book of Dignitaries; Containing Rolls of the Official Personages of the British Empire* (London: Longman, 1851), 167.
[103] J. Barrow to R. Hay, 24 November 1834, in *HRA* 1, vol. 17, 609.
[104] Aberdeen to R. Bourke, 21 December 1834, in *HRA* 1, vol. 17, 608–9.
[105] *Correspondence with the Secretary of State Relative to New Zealand*, 69.
[106] J. Busby, 10 October 1835, *Report for the Select Committee of the House of Lords Appointed to Inquire into the Present State of the Islands of New Zealand*, 245.

allow British law to be applied in New Zealand.[107] However, newspaper commentaries were becoming so routinely antagonistic towards the Residency that James developed something of an immunity towards them. In addition, in his view, he had reached an important milestone for New Zealand in securing a means by which locally made ships could be registered, and at the same time (again, in his view), had fostered a sense of pan-tribal cooperation that bode well for the future.

Amidst the 'perpetual turmoil' James experienced in getting a national flag selected and confirmed, he was also trying to squeeze in some time to manage his personal affairs. In addition to the imminent arrival of his first child, he was giving hasty consideration to a lengthy piece of correspondence that had arrived with the *Alligator*, informing him of financial challenges involving the family back in New South Wales. 'I seize a few moments to write a line to you,' he told William, by way of reply, 'although I am so confused I fear they will be very unsatisfactory'. The issue causing so much concern was Bourke's rather underhand decision to renege on their father's contract with the colonial government and force him to accept a reduction in pay, while expecting him to undertake even more work than before. James was 'vexed' and 'amazed' that Bourke could have breached his father's long-standing agreement with the state, but it was the Governor's prerogative, however much of a 'flagrant injustice' the Resident considered it.[108] Bourke's decision was based on his belief that John was making insufficient progress in his work, and now needed supervision, which was an added cost to the Government.[109] However, James was most likely unaware of this, and joined in the outrage of his siblings that for no apparent reason their father was apparently being ill treated by the Governor.

The other family matter at this time was the birth at Waitangi of John Busby – the first child of Agnes and James.[110] Marianne Williams (Henry's wife) had assisted in the delivery, and remained at Waitangi for a few days afterwards in order to see that Agnes recovered sufficiently.[111] The elated father wrote to his brother, Alexander, describing the arrival of the child. After completing a full page on 'my first bairn's birth', he read it out to Agnes, who 'actually tore it up', and said that James's family 'had no business to know anything more than . . . [that he was] "the happy father of a most lovely baby"'. James described his son as 'a hearty feeder', 'getting as plump as could be desired', and 'a very fine little fellow'.[112]

---

[107] *Hobart Town Courier*, 4 April 1834, 2.
[108] W. Busby to A. Busby, 15 April 1834, in *BFR* 2, 458.
[109] R. Bourke to Stanley, 23 December 1834, and enclosure, in *HRA* 1, vol. 17, 439–42.
[110] *Sydney Herald*, 26 June 1834, 2.
[111] H. Williams, in *The Early Journals of Henry Williams*, 369.
[112] J. Busby to A. Busby, 17 May 1834, in *HRA* 2, 466–7.

7

Trouble at Home

With a newborn child, a house, servants, and a job that was as close as any he had had to fulfilling his aspiration for status and influence, James had good reason to feel that his life was finally on a deserving course – one that matched his skills and ambition. It was an optimism that was not universally shared, however. When the trader Joel Polack cast his sagacious eye in the Resident's direction, his assessment was altogether more severe. '[U]nversed in the language, customs, or habits of the people – retiring within himself, avoiding the respectable class of Europeans, and choosing a locality distant from the natives and traders, the character of Mr Busby as a British Consul was early lost,' he alleged, before observing that 'the native tribes on whose land he took up his residence, treated him with indifference . . . The conduct of these unruly tribes among whom the Resident located himself, was disgraceful.'[1]

Just how precarious James's position was became apparent in the closing minutes of 30 April 1834. One of his servants woke the Resident just before midnight to inform him that some people had broken into the storeroom close to the house. James leapt out of bed, put a duvet over his shoulders, and rushed towards the hut, where the silhouettes of two men were visible. One of them heard the approaching Resident and fired a shot in his direction. Although James later concluded that this shot was a blank, at the time he had no way of knowing, and so he quickly retreated to the house.

Inside, there was panic. Agnes, who was unable to move from the bed, was 'greatly agitated' by what was going on outside,[2] while James scoured the rooms in the dark for a weapon. 'I had no arms in the house with the exception of a fowling piece,' he later recounted, 'and had even left my shot belt in the store-room which they were breaking into.' One of the servants managed to get to the storeroom without being noticed, find some ammunition, and bring

---

[1] Polack, *New Zealand* 2, 221.
[2] M. Williams in *BFR* 2, 460.

it back to the house. James loaded his shotgun and went to the kitchen window to see if the burglars were still in the grounds. Another shot was then fired at the house, but from a different direction. James had no way of knowing how many assailants were outside, or how well armed they were. Concerned for his wife and child, he moved closer to the bedroom when another shot was fired at the house. This time it hit a doorframe, causing a splinter of wood to deflect into his face. 'I felt more from the blood trickling down my face than the pain,' he later wrote.[3] Soon after, the burglars tore away the raupo (a form of reed) walls of the storeroom and stole most of its contents. (The damage done to the doorframe remained until 1933, when parts of the house were renovated.)[4]

James had no way of knowing if others were still lurking outside in the dark, or whether those who had fired at him might return. He decided to send one of his servants to Henry Williams's house – around two kilometres away – to raise the alarm. 'A little after midnight', Williams noted in his journal later in the day on 1 May, '[I] was awoke by a Messenger (an English man) from Mr Busby to say that the natives had broken in the windows of his house and had been firing guns, that his Master and the whole household were in a state of alarm.'[5] Williams immediately raised the alarm and woke up everyone on Paihia. He also sent for the doctor on a ship in the Bay, and dispatched his wife to comfort Agnes.[6]

The event had symbolic as well as security implications. An attack on any settler property in the Bay of Islands was a comparatively rare occurrence, largely because local chiefs did not want to discourage the commercial benefits settlers brought to the area. However, in this instance, guns being fired at the King's representative in New Zealand, one shot of which very nearly killed the Resident, represented a challenge to the entire European presence in the country. And what did it say for the implicit guarantees of protection that local chiefs had offered if such a brazen and prolonged attack could have taken place?

Having failed to find the perpetrators after an initial search,[7] Williams sent messengers to chiefs at Waimate, Kerikeri, Whangaroa, and elsewhere, asking them what they intended to do, and was confident that the offenders would be caught in the next few days. This reaction to an assault on a European was unprecedented in the Bay of Islands, in both scale and intensity. The fact that chiefs from other regions were drawn into the matter is also

---

[3] J. Busby to Colonial Secretary, 3 May 1834, in *BFR* 2, 459.
[4] McLean, 'The Garden of New Zealand', 27.
[5] H. Williams, *The Early Journals of Henry Williams*, 369.
[6] Ibid., 369–70.
[7] *Sydney Herald*, 26 June 1834, 2.

indicative of how seriously Williams regarded the episode, and especially the need to rectify the wrong that had been perpetrated against James.

During the day, a sense of quiet, but not calm, returned to the area. Williams stationed men in and around the Resident's house, as much to relieve James's and Agnes's anxiety as to fend off any potential return of the assailants. Williams himself was also armed, but perhaps in keeping with his beliefs, his weapon of choice was a rake, which he thought 'would do very well either to keep off or draw to my opponent; at all events it would be a weapon they would not be well prepared for'.[8]

A reprieve of sorts from the fear of a further attack came in the form of the chief Titore, who arrived at Waitangi on the morning of 3 May. The missionary William Colenso described him as 'one of the most powerful and best of the many Ngapuhi chiefs of high rank'.[9] Williams went over the recent attack on the Resident with the chief in some detail, hoping to elicit his support to apprehend the offenders. However, at the conclusion of the discussion, the chief responded that there was little he could do until the identities of the perpetrators were known. The names of various possible suspects had been proposed, but this was largely idle conjecture, and over the next few days Williams became increasingly frustrated at the lack of cooperation and even apparent concern among local Māori.[10]

On 6 May, a group of local merchants, including Mair, Powditch, Clendon, and Polack, wrote to James, advising him that Māori attacks on the possessions of Europeans in the region had been on the increase, and warned that 'should this last attempt upon your premises be suffered to pass without the fullest determination being manifested to enforce satisfaction . . . the persons and properties of persons residing in this country . . . will be left to the arbitrary caprice of every savage's horde'. The authors of this letter went further, expressing their view that the Resident would be guilty of deceiving both Māori and settlers if he proved unwilling or unable to achieve some form of redress for this act, and warned him that 'you will cause us to doubt the intention of our government in appointing you', if justice did not prevail.[11]

Three days later, James responded to this letter of discontent. He was taken aback by its 'extraordinary character', but told its authors that he could take no notice of it, on the basis that local chiefs had 'hastened almost with one accord, to express to me their abhorrence of the late attack upon my

---

[8] H. Williams, *The Early Journals of Henry Williams*, 370–1.
[9] W. Colenso, *The Authentic and Genuine History of the Signing of the Treaty of Waitangi* (Wellington: Govt. Printer, 1890), 24.
[10] H. Williams, in *The Early Journals of Henry Williams*, 371.
[11] Letter from colonists to J. Busby, 6 May 1834, in Marshall, *A Personal Narrative of Two Visits to New Zealand*, 349–50.

house, and attempt upon my life – and to assure me that they would use every means to search out and bring to punishment the guilty parties'.[12] Privately, James was furious at this complaint, telling his brother that he found it 'most insulting', and accused most of those who put their name to it of not having 'sense enough to perceive the character of the letter they have signed'.[13] James had missed the point entirely. Promises from the chiefs that order would return to the region were one thing, but as far as these settlers were concerned, they did little to mitigate the mounting threat they believed some Māori in the region represented.

Once the initial shock of the attack had subsided, the Resident downplayed the episode as little more than an anomaly: 'Till the late occurrence I considered this the safest country in the world, and after the uneasiness of the first few nights have been got over, I still feel as secure as I could in any part of the bush of New South Wales.'[14] However, few settlers shared this confidence, and discontent continued to ferment. While Williams continued to plead with several of the chiefs in the area to help find the offenders, on 7 May, a meeting was held by some of the masters of the ships in the Bay, together with various merchants based in Kororāreka. They decided to appeal directly to Bourke to give the Resident sufficient powers 'to support the dignity of his office'.[15] As it stood, James's position was perceived as being of little practical use to the country.

James was largely dismissive of these gatherings and protestations. Instead, he invested his hopes of resolving the matter through convening a meeting of chiefs, which would discuss the attack and serve up a remedy. The conference took place, but after a series of often lengthy speeches from the chiefs condemning the attack, the names of the culprits were still not forthcoming. There was one development which gave James cause for hope, though. Williams reported how those Māori at the meeting 'seemed much concerned and disposed to . . . reside more closely to Mr Busby as his protectors', as a form of personal guard.[16] Polack was more cynical about the Resident's conference of chiefs. 'They made many speeches with the usual intention of never carrying them into effect,' he observed, before identifying the main suspect – a minor chief named Rete.[17] James's immediate concern, though, was not so much the apprehension of the burglars, but the way in

---

[12] J. Busby to Resident Traders of the Bay of Islands, 9 May 1834, in Marshall, *A Personal Narrative of Two Visits to New Zealand*, 350–1.
[13] J. Busby to A. Busby, 17 May 1834, in *BFR* 2, 467.
[14] Ibid.
[15] Cited by H. Williams, in *The Early Journals of Henry Williams*, 371.
[16] H. Williams, in *The Early Journals of Henry Williams*, 372.
[17] Polack, *New Zealand* 2, 222.

which this episode might be relayed to his superiors in Sydney. Nervous that he could face further ridicule, he wrote to MacLeay, warning of the 'exaggerated accounts' that would probably be published in the press, and crafted his own version as a corrective.[18]

It was at this time that Edward Markham, an English artist and traveller, provided a rare impression of James and Agnes. 'Mrs Busby is very pleasant', he assessed, while James was 'rather too formal, and Religious for me to be quite at my ease with, but was particularly kind and civil'. Markham felt that there were '[t]oo many prayers at Why tanghie [Waitangi]' for his liking, but considered his reception by the Resident overall as 'good and a glimpse of Civilization', and that on every occasion he visited James, he was always warmly welcomed. Others echoed this view of James's piety, but with more favour. Marshall described, for example, how it was 'pleasing to hear that Mr Busby, by constant and unremitting attendance in his place in the church on every successive Lord's Day, lends his official sanction to the sacred observance thereof'.[19] But to Markham's mind, whatever the Resident's personal propriety, there was no escaping the predicament he appeared to be in: 'He has not Devil enough for the situation. It requires a Man of some Nouse. His Orders are few, his duties undefined and his Instructions few.'[20]

In his personal correspondence, James revealed that he had shaken off the stress of the attack on his house within a few weeks,[21] but a month later, the offenders had still not been identified.[22] In early June 1834, a deputation of Māori from Kawakawa visited the mission station at Paihia. The group comprised 400 armed warriors, and on reaching their destination, a message was sent to James, inviting him to meet them, and offering their services in identifying and capturing those who had attacked the Resident. However, there were political currents running beneath these visitors' stated motive. Firstly, their presence at Paihia served as a warning to local tribes of how powerful they were. Visiting the Resident was the perfect pretext for parading their military might in unfriendly, if not hostile, territory. It also presented an opportunity for them to feign surprise that local Māori had not apprehended the suspects, thus implying either their incompetence, or worse, complicity. It was the sort of tactical political jostling that, even if James fully appreciated it, was well beyond his means to manage. The Resident was reduced to being a spectator at this diplomatic dance that was choreographed according to the rules of a system that was still largely foreign to him.

---

[18] J. Busby to Colonial Secretary, 15 May 1834, in *BFR* 2, 463–4.
[19] Marshall, *A Personal Narrative of Two Visits to New Zealand*, 248.
[20] Ibid., 65.
[21] J. Busby to A. Busby, 17 May 1834, in *BFR* 2, 467.
[22] J. Busby to Colonial Secretary, 7 June 1834, in *BFR* 2, 474.

With the meeting complete, the hapū from Kawakawa returned home, no doubt satisfied with their mission to Paihia. James, though, was still none the wiser as to who was responsible for the attack on his house, and was aware that if the culprits were not found, it would reflect poorly on how his authority was perceived. The incident had certainly left its mark in the region, with James informing MacLeay in July that 'the Natives throughout the Country are still in a high state of excitement and agitation; mutual accusations and recriminations having passed between the most powerful rival Tribes; and all parties have been engaged for some for some weeks past in strengthening their pahs and forts, or in constructing new ones'.[23]

It was only inadvertently that Rete's guilt was eventually revealed. Five months after the attack, he beat his wife, who took her revenge by informing anyone who would listen that her husband possessed a rug that had been stolen from James's storeroom. Rete was brought before James by a young chief, and relative of Titore, Hone Heke. Rete initially denied the theft, at which point Titore intervened and said that if Rete did not admit his guilt, he (Titore) would go to Sydney, along with another local chief, Tamati Waka Nene, and become slaves in New South Wales.[24] Shocked at this suggestion, Rete confessed, but then claimed that he had removed the rug from the house of Dr Ross, who lived near the Resident. However, the doctor pointed out that it was not his rug, to which Rete injudiciously replied, 'Perhaps Dr Ross stole it from Mr. Busby!' Realizing his story was falling apart, Rete finally admitted his guilt. All that now remained, as far as the chiefs were concerned, was to decide on a suitable punishment. On 30 October, Māori leaders from the region again assembled at the front of James's house to deliberate on the matter.

Execution was an early suggestion proposed to remedy Rete's transgression, but the meeting eventually settled on Titore's recommendation (which had been suggested to him by Henry Williams): that the offender forfeit his land at Puketona (around fourteen kilometres from Waitangi). In addition, Rete and his whanau would have to leave the region.[25] The land in question would be handed over to James, and would become Crown property. This way, restitution was made, and justice was seen to be done. Williams also identified another positive aspect of this episode: that the attack on the Resident's house was neither politically motivated, nor driven by personal feelings towards James, but rather was prompted purely by greed.[26]

---

[23] Ibid., 475–6.
[24] J. Busby to A. Busby, 17 November 1834, in *BFR* 2, 497.
[25] G. W. Rusden, *History of New Zealand* 1 (London: Chapman and Hall, 1883), 178–9.
[26] Marshall, *A Personal Narrative of Two Visits to New Zealand*, 294.

For more than a year, the Resident's dominion (such as it was) had extended to little more than the Bay of Islands and its immediate hinterland, while other parts of New Zealand were still a foreign country when it came to the significance of his presence. It was elsewhere in the country, though, that a situation emerged in 1834 that debunked any presumption that James exercised even the slightest authority over the vast majority of New Zealand that lay outside the small radius of his house at Waitangi.

On 29 April 1834, the barque *Harriet* was wrecked during a storm at Cape Egmont, on the Taranaki coast. On board was the whaler (and former convict) John Guard, his wife Elizabeth, and their two children, as well as a crew of twenty-eight men. All survived the stranding and managed to clamber to shore. As they tried to establish rough shelters to shield themselves from the weather, a party of local Māori descended on them, killing and eating twelve of the crew, and holding the rest captive until a ransom was paid. John and five others were permitted to leave in order to obtain payment, and eventually reached Port Nicholson,[27] where he arranged for the *Joseph Weller* to come to the rescue. Another storm intervened, however, and the rescue mission was aborted as the ship that was meant to save the captives was itself blown off course, and eventually was forced to head to Sydney, where Guard desperately pleaded for assistance from Bourke, while the whole sorry episode to this point became public knowledge.[28]

The bare bones of the story were embellished by a media that gorged on the lurid details obtained from those who had survived the event. And of course, James's role in this (or rather, his lack of a role) inevitably became a point of focus.[29] Bourke reacted immediately to the crisis, but in the process he largely bypassed consideration of a possible part that James might play. 'I called a meeting of the Executive Council to consider what measures were to be adopted under the circumstances,' he later informed the Colonial Office. The decision was reached that a military response was the only suitable way of dealing with the crisis. The HMS *Alligator*, with a detachment of troops, was sent directly to the location where the captives were being held, with instructions to effect a rescue.

Bourke used this episode to push for the 'urgent necessity' of having a naval vessel stationed full-time in the region for the purposes of securing trade and for the 'repression of the numerous outrages which are so frequently committed both by Europeans and natives'. James was not quite forgotten, though. Bourke recommended that the Resident 'be withdrawn from New Zealand, and the

---

[27] W. H. J. Seffern, *Chronicles of the Garden of New Zealand Known as Taranaki* (New Plymouth: W. H. J. Seffern, 1896), 13–16.
[28] S. Marsden, in *The Letters and Journals of Samuel Marsden*, 508–9.
[29] *Sydney Herald*, 21 August 1834, 2.

British Subjects settled there to be warned that they are altogr. without the pale of British protection, unless at least one ship of War be stationed permanently in these seas'.[30] There was no discussion with James, no alternatives considered, just this stark ultimatum: either the Colonial Office authorize sufficient force to protect British interests in New Zealand or the Resident would cease to have the support of the New South Wales government.

The press endorsed Bourke's decisiveness, and praised his administration for acting 'with spirit in thus taking up the cause of the Ship Masters and others, who have been plundered by the savages of New Zealand', adding that there was 'no reason why they should be allowed to commit such depredations with impunity'.[31] James did not even rate a mention in the newspapers, and why would he? After all, he was hundreds of kilometres away from where the captives were being held, and was entirely bereft of any means of assisting in their rescue.

Bourke's formal request to the Colonial Office that James be recalled from his post was an unusual reaction to the situation. It was certainly no panicked announcement made in the heat of the moment, as he wrote this recommendation almost a month after the Executive Council meeting where the matter was discussed. It is likely that the Governor wished to make James a scapegoat in case the Colonial Office decided to point the finger at the New South Wales administration for the failure of its New Zealand policy that this event could be seen as representing. The only concession to James's position as Britain's official representative in New Zealand during this episode was a dispatch MacLeay sent to him on 29 August, advising him retrospectively of the rescue mission to Taranaki. In a slightly demeaning manner, James was instructed to inform the chiefs in the Bay of Islands of what had happened with the *Harriet*, and to 'impress upon them the propriety and necessity of making common cause with the British in repressing the barbarity of their countrymen'.[32]

What ultimately saved the Residency from being terminated was the disastrous outcome of the rescue. The captives themselves were saved, but once they were out of harm's way, the community that had held them hostage was fired on by British troops, causing an unknown number of casualties. Marshall offered a grim account of the aftermath: '[i]n less than an hour after, nothing was discernible of the poor New Zealanders' town, but blazing ruins and burning embers'.[33]

---

[30] R. Bourke to Stanley, 23 September 1834, in *HRA* 1, vol. 17, 544–5.
[31] *Sydney Herald*, 28 August 1834, 2.
[32] A. Macleay to J. Busby, 29 August 1834, in *BFR* 2, 482.
[33] Marshall, *A Personal Narrative of Two Visits to New Zealand*, 182; T. Ballantyne, 'Humanitarian Narratives: Knowledge and the Politics of Mission and Empire', *Social Sciences and Missions* 24, nos. 2–3 (2011): 252–3.

As James had been deliberately and formally excluded from all involvement in the rescue, there was no way he could now be implicated by Bourke in the subsequent atrocities committed by the crew of the *Alligator*. When Guard was later questioned about the rescue and was asked how he envisaged Māori would be civilized, his reply reflected poorly on Bourke's overall command of the rescue, but not at all on James. 'How would I civilize them?' Guard replied rhetorically in a way that raised doubts about Bourke appointing him to help lead the rescue, 'shoot them to be sure! a musket ball for every New Zealander is the only way of civilizing their country!'[34]

In a letter to his father, James emphasized Guard's dubious reputation and the threats he made to various Māori, and pointed out an important fact that was effectively overlooked in the later inquiry: that one of the Māori from the settlement that was savaged by the troops from the *Alligator* had made his way to the Bay of Islands to seek the Resident's protection from further violence by Europeans of Guard's ilk.[35] Unsurprisingly, the New South Wales press took a different view, portraying the murderous retaliation on the Māori settlement as some sort of righteous retribution which served as a message to the rest of the Māori population 'that however much the King of England wishes to cultivate friendship with the New Zealanders [Māori], he will feel indignation at a repetition of such cruelty to his subjects, and severely punish the offenders'.[36]

In accordance with the instructions Bourke had issued, the *Alligator* made its way to the Bay of Islands after the rescue, reaching its destination on 25 October. Henry Williams was informed of the troops' attack on Māori in Taranaki, and privately lamented what had transpired. He was also aware that such a dramatic course of action would have repercussions.[37] Indeed, already, information on the assault had reached the Bay of Islands via a network of Māori messengers, and there was some trepidation rippling through local Māori communities – so much so that James advised the *Alligator's* captain – Robert Lambert – not to allow the troops on board to go on shore. Apparently, various chiefs in the area had pleaded with the Resident for this arrangement, fearing that they might share a similar fate to their compatriots in Taranaki.[38]

Two days later, James met with the captain and senior officers from the *Alligator* and informed them about Pōmare, who was again proving troublesome as far as some settlers were concerned. The latest allegation was that he was now possibly harbouring a Māori sailor who had fled from service on a ship.

---

[34] J. Guard, in Marshall, *A Personal Narrative of Two Visits to New Zealand*, 162.
[35] W. Busby to G. Busby, undated, *c.* October 1834, in *BFR* 2, 487.
[36] *The Sydney Monitor*, 6 December 1834, 4.
[37] H. Williams, in *The Early Journals of Henry Williams*, 397–8.
[38] *BFR* 2, 489.

One of the officers, perhaps still euphoric from the power exercised in Taranaki, suggested that Pōmare's settlement be shown the force at the *Alligator*'s disposal. Williams intruded on this discussion and insisted as firmly as he could that no such action should take place, and that as far as Pōmare was concerned 'upon my word . . . he should not be touched'.[39] Lieutenant Thomas Woore,[40] one of the officers from the *Alligator*, left an account of this discussion which gives an impression of how tense the mood was during this meeting. 'Mr Williams was so distressed that he could not speak, and paced the room in great agitation,' he wrote. 'The situation was relieved by Mrs Busby announcing that dinner was ready; and we all set to, but with less appetite than we had known for a long time.'[41] For his part, James retained a calm demeanour throughout the discussions and helped tilt the view of the meeting away from military action. It was not a foregone conclusion that the Resident's will would triumph, though. The complicating question was whose authority was greater: a naval captain under direct orders from a colonial governor, or the country's Resident?

Having championed restraint and a diplomatic solution, though, the following day James experienced a change of mind. Looking on the debit side of the situation, Pōmare had stolen another boat — this one belonging to a visiting captain — and was now offering refuge to four of the captain's crew who had absconded from their ship. To compound the Resident's concerns, some of Pōmare's men had also just robbed a local store, and when its owner chased the thieves, they fired back at him. James realized that the presence of the *Alligator* afforded him a rare opportunity of showing everyone in the region that he was able to impose his rule after all. He sent a note to the ship's captain with a list of demands he expected to be fulfilled by the errant chief. The boat had to be returned, the deserting sailors rounded up and handed back, and the thieves identified and suitably punished. Pōmare would be given three days to fulfil these demands, and if he failed to do so, his pa would be obliterated by the *Alligator*'s guns.

Williams was shocked by how suddenly the Resident had become bent on vengeance. 'Found Mr Busby very resolute in requiring the lives of the three offenders, that the offence was not against him but against the British Government,' he recorded in his journal. 'We could not see that the offence was worthy of death and should he persist in his present ideas, we must certainly come forward on behalf of the Natives generally, as it was a most

---

[39] H. Williams, in *The Early Journals of Henry Williams*, 398.
[40] *The New Holland Journal: November 1833–October 1834* (Sydney: State Library New South Wales, 1994), 511.
[41] T. Woore, in *BFR* 2, 489.

serious question affecting the whole.'[42] Williams was determined to keep the peace, almost at any cost, but such a stance was now putting him on a collision course with James. A confrontation was averted only because the *Alligator*'s captain had meanwhile decided to take matters into his own hands and ignored the Resident's demands. The stolen boat was recovered, but not so the deserters, while the thieves remained unidentified and unpunished. Most likely, the captain's decision to retrieve the boat and do no more was a way of acceding to at least one of the Resident's demands, while at the same time side-stepping the need for further military action, especially knowing how calamitous the recent encounter at Taranaki had been.

James's about-turn on using military force – or the threat of it – as a way of demonstrating his potential power was understandable after more than a year of relying (often in vain) on the goodwill of others to prop up the reputation of Residency. With the imminent departure of a naval vessel, he realized that such an opportunity would not present itself again in the short term. However, the failure of the *Alligator*'s captain and officers to acquiesce to his plan for delivering an ultimatum to Pōmare had the effect of confirming to anyone who was paying close enough attention that James remained hopelessly lacking in his ability to enforce his will over anyone.[43]

It was not until 17 November that James finally found a moment to write to Alexander.[44] This letter remains the best surviving insight of James's view of his posting to New Zealand to this time, and even by the standards of his previous correspondence with his siblings, it is remarkable for its length and its candour. He firstly addressed the burglary at the Residency six months earlier, informing Alexander that those who were unfamiliar with the true nature of Bourke would be surprised to learn that the Governor had not even had the courtesy to reply to two letters James had sent him detailing the nature and seriousness of the attack. James had told Williams of this, and in response, the missionary tried to play the devil's advocate, suggesting that James's letters had not reached Sydney. However, the Resident was easily able to counter this by observing that all the other correspondence he had sent to New South Wales on the same ship had reached its destination. There was only one conclusion James drew from the silence emanating from the Governor's office: 'I . . . believe that the same dishonest fear of incurring the responsibility necessary to a faithful discharge of his duty which characterized his proceedings in other matters, will prevent his doing anything in the present occasion.'[45]

---

[42] H. Williams, in *The Early Journals of Henry Williams*, 398.
[43] J. Samson, 'The 1834 Cruise of HMS *Alligator*: The Bible and the Flag', *The Northern Mariner/Le Marine du Nord* 3 (1993), 38.
[44] J. Busby to A. Busby, 17 November 1834, in *BFR* 2, 495.
[45] Ibid., 496.

The extent of the acrimony James felt towards the Governor was unmistakable. When he learned that Alexander and their father had been to dinner with Bourke recently, James was furious, and made sure his sibling knew it:

> I must say that it has given me great pain to find that you and my father would go out to dine with the Governor. I am certainly more out of the way than either of you, but if I were to go to Sydney tomorrow, I would flatly decline any invitation he might send me. Whatever allowances may be made for differences of opinion on public matters, I am persuaded it is a duty to resent so flagitious a personal injury. Justice to the 'public interests', forsooth![46]

Having tapped his pent-up sense of grievance towards Bourke, James now poured his scorn on a host of other officials, naming them individually and then detailing their shortcomings. Never before had he targeted so many people in such a fit of accusatory bitterness, but they were obviously all still playing on his mind more than a year after leaving New South Wales. Such an outburst, despite the fact that it was only shared with a sibling, exposed a raw nerve James had in relation to his colleagues as well as superiors in Sydney – one that twitched whenever it was touched. He described them variously a 'pettifogging', 'lazy', 'immoral', 'untrustworthy', 'incompetent', 'infamous', and 'disgraceful', and at their head was the Governor, whom he styled an 'evil-doer'.[47]

To his superiors in Sydney, James tried to convey the impression of containing whatever crises emerged in New Zealand. To do otherwise would be to give his critics (in the media and the government) renewed reason to question his future as Resident. To his brother, however, he referred to the lack of force at his disposal as having led to 'a crisis of British affairs in this place'.[48] He described the British Government as keeping him 'with less protection than any other European possessing property in the Bay of Islands', and assessed his situation as 'impossible'.[49] The missionaries, he explained, achieved some degree of security through living in groups (although the respect with which most were regarded stemmed from the integrity of their actions much more than their living arrangements). Traders, builders, and others were also afforded a sort of protection on the basis that their skills

---

[46] J. Busby to A. Busby, 17 November 1834, in *BFR* 2, 498.
[47] Ibid., 499.
[48] J. Busby to A. Busby, 17 November 1834, in *BFR* 2, 497.
[49] Ibid., 500.

were required in the region. But James was finally putting into words what he must have realized for some time: that he was effectively surplus to requirements – something that he was reminded of daily by his inability to command the sort of influence other settlers did.[50]

In Sydney, Bourke had now fixed in his mind the idea that the Empire's interests in New Zealand could only be secured through a warship being permanently stationed in the region. He believed that trade with New Zealand as well as the settlers' welfare in the country were at growing risk from instability if the status quo remained. And when it came to James's role, the Governor advised the Colonial Office of his serious doubts about the continuation of the position. 'The authority of the Resident in the Bay of Islands', he wrote, 'is, I am sorry to say, almost totally disregarded by Europeans frequenting his station, and he has failed to form so close a connection with the Native Chiefs as to command their aid when occasion required to restrain lawless violence or fraud.' This was a serious indictment of the credibility of the Resident (both the position and the person occupying it), but Bourke was not finished yet. He pointed out that James had no legal authority to apprehend and commit for trial in New South Wales any British subjects who broke British laws in New Zealand. This was hardly news, as the conditions of James's appointment two years earlier had made this explicit, and nothing had changed in the meantime to alter this situation. Still, though, Bourke felt it necessary to remind his superiors of exactly how ineffectual James had become. '[T]he state of affairs in the northern part of the Northern Island', he continued, 'where it was hoped Mr Busby's presence would have been advantageous seems to be in no respect improved, nor likely to be so, nor has he been able to accomplish any of the objects pointed out to him in any of the instructions . . . as the matter now stands the appointment is ineffectual.'

Finally, Bourke's, underlying motive was coming into view. His extended criticism of the Resident was his means of inuring himself to any future criticism that could be directed at him if or when James's role toppled over into a mess of impotent failure. Bourke needed to distance himself now from the impending disaster he foresaw, rather than be forced into a position of justifying his role after the event. In the process, James was thus being abandoned by the one official on whom he most depended. The Governor laid the responsibility for any future failure of Britain's New Zealand policy clearly in the lap of the Colonial Office, citing its previous refusal to provide the Resident with some sort of military support as the basis for the present lack of success. His final recommendation on the matter was his strongest to date on the future of the Residency in New Zealand: 'if measures . . . for giving

---

[50] J. Busby to Colonial Secretary, 29 November 1834, in *BFR* 2, 503.

effect to Mr Busby's commission cannot for sufficient reasons be adopted, it will be more creditable to withdraw him altogether'.[51]

The Colonial Office was not persuaded by Bourke's suggestion that the Residency be abolished. On the contrary, several months before Bourke's treacherous letter had reached the British capital, senior colonial officials in London had already issued instructions for an initiative they felt would go some way towards remedying circumstances in New Zealand in the short term at least: they recommended the appointment of an additional Resident.[52] It was an ill-conceived decision, in that rather than addressing the absence of any means of enforcing the incumbent's will, the Colonial Office simply determined that appointing another Resident who was similarly without any force to back his decision would somehow represent an improvement in the standard of Britain's presence in New Zealand.

The person who had lobbied for the role to be created (for himself) was Thomas McDonnell, a former lieutenant in the Navy who in January 1831 had bought a ship and some land in Hokianga.[53] On a return visit to England in 1834, he had occasion to deliverer an address before the Royal Geographical Society,[54] in which he laid out – in true imperialist spirit – the opportunities New Zealand presented to Britain. If only Māori 'could have justice administered, their rights recognised, and their property secured by good and wholesome laws, they would, I am convinced, prove good subjects, and become a valuable acquisition to the colonist', was his assessment of the prospects for the country if further official British intervention was to take place. The territory itself was also depicted in a manner that was designed to tantalize. 'I have been in most parts of the globe,' McDonnell boasted to his audience, 'but never did I experience a finer or a more equalised climate.' All that this idyllic land needed was 'colonising to render it flourishing in every vegetable production of nature; in fact, there is an abundant and a never-failing supply of all the necessaries, and most of the comforts of life, in New Zealand, were her population twenty times more numerous than it now is'. New Zealand would become 'among the most respectable of the colonies of Great Britain; and that, too, without expense to the English Government. She will become the garden, the depot, and the granary of the Pacific.'[55]

---

[51] Ibid., 504.
[52] T. Spring Rice to R. Bourke, 8 July 1834, in *HRA* 1, vol. 17, 472–3.
[53] J. Nicholson, *White Chief: The Colourful Life and Times of Judge F. E. Maning of the Hokianga* (Auckland: Penguin, 2006), 31, 43,75; J. Binney, 'Tuki's Universe', *NZJH* 38, no. 2 (2004): 222.
[54] The address was delivered on 10 March 1834. A derivative map of New Zealand which he produced at this time was published in London on 31 October 1834. See 'Chart of New Zealand. / by Lieutenant Thomas McDonnell, RN; engraved by James Wyld', Libraries Australia, Ref. 44630284.
[55] T. McDonnell, *Extracts from Mr. M'Donnell's MS Journal* (London: James Moyes, 1834), 10, 11–13, 22–3.

While in London, McDonnell arranged to meet Stanley to present his idea for New Zealand to have two Residents. After all, why not? There was no formula that prescribed one Resident per territory, and if recent reports from Bourke and James were anything to go by, one was clearly not enough for New Zealand. James had represented the situation in the country (or at least the Bay of Islands region) fairly, but had decided not to minimize some of the challenges of the post in the hope that this would incline colonial officials to granting him some sort of supporting military force. However, there was little eagerness among officials for giving a Resident troops. Sustaining even a small number of soldiers was expensive,[56] while the very point of having a Resident posted to a place of interest to the Empire was that he would work through liaison and diplomacy rather than the threat of force.[57]

McDonnell's proposal was that he serve in New Zealand as an 'Additional' (and unpaid) Resident – a proposal that immediately appealed to the parsimonious mandarins in the Colonial Office. As well as promoting an alluring vision of New Zealand in the near future once it was presumably drawn into the British imperial family of colonies, he was offering another official presence in New Zealand for no extra cost or any military commitment. McDonnell justified the need for such an appointment by the fact that he was based in Hokianga, which was at an 'extreme distance' from the Bay of Islands, and was therefore implicitly beyond the incumbent Resident's influence.

On the strength of this meeting, the Colonial Official agreed to the appointment, and instructed Bourke to enact the decision to install an Additional Resident. It was a poorly considered move by London officials. There was no consideration of the potential impact it might have on perceptions of James among settlers and Māori. Could another Resident give the impression, for example, that the sole authority that James represented was now compromised? McDonnell's role was meant to be 'subordinate to that held by Mr Busby', but in practice the logistics of the arrangement militated against this.[58]

As McDonnell commenced his journey back to New Zealand, Bourke was already at work on another dispatch to London which he hoped would undermine James further among colonial officials. On 1 February 1835, the

---

[56] J. Gallagher and R. Robinson, 'The Imperialism of Free Trade', *The Economic History Review* 6, no. 1 (1953): 115; P. J. Cain and A. G. Hopkins, 'The Political Economy of British Expansion Overseas, 1750–1914', *The Economic History Review* 33, no. 4 (1980): 463–90.
[57] As examples from elsewhere in the Empire, see D. MacIntyre, 'Britain's Intervention in Malaya: The Origin of Lord Kimberley's Instructions to Sir Andrew Clarke in 1873', *Journal of Southeast Asian History* 2, no. 2 (1961): 47–69; M. H. Fisher, 'Indirect Rule in the British Empire: The Foundations of the Residency System in India (1764–1858)', *Modern Asian Studies* 18, no. 3 (1984): 393–428.
[58] T. Spring Rice to R. Bourke, 8 July 1834, in *HRA* 1, vol. 17, 472–3.

Governor wrote to Thomas Spring Rice, the Secretary of State for War and the Colonies, informing him that the Resident had 'failed to obtain any considerable degree of respect among the New Zealanders [Māori]'. James had pleaded with Bourke for just two soldiers to be posted to the country to support him, but Bourke was now making plain his opposition to the idea, citing cost as the main reason, but also mentioning James's apparent failure to make his influence felt in the country as a more fundamental problem with the Residency.[59]

What made Bourke's opposition to allocating troops to New Zealand to support the Residency inexplicable, if not suspicious, was how little such an allocation would impact on the overall British military presence in New South Wales. At the time Bourke was claiming that his government could not afford two soldiers to be deployed in the Bay of Islands, there were more than 2,100 troops stationed in New South Wales and Tasmania.[60] Deploying two soldiers would make no noticeable difference to this number, and likewise would incur a negligible cost to the government. Expenditure was just a pretext for Bourke, though – the justification that excused a policy that was well on its way to draining the life-blood from the Residency in New Zealand.

And there was little James could do to thwart this strategy. Every letter he wrote to the Colonial Office would first have to be read by senior officials in Sydney, including the Governor, and Bourke frequently took the opportunity to append covering letters to James's correspondence in order that officials in Downing Street would be able to interpret the Resident's communications with the benefit of the Governor's assessment of them. James had no right of reply because the contents of this correspondence between Bourke and London were only occasionally made known to him, and then only several months or even years after the event. It was an arrangement that was inherently prone to weakening the Residency as time went on, especially if there were insufficient accomplishments for James to claim some sort of success in the role.

Political changes in England were also beginning to make themselves felt at this time when it came to the New Zealand question. In April 1835, Lord Glenelg assumed the role of Colonial Secretary – a position he was to retain until February 1839. He proved to be considerably more conscientious and inquisitive than some of his predecessors, and was prepared to delve deeper into the details of British colonial policy. Six months after his appointment, Glenelg stood back and surveyed the already tarnished arc of James's career as Resident. He read over the many dispatches and enclosures from Bourke, and sifted through the protracted correspondence from the Resident to

---

[59] R. Bourke to T. Spring Rice, 1 February 1845, in *HRA* 1, vol. 17, 645–6.
[60] *Reports from the Committees. Army (Colonies)*, vol. 6, session 19 February–10 September 1835 (London: House of Commons, 1835), 89.

various officials. He then set about assembling the lengthiest assessment yet made by a Secretary of State on James's time in New Zealand. It was a defining moment for the Residency as it represented the clearest statement to date on the dissatisfaction with which the Residency was regarded by those at the highest levels of the British government. Glenelg's ominous judgment was that 'little if any advance towards Civilization has been made by the Natives amongst whom Mr Busby has been residing, and that he has failed in establishing any influence over his own Countrymen resorting to New Zealand'.[61]

What followed was a review of the entire policy and history of the Residency. Glenelg did not regard Bourke as being immune from criticism either, noting that the New South Wales Governor had been among those who had lobbied for a Resident to be appointed to New Zealand in the first place, and had approved James's selection to the post. And it was a position that was needed, as Glenelg reminded Bourke, for establishing some form of British authority in New Zealand, with the primary aim of preventing both 'the aggressions of the Natives', and 'the lawless violence of European depredators'. This had been a priority for the Colonial Office, but Glenelg acknowledged that the failure of previous British governments to provide adequate means for the Resident to achieve this represented something of a failure, although it was insufficient in itself to account fully for James's shortcomings in the role. Indeed, the Colonial Secretary threw James's words back at him, recalling that the Resident was 'the least protected of any individual in the Bay of Islands, if not in all New Zealand'. Glenelg then expressed his inclination that James be withdrawn as Resident, but that he would not act on that inclination until he had appealed to Parliament to provide the Resident with the powers and means of enforcement that James had been pleading for from the commencement of his appointment.

But how best could the British government deal with the situation as it stood now? Glenelg conceded that he was contemplating supporting the Resident with the means that would enable British subjects in New Zealand to be controlled to some extent (although falling well short of any assertion of British sovereignty over those subjects in the country), and that would encourage Māori to pay more deference to the Resident. And once again, Glenelg drew on history to highlight previous errors of judgment. This time he recalled the position taken by the New South Wales Executive Council in 1831, which had been explicit in arguing that a military guard to back the Resident in New Zealand was 'indispensably necessary'. However, Glenelg came to Bourke's defence in this matter, backing the Governor's claim that the costs would be too great to bear.

---

[61] Glenelg to R. Bourke, 28 October 1835, in *HRA* 1, vol. 18, 170–4.

James had previously proposed that he be allotted two constables to enable him to achieve what his superiors expected of him, but Glenelg cast doubt on the efficacy of such a scheme, arguing that it would not give the Resident the hoped-for authority to deal with those around him. The Colonial Secretary instead approved the expenditure of an additional £300 annually from the New South Wales budget to provide whatever type of assistance Bourke decided was best to prop up the Residency.

Overall, though, the tone of Glenelg's assessment was grim. He noted that James's area of influence (such as it was) appeared to be 'confined to a single spot where he had fixed himself; and that, after a residence there of more than a year and a half, he had failed to obtain the confidence of the Chiefs, or even to acquire a knowledge of them or their Country'. Whether this shortcoming was the fault of James or the circumstances in which he was placed was a matter Glenelg left Bourke to determine. This put Bourke in an awkward position. If he decided that James had indeed been deficient for the task, then the Colonial Secretary recommended that there was 'no alternative but to remove Mr Busby to some other Office for which he may be better fitted, and to appoint another officer more calculated to fill the office of Resident'. However, if it proved to be a lack of sufficient support that was at the heart of James's apparent failure as Resident, then it was up to Bourke to devise a means of remedying this.[62]

Bourke had been given free rein to decide on James's future. It was not quite what he expected, as his preference had been for London to make a decision, and thereby absolve him from any immediate responsibility. The chances are that Bourke would have chosen to recall James had the status quo prevailed in New Zealand. However, James was saved by an upsurge of volatility in the country that put British lives at risk, and which left Bourke concluding, with great reluctance, that it was preferable to leave the Residency as it was.

James found out about Bourke's scheming to bring an end of the Residency in March 1835 through a letter from the Governor. He at once told Alexander of this threatening development, but instructed his brother to keep the matter absolutely secret. If the Sydney press got hold of the story, it could damage his career irreparably, so James's approach seems to have been one of keeping the Governor's intention to abolish the post private, in the hope that it might subside in time.[63] James had heard nothing from London to indicate that his role was at risk, but was given a hint that the situation was not good from MacLeay, who confidentially warned James that the

---

[62] Ibid.
[63] J. Busby to A. Busby, 23 March 1835, in *BFR* 2, 539.

dispatches 'would not be very satisfactory', and that the New South Wales government had been 'left in a very unpleasant predicament with respect to New Zealand'.[64]

At the same time as he was grappling with Bourke's hostility towards him, as well as some criticism of him from a handful of local settlers, and the mysteries of working with Māori, James could take some comfort from the fact that the family's financial affairs looked to be improving. His father had managed to sell Rockwall – the folly that had just about driven the Busbys bankrupt and that had been one of the reasons for the fierce rift that had opened up between the two men that was only very slowly beginning to narrow. James described the sale as something giving him 'great satisfaction', and hoped that his parents would now leave Sydney and move somewhere in the colony's countryside, where the cost of housing was considerably cheaper. James reminded Alexander that the sale also gave their father the opportunity finally to settle some of the long-standing debts that he had accumulated over the previous several years.

James's greatest solace, and the counterweight to the myriad challenges he faced, was his wife. 'I have often reflected with gratitude on the goodness of God in providing me such a help-meet in my circumstances,' was how he expressed his appreciation for Agnes. He later wrote that his only regret was that he did not have a steed for her so that the two of them could enjoy a ride together.[65] This small detail in a way encapsulates the nature of James's Residency at this time. The things he hoped for were small in scale, and he must have felt at times as though they were almost within reach. But the emphasis is on 'almost'. He found that in so many areas of his role, he was never quite able to achieve what he otherwise felt he could have, if only he had received a little additional support. However, by early 1835, there were no longer any doubts in his mind about the chances of more resources being sent to him from across the Tasman Sea. James now accepted that he was practically marooned in the Bay of Islands, and if he had not received the support that he had repeatedly implored officials to supply for more than two years, there was little chance of it coming now. Bourke's increasingly overt opposition to the Residency only served to confirm this view. Whenever James gave thought to his Residency, he knew that this was as good as it would get, unless something dramatic was to happen.

Instead of drama, though, James was delivered pantomime. Rete, who had nearly killed him, who had concealed his responsibility for burgling the Residency for months, and who had finally forfeited some land to the Crown

---

[64] Ibid., 540.
[65] Ibid., 541–3.

as punishment, was again appearing in James's sights as an unwelcome presence. Part of the problem rested with two very different perceptions of the law and its functions. James had brought with him a very rigid understanding of the law, of the sort that applied in Britain. When sentences were passed, they were adhered to strictly, and aimed in equal measure to act as punishment and deterrent. British law did not apply to Māori in New Zealand at this time, but when Rete had been punished by James (which had only been possible with the consent and assistance of local chiefs), the Resident had every reason to expect that the sentence – the forfeiture of land to the Crown and the banishment of the guilty from that land – would be upheld. The Māori approach to justice was different, however. It was not that the punishments doled out were any less severe (frequently, the contrary was more likely to be the case), but there was more elasticity in their application. If the affected community gradually felt a degree of clemency towards the convicted person, then whatever sanctions were applied might be eased or even removed altogether. To a degree, the character of the person found guilty could come into play. The genuinely penitent might earn some sympathy from the community, and occasionally, the audacity of the offender in challenging the terms of the punishment could work in their favour.

Rete fell into the category of the latter: someone who was determined to overcome their sentence not through contrition, but through persistently testing the boundaries of their sentence. On 11 May 1835 an increasingly exasperated James wrote to MacLeay, explaining how Rete, whom James had imagined had been evicted for good from the area, was now defying that penalty. The errant chief was still 'in the habit of passing and repassing formerly within a quarter of a mile of my residence', he complained. 'About three weeks ago I was passing some fishing huts upon the land which I had purchased within the above distance of my house when I found a party of Natives to whom the huts formerly belonged, including Rete, sitting there.' James's reaction was astonishing, and he was not reticent in informing MacLeay of his surprising response: 'I passed on without making any observation, but on the departure of the parties I burnt down the huts.' He justified that action on the basis that when he had purchased the land, he had agreed for those Māori who had used the huts near the water for fishing to maintain this right. It was not something that Māori had insisted on, and neither was it written into the purchase agreement, but James had made the offer as an act of grace. However, Rete abused this privilege as far as James was concerned, hence the Resident's decision to torch the huts in response.[66]

---

[66] J. Busby to A. MacLeay, 11 May 1835, in *BFR* 2, 549.

Such impetuosity immediately worried local missionaries – those judicious sentinels of the settler presence in the country, whose efforts to maintain peace and order were a constant reminder to the Resident of how much could be achieved without the sort of military presence he had long argued was crucial. '[M]uch ill-will' was excited by James's rash action, and threats of retaliation were voiced by some Māori in the Bay of Islands in response. James was unrepentant, however. He told MacLeay that '[s]everal of the Natives whom I have always considered well disposed have come to me to remonstrate, but I have told them that if Rete visits any other hut upon my land I will burn it also; and that I will not allow any person to have a hut upon my land who continue to befriend him'.

At this moment, James's judgment had faltered. Unleashing pent-up indignation might have been temporarily satisfying, but it did nothing to convey among the local population any sense that James was suddenly in control of things. He could not see the short-sightedness of his actions, though. He thought it strange that the missionaries did not back his actions (they had even gone as far as suggesting that the Resident may wish to consider making some sort of reparation to prevent the situation from being further inflamed).

James was not convinced that the missionaries knew what was best for the Residency, and to a degree, he was right. The success of the Church Missionary Society in most of the areas in Northland where they had operated could be attributed partly to the emphasis they placed on maintaining peace. They were not appeasers – far from it – but in general, they stuck determinedly to Christ's injunction about the peace-keepers being blessed. However, the authority they wished to establish was spiritual, and focussed on the world to come, whereas James's attention was very much on the temporal.

James's hopes rested with establishing a new form of civil order throughout the country (despite the fact that he had not yet visited any Māori communities outside of Northland). He hoped to convene a confederation of chiefs that would assemble and parley on matters of national importance. For James, the troublesome episodes involving minor chiefs like Rete – as irritating as they were – were nevertheless to be regarded as temporary anomalies. The task of forming a type of chiefly government was the grand objective. However, after two years in the country, what progress towards this goal was there to show? The lack of any breakthrough in the establishment of this confederation was not lost on James. He wrote to MacLeay in May conceding as much:

I have not ventured to absent myself from my family for a single night; and it is not by confining myself to one spot that I can either acquire a knowledge of the Chiefs, or obtain their confidence. I ought to have a knowledge of the country to qualify me to be useful to them; and I am confident it is an object worthy of attention to obtain a knowledge of the capabilities of the country with reference to its connection with Great Britain.[67]

This vision was thus laid out by James for his superiors in Sydney and London to examine. However, its apparently grandiose scale was subverted by the very next line in the letter, in which James argued that the whole scheme was not practicable as long as the Resident and his family remained undefended. He therefore asked for two constables, which would provide the necessary security to enable the proposed congress of tribal leaders to take place.[68] It was too easy a fix, and left the impression that the promise of a great political step forward in New Zealand was a ruse by James to secure the services of the constables. James was genuinely committed to a confederation of chiefs, but the awkward way he juxtaposed this plan with the repeatedly rejected plea for armed support for the Residency gave the impression that the promotion of the former was designed to lure officials to endorse the latter. Unsurprisingly, the request was met with silence.

It was not that officials had lost interest in New Zealand. On the contrary, MacLeay was busy putting the finishing touches to the instructions for McDonnell, which at the very least he hoped would ameliorate some of the challenges James had either mentioned directly or alluded to over the past two years. McDonnell was in Sydney in June 1835, preparing to return to Hokianga, where he would resume his shipping business and commence his pseudo-official functions as Additional Resident.

The contents of MacLeay's message to McDonnell were similar to that sent from the Colonial Office in July the previous year, but the New South Wales official added a few extra details he felt would be useful. The whole plan was based on the belief (however superficially some held to it) that because Busby could not attend to the interests of all the European settlements in the country, it made sense that he have someone assist him. But then, why stop at one? Why not have several Additional Residents – maybe even one for each settler community? And more importantly, if the existing Residency was struggling to achieve any progress because it was denied the means of enforcing its will, how could officials hope to accomplish anything different by replicating such a failed system? It was not as though McDonnell had impressed officials to such an extent that they saw him as the antidote to New Zealand's problems. It was more a case of an opportunist who had convinced the Colonial Office that he could offer some protection for British interests in a part of New Zealand that was relatively remote from

---

[67] Ibid., 551–2.
[68] Ibid., 551.

James's base in the Bay of Islands. And with no attendant cost, McDonnell's scheme came across as something which, regardless of how marginally successful it might be, would place no burden on the British government or that of its colony in New South Wales.

MacLeay was explicit in his letter that McDonnell would under no circumstances be able to override James's authority, and insisted that McDonnell maintain a regular correspondence with the incumbent Resident. Furthermore, the Additional Resident was instructed not to write directly to officials in Sydney or London, and instead direct any concerns or queries to James. McDonnell's main task would be to improve the state of order among settlers in the Hokianga region, relying on 'moral influence' rather than 'personal collision'. The latter option would only end up diminishing his authority, as MacLeay was well aware from James's experiences in the Bay of Islands.[69]

As winter arrived in the region, the frequency of ships visiting diminished, and drunkenness and the ensuing disorder in Kororāreka dropped accordingly, with sailors more inclined to stay in the public houses rather than roam outside in the increasingly chilly evenings. In July, with the Bay of Islands having quietened down from the height of summer trade, James put his mind to his family's situation in New South Wales, and Bourke's role in their fortunes. The Resident was effectively jammed between his official position, in which he was directly answerable to the Governor, and his loyalty to his family, over whom Bourke exercised authority as John's employer.

This awkward amalgam of personal and professional relationships came to the fore in mid-1835, when John and Sarah Busby were visited by a friend, Anna Thomson. Anna was married to Sir Edward Deas Thomson (who two years later took over from MacLeay as the New South Wales Colonial Secretary).[70] Anna was also notable in Sydney society for being one of Bourke's daughters, and so the fact that she was meeting James's parents was significant, given the rift that existed between John and the Governor. And it appears that the visit was not entirely social. Anna made some 'disclosure' to the Busbys in relation to John's recent dispute with the Governor over the salary he was receiving. Whatever was said, James suggested that it was 'for the purpose of lessening my father's ill will to General Bourke'. At the same time, the Governor had been encouraged to adopt a more conciliatory approach to John by Thomas Spring Rice, the British Colonial Secretary, who had in turn been lobbied by the Busbys' long-time friend, Buxton, whose influence James assessed to be 'of immense importance'.[71]

---

[69] A. MacLeay to T. McDonnell, 29 June 1835, in *BFR* 2, 554–6.
[70] S. G. Foster, *Colonial Improver: Edward Deas Thomson, 1800–1879* (Melbourne: Melbourne University Press, 1978), 37.
[71] J. Busby to A. Busby, 23 July 1835, in *BFR* 2, 560.

With this small olive branch extended to the Busbys by Bourke, albeit reluctantly, James would have felt some relief that at least one source of conflict affecting the family had been clipped. He now allowed himself to ruminate about his parents' future. James's wish for them was that they enjoy a quieter life for however many years they had remaining. 'Were my father once rid of the Government and he to settle at Hunter's River in a little cottage of his own building,' he told Alexander, 'you and Willie and John might form some arrangement by which you might have a sheep station in a not very distant place and one of you might be with the old people and one each at the stations, moving about as circumstances or pleasure might require.'[72]

It was the sort of consideration of his family's circumstances in New South Wales which the winter months gave time for James to contemplate. Otherwise, his days were occupied with banalities. He acquainted Alexander with the tedium of his post, complaining how his time was 'frittered away in the most trifling engagements you can imagine. I can get nothing worthy naming done in the way of improvements either by the Natives or Europeans.' However, the absence of pressing problems gave James the opportunity to assemble his thoughts about the future of the country. The routines and rhythms of the Residency offered a kind of stability, but to the same extent, they stifled some of James's innate ambition. Admittedly, the turbulence of his first year in the country had settled considerably. In July 1835, he wrote how previously, for example, he suffered from frequent thefts, and would often have to remain up all night to keep a watch over his house and possessions. Now, though, such apprehensions had gone, and in recent months he had not experienced even one instance of theft. Yet James had a yearning for more than just the status quo. In his mind's eye, he foresaw New Zealand being cut free from the moorings of a Residency and heading in the direction of a fully fledged British dependency.[73]

James's long-held faith in the relentless progress of all things was no doubt at the core of this vision, but what gave it a more defined form was a series of recent experiences that had convinced him that his authority – which was initially more proclaimed than acknowledged or respected – had finally taken root. As 'proof' of this, he cited an example in which he settled a land dispute involving a chief who was claiming ownership of a block of land that had belonged to a recently deceased settler. 'Two years ago', James noted, 'there would have been a general scramble for the man's effects', but now, '[t]he moment my name was mentioned everything was considered sacred'.[74]

---

[72] Ibid.
[73] Ibid., 561.
[74] Ibid.

Despite James's confidence, the Residency had not suddenly turned a corner, and was still very much a work in progress. It remained geographically insular, and its authority continued to rely only on the consent of those prepared to submit to it. Neither had there been any modification to the terms of his posting. The policies of the New South Wales Government and those of the Colonial Office had remained unchanged in their fundamentals. Instead, James's improved morale came from unexpectedly finding that settlers and Māori were prepared to adhere to his will at times, and that he was no longer being brushed aside as irrelevant, as he had been earlier on in his Residency. He was finally growing into the role, and if recent experience was anything to go by, he had good reason to be hopeful about the future.

8

Independence

By the winter of 1835, James had in some ways become discontented with the status quo of his Residency. He was determined to nudge New Zealand closer to Britain – perhaps turning it into a dependency, with all the military, financial, and bureaucratic infrastructure that would entail. Of course, he presumed that he would be at the helm of this new state, captaining it regardless of what form it assumed. A note that reached him on 3 August 1835, however, tore into pieces the grandiose picture he had assembled for New Zealand's future, and his commanding place in it. It was from McDonnell, who had just returned to New Zealand, clutching the details of his appointment as Additional British Resident. As soon as he was settled again in his house, he had written to James, informing him that he was 'executing a contract with my Lords of the Admiralty' to assume his new role.[1] This completely blindsided James, as did the arrival at the same time of a bundle of dispatches from MacLeay that contained details relating to the Additional Resident's appointment.

It was subversion of the worst kind as far as James was concerned. After taking a few days to digest the implications of this new appointment, and to calm his nerves, he wrote to MacLeay, spelling out his concerns over McDonnell's posting. James depicted this development overall as being 'dangerous to British interests in this part of the world', before going on to assess in some detail precisely why he believed the Additional Resident would be unnecessary and even harmful to the country. He attacked McDonnell's claim that the role was needed in the Hokianga region because of its 'extreme distance' from the Bay of Islands, pointing out to MacLeay that the distance between the two locations was no more than sixty kilometres, and that chiefs from the region had always been happy to meet with him when invited, thus leaving the impression that McDonnell had been circumspect with the truth when applying for the position.

---

[1] T. McDonnell to J. Busby, 3 August 1835, in *BFR* 2, 562.

James also suggested that it would be impossible for his counterpart to separate his political functions from his 'commercial speculations', especially as McDonnell was known to have had 'collisions in matters of trade' in the past. The risk in all this was that the Crown's reputation would be tarnished by the Additional Resident's partiality in his business dealings. When he had heard that the trader was returning to New Zealand (and before he was aware of his appointment as Additional Resident), James was anxious about McDonnell's plans to claim hundreds of acres of land as a result of transactions with some local chiefs that were not as comprehensive and binding as they could have been, and with a payment of about 10 per cent of the actual value of the land according to James's calculations. He stopped short of accusing McDonnell outright of fraud, but the implication was clear enough.[2]

James's lengthy response to McDonnell's appointment was logical, factual, and ought to have raised serious doubts about the decision both to have an Additional Resident in the first place, and to have McDonnell fill the role. However, as good as James's appeal was, it was made after the fact of McDonnell's appointment. He was consequently stuck with his off-sider, and would somehow have to accommodate the fact of there now being two official British representatives in the country.

When it came to seeking solace amid the vicissitudes of his Residency, James was cultivating an increasing interest in what he referred to as 'metaphysics', and had been sending copies of books he had read on the topic to Alexander, in the hope that his brother could be likewise enlightened. The works in question were principally Christian books dealing with 'that wisdom that cometh from above'. James recounted how profound and dramatic an effect these works had on him: 'I went to bed with my hair almost on end with the prospect which presented itself on endeavouring to look into the womb of time, no, of eternity.'[3] This private confession to his brother gives a glimpse into the intensity of James's faith. One of his favourite books was *Evidence of the Truth of the Christian Religion Derived from the Literal Fulfilment of Prophecy*, by the Church of Scotland minister Alexander Keith. It was a volume that encouraged readers to dispense with the 'apathy of nominal Christians, in the present day', and to embrace 'the zeal of those who first became obedient to the faith'.[4]

Despite the depth of James's profession of faith, and the intensity of his adherence to it, it was a subject he raised only rarely in his correspondence. On the whole, his letters to family members tended to be dominated with

---

[2] J. Busby to A. MacLeay, 7 August 1835, in *BFR* 2, 562–4.
[3] J. Busby to A. Busby, 5 September 1835, in *BFR* 2, 564–5.
[4] A. Keith, *Evidence of the Truth of the Christian Religion Derived from the Literal Fulfillment of Prophecy* (Edinburgh: Waugh and Innes, 1826), 14.

information about his Residency, together with concerns about their progress in New South Wales. Apart from the rancorous relationship with his father which had resulted in communication between him and James almost drying up completely, letters between the others of the family continued to flow freely. However, in September 1835 James divulged that there had been an inexplicable cooling of relations between him and George. His elder sibling had not written to him in over a year. Thirteen months earlier, James's son had been christened, with James naming George as the godfather. Yet when advised of this in a letter, George had not replied, and there had been silence since. James speculated that George might have become annoyed over an outstanding debt of £120 that James owed him, but this was just a guess. He proposed to Alexander that if the debt was indeed the issue that had led to George shunning him, then he was prepared to repay it with interest if that would resolve the matter, but that he would be 'sorry' if the situation got to that point.[5] But whatever the reason, George continued to ignore James's letters, leaving the Resident confused and disappointed at this treatment from someone who in previous years had been his closest confidant. At the same time, James was welcoming another child into the house – his daughter, Sarah, who was born on 23 September, and who was 'thriving admirably', as was Agnes.[6]

On the political front, James felt he was making some headway. Robert Hay, the Permanent Under-Secretary of State for the Colonies, had agreed to receive some of the Resident's communications directly, so as to bypass the increasingly adverse commentary being made on it by the New South Wales Governor. James saw this as 'a most important point gained', principally because he would now be able to fashion his reports for officials in London, rather than worrying about wording them to placate Bourke. However, the presence of the Additional Resident was still at the forefront of James's concerns at this time. Although he would never be imprudent enough to say so publicly, in one letter to his brother, James characterized McDonnell's appointment as a 'shameful transaction' that 'disgraced a Minister of the King'. Since returning to Hokianga six weeks earlier, McDonnell had not communicated at all with James, apart from the note he had sent him at the beginning of August, advising that he was assuming this newly created role.[7]

However, McDonnell could not simply be ignored in the hope that he would somehow recede into the political background. Instead, the new appointment spurred James to seek other ways by which he could prove to his superiors

---

[5] J. Busby to A. Busby, 8 September 1835, in *BFR* 2, 565–6.
[6] J. Busby to A. Busby, 10 December 1835, in *BFR* 2, 601.
[7] J. Busby to A. Busby, 8 September 1835, in *BFR* 2, 566.

that he, and he alone, was sufficient for British interests in New Zealand to be served. One of these opportunities unexpectedly arrived at his house on 6 September in the form of a delegation of settlers who were seeking an end to the importation of spirits into the country. They presented the Resident with a resolution prepared at a public meeting that had been convened specifically for this purpose.

The previous month, James had gathered a small group of merchants and missionaries in the Bay of Islands and founded the New Zealand Temperance Society. But the initiative had soon dropped down on the list of James's priorities.[8] However, the resolution presented by the group of settlers in September reinvigorated this commitment to a form of prohibition. It was a principled cause that was not based on any monetary gain, and one which James believed would be welcomed not only by his superiors in Sydney and London, but also by the missionary organizations, whose influence he depended on to some extent. Although completely bereft of a means to monitor or enforce such a measure, he could cast any pronouncement he made regarding the regulation of alcohol in the region as being in anticipation of acquiring more formal legislative powers at some point.

There were practical as well as moral reasons for such a ban to be introduced. Drunkenness was becoming a serious threat to order in the Bay of Islands – to the point where some captains were now considering sailing to other harbours in Northland to conduct trade. In the preceding twelve months, there had been a noticeable decline in shipping in the Bay of Islands, and James attributed this in part to the difficulties captains were having with the alcohol-fuelled disorder that their crews indulged in once on shore.[9]

James was also concerned with the effects of alcohol on Māori in the region. The Resident reported to MacLeay on 10 September that '[i]nstances have occurred of Natives whose general conduct and demeanour are quiet and respectful, having while under the influence of spirits proceeded to acts of violence which would justify the apprehension of the most alarming consequences, were the use of spirits to become general among them'.[10] Implicit here was the fear that disorder might gain the upper hand, at least in the Bay of Islands, which could have a destabilizing effect on the Residency.

There was one obstacle in an otherwise clear path to prohibition, however, that James could not dismiss. If the mooted ban was introduced, with the backing of the missionaries and a group of upstanding settlers, and even supported by certain chiefs in the area, yet could still not be sufficiently

---

[8] New Zealand Temperance Society, *Report of the Formation and Establishment of the New Zealand Temperance Society* (Paihia: Church-Mission Press, 1836), 1–8.
[9] J. Busby to A. MacLeay, 10 September 1835, in *BFR* 2, 567.
[10] J. Busby to A. MacLeay, 10 September 1835, in *BFR* 2, 567.

enforced, then there was no chance that any other attempt at imposing rules of any sort would work. As he began to reflect on the consequences of the potential failure of such a prohibition, James's initial enthusiasm began to drain. He therefore decided to pause to weigh up his options, rather than take what might be hasty action.

Meanwhile, through his trading networks, McDonnell had heard about the Resident's decision to proceed with a ban on spirits. Quickly calculating the advantages to his own career, McDonnell decided to mimic this move. He advised Bourke in a letter (to which James was not made privy) that he had discussed a liquor ban in Hokianga with some of the British settlers in the area, and with the local missionary, the Rev. William White (whose tenure as superintendent of the Hokianga mission was about to come to an end following allegations of sexual assault and rape).[11] And as James had done in the Bay of Islands, McDonnell turned to local chiefs and missionaries to galvanize support for 'his' initiative, citing (with less conviction than the Resident) the great benefits to the country that would be conferred by prohibition. When Bourke received the Additional Resident's letter, he informed the Colonial Office not only that he had given his approval to the measure, but also that he had issued 'notice of the Law in the Government Gazette of this Colony, and instructed Mr McDonnell how to proceed with regard to it'.[12] This was an unprecedented and legally highly questionable move that can only be explained in political terms, in that it was a way for the Governor to show his favour for McDonnell over James.

When James's report on the possibility of a similar ban in the Bay of Islands reached Bourke, containing the Resident's suggestion for careful consideration before taking any further steps, the Governor seized on it, expressing his 'surprize' that James had cautioned against the 'law'. Even the perennially ambitious Resident had not referred to this initiative as a law, and had reservations about such moves precisely because they lacked the sort of enforcement that laws carried with them. Yet, far from supporting James's prudence, Bourke persisted with gaining political mileage from the proposed liquor ban. He labelled the Resident's reticence 'altogether unsatisfactory', and then told the Colonial Office that he had subsequently directed James not to discourage 'such a law', citing the implementation of a similar measure in Hokianga.[13]

This impression created by Bourke was entirely (and deliberately) misleading. James's hesitation had been partly procedural. He had agreed in

---

[11] A. Wanhalla, 'The "Bickerings" of the "Mangungu Brethren": Talk, Tales and Rumour in Early New Zealand', *JNZS* 12 (2011): 13.
[12] R. Bourke to Glenelg, 10 March 1836, in *HRA* 1, vol. 18, 352.
[13] Ibid.

principle to the ban, but first wanted formally to approve a resolution to that effect. He was reluctant to avoid being led by a group of settlers to a decision that 'might subsequently place me in a false position as British Resident'.[14] Having slowly and with great difficulty accumulated some political capital in his role, James was sensitive to the risk of expending it freely, and potentially fruitlessly. As he explained to MacLeay, these 'rude essays in the act of Government' – as he described the resolution submitted to him – required the backing of the colonial authorities in New South Wales. 'It would in fact be dangerous and unjust', he cautioned, to promise the settlers that a prohibition on spirits would be put in place, and then be unable to deliver on that promise.[15]

There was an important coda to this episode which offers another possible reason for James stalling progress on the resolution. He was hopeful that he would shortly be 'invested with legal authority, and some means of enforcing it'[16] – a hope based on a vague allusion Glenelg had made of his plan to introduce a bill to the House of Commons that would in some way address the New Zealand situation, and change the nature of the Resident's role.[17] For a number of reasons, though, the following year, Glenelg had a change of heart. 'I was induced by various considerations', he told Bourke, 'to refrain from attempting to execute in the late Session my purpose of making more effectual provision for the protection of the Inhabitants of New Zealand against the misconduct of British Subjects. I have not, however, abandoned that design.'[18] The door was not completely closed on the idea, but it now remained at best a distant possibility. Certainly, subsequent events proved that the promise of the Resident finally being able to govern rather than just liaise was an entirely forlorn one.

But in September of 1835, James was practically convinced that change in his powers was just a matter of time. In a letter marked 'Private and Confidential', he prematurely informed MacLeay that month that a decision on the Residency by the British government would be arriving in Sydney shortly, and that in order not to cause undue delays, some of the details of his authority, and of the way the country would be governed, were best sorted out sooner rather than later. Central to James's suggestion was where the balance of sovereign power ought to lie in the country. Here, for the first time, he laid out the rudimentary constitutional principle which he believed ought to

---

[14] J. Busby to A. Busby, 8 September 1835, in *BFR* 2, 566–7.
[15] J. Busby to A. MacLeay, 10 September 1835, in *BFR* 2, 568.
[16] Ibid.
[17] Such a bill was alluded to by Glenelg in Glenelg to R. Bourke, 28 October 1835, in *HRA* 1, vol. 18, 172. Also see S. Cheyne, 'Act of Parliament or Royal Prerogative: James Stephen and the First New Zealand Constitution Bill', *NZJH* 24, no. 2 (1990): 184.
[18] Glenelg to R. Bourke, 26 August 1836, in *HRA* 1, vol. 18, 506.

apply as the basis for Britain exercising a more direct and formal presence in the country: 'For the British Government to take upon itself to frame and give effect to regulations for the conduct of trade in this country would be a decided assumption of authority which of right belongs exclusively to the Natives.'[19]

James was adamant that Māori sovereignty ought not to be impeded by any moves undertaken by colonial officials to affirm British control over some of the New Zealand population. He proposed that a division of authority and jurisdiction be formalized through a treaty between the Crown and chiefs, and that the Residency would continue, but with constables to enforce its decisions, and that it would all be funded through levies placed on ships visiting the country. This last suggestion was important because it would mean that no costs would be incurred by the British government.

James's faith in his imminent assumption of some form of authority also led him to assume a more didactic tone with McDonnell. On 6 October, he dispatched a letter to him, chastising him for sending copies of their correspondence directly to Sydney. James was worried that the New South Wales Governor would build up a mistaken impression of what was happing in New Zealand. He then made clear his view of McDonnell's recent actions: 'I think it may be important to lose no time making you aware that I have resolved to recognise no law which can in any way affect the persons or property of British subjects unless it proceeds from an assembly of all the Chiefs . . . in their collective capacity.' This argument exposed James, though, to the same sort of criticism that he was levelling at McDonnell: making decisions based on the consent of only some chiefs, rather than all. The Resident anticipated this, and so advised McDonnell of his intention 'to convene such an assembly at this place [Waitangi] . . . once every twelve months and occasionally as circumstances may make it desirable' in which chiefs from around Northland would gather to assist in the government of the region.[20]

McDonnell's attempts to emulate something along these lines, albeit on a more localized scale, were condemned as 'inconsistent' by James. The Resident wrote to McDonnell, recommending him to 'retrace your steps', and 'abstain as much as possible . . . from acting or encouraging others to act in the spirit of the Resolutions of which you have transmitted a copy to me'. James knew he was not vested with the authority to order the Additional Resident directly, but this was as good as issuing a binding instruction, especially as he then informed McDonnell of the Bill he thought was about to be passed, empowering him with real powers.

---

[19] J. Busby to A. MacLeay, 10 September 1835, in *BFR* 2, 572.
[20] J. Busby to T. McDonnell, 6 October 1835, in *BFR* 2, 577.

In writing his response to this forceful letter, McDonnell knew that he was replying for two readers: the Resident in Waitangi and the Governor in Sydney. With this in mind, his reply was a mixture of oleaginous concessions and pointed disagreement. He 'innocently' claimed he had simply been following Bourke's instructions, and noted that the measures he had implemented in Hokianga were practically the same as those James had proposed for the Bay of Islands. He then claimed, disingenuously, that he had 'no immediate mode of communicating' with the Resident, and so was forced to act independently for the good of British interests in the country.

Then, with the justifications dispensed with, McDonnell attacked directly and bluntly James's plan of a gathering of chiefs to aid with the government of New Zealand, in a way that was designed to appeal to Bourke's existing concerns about the Resident. McDonnell argued that the chiefs were 'not yet sufficiently civilised to be trusted with such a power, which their very ignorance and avariciousness must lead them to abuse'. This went against James's experience of the chiefs he had encountered, but it was not the end of McDonnell's case. 'I trust you will permit me to observe', he continued haughtily, 'that I consider it utterly hopeless your being able to congregate the whole of the chiefs of New Zealand at any one place for the purpose of enacting any law, though their acquiescence may be separately obtained by which the object you have in view might be ultimately gained.'[21]

McDonnell's approach of playing to an audience of his superiors in Sydney paid off. On receiving this letter, Bourke promptly issued a notice, advising the captains of all vessels trading in New Zealand that a 'law' had been agreed to by the Hokianga chiefs, that 'prohibited the importation of Spirits into their District', and that 'enacted that any [spirits] which may in future be attempted to be landed, as well as the Boats employed in disembarking the same, shall be confiscated'.[22] The New South Wales government was now explicitly threatening to exert its authority to enforce a New Zealand 'Law', as Bourke put it. McDonnell would have been encouraged by this level of support in equal measure to the dismay James would have felt for not having ever received such backing from his superiors. It was a manifestly unjust decision by the Governor, but calculatedly so. Based on subsequent events, Bourke probably had no intention to enforce his 'Law', but it was the gesture rather than the fulfilment that mattered.

McDonnell's letter to the Resident had been written in a deliberately condescending way, but despite such provocation, James decided that there was no benefit in maintaining the tit-for-tat exchanges with the Additional

---

[21] T. McDonnell to J. Busby, 10 October 1835, in *BFR* 2, 578.
[22] Notice of the Law, 28 October 1835, in *HRA* 1, vol. 18, 825.

Resident. Consequently, he directed his reply to MacLeay, who he hoped would act as some sort of arbiter in the matter. James highlighted the fact that McDonnell was pretending to settlers and Māori in Hokianga that he was capable of exercising some legislative authority, and worse still, that he had wielded this falsely claimed power in an abusive way, with a hint that the Additional Resident was even using his role for pecuniary interests. In contrast, James cast the execution of his own role as having been highly principled, and reiterated that any steps towards British rule in the country could only commence if the chiefs were involved in some way in their collective capacity.[23] However, as much as this relationship between the Resident and the Additional Resident was becoming increasingly abrasive, the New South Wales authorities were untroubled by this development. There was no rebuke given to either man, and MacLeay did not seem in any rush to resolve the rift. Consequently, the acrimony remained, and for James, it became another standing challenge for him to contend with.

If a Downing Street official, fresh to New Zealand affairs, glanced at the state of the country in September 1835, he could be forgiven for concluding that as far as its Residency was concerned, it was all business as usual. Yes, there were small crises from time to time, but they had tended to be more alarming to James than his superiors. The Residency was far from perfect, but also far from exceptional in imperial experience. However bumpy the path sometimes was, colonial officials were satisfied that James was broadly achieving what they hoped he would. The process of policy formation for New Zealand, such as it was, remained guided by the principle of minimal intervention tempered by developments on the ground. What mattered more than the specific impetus behind policy adjustments – whether it originated from the core or periphery – was the maintenance of a rough equilibrium when it came to upholding peace and order (at least among British subjects) in New Zealand.

Managing any disruption to this equilibrium became an end in itself for the Colonial Office, and in general, the network of intelligence flows through the Empire ensured that there were few surprises when it came to events that might risk upsetting the status quo. It was a robust and long-tested system, but it was far from foolproof. The law of unintended consequences – no respecter of British might – wormed its way into New Zealand affairs in 1835, having burrowed from an unexceptional event fifteen years earlier. In 1820, the great Ngapuhi chief Hongi Hika (described at the time as 'New Zealand's cannibal Napoleon' for his series of spectacular military conquests)[24] had visited England with the missionary Thomas Kendall. While in Cambridge,

---

[23] J. Busby to A. MacLeay, 10 October 1835, in *BFR* 2, 579.
[24] Hurstbouse, *New Zealand, or Zealandia* 1, 21–2.

principally to meet the Rev. Samuel Lee, who was Professor of Hebrew at the University of Cambridge,[25] Hongi was introduced to Baron Charles De Thierry – an eccentric noble of an immigrant French family. This meeting between the entrepreneurial chief and the ambitious aristocrat resulted in a (dubious) transaction in which De Thierry received approximately 40,000 acres of land in Northland in return for a payment of tools and probably muskets.[26]

Three years later, De Thierry had written to Bathurst indicating his intention to establish a British colony on the land and seeking clarification of the rights and protection that would be offered to those settling there.[27] De Thierry received a curt reply from Wilmot-Horton, which concluded with the point obvious to everyone except De Thierry, that New Zealand was not a Crown possession.[28] The Baron persisted with pleas to the Colonial Office until April 1824, when repeated rejections finally made him accept the futility of seeking government sanction for his proposed colony, and so he shelved the idea.

However, in 1835, the idea of planting a colony in New Zealand again flared up in De Thierry's imagination. In May, he wrote to the British king, William IV, citing the *Harriet* episode as the pretext for his planned intervention in the country. His intention was to form what he envisaged as an 'Independent Government, not only for the security of my property, but also for the safety of the families who might accompany or follow me, and in consequence of the repeated and earnest prayers of several native Chiefs, who have from time to time invited me to rule over them and thus to ensure their future peace and prosperity'.[29] Such requests were not uncommon, but what separated De Thierry's appeal from all the others was the preposterous rationale behind his request, and his extraordinarily inflated, almost delusional self-importance:

> By right of purchase of many Chieftaincies, I am a New Zealand Chief and a Sovereign Chief, in which character I treat with the Government of New Granada, and I assume my own flag; but that flag (though that of a descendant of Charlemagne) is an infant needing parental care and protection, and it is from the best parent of all Englishmen, and from the most able to protect, that I ask, for New Zealand, as for myself, family, and adherents, the Protection of the King of Great Britain.[30]

---

[25] *The Missionary Register* (1840), 231.
[26] R. FitzRoy, *Narrative of the Surveying Voyages of His Majesty's Ships Adventure and Beagle* 2 (London: Henry Colburn, 1839), 586; P. Moon, *A Savage Country: The Untold Story of New Zealand in the 1820s* (Auckland: Penguin, 2012), 66–7; C. De Thierry, *Historical Narrative of an Attempt to Form a Settlement in New Zealand* (Auckland: Auckland Library, Ref. no. GNZMS 55, c. 1857), 116.
[27] C. De Thierry to Bathurst, 2 December 1823, in *Historical Records of New Zealand* 1, 614–15.
[28] R. Wilmot-Horton to C. De Thierry, 10 December 1823, in *Historical Records of New Zealand* 1, 615.
[29] C. De Thierry to King William IV, 12 May 1835, in *HRA* 1, vol. 18, 823.
[30] Ibid., 823.

And as if this was not audacious enough, De Thierry requested that the King supply him with 200 soldiers, plus officers, to secure the settlement.

Finding no support in Britain for his schemes, De Thierry wrote to James, making absurd claims about assuming sovereignty over New Zealand, and threatening that he would arrive 'with strength to maintain and power to resist'.[31] Was this bluster or was there something more substantial that enabled the baron to make such ominous comments? There was no way of James knowing for sure, which added to the Resident's anxieties.

To the missionaries in the Bay of Islands, De Thierry penned a similarly brash letter. He claimed that he had been 'invited by many chiefs' to come to country, and that he had 'declared the independence of New Zealand – that is, my own independence as Sovereign Chief, including all who may find it in their interest to benefit by it, and who may prefer wealth to poverty, honour to degradation, or happiness to misery'. He then warned that if he was not welcomed cordially, he would land as an enemy, using force.[32]

James's immediate reaction was to write to MacLeay within a day of receiving the baron's 'extraordinary' letter. 'I confess that my first impression . . . was that it was the production of a madman,' was how he recounted his reaction. However, after rereading De Thierry's letter, James was convinced that 'there might be sufficient method in the madness of the man to be productive of much mischief', and so he took it upon himself to do whatever he could to frustrate the Baron's plans. Interestingly, James did not refer to De Thierry's threatened arrival as part of some greater strategic plot involving France, but instead was worried solely by what De Thierry was capable of doing in New Zealand as an individual, and that 'having obtained a footing in this country . . . he might sufficiently extend his influence amongst the Natives to give occasion for . . . disquietude'.[33]

James also knew that in the rumour-riddled settler communities of the Bay of Islands, he needed to act promptly and decisively to extinguish any talk of French intervention, or of some other threat to the Residency. On 10 October, he issued a public proclamation that detailed what had happened, and what he intended to do about it. He began by announcing that he had received a formal declaration from a person who styled himself as 'Charles, Baron de Thierry, Sovereign Chief of New Zealand, and King of Nuhuheva' who intended to form a sovereign state in New Zealand in his own name. De Thierry was currently in Tahiti, apparently waiting for 'an armed ship' from Panama to arrive, so that he would have the means to proceed to the Bay of Islands and assert his sovereignty.

---

[31] C. De Thierry to J. Busby, 14 September 1835, in J. D. Raeside, *Sovereign Chief: A Biography of Baron De Thierry* (Christchurch: Caxton Press, 1977), 110.
[32] C. De Thierry to H. Williams, 14 September 1835, in Raeside, *Sovereign Chief*, 111–12.
[33] J. Busby to A. MacLeay, 10 October 1835, in *BFR* 2, 581.

James alluded to the offer De Thierry had made to pay missionaries to work for this independent state as magistrates, and to induce other settlers to move to his colony, but disabused British subjects in the country of any interest in this scheme, denouncing De Thierry's 'insidious Promises' as capricious nonsense.[34] It was the duty of all British settlers, he insisted, to exert whatever influence they could to counteract the baron's 'Avowed Intention of Usurping a Sovereignty' over the country. James still felt that such measures might prove inadequate, and so announced that he would call together local chiefs in order that they might act collectively to protect their independence.[35] This was it: James's manifesto for New Zealand. A meeting of chiefs from Northland would be convened, with those present declaring their determination to withstand whatever attempt might be made to usurp their independence. An added advantage of this idea was that it would all but eliminate McDonnell's influence,[36] and deprive Bourke of a basis for continuing to favour the Additional Resident.[37]

Bourke was hardly likely to approve such a scheme, though, and so James decided to play up the threat of a French invasion and its supposed risk to British interests in New Zealand as a way of distracting the attention of officials from the details of his proposed declaration. Hence James went ahead with drafting and obtaining the signatures of chiefs for his Declaration of Independence without even informing his superiors, let alone obtaining some sort of permission.

The response when news of the Declaration of Independence reached Sydney was predictable. Burke was irate at only being informed of the Declaration after the fact, and wrote to the Colonial Office, claiming that the Resident's views were at odds with those of the missionaries and settlers in New Zealand, as well as with the government of New South Wales.[38] James had trespassed on the tolerance of his superiors, and while he saw the Declaration as a new dawn for New Zealand, it also came to represent the sunset of his career.

The Declaration's text was plainly written (by James's standards) – avoiding the tendency towards legalism in important documents that had previously been his preference. Part of the reason for this can possibly be attributed to the fact that Henry Williams was involved in the document's translation, and so may have drawn the Resident's attention to the need to have a more

---

[34] J. Busby, 10 October 1835, in *Report from the Select Committee of the House of Lords, Appointed to Inquire into the Present State of the Islands of New Zealand* (London: House of Lords, 1838), 444–5.
[35] Ibid.
[36] Ross, 'Busby and the Declaration of Independence', 106–7.
[37] R. Bourke to Glenelg, 10 March 1836, in *HRA* 1, vol. 18, 354.
[38] Ibid., 353.

straightforward set of provisions. It is also probable that James took a cue from the address he had delivered to Māori when he arrived in the country in 1833, which was simple in its construction and straightforward in its language.[39]

Although Williams, and possibly other missionaries, were involved in the Declaration's translation, curiously, the final version of the Māori text – the one which the chiefs signed – was written by Eruera Pare Hongi.[40] Exactly why Hongi was brought in to act as scribe is unclear, but it may have to do with the high regard he was held in by the missionaries because of the extent of his literacy, or that in having a Māori write out the translated text, there would be one less reason for the signatories to be suspicious of it. Far from merely serving as a scribe, though, Hongi improved the Declaration's phrasing and expression, whilst maintaining its integrity as a translation of the English text.[41] However, the faith in Hongi's skill in polishing Williams's translation is not universal, with the language used in the Māori text later described by one Māori language expert as 'awkward'.[42]

The agreement consisted of four operative articles, and was just over 300 words in length. And despite its title, it bore little resemblance at all to the United States' Declaration of Independence, which had been written fifty-nine years earlier, with all its Enlightenment references to liberties, natural rights, and utilitarian goals.[43] If James had been aware of the American counterpart, he made no reference to its contents or philosophies in his Declaration. Rather, his preference was to address the issues that he saw as more practical and immediate. Here was a document that owed its contents and orientation largely to the set of circumstances James had encountered in just over two years of living in a small part of the country. To a large extent, he did not need to look back on the glories of the British constitution or the American Declaration of Independence for inspiration because this was more a practical manifesto than a wistful meditation.

The first article of the New Zealand Declaration of Independence referred to the chiefs of Northland who had assembled at Waitangi to declare the country's independence. This group would thereafter be known as the United Tribes of New Zealand. However, in no way could the Northland chiefs be said

---

[39] J. Busby, 17 May 1833, in *Church Missionary Register* (1834), 265–6.
[40] P. Parkinson, 'Our Infant State: The Maori Language, the Mission Presses, the British Crown and the Maori, 1814–1838' (PhD thesis, Victoria University of Wellington, 2003), 128, 208.
[41] *He Whakaputanga Me Te Tiriti: The Declaration and the Treaty. Report on Stage 1 of the Paparahi o Te Raki Inquiry, Wai 1040* (Wellington: Waitangi Tribunal, 2014), 163.
[42] M. Mutu, in *He Whakaputanga Me Te Tiriti*, 171.
[43] R. Hamowy, 'Jefferson and the Scottish Enlightenment: A Critique of Garry Wills's *Inventing America: Jefferson's Declaration of Independence*', *The William and Mary Quarterly: A Magazine of Early American History* 36, no. 4 (1979): 503–23.

to represent the entire country, and so a codicil was added to the agreement which clarified that those chiefs who were unable to attend the initial signing nonetheless fully agreed with the Declaration, and in signing it, would join 'the sacred Confederation'.

Article Two was at the heart of the Declaration. In it, '[a]ll sovereign power and authority within the territories of the United Tribes of New Zealand' was declared to reside 'entirely and exclusively in the hereditary chiefs and heads of tribes in their collective capacity'. In addition, the signatories would 'not permit any legislative authority separate from themselves in their collective capacity to exist, nor any function of government to be exercised within the said territories, unless by persons appointed by them, and acting under the authority of laws regularly enacted by them in Congress assembled'. This excluded even British authorities from having any formal jurisdiction in New Zealand unless first approved by the Confederation. Far from easing the route for the incremental increase in British authority in the country, James had cut it off at the pass. The provision affirming Māori sovereignty over New Zealand was absolute (albeit exercised in an as yet untested collective capacity). As much as this was outwardly a signal to the French that New Zealand was not available for the taking, so too was it a signal to Britain that it could not ignore Māori sovereign rights over the country. In this sense, the Resident was representing in a collective form for the whole of New Zealand the sort of authority the chiefs had exercised over their own territories for centuries.

The following article summarized how this new collective would operate. James envisaged this grand coalition of chiefs gathering at Waitangi every autumn (presumably after the labour-intensive harvests were over) to act as a nascent parliament,[44] devising and passing laws 'for the dispensation of justice, the preservation of peace and good order, and the regulation of trade'. However, such acts of inter-tribal unity went against the grain of long-standing political differences between various tribes, and so the Resident also proposed in this provision that chiefs from outside the Northland region be invited to 'lay aside their private animosities' in the interests of 'the safety and welfare of our common country', and join the Confederation of the United Tribes.

The Declaration's fourth and final article was written mainly for the benefit of senior colonial officials. In it, the Māori signatories noted their intention to send a copy of the agreement to the King, and thanked him 'for his acknowledgement of their flag; and in return for the friendship and protection they have shown, and are prepared to show, to such of his subjects as have settled in their country, or resorted to its shores for the purposes of trade'.[45]

---

[44] Ross, 'Busby and the Declaration of Independence', 84.
[45] *The Declaration of Independence, He Whakaputanga, 1835*, Archives New Zealand, ref. IA9-1.

But what about the Māori signatories? Did they have a common stance on the agreement, and did they even understand it in the way the Resident had intended them to? The implicit presumption that the chiefs who acceded to the Declaration interpreted its provisions in precisely the same way that James had was almost universal whenever the topic was addressed in later works.[46] However, the fact was that for more than a century and a half after the Declaration was signed, Māori understandings of the agreement – passed down orally through generations – were concealed behind the facade of 'proper' histories. It was only in the early 2000s that this indigenous perspective began to enter the public domain.

Individually, the aberrations in the translation might seem on the surface to be little more than a case of faintly varying shades of meaning. However, these shades, when combined, gave the Declaration a different complexion to some of its Māori signatories. Even the agreement's title in Māori, for example – 'He Whakaputanga' – had connotations of 'emergence' rather than the abruptness of a 'declaration', while the Resident's role in the Declaration was cast as that of 'a foreign political adviser'.[47] In addition, the agreement was seen by some Māori signatories as a sacred covenant as much as a constitutional arrangement.[48] And far from creating a new nation state, as James believed his Declaration had accomplished (in word if not yet in deed), the notion of a single Māori nation as far as the chiefs were concerned (socially, culturally, and linguistically, though not politically) already existed. The Declaration was thus more a case of Māori 'emerging onto the world stage',[49] than undergoing any fundamental change to their own body politic.

The Declaration of Independence was initially signed by thirty-four chiefs. The figure of thirty-five is sometimes cited, but the additional name was actually that of the person who inscribed the names of the chiefs.[50] It was witnessed by two missionaries (Henry Williams and George Clarke) and two merchants (Mair and James Clendon), and signed by James.[51] Strangely, there is a dearth of extant evidence on the discussions that took place at the time of its signing. Neither Williams nor the Resident recorded the content of the

---

[46] As examples, see T. Ballantyne, *Entanglements of Empire: Missionaries, Māori, and the Question of the Body* (Auckland: Auckland University Press, 2015), 232–4; Sinclair, *A History of New Zealand*, 52; Petrie, *Chiefs of Industry*, 58; Belich, *Making Peoples*, 181; Orange, *The Treaty of Waitangi*, 21; Ward, *A Show of Justice*, 24–5.

[47] *He Whakaputanga Me Te Tiriti*, 154, 161.

[48] H. Sadler, *Ko Tautoro, Te Pito o Toku Ao: A Ngapuhi Narrative* (Auckland: Auckland University Press, 2014), conclusion.

[49] N. Aldridge, in *He Whakaputanga Me Te Tiriti*, 187.

[50] J. Binney, *The Legacy of Guilt: A Life of Thomas Kendall* (Auckland: Oxford University Press, 1968), 192.

[51] J. Busby to R. Hay, 2 November 1835, in *Report from the Select Committee of the House of Lords, Appointed to Inquire into the Present State of the Islands of New Zealand*, 179.

negotiations, and even in Māori oral history there is no detailed, consistent record.[52]

With the Declaration freshly signed by the end of October 1835, it was now time for the Resident to deal firmly with De Thierry. The following day, he composed a letter to the baron which was intended to deter him from pursuing his fantasist vision of usurping sovereignty over the portion of land he had purchased. James needed this letter to sink the Frenchman's ambitions to the point that they would be beyond salvage at any time in the future. Accordingly, the text of the Resident's message was vehement, but unfortunately, it was also misleading in parts. James commenced by falsely claiming that his Declaration was an initiative of the British government, and that as a result of Māori consenting to it, British law now applied to Māori and settlers alike in New Zealand. However, in the next sentence, he asserted (paradoxically) that Māori independence from foreign rule and laws had been upheld by the agreement and could not be interfered with.

James then proceeded to hack away at the basis for De Thierry's wish to be involved in New Zealand. He alleged that the Baron had short-changed the vendors of the land he had purchased a decade and a half earlier, and had therefore forfeited his rights to any lands in the country. This was followed by a caution that supposedly emanated from the chiefs who signed the Declaration: 'they request me to warn you against approaching their lands, in whatever capacity you choose to represent yourself'. From this veiled threat, James's language only became terser. He highlighted the 'utter hopelessness' of De Thierry's cause, and even accused him of 'criminality'. And just in case the message had still not quite penetrated the Baron's mind, James finished his letter with another, even stronger threat: 'should you present yourself . . . you may be sure of meeting with the most spirited resistance from the whole population – a population with whom warfare in its fiercest form has been a sport, and who are far from being ill-provided with arms and ammunition'.[53]

James might have believed he had a achieved a victory over De Thierry, but Polack astutely noted that it was only the baron's failure to arrive in New Zealand when he had threatened to (De Thierry eventually reached Hokianga on 4 December 1837) that saved the day for the Residency. 'Had the adventurous "King of Nuhuheva" arrived,' he observed, 'Mr Busby would have soon found that a few blankets and firearms well distributed, would soon have visibly displayed the characteristic spirit of the New Zealanders in its true light, and scarce a respectable European would have stood up in defence of that

---

[52] *He Whakaputanga Me Te Tiriti*, 167. James continued to seek support for the Declaration, including from locations outside of Northland, and by 1839, a total of fifty-two chiefs had put their names to the agreement.
[53] J. Busby to C. De Thierry, 30 October 1835, in *BFR* 2, 583.

gentleman [James]. They would gladly have embraced any social form of government, however oppressive for the protection of their property, rather than the law of force, which has hitherto agitated the country.'[54] There was some truth to this assessment. Regardless of the extent to which James believed he was in control of the situation regarding the De Thierry 'threat', circumstance as much as strategy was the key saviour for the Residency.[55]

Bourke took some time to consider the implications of the Declaration before reporting on it to Glenelg. The New South Wales Governor claimed that James had 'mixed up with the Declaration of Independence a matter totally unconnected with the protection of the Islands from foreign usurpation',[56] and that the possibilities for the British government asserting more formal levels of jurisdiction over its inhabitants in the country were curtailed by the agreement. Indeed, the Governor made the rather feeble argument that his earlier 'law' prohibiting the importation or selling of spirits in Hokianga (which was never implemented and manifestly was not a law) was undermined by the chiefs' assertion of total sovereignty in the Declaration.[57]

Glenelg put on record his 'entire concurrence' with Bourke, asserting that 'however upright may have been his [James's] motives, he judged unwisely and acted with great indiscretion'. The counterpoint to this condemnation of the Declaration's effect of excluding direct British jurisdiction in New Zealand was Glenelg's satisfaction with the way James had dealt with De Thierry: 'Every motive of humanity and of National policy combined in favour of Mr Busby's efforts to defeat the attempts of the person calling himself the Baron de Thierry, to establish Sovereignty over the New Zealanders.' Glenelg suggested that had De Thierry been successful in his aims, then 'a new and dangerous power' would have been introduced in the region, and that the consequence of this would soon have been 'the depopulation of New Zealand, or at least the extinction of the Aborigines'.[58]

It is difficult to take Glenelg's comments at face value. He would have been fully aware that the French posed no threat to New Zealand,[59] and so his statement about the dangers of De Thierry being at the vanguard of intervention by a 'a new and dangerous power' does not ring true.[60] Glenelg's assessment

---

[54] Polack, *New Zealand* 2, 430–1.
[55] *BFR* 2, 584.
[56] R. Bourke to Glenelg, 10 March 1836, in *HRA* 1, vol. 18, 353.
[57] Ibid., 354–5.
[58] Glenelg to R. Bourke, 26 August 1836, in *HRA* 1, vol. 18, 506.
[59] Adams, *Fatal Necessity*, 52–3; G. Martin, 'Two Cheers for Lord Glenelg', *Journal of Imperial and Commonwealth History* 7, no. 2 (1979): 213.
[60] He was known to be a charlatan. See T. W. Nechtman, *The Pretender of Pitcairn Island: Joshua W. Hill – The Man Who Would Be King Among the Bounty Mutineers* (Cambridge: Cambridge University Press, 2018), 278.

of the Declaration was more an exercise in politics. Having chastised the Resident for formally affirming the sovereignty of Māori over the country, he needed to balance the ledger so that Bourke did not interpret his response as being universally unfavourable towards James. Given Bourke's previously expressed criticism of James, Glenelg risked prompting further condemnation of the Resident from New South Wales if he failed to draw attention to the good James was doing. Glenelg's message was thus a balancing act, with France – the old enemy – serving as a useful pretext to justify at least some elements of the Declaration.

There were other potential repercussions of the Declaration that James must have been aware of, but that he avoided committing to paper for obvious reasons. Principal among these was how it might affect New Zealand's relationship with Britain. If New Zealand was now a sovereign and independent state, then British attempts to regulate its citizens or shipping in the territory would become much more legally questionable. This point was brought to the attention of the British government by Dandeson Coates and the Rev. John Beecham, who were testifying before the House of Lords Select Committee enquiring into New Zealand. They made explicit what had probably occurred to just about everyone who had read the Declaration – that any act which infringed on New Zealand's newly defined and declared national sovereignty would be 'one which the British Government cannot warrantably adopt'.[61]

Among the imbroglio of opinions and positions on the Declaration, understandably, James's was the most acclamatory. He saw this development in almost providential terms, and in a lengthy dispatch to Bourke, written on the final day of October 1835, as the glow of the agreement's signing still hung in the air, the Resident spelled out the specifics of the Declaration, and how he saw it functioning. Where sovereign power lay was axiomatic. All powers of government would be vested solely with the chiefs. However, whereas the text of the Declaration referred to hereditary chiefs, James also foresaw chiefs emerging whose power was not determined by birth, but by their 'talents and conduct', and who grew to have authority within their communities. It was as though the Resident saw an embryonic form of democracy sprouting from the terrain of traditional Māori hereditary leadership. Exactly how this would emerge and propagate was unknown, but it suggested James conceived of an evolutionary approach to indigenous rule in the country, in which the Declaration served as a major step towards the goal of a chief-governed nation. This was to be no contrived construct, but one that 'naturally springs from the actual condition of the people', as he put it. It would promote

---

[61] D. Coates and J. Beecham, in *Report from the Select Committee of the House of Lords, Appointed to Inquire into the Present State of the Islands of New Zealand*, 246.

'the improvement of the people themselves' and offer a 'degree of safety and protection' to settlers in the country.[62]

The Resident had taken on a 'weighty responsibility' in formulating the Declaration, as he informed Bourke, but there was no alternative as far as he could see. Without such an initiative, James could see the entire balance of power in New Zealand shifting: 'looking to the actual condition of this people, if left to themselves, I felt satisfied that if such a man [De Thierry] . . . were to arrive among them even with a score of determined men, and a few hundred pounds worth of property, he might achieve the Sovereignty of the Islands'. Perhaps this was not as exaggerated as it might have appeared to Bourke and his officials. James had received intelligence relating to the plans one tribe near North Cape was making to attack an historic rival in Tauranga. In James's estimation of the situation, all that it would take would be for De Thierry to offer assistance to one of the belligerents, after which the baron 'would be strengthened by the continued accession of individuals and Tribes, till he could overrun the Islands, and while overcoming any opposing force, he could consolidate his authority by a skilful management of jealousies and rivalries'.[63] And with growing British interests in the country – both through settlement and trade – the chances of a British collision with De Thierry and his growing band of tribal supporters could heighten. James could confidently claim now, though, that those chiefs who had signed the Declaration were 'perfectly unanimous in asserting their determination not to permit the landing of the Baron . . . nor to submit to his government'.[64]

However, the Resident was astute enough to accept that a balance had to be established. In preventing De Thierry from establishing some form of sovereignty in New Zealand by means of the Declaration, James had successfully avoided the need for the British government to intervene more forcefully in the country. He saw himself '[a]cting upon the firm belief that HM Government would in no degree seek to promote the ascendance of British power or the extension of British interests at the sacrifice of the just rights of the Natives'. He knew that Britain would not intervene militarily for economic as well as policy reasons, and so his Declaration achieved the desired effect of fending off the presumed threat of French intervention without the need for a single British soldier or ship being sent to the country.[65]

On the matter of property rights, James was convinced that his Declaration would serve to protect Māori interests. He explained to Bourke how each tribe exercised a form of exclusive ownership over their territory, and that within

---

[62] J. Busby to R. Bourke, 31 October 1835, in *BFR* 2, 587.
[63] Ibid.
[64] J. Busby to R. Bourke, 31 October 1835, in *BFR* 2, 587–8.
[65] Ibid.

each tribal territory, land was held communally rather than in individual allotments. In confirming these property rights, James saw the Declaration as being entirely consistent with British law, in which the respect for property was almost sacrosanct, without upsetting traditional Māori notions of land tenure.

Underlying the importance of such principles was the practical fact of the country's demographic composition, in which settlers made up less than 1 per cent of New Zealand's population.[66] Given this enormous imbalance, there was no point in trying to impose on Māori a system which they may not have wanted. Instead, James favoured a more conciliatory approach when it came to the possibility of introducing British law into New Zealand. He hoped that with the conclusion of the Declaration, 'the chiefs might be led to enact and to aid by their influence and power the enforcement of whatever laws the British Government might determine might be advantageous to the country'. Any attempt to govern Māori directly through usurping chiefly power 'would make it necessary to overawe them by an army capable of crushing all resistance that the whole country might be able to offer', and would end up with an 'evil' situation in which the minority held sway over the majority through force. In contrast to such a terrible prospect, James held up his Declaration as 'the most effective mode of making the country a dependency of her British Empire in every thing but name'.[67]

However, the Declaration's subsequent ineffectiveness even in maintaining, let alone improving, order in the country, the failure of the Confederation to meet even once to pass laws, and violent rivalries that burst out between some of the signatories within two years of the agreement being concluded, along with a lack of official backing from Britain and New South Wales, collectively contributed to the Declaration's downfall as far as colonial officials were concerned. Sir George Gipps, Bourke's successor as New South Wales Governor from February 1838, depicted the agreement as a 'concocted manoeuvre' by which the Resident fended off the advances of De Thierry. As for its content and wider purpose, Gipps comprehensively denounced it in 1840. He claimed Māori had not understood the Declaration, they were incapable of legislating as James had envisaged, and that overall, it was 'a silly as well as an unauthorized act . . . it was, in fact, as I have said before, a paper pellet fired off at the Baron de Thierry'.[68]

---

[66] J. Beecham, *Remarks upon the Latest Official Documents Relating to New Zealand* (London: Hatchards, 1838), 15.
[67] J. Busby to R. Bourke, 31 October 1835, in *BFR* 2, 88.
[68] G. Gipps to J. Russell, 9 July 1840, in *Great Britain Parliamentary Papers [GBPP] 1841* (311) (London: House of Commons, 1841), 75.

9

Visitors and Schemers

James's Sydney superiors were uncertain about the Declaration's exact status in New Zealand, unconvinced of its legality, and unenthusiastic about its prospects. It received a mixture of condemnation and heavily qualified acknowledgement from colonial officials, but never outright endorsement. Internationally, the response was limited to a few brief formal pronouncements, in keeping with the low priority New Zealand was generally afforded by most other countries. France later acknowledged the Declaration as one of a series of acts that confirmed Britain had not sought to establish sovereignty over New Zealand prior to 1838,[1] and the United States Senate Committee on Foreign Relations belatedly recorded that the confederation was 'a convention of chieftains who declared their independence . . . and who also declared that . . . all sovereign power and authority was vested exclusively in the hereditary chiefs and heads of tribes collectively'.[2] However, these responses to the Declaration came years later in some instances, and were no advantage to James's claims of the agreement's central importance to New Zealand in 1835.

In a letter to Bourke written a week after the Declaration's signing, James expanded on his thoughts about how the provisions of the agreement would be enacted. This moment should have felt like the crowning achievement of his Residency to this point, and the fulfilment of his long-held desire for status, but James's mood seemed to have been dampened, primarily because his grand scheme was being hobbled by a lack of funds. The authorities in Sydney would not pay for the planned parliament building for the chiefs, and he had so little money of his own that he was forced to admit

---

[1] B. Kingsbury, 'The Treaty of Waitangi: Some International Law Aspects', in *Waitangi: Maori and Pakeha Perspectives of the Treaty of Waitangi*, ed. I. H. Kawharu (Auckland: Oxford University Press, 1989), 123–4.
[2] *Compilation of the Reports of the Committee on Foreign Relations, United States Senate, 1789–1901*, First Congress, first session to Fifty-Sixth Congress, second session (Washington, DC: United States Senate, 1901), 11.

to Bourke that 'I am destitute of the most necessary accommodation for my own family'.[3]

It was just a week since the Declaration had been signed, but already a hint of pessimism was detectable. It was as though James felt that his attempts to embroider the chiefs of the region into a single fabric of government was already unravelling. He was sensitive enough to local circumstances to realize that his lofty vision for the confederation would not materialize in the short term in the manner he had wished. And perhaps, in some corner of his mind, that was his intention all along. The Declaration had deterred De Thierry (or so he believed), and had given him the upper hand over McDonnell; unencumbered by these two threats, James's position was consolidated accordingly. This may be too cynical an assessment, but it is worth noting that even at the time the Declaration was being drafted, James's faith in the process of assembling chiefs in order to rely on their collective authority had already begun to taper off, and in his remaining five years as Resident, such gatherings were seldom held, poorly attended when they were convened, and operated only informally.

At the end of November 1835, James launched a fresh attack on the Additional Resident, which, in addition to revealing that his animosity towards McDonnell remained undiminished, was an inadvertent concession that the Confederation of Chiefs was not regarded by the Resident as really exercising the sort of sovereign authority that the Declaration asserted it possessed. If the Confederation was indeed what it was asserted to be on paper, then McDonnell's role would have been redundant, and his power eviscerated. This was not the case, though. McDonnell still had Bourke's support, and as long as the New South Wales Governor could use the Hokianga shipbuilder as someone to play off against the Resident from time to time, he served his purpose.

James denounced the Additional Resident as 'unfit for employment' in a letter to MacLeay on 30 November. He cited an inherent conflict of interest in McDonnell's role, pointing out that the Additional Resident was 'accredited as a Political Functionary to the very individuals with whom he is liable to come into collision in matters of Trade'. Added to this was a question hanging over the propriety of a major land purchase McDonnell had made, and the general impression James had that McDonnell's role was 'inconsistent with the honour of the Government'. Underlying these concerns was a much more serious one for James. He maintained that McDonnell's continued exercise of the functions of an Additional Resident was 'unnecessary', and 'likely to counteract in a very important degree my influence and usefulness'.[4] It was

---

[3] J. Busby to R. Bourke, 6 November 1835, in *BFR* 2, 594.
[4] J. Busby to A. MacLeay, 30 November 1835, in *BFR* 2, 595–6.

now a month since the Declaration had been concluded, and it had done nothing to elevate James's authority to the point where he was no longer troubled by McDonnell.

If the Declaration was insufficient for the Resident to overcome McDonnell's influence, would it be any more effective against De Thierry? For a short while, James thought he might have to confront that question. On 2 December, a breathless runner emerged from the scrub-lined path that led to the track that linked the Bay of Islands to Hokianga. He carried a message from McDonnell, alerting the Resident to intelligence about a ship that had been sighted, and which was suspected to be De Thierry and his party, ready to assert the Baron's 'sovereignty'. It turned out to be a false alarm, though, and so one purpose of the Declaration – to deter De Thierry – remain untested.

In the meantime, the sense of political ascendancy that McDonnell felt he had been experiencing, courtesy almost entirely of the encouragement he had received from Bourke, took another step forward. In December 1835, James was at home in Waitangi when a letter from McDonnell arrived, dated the fourth of the month. The Additional Resident had found himself confronting an episode of lawlessness, and – exaggerating probably more for effect than from trepidation – McDonnell explained how it was his 'melancholy duty' to inform James of 'one of the most inhuman and aggravated murders that ever disgraced the annals of crime'.

It turned out that Gibson Bragg, the captain and owner of the schooner *Industry*, had been killed by members of his crew while en route from Launceston to Hokianga around ten days earlier. The four alleged perpetrators of the murder were being held in custody by McDonnell, who described them (in keeping with his penchant for hyperbole) as 'as desperate a gang as ever were let loose on mankind'. The Additional Resident arranged some sort of trial and pointedly told James that he needed no assistance from him because he had the situation entirely under control. And to top off this absurd narrative, McDonnell announced, 'I have . . . fearlessly put down the turbulence and seditions and prevented the commission of a crime by decisive measures.'[5]

To Bourke, his patron, McDonnell revealed his other, even more treacherous face. Having rehearsed his status as some sort of hero for apprehending the suspected murderers, he informed the Governor how the Resident had treated him unjustly, and that his brave actions should have elicited praise rather than incited envy from James.[6] Then, at his duplicitous best, McDonnell thrust the knife as deeply as he was capable into James's back:

---

[5] T. McDonnell to J. Busby, 4 December 1835, in *BFR* 2, 598–9.
[6] T. McDonnell to R. Bourke, 4 December 1835, in *BFR* 2, 599.

I only wish that Mr Busby instead of attempting to deprecate my authority here and throw it into contempt among the Natives Chiefs and Europeans (which I am happy to state he is powerless to accomplish) that he would be a little more practical in his own measures . . . I have given him my unqualified support and assistance and shall continue to do so.[7]

However, not only did McDonnell's foray into the realm of judicial power fail to win the direct endorsement of Bourke, it also fell foul of Tasmanian authorities. When those apprehended for the murder were finally put on trial, the report on McDonnell's involvement was stinging:

A '*Mr McDonnell*', who signs himself '*additional British Resident of New Zealand*', seems to have taken upon himself extraordinary authority in this matter. He not only took examinations, on oath, with all the accompanying forms of a British Magistrate, *which he is not*, and the affectation of his '*additional British Resident*' is another specimen of 'pre-eminent humbug'.[8]

McDonnell had more schemes up his sleeve, though, to undermine the Resident. On Christmas Eve 1835, he announced that he had formed a committee of chiefs, presumably mimicking James's Confederation of Chiefs. This committee had been convened by the Additional Resident to conduct a 'trial' over what he saw as a 'disgusting' matter. The suspect in this hearing was the Wesleyan missionary William White. White and McDonnell had long been at odds with each other as the missionary had tended to side with local Māori, who were rightly worried that some timber-traders (including McDonnell) were endeavouring to wrestle their land from them.[9] White suddenly found himself accused of 'an attempt to commit rape', with McDonnell clearly relishing the chance to inform James of '[t]he shameless conduct of this human brute, who under the cloak of religion, gloated his propensities by wrecking more effectually the soul he was sent to save'.[10] White's guilt or innocence over the alleged sexual misconduct was never clearly established, either in McDonnell's dubious trial or in the later investigation conducted by his parent missionary body. However, this episode yet again plainly exhibited McDonnell's preparedness and ability to exercise his will in defiance of the Resident and the provisions of his Declaration.

---

[7] Ibid.
[8] *The Tasmanian*, 8 January 1836, 7.
[9] A. Wanhalla, 'The "Bickerings" of the "Mangungu Brethren"', 14. Details of the White 'trial' are contained in 'General Report of a Committee appointed by the Conference of 1837 to Examine Charges Alleged against the Rev. William White', 26 February 1838 to 8 March 1838, Wesleyan Society Minutes, 1821–67, qMS-2179, ATL.
[10] T. McDonnell to J. Busby, 24 December 1835, in *BFR* 2, 600.

On the personal front, James was pleased to be able to inform Alexander that he had heard from their older brother, George, after more than a year's silence. The reason for such a long interval during which there was no correspondence between James and George was that the latter had got into some serious financial difficulty with a bank, and was almost ashamed of letting the family know. As soon as he discovered this, James sent his brother detailed instructions on how to manage George's debts and deal with the bank.[11] The irony was not lost on James, though, that while he was dispensing advice on remaining solvent to George, his own financial situation was far from bright. After reconciling his various accounts, and including his salary, he calculated that he was in debt by £400. 'It is really frightful to contemplate it,' was his summary of his circumstances. He had been forced to sell one of his horses to a local missionary, and was still trying to pay off debts extending back to his time in Scotland. His house remained unfinished, and his young family was having to do without certain basics in order that they not fall further into debt. Yet James seemed confident about his future. He had plans in the longer term to add to his number of livestock,[12] and in late December, he received a remarkably contrite letter from McDonnell. For the first time, the Additional Resident was sending correspondence to James, and asking the Resident to forward it on to Sydney. He was also much more conciliatory in tone, as though McDonnell was seeking to regain James's goodwill.[13] Whether this was a genuine shift in sentiment or more subterfuge, James had no way of knowing, and so he continued to maintain a distant professionalism when responding to the Additional Resident.

On 21 December *HMS Beagle*, captained by Robert FitzRoy, dropped anchor in the Bay of Islands. FitzRoy was enthused with the location. Paihia was a 'pretty spot', and the harbour was in 'an amphitheatre of verdant hills'.[14] The Captain went ashore with his passenger, the naturalist Charles Darwin, and spent a few hours at James's house, which an unimpressed FitzRoy dismissed as being '[l]ike most of the missionary dwellings . . . a temporary boarded cottage, intended only for present purposes'.[15] After meeting James, FitzRoy described the Resident as an 'isolated individual . . . encircled by savages, and by a most troublesome class of his own countrymen'.[16]

When it came to the recently minted Declaration of Independence, FitzRoy observed that '[m]uch had been done by words on paper', but 'the efficiency

---

[11] Ibid., 603.
[12] Ibid.
[13] Ibid., 604.
[14] FitzRoy, *Narrative of the Surveying Voyages of His Majesty's Ships Adventure and Beagle*, 575.
[15] Ibid., 576.
[16] Ibid.

of their authority, "in a collective capacity", was yet to be discovered. No "executive" had been organized; the former authorities – each a chief in his own territory – hesitated to act as they had been accustomed, owing to a vague mystification of ideas, and uncertainty as to what they had really agreed upon.' And about James himself, the captain was brutally frank: 'the authority of Mr Busby was absolutely nothing, not even that of a magistrate among his own countrymen; so of course he could have no power over the natives'. Even as an arbiter of local disputes among 'so mixed and turbulent a population', the Resident was deemed to be ineffectual.[17]

It is telling that a visitor to the area for a few days, unversed in local politics, unfamiliar with the history of the relationship between the Resident and his New South Wales superiors, and unaware of the nature of Māori politics or society, was able to come to such an accurate conclusion on the deficiencies of the Declaration and its author. One reason for FitzRoy's keen appreciation of the situation on the ground in New Zealand is that during his brief stay, he received a stream of complainants from Māori and settlers, each of whom had a particular grievance they wanted settled. They assumed that FitzRoy, being a naval captain, would have the requisite authority to assist them. He referred all of these complaints to the Resident, and stated that his involvement would be limited to supporting whatever decisions James made. However, he found the Resident 'unwilling to take any steps of an active kind, not deeming himself authorised to do so'. This did nothing to placate the aggrieved parties, and obliged FitzRoy to refer them 'to the only real, though not nominal, authority, in the place, that of the missionaries'.

FitzRoy sensed (as had others previously) that the fault in most of the grievances between Māori and settlers lay with the latter. He was so affected by what he witnessed in the Bay of Islands that he argued that a proper British authority in the country – one that was armed – was required, 'with a definite degree of control over the licentious, or ill-disposed portion of their own countrymen, who, in those remote regions, are disproportionably numerous, and now able to do pretty much what they please'.[18] And as a result of the Resident refusing to intervene in disputes, FitzRoy observed that 'disorder, with "club-law", was prevailing and likely to continue'.[19] If FitzRoy's passing record of the Residency is anything to go by (and his authority and accuracy were highly regarded),[20] then James's Residency was barely functional.

---

[17] Ibid., 590.
[18] Ibid., 590–1.
[19] Ibid., 592.
[20] P. Moon, *FitzRoy: Governor in Crisis, 1843–1845* (Auckland: David Ling, 2000), 52–3; *Proceedings of the Royal Society of London, 11 January 1866–23 May 1867* (London: Royal Society, 1867), 23.

For the twenty-six-year-old Darwin, politics was less of an interest. On 23 December, he travelled with James up the Waitangi River towards Waimate North. A few Māori accompanied the party, with Darwin observing that they were on very good terms with the Resident. Darwin was optimistic that under the Resident's guidance, 'the moral state of the people will rapidly improve'. However, as the *Beagle* departed the Bay of Islands, he also reflected on the general condition of the country, which seemed to militate against this earlier optimism; he depicted New Zealand as 'not a pleasant place', principally because it was populated by Māori who lacked the 'charming simplicity' of their Polynesian counterparts in Tahiti, and settlers who were 'the very refuse of society'.[21]

As a parting gesture, James gave Darwin a letter of introduction to his long-standing friend in Sydney, Alexander Berry.[22] The Resident had been gratified to have someone outside the claustrophobic community of settlers in the Bay of Islands to talk with, but although James's letter of introduction for Darwin was a courteous gesture, the Resident did not seem to have warmed to the naturalist. About a fortnight after Darwin's visit, John Busby jnr mentioned in a letter to George that James had 'found Mr Darwin very difficult to talk to, and that he seemed more interested in the shrubs and trees than in the future of New Zealand'. Knowing his brother's personality, John added 'how James must have bored him!' There were other occasional glimpses of this encounter that flicker from the letter. Agnes liked Darwin because he engaged with her son – with the naturalist playing 'tag with the best of them' at a children's party organized by local missionaries.[23]

After a lull of a few months, the Australian press had returned to publishing hostile assessments of the Residency. De Thierry's plans for New Zealand (following on from his scheme to build a canal in Panama) were an easy target to ridicule. In January 1836, a journalist writing for the *Australian* mockingly noted that this was the person 'who is now threatening to dispute the sovereignty of New Zealand with King Busby'.[24] Both men allegedly had their absurd pretentiousness in common, and the newspaper relished exaggerating these for the amusement of its readers. The same month, the *Sydney Gazette* addressed De Thierry's aborted plan to establish a settlement on the land he had purchased back in 1820. 'New Zealand is likely to be the theatre of a curious contest for supremacy, between Mr Resident Busby, and a white man, calling

---

[21] C. Darwin, *Journal of Researches into the Geology and Natural History of the Various Countries Visited by HMS Beagle* (London: Henry Colburn, 1839), 502–3; 512–16.
[22] J. Busby to A. Berry, 29 December 1835, in *The Correspondence of Charles Darwin. Vol 18* (Cambridge: Cambridge University Press, 2010), 327–8.
[23] J. Busby to G. Busby, 15 January 1836, in *BFR* 2, 628–9.
[24] *The Australian*, 15 January 1836, 2.

himself "the King". Some hungry natives, it is thought, will end the matter by eating both!'[25] The *Tasmanian* portrayed the Declaration of Independence and its author as an example of 'more humbug', and rubbished its significance: 'Mr Busby calling himself *"British Resident"* at the Court of the *"Sovereign Chief"* of New Zealand, has published a manifesto calling upon the chief to resist His Majesty, Baron de Thierry.'[26] Despite misunderstanding the nature of the Confederation that the Declaration nominally established, such articles nonetheless reduced James's credibility, and raised questions about the seriousness of the impending encounter between him and De Thierry. These men appeared as two caricatures of hopelessness – petty officials at the extremities of their respective empires, dreaming of a power and status they would never attain – a fact apparent to everyone except themselves. This perception of the state of affairs in New Zealand resembling a farce might have been mildly entertaining to the Australian public, but it had a corrosive effect on the reputation of the Residency. If James's role could be held up for such sustained popular ridicule, there was little incentive for the Governor to stick his neck out to support the Resident.

At the same time, James was having to contend with the damaging consequences of McDonnell's latest rapacious scheme – one that threatened to engulf parts of Northland in war. It had started with Henry Williams warning off two speculators (who were apparently backed by McDonnell) from proceeding with the purchase of a section of land south of Hokianga that Williams claimed had been promised to the mission by its Māori owners. Most likely, McDonnell had anticipated what he saw as missionary meddling, and had enlisted the support of the Ngapuhi chief Waikato to support the claim of the speculators. Waikato declared that he was one of the owners of the land in question, and with the prospect of a lucrative payment if the sale went ahead, he was perturbed by what he saw as Williams's interference in the proposed transaction. He wrote to the Resident, claiming ownership of the land on the basis of a whakapapa (genealogical) connection to it. He then warned James that 'it is my full determination never to give up on my claim to my own lawful property but with the loss of my life and that of my family'.[27] It was a chilling ultimatum. Here was a chief threatening to defend to the death his right to sell land he claimed was his. Had it been almost anyone else opposing the sale other than Williams, the Resident would probably have sided with Waikato. However, Williams's reputation and judgement in such matters were unimpeachable, and this created a dilemma for James.

---

[25] *SGNSWA*, 9 January 1836, 2.
[26] *The Tasmanian*, 8 January 1836, 7.
[27] Waikato, in *BFR* 2, 631.

McDonnell hoped that the purchase would proceed so that he would have an additional supply of timber for his business. To advance the sale, he wrote to Titore and Tareha, calling on both chiefs to support it.[28] The Additional Resident knew that passions would be inflamed by his letters, and within a week, tension was beginning to spread through the entire region. The insults, battered pride, and questions over ancestral rights to land were adding up to the possibility of armed conflict – so much so that James now regarded the situation to be grave. For the Resident, the one faint silver lining to this darkening cloud was that here, at least, was an indisputable justification for having some force put at his disposal. The protection of settlers and Māori could 'no longer be deferred', as he insisted to MacLeay.[29]

James was determined to disentangle the conflicting Māori claims of ownership to the disputed land as a means of forestalling a potential conflict. He travelled to the site and spent hours discussing the ancestry of various descendants, and through this process, determined that Waikato's claim to the land in question was trumped by others with closer ancestral ties to it. With this information, the Resident convened a meeting with the affected parties on 12 January 1836, where he hoped the dispute could be given a good airing and then be resolved amicably rather than aggressively.[30]

It must have made perfect sense to James: bringing the two opposing groups together to resolve the dispute. But in getting each side to evoke ancestors and histories as the basis for their claims, the Resident was entering dangerous territory. This was never going to be simply a matter of comparing lineages in order to determine outright ownership. James may have been adhering to the principles of intestacy as he understood they applied in Britain, but for Māori, affiliation was no mere case of calculating property rights.[31] In opening up issues of tribal belonging, and prodding around for his proof, James risked exposing cultural sensitivities that could easily result in conflict.

Unexpectedly for the Resident – who had hoped for the meeting to resolve the dispute – insults began to be traded between the two main rival Māori claimants to the land. James intervened in this increasingly heated discussion in an effort to bring talks back to the topic, but it was no use. The exchanges were getting 'very angry and abusive'. One elderly Māori, exasperated with the course that the meeting was taking, approached Waikato's party and asked if any of them could name an ancestor of theirs who was closely associated to the disputed territory. As he was finishing his challenge, one

---

[28] T. McDonnell to Titore and Tareha, 11 January 1836, in *BFR* 2, 632.
[29] J. Busby to A. MacLeay, 18 January 1836, in *BFR* 2, 633.
[30] Ibid., 634.
[31] T. Kingi, 'Maori Landownership and Land Management in New Zealand', *Making Land Work* 2 (2008): 132–5.

of Waikato's men stood up and pushed the elderly opponent back to his own group.

From here, the meeting went from disorderly to dangerous. Waikato's party, which appeared to have come unarmed, sprang to their feet as the pushing and shoving began, and rushed off a short distance to where they had hidden their weapons. Sensing what was happening, the opposing group ran to try to prevent them retrieving their guns, but were unsuccessful, and within moments, shots were being fired by Waikato's men as they charged towards their enemy. 'In an instant my house and kitchen were filled with Noa's party and the floors were covered with the blood of the wounded men who were also carried in,' James recalled. The situation was fast descending into a potential massacre, and drastic measures were needed to try to wrestle some control of the situation. The Resident and a few others took desperate action to halt the bloodshed:

> Mr Baker, one of the Missionaries, Mr Mair and myself, kept back the most forward of Waikato's party from advancing from the position they had taken up to one from which they could fire upon those who had not been able to crowd into the house. In this we were at last assisted by Waikato himself, to whom I called out by name that this outrage was against the King of England, and would be so considered.[32]

As James was yelling out to the assailants in a frantic attempt to stop them from firing on his house, William Williams was frantically trying to keep those Māori in the Resident's house who were armed from rushing outside to engage the attackers. Williams's decision was a turning point. The aggressors sensed a stalemate was approaching, and not wishing to remain on the exposed area of land around James's house in case reinforcements for the Resident from other hapū arrived, they abandoned their assault and left, taking their injured with them.

The damage done by this encounter was not confined to relations between the parties in the dispute. Other Māori in the region could be forced to choose sides if the conflict spread, the Resident's authority had been ravaged in the eyes of just about everyone, and the idea of a coalition of chiefs legislating for the collective good of the country was in tatters. Those Māori who had attended James's meeting in good faith now demanded justice for being attacked, but the Resident's response was a hollow one. All James could say was that he would delay any decision about how he would respond until the King determined 'whether justice should be done by his [the King's]

---

[32] J. Busby to A. MacLeay, 18 January 1836, in *BFR* 2, 634.

Government, or by the Government of this country [New Zealand] alone'. Once this jurisdictional issue was resolved, James promised to assemble the Confederation of Chiefs 'to see justice administered'. It was no use, though. The chiefs made it clear to James that they would no longer attend any meetings he convened at his house. There was no Confederation left as far as they were concerned.[33]

In the days that followed this catastrophe, small groups of Māori approached the Resident. Each was armed, and spoke not of cooperation or even of reconciliation, but of retribution. James now realized that Waikato and his party had attended the meeting at the Residency with just one purpose in mind. They had 'made deliberate preparations for the attack which took place'. The quandary that the Resident now faced was how to deal with an offence on this scale. Almost by instinct, he was guided more by high-minded principles of justice than pragmatism:

> this insult upon the British Government should be taken up as a national question, and the Tribe from which it proceeded should be thoroughly humbled, and the persons who fired the shots which took effect brought to that punishment which is authorised by the laws of God and man for the crime of murder.[34]

Bringing the perpetrators to some sort of justice was a nearly impossible expectation. James hoped that the Confederation would wield some influence in the matter, but in the same breath acknowledged that its authority only existed in theory. The Resident had to concede to the government in Sydney that there was a real risk of both groups of Māori involved in the fracas calling on allies to boost their numbers and seeking revenge.[35]

For James, this was the same technique he had deployed almost since the time he set foot in New Zealand: make a claim that some sort of calamity was imminent, and press for military involvement as the only antidote. However, with each effort to pressure the New South Wales government in this way, James's reputation slid down further in the view of his superiors. Not only had all his previous warnings of dire consequences failed to materialize as he had prophesied, but on every occasion that he had pleaded for support, he had not received any.

Precisely because he believed that if he conveyed a sense of crisis to his superiors frequently enough, they would eventually supply him with some

---

[33] Ibid., 635.
[34] Ibid., 636.
[35] Ibid.

measure of enforcement, James was increasingly falling into the habit of omitting any mention of his successes. To do otherwise would risk creating the impression that circumstances were not so close to the brink of chaos as he made them out to be. For example, the day after the confrontation at the Residency, James walked to Paihia. Although he did not put this episode in his report to his superiors in Sydney, it reveals how he was able to deal with challenges in the absence of any force backing him up. A group of Māori from Kawakawa had congregated in the missionary settlement, seemingly intent on retribution for the fighting that had broken out the previous day. As James approached them, they huddled together in formation, and performed a vigorous haka. The Resident stood his ground, and when they had finished, he walked up to the warriors and talked with them, quelling their passions in the process. In the words of the family's oral history of this event, '[h]is manner more than his words quietened them'.[36] Yet instead of trumpeting his triumphs, he increasingly played the role of an official with great potential, but one constantly undermined by the lack of any means of achieving this potential.

The security situation in the region was complicated on this occasion by the convoluted loyalties of local Māori. Allegiances and divisions among tribes occurred along traditional lines, but could also be cut in another way, depending on their affiliation or opposition to local missionaries. As the issue of loyalties was becoming more knotted – with each party trying to assess how it would gain from particular combinations of alliances – the Resident again used the heightened state of regional tensions to call for assistance, but this time with the added point about the fate of the Confederation: 'were I to call a meeting of the Chiefs it is probable that most of them who are disposed to peace would decline to attend; and that amongst those who should be present the agitation of the question for which they were brought together, would lead to a repetition of the late outrage upon a more extended scale.' This was another example of James highlighting a failure of his own policy with the aim of securing more support from Sydney. He thus suggested at the end of this assessment of the tense situation in the Bay of Islands that '[t]he question . . . of British interference, can no longer be deferred, and the cause of humanity ignored'.[37]

James had now raised the stakes. He was exposing the collapse of his flagship policy – the Confederation of Chiefs – for the sake of pressing for military support. And it was a riskier policy than he may have realized. Not only was he repeatedly drawing attention to the failure of his ideas, but he was also reminding colonial officials in Sydney and London that it was he who was

---

[36] Busby family history, in *BFR* 2, 637.
[37] J. Busby to A. MacLeay, 26 January 1836, in *BFR* 2, 638.

presiding over a security crisis in New Zealand – one that directly threatened British interests in the country. The other flank that James had to protect was that involving his relationship with the Additional Resident. One of the unintended consequences of so many chiefs converging in the Bay of Islands was that some of the correspondence McDonnell had sent to various potential Māori allies ended up in James's hands. When the Resident read McDonnell's letters to Titore and Tareha,[38] he was indignant and wrote at once to his off-sider, lecturing him on the history of inter-tribal wars in Northland, and then accusing him of having allowed himself to be misled over the land ownership dispute that was at the root of the conflict.[39] McDonnell backed down, and James was subsequently able to place this correspondence before Bourke as a means of vindicating his stance.

On the back of these events, later in February 1836 James specified what sort of assistance he expected from Sydney. A hundred British troops would be an absolute minimum, he estimated, and they would have to have access to rockets and heavy artillery. However, such a request did not even enter into the realms of possibility as far as any of his superiors were concerned; this reveals the extent to which James continually overestimated the preparedness of colonial officials to acquiesce to his demands.

Still, though, he persisted with his vain attempts at lobbying the New South Wales government. The following month, he sent another dispatch to MacLeay, emphasizing that 'the opinion of the Missionaries coincides with my own as to the precarious state of the country, and the hopelessness of effecting any improvement under the present system'. He endeavoured to add weight to these concerns by claiming that the missionaries were preparing a petition to send to the British government, demanding that 'a British Force should be employed for the maintenance of peace and good order'.[40] This was little more than a variation of his previous theme of issuing vague warnings or expressing deep concerns over the state of affairs in New Zealand, and met with the same dismissals from Sydney.

James was going further now, though. He was seeking Bourke's permission to travel to London to address the issue of financing a force in New Zealand to support the Residency. In his absence, James proposed that his brother, Alexander, would serve as acting Resident in New Zealand (or failing that, some of the local missionaries could move into his house at Waitangi so that the authority of the Residency could continue to be upheld).[41] In the meantime,

---

[38] Tareha was another powerful regional chief. K. Shawcross, 'Review of Narrative of a Residence in New Zealand: Journal of a Residence in Tristan da Cunha', *JPS* 76, no. 2 (June 1967): 237.
[39] J. Busby to T. McDonnell, 9 February 1836, in *BFR* 2, 640.
[40] J. Busby to A. MacLeay, March 1836, in *BFR* 2, 648.
[41] Ibid., 648.

Agnes and the children had left New Zealand for the safety of New South Wales – a sure sign that he was not merely posturing in his claims about the mounting danger in the country.

James had some reason to feel confident about this plan. Even though it would be circumventing Bourke's authority to some extent, and even though an absence from New Zealand might expose how little would change if the country was without a Resident, this was nonetheless a tested technique for him. He had secured the Residency in the first place exactly by going over the heads of his superiors in Sydney, and dealing directly with senior politicians and colonial officials in London. He was also coming to terms with the fact that he had pushed Bourke as much as he could to change his stance on providing some means of enforcement for the Residency, and the Governor would not be budged any more.

Bourke saw the hostilities as 'not . . . unexpected', and not of a sufficient magnitude or threat to British interests in the country to induce him to alter the existing policy on New Zealand in any way,[42] but the support of local missionaries at this crucial juncture gave James extra reason to feel hopeful in the course of action he was planning to take. It was rare for missionaries to descend into politics, but on 13 May, a letter signed by most of the senior missionaries in the region stressed that they could see 'no prospect of an improvement under the present system on account of the inefficiency of power possessed by the British Resident' to deal both with the lawlessness of some British subjects, and those 'evilly disposed Natives who are frequently stirred up by them to acts of violence'.[43]

Around May 1836, James composed a long letter to Alexander, which ranged across politics, family matters, finances, and the future. It is the best extant source on how the Resident saw his position in the wake of the Declaration. He believed that Bourke was looking for any pretext to dismiss him as Resident, and that he was prepared to challenge the Governor 'at the very highest authority known to the Constitution'. James also was convinced of his own superiority in the art of politics. Having received a 'wantonly insulting' dispatch from the Governor, he proudly boasted to Alexander, 'I have so completely foiled him on every point that I can easily conceive the difficulty he must feel in expressing his spleen'. James may well have won on points in this exchange, but this triumphalism indicates that his understanding of the nature of politics was confined to a narrow notion of trumping an opponent's arguments.

In this letter, James also told Alexander of his plans to go to London, and in his absence, suggested that Alexander serve as acting Resident for around a

---

[42] R. Bourke to J. Busby, 23 March 1836, in *BFR* 2, 649.
[43] Cited in *BFR* 2, 649.

year, which he commented would be 'a very gentlemanly way for you to pass your time'. It was a sardonic line, especially given the extent to which James had discussed the intractable problems of the Residency with his brother. However, James was adamant that he had to travel to England,[44] even though had no plan for what to do if Bourke did not grant him permission.

It would be at least a month before James could expect a reply from Sydney, and in the meantime he decided to explore some of the country beyond the Bay of Islands – presumably something that as Resident to New Zealand he ought to have done at some time in the preceding three years. The main sources outlining the journey are a family history and correspondence between James's siblings. The route of the journey was determined by terrain, weather, areas of interest to the Resident, and the assistance that missionaries could offer him in certain locations. It was unusual for settlers to make long expeditions, and especially so during winter, but circumstances had opened up the opportunity for James, and he was not to be deterred.

James's expedition was across land, primarily because of the unavailability of any vessels that could have transported him to some of the destinations more conveniently. He and his party commenced the journey on horseback, travelling south for around eighty kilometres to Whangarei, and from there, another sixty kilometres southwest to Kaipara. Struck with the prestige and perhaps the novelty of a visiting representative of the British Empire, for the next leg of the route, the Resident was accompanied by an entourage of thirty men from a hapū in Kaipara, which travelled with him to Onehunga – a distance of about 180 kilometres.

From Onehunga, which four years later would become part of the settlement known as Auckland, but which at this time was still sparsely populated by the local iwi – Ngati Whatua – James and his party undertook another lengthy trek. They headed 110 kilometres southeast to Thames, then through Tauranga to Maketu – a journey of a further 150 kilometres. From Maketu, it was a relatively short passage of fifty-five kilometres to Rotorua, where James met with the missionary Thomas Chapman, who had established a mission at Te Koutu the previous year.[45]

Again, the Resident's presence was a source of prestige for his host community. On the next leg, James was accompanied by a contingent of men from the local tribe, Te Arawa[46]. This party trudged through the cold terrain to Lake Taupo, eighty kilometres to the south, and on arrival, was met with

---

[44] Ibid.
[45] A. Matheson, 'Wharekahu C. M. S. Mission Station, Maketu. The Chapmans, 1845–1861,' *Historical Review* 49, no. 1 (2001): 49.
[46] P. Andrews, *No Fear of Rusting: A Biography of the Rev. Thomas Chapman* (Rotorua: Rotorua & District Historical Society, 2001), 84.

an enthusiastic reception. The account of the Taupo visit was handed down through the family, probably because of the cultural contrasts it accentuated:

> During the first night that James slept in a Maori whare in the pah, he was horrified to find that, according to ancient Maori custom, some of the fairest of the Chief's daughters were sent to keep him company. Greatly upset, James told them to go (a fearful insult in Maori eyes) and reluctantly, and very downcast, they left. But when they reappeared in the Maori sleeping 'hall' and told of their failure to please, the Chief, thinking that James had returned them to 'store' as there were too few for his exalted station, promptly sent them back again, plus several more.[47]

It was the sort of hospitality James had no interest in, and even though he risked causing considerable offence in rejecting the offers of 'company', he held his ground, explaining to the chief that 'British gentlemen with one wife already, simply did not do these things'.[48]

The final stage of the expedition was to Wairoa, roughly 200 kilometres east, from where the Resident returned to the Bay of Islands, arriving around 15 June. It had been an exhausting undertaking, and judging by how little he commented in correspondence on what he discovered in the other tribal territories he visited, it was also an unproductive one for James. However, one innovative idea did occur to him during his travels: the need for Britain to conclude a treaty with chiefs throughout the country. James suggested to MacLeay that if he was given permission to travel to London, he was certain he would be given the powers to negotiate such a treaty, which would form 'the basis of a Government capable of maintaining His Majesty's subjects and the Natives in peace and good order, and of affording full protection to lives and property'.[49] A treaty would be a significant departure from existing British policy, and entail considerably more financial and political commitment – of the sort that James had been complaining for years had been lacking. However, it was more a suggestion made in passing than something that the Resident appears to have given any deeper consideration to. He did not resort to one of his lengthy reports to expand on the idea, and neither did he pursue it further in subsequent letters to his superiors.

It was another twist in the McDonnell saga, however, that drew James's attention back to more immediate concerns. In July 1836, the Resident was astonished to discover that McDonnell had convened a form of court in Hokianga, where the missionary William White was on trial for 'loose and

---

[47] Family history of the event in *BFR* 2, 669.
[48] Ibid.
[49] J. Busby to A. MacLeay, 18 June 1836, in *BFR* 2, 671.

immoral conduct'.⁵⁰ While Bourke was indifferent to the whole issue,⁵¹ James viewed it as another incursion on his authority, and his attitude towards McDonnell became even more antagonistic as a consequence. McDonnell's increasingly capricious and unilateral decisions as Additional Resident were threatening to endanger security in the region, and so James resolved to travel there to see what he could do to calm things down.

On the way, however, he was diverted by an unusual circumstance. He met a young Māori who informed him that a special meeting was about to take place, where the rites of 'witchcraft from the American negroes' and 'voodooism' were to be imparted to local Māori. With his Christian sensibilities shaken, James was led through the forest until he came to a clearing. There, he saw around thirty Māori seated in a circle, being instructed by four blacks, who had assembled some sort of altar. There were also a handful of 'undesirable' European sailors present, and it appeared to the Resident that several of the participants in these rites were extremely drunk. Infuriated at this scene, James commanded that the meeting end immediately, and indeed it did, with the Māori present dispersing at once. The Resident's righteous authority brought this heresy to an end, but he later discovered that other similar meetings had been held in the region.⁵²

This episode was striking for the sort of insight it provides into the influence of black Americans on the religious beliefs and rites of some Māori communities, of the type that barely gets mentioned in any other European accounts of the era. It is also unusual because commenting on any aspect of Māori culture was rare for the Resident. His correspondence – both personal and professional – was largely bare of any description of Māori society. He seemed hesitant to probe the culture, preferring instead to assume that it would eventually conform to that of the more upright Britons in New Zealand.

It was only when he discussed this matter with the Wesleyan missionary Nathaniel Turner en route to Hokianga that James was startled by an even more unexpected development: McDonnell had suddenly resigned as Additional Resident.⁵³ The person who most immediately had appeared to James as a threat to his position as Resident was now back to being an ordinary settler, with no official responsibilities. James was once more the sole representative of British interests in the country, and even Bourke, who had seen McDonnell's appointment as potentially tempering some of James's more grandiose visions, appeared relieved at the resignation. In a dispatch to London, the New South Wales Governor depicted McDonnell as someone with a 'sanguine and hasty

---

⁵⁰ Cited in *BFR* 2, 673.
⁵¹ R. Bourke, in *BFR* 2, 674.
⁵² Ibid., 677–8.
⁵³ Ibid., 678.

temperament', and doubted the impartiality of the reports that this 'Assistant' had previously sent.[54]

The Governor's comments about McDonnell were largely an exercise in face-saving, and Bourke's animosity towards James did not abate as a consequence of McDonnell's departure. If anything, it worsened. In early September 1836, the Resident received a blistering letter from Bourke. The Governor condemned James's 'style of language' as 'totally uncalled for and unwarrantable'. And for the benefit of his own superiors, Bourke continued with his castigation: 'It is not for you to state that you cannot act upon your instructions without compromising the honour of the British Government, or that you consider your office in abeyance whilst you remain in receipt of the salary paid to you for discharging its duties.' Bourke accused James of taking 'rash and impudent measures', and on these bases refused the Resident's request to travel to London to lobby for greater support for his role in New Zealand.[55]

Within days of receiving this caustic dispatch from Bourke, a rambling letter arrived from De Thierry. The baron reminded James that New Zealand was not a British possession, and that he still intended to take possession of the 40,000 acres of land he believed he owned in the country.[56] Unlike with similar statements made by De Thierry the previous year, on this occasion James was neither perturbed nor panicked by the possibility of his arrival. The baron's bluster was just that, as far as James was concerned, and besides, the far greater risk to the Residency's future was now coming from Sydney and London. James felt wounded by Bourke's most recent missive. He told his brother that the Governor's assessments showed 'such total want of ordinary discretion and destitution of all moral principles as would disgrace the lowest office under the Government'. This much was an understandable reaction, but what followed was less explicable. James revealed his extraordinary plan to have Bourke fired. He threatened to release to the Colonial Office all the correspondence which the Governor had withheld from London, and in so doing, either embarrass Bourke into a resignation, or force his superiors to recall him.[57]

Not only was the Resident now setting himself on a direct collision course with the Governor, but he was also grossly overestimating the impact this correspondence might have in London. New Zealand was not a British possession, and was barely administered by an under-supported and under-resourced Resident. The reason for this was precisely because the country

---

[54] R. Bourke to Glenelg, 13 September 1837, in *HRA* 1, vol. 19, 90.
[55] R. Bourke to J. Busby, 22 August 1836, in *BFR* 2, 679.
[56] C. De Thierry to J. Busby, 30 August 1836, in *BFR* 2, 679–80.
[57] J. Busby to A. Busby, 9 September 1836, in *BFR* 2, 682–3.

was not a priority for the British government, and had not been since the British learned about its existence almost two centuries earlier. James continued to labour under the related illusions that New Zealand was more important to Britain than was the case, and that as Resident he was accomplishing more than any other individual was capable of.

If James's confidence was wavering at this point, he certainly revealed no signs of it, and a few weeks later, his faith in the rectitude of his stance was shored up by the arrival of a letter from the old family friend and patron, Haddington. The earl was responding to concerns James had expressed to him the previous year, and was able to inform James that he had been in direct communication with the Colonial Office about the New Zealand situation. Glenelg had told Haddington that he had authorized £300 to be spent annually to provide a constable to support the Resident.[58] This was news to James. Although the instruction for this expenditure had been sent to Bourke in October 1835, the Governor had not only failed to act on it but had also concealed it from James. Haddington had anticipated that this might be the case, and noted – correctly – that 'it is just possible' that the Resident had not been informed of this development.[59]

James was indignant at Bourke's duplicity. On the one hand the Governor was critical of the Resident's near-impotence in New Zealand, while on the other he was covertly withholding funds he had been instructed to provide for a constable to support the Resident. It was an act of personal as well as professional subversion as far as James was concerned. He replied to Haddington, referring to the overall state of the relationship between himself and Bourke as a 'struggle' and 'crisis', in which he endured 'persecution' from the Governor. Over several pages, James then provided a potted history of his Residency and the catalogue of challenges he had faced.[60] Having a contact such as Haddington, who had direct access to senior officials in the Colonial Office, was more important for James now than at any previous time.

How worried was James really about losing his job? He was apprehensive at times, and with good reason, given Bourke's hostility towards the Resident. He was also anxious by nature, which could give the impression to others that he was fearful of his tenure being cut short. But sometimes it is the smallest of actions that can disclose the inner workings of a person's mind. In this case, after James had discharged his frustration and anger in his letter to Haddington, he began extending his garden at Waitangi, including building a shed on the perimeter of the property, and planting roses and more grape

---

[58] This authorization was contained in Glenelg to R. Bourke, 28 October 1835, in *HRA* 1, vol. 18, 173.
[59] Haddington to J. Busby, 20 April 1836, MS 46, Auckland Museum Library, 24.
[60] J. Busby to Haddington, 28 October 1836, in 'James Busby Official Letters to Various People', Auckland Museum Library, MS 46, 55–9.

vines.⁶¹ These were not the actions of someone who was anticipating an imminent departure, but rather those of a person who saw a future tied to this specific location. He was much less troubled by Bourke's opinions now, and when writing about his situation to Alexander on 14 November he remarked that overall, his situation 'looks well'.⁶²

Still, though, the underlying problem that bedevilled the Residency remained. A brief visit to New Zealand at the end of 1836 by the British Quaker missionary Daniel Wheeler confirmed what most people knew: that James was 'wholly destitute of power', even though Wheeler regarded the Resident as 'an amiable man, upright in all his dealings with the people, and decidedly desirous of promoting in others that which he conceives to be the duty of man'. The missionary was also aware that being without formal power did not make James's role redundant. On the contrary, he considered that '[m]en of his general character are greatly needed to improve the present state of things as regards the best interests of the natives; while the bad example of licentious foreigners might be checked, and their influence to a considerable extent diminished'.⁶³

In 1837, the House of Commons Select Committee on Aboriginal Tribes on British Settlements reported its findings. It had been convened to consider the measures that should be adopted by the British government in relation to the native inhabitants in countries where British settlements had been established, 'in order to secure to them the due observance of Justice, and the protection of their Rights; to promote the spread of Civilization among them; and to lead them to the peaceful and voluntary reception of the Christian Religion'.⁶⁴ The emphasis of the Committee's report extended beyond indigenous peoples that found themselves part of the Empire, to encompass those who happened to be in the vicinity of British settlements outside the Empire, which included New Zealand. The evidence of various missionary organizations featured prominently in the deliberations, and cast a light on New Zealand's situation that exposed the crevices in which they felt sin had gained a stronghold. The Australian penal settlements were depicted as the source of 'incalculable mischief to this whole quarter of the world', with escaped convicts acting as 'the pests of savage as well as civilized society'. In New Zealand there were estimated to be at least 150 runaway prisoners at any one time, who were 'counteracting all that was done for the moral improvement of the people, and teaching them every vice'.⁶⁵

---

⁶¹ W. Busby to G. Busby, 16 November 1836, in *BFR* 2, 695–6.
⁶² J. Busby to A. Busby, 14 November 1836, in *BFR* 2, 699.
⁶³ D. Wheeler, *Memoirs of the Life and Gospel Labors of the Late Daniel Wheeler: A Minister of the Society of Friends* (Philadelphia, 1850), 474, 480.
⁶⁴ *Report of the Parliamentary Select Committee on Aboriginal Tribes (British Settlements)*, 1.
⁶⁵ Ibid., 16.

The committee had little appetite for the various colonizing schemes that had been touted to establish British communities in parts of the South Pacific, but noted that the alternative in New Zealand's case – a Residency – was ineffectual. Unless a British official had the power to apprehend suspects and put them on trial 'on the spot', there was the risk of 'brigands triumphing', and a 'new race of buccaneers' appearing that would come to dominate the region.[66]

The Committee seemed to be endorsing the very policies that James had been pressing for since his appointment to New Zealand. However, it would be mistaken to see the Report as some sort of boost for his besieged career. On the contrary, the problems of crime and disorder in New Zealand, the challenges of civilizing Māori, and the claim made by the Committee (which was clearly swayed by missionary testimony) that only the missionaries were a force for good in the country cumulatively debilitated the Resident's reputation. After all, if James had presided over the deteriorating situation New Zealand appeared to be in, what good was he?

Like any such undertaking, the Committee's report was only as good as the evidence presented before it. Crucially for James (although obviously not for the members of the Committee) he was not present to testify, and so a major source of information about New Zealand was missing from the findings. The importance of the report lay in the way it helped to forge British policy on New Zealand, which was still slight and vague because the country was not part of the Empire, and so was still not a direct responsibility of the British government.

Closer to home, another twist in colonial politics was threatening to upset the channels of communication that James had relied on. On Boxing Day 1836, MacLeay received notice from the Governor that he was about to be replaced as Colonial Secretary by Edward Deas Thomson, who was Bourke's son-in-law. MacLeay had been opposed to some of the Governor's legislative initiatives, while Bourke had found his Colonial Secretary to be uncooperative on occasion.[67] The relationship had broken down in recent months, and on 3 January 1837, Bourke wrote to Glenelg, confirming the decision.[68]

Six days later, William informed James of this development (in a letter that was taken from Sydney to the Bay of Islands by Agnes, who was finally returning to Waitangi). He described how their father's attempts to get a payment he was entitled to from the colonial government had suddenly become very difficult, no doubt as a consequence of the now-ostracized MacLeay having been an advocate of the Busbys before the Governor.[69] A

---

[66] Ibid., 16, 129, 130.
[67] S. G. Foster, 'A Piece of Sharp Practice? Governor Bourke and the Office of Colonial Secretary in New South Wales', *Australian Historical Studies* 16, no. 64 (1975): 402–24.
[68] R. Bourke to Glenelg, 3 January 1837, in *HRA* 1, vol. 18, 638.
[69] W. Busby to J. Busby, 9 January 1837, in *BFR* 3, 739.

crucial ally in the New South Wales administration was now gone, and the replacement was inevitably going to be more inclined to support the Governor than the Resident and his family.

Another surprise departure followed shortly afterwards, and gave James cause for renewed optimism. On 30 January, Bourke formally tendered his resignation as Governor. He had previously threatened to leave if the Colonial Office did not support his handling of his senior staff (which included the dismissal of MacLeay, the attempted dismissal of another official, and a controversial appointment). London did not offer unequivocal support (more out of habitual caution than from any desire to test the Governor's will), and Bourke resigned as he had promised (although his motives may also have included the possibility that he was growing increasingly disillusioned with the role). However, as was protocol, Bourke was required to continue acting as Governor until a replacement arrived, which was not due until December.[70] James had lost an ally in MacLeay, but within weeks he had also seen his greatest opponent step down. But whatever jubilation the Resident might have felt over Bourke's resignation was soon swamped by a large, close, destabilizing, and deadly threat: full-scale war in Northland.

James first learned of this outbreak of fighting in the region via a message from Samuel Marsden (now aged seventy-one), who had landed at Hokianga on 23 February 1837, in what would be his final visit to New Zealand. The parson immediately found himself in a war zone. Pomare and Titore – two of the most powerful leaders in the pantheon of regional chiefs – were at war with each other. One consequence, Marsden observed, was that 'the whole island was in the greatest commotion'. What made this conflict so dangerous was that both of the chiefs were dragging in supporters from further afield to augment their forces. Marsden and Henry Williams pleaded with the combatants to cease hostilities, but their efforts met with no success at all.

The dangerous complication in this conflict was that some British subjects had become involved. Marsden recorded 131 Europeans in Pomare's pa, and possibly just as many in Titore's. These Britons were 'generally men of the most infamous characters, composed of runaway convicts and sailors, and publicans who have opened grog shops in the *pas*, where every scene of riot and drunkenness and prostitution are carried on daily'.[71] It was only a matter of a few weeks until news of this crisis reached New South Wales, where popular sentiment (if the press was anything to go by) was turning even more firmly against the Resident. 'Every day shows, more imperatively,' wrote the *Colonist*'s editor on 26 January 1837, 'the necessity for some measures to be pursued relative to the protection of British subjects and property at New

---

[70] *Sydney Monitor*, 1 February 1837, p. 2.
[71] S. Marsden, in *The Letters and Journals of Samuel Marsden*, 524.

Zealand'. So inconsequential was James's role now seen to be that he was not even mentioned in the article. It was as though Britain was doing nothing to secure peace and stability in New Zealand: 'Why should such a country as New Zealand, beautiful and fertile beyond praise, be allowed almost to lay waste – a receptacle for crime – a place of refuge for runaway convicts and speculating defaulters? Let the British Government be assured, that if they do not quickly decide upon some line of conduct, there are other nations who will save them the trouble, and deprive them of that territory.'[72]

War in the region, a hostile press in Sydney, and the mysterious motives of the French in New Zealand waters were challenges that James had little chance of influencing. The fact that these 'crises' had converged at one time simply drew attention to the Resident's incapacity to do much more than correspond with his superiors about them. By March 1837, James's predicament was worsening. Around the middle of the month, Polack delivered a letter to Marsden, to pass on to the authorities in Sydney. Late in the evening of 9 March, Polack's house in the Bay of Islands had been attacked by a small mob, which consisted of an escaped convict, a 'pugilist', and a 'grog-seller'. Polack ended up shooting at them. However, he was overpowered, dragged outside, and brutally beaten. The next morning, Polack managed to reach James's house where he pleaded for protection. Yet, according to Polack, the Resident 'refused in any way to interfere', and then chastised him for having fired at the attackers.

Polack was utterly disillusioned. 'Mr Busby who saw the disfigured and disabled state I was in refused even to return with me. As for protection he could give me none.' Feeling abandoned by the Resident, Polack told Marsden that he was 'disgusted at conduct so heartless',[73] and wrote to the New South Wales administration condemning James in the strongest terms. Neither Marsden, nor Henry Williams, who also saw the letter, seemed particularly perturbed by its contents, and James, too, initially brushed off Polack's concerns. The war raging in the Hokianga region was expanding in scale, and dwarfed the concerns of any single settler.

In the weeks that followed, skirmishing between various Māori factions in and around the Bay of Islands increased, and added to the climate of fear among settlers that the region was about to descend into violent anarchy. On 5 May 1837, as the fighting intensified, James wrote a lengthy letter to Alexander, in which he dealt with various aspects of the crisis he found himself in with surgical precision, but without regard for the wider circumstances. He denounced Polack as 'a great knave' who was 'universally detested here', and claimed that the lower sort of settlers in the Bay of Islands regarded the

---

[72] *The Colonist*, 26 January 1837, 3.
[73] J. Polack to S. Marsden, c. 11 March 1837, in *BFR* 3, 750–1.

merchant as being 'as great a rogue as the worst of them'. But Polack was the least of his worries. James's domestic help had abandoned him and his family over the past few months, his father had been publicly humiliated by Bourke in a manner that James outlandishly claimed was 'unprecedented in the annals of public employment', and New Zealand looked to be in 'a state of civil war', with 'armed parties . . . constantly in motion'. James admitted he was helpless in this situation, but also regarded himself as blameless. In an extraordinary act of self-justification, he rounded on the missionaries, alleging to Alexander that they had shown him insufficient respect, and that they were in the habit of resolving disputes without consulting with him first.[74] This was followed by a remarkably candid assessment of their respective powers:

> I came here to assume an authority which they already possessed, but so far from being able to assume a commanding attitude, I was literally thrown upon them for the most necessary assistance in the most trivial affairs. They had the command of whatever means they judged necessary for the effectual performance of their duty . . . while I was not only without an individual upon whom I had a right to call for information, but absolutely destitute often of the means of moving from place to place, to acquire it for myself.[75]

Some of the blame for James's dependence on the missionaries lay with the colonial authorities in Sydney (and to a lesser extent London), who had willingly starved him of the means of enforcing his decisions. On the whole, the missionaries had offered him unwavering support.

Reference was also made in James's letter to the recent petition signed by local settlers and submitted to the British government pleading for some form of military presence in the territory. Although the motives of the petitioners were entirely in accordance with his own, the fact that he had not initiated the appeal meant that he was reluctant to lend his support to it. This was a trait that he had failed to modify, regardless of the circumstances he faced. The rectitude of an idea was nearly always less important than its proposer. In the case of the petition, James was dismissive, assuring his brother that 'all the wits of the Missionaries here were brought into requisition to produce it. I heard that it was such a production as that no person in the Bay of Islands was capable of.'[76] This was a snide reaction to a document that urged precisely the sort of support the Resident himself had been seeking.

---

[74] J. Busby to A. Busby, 5 May 1837, in *The Life of Henry Williams* 3, 760–2.
[75] Ibid., 763.
[76] Ibid., 763–4.

James had more to say shortly after this letter had been sent. On 7 May he wrote to William, and in the intervening forty-eight hours, the Resident's mood had slipped noticeably. 'The war news grows worse; and my news likewise,' he lamented. 'I grow quite disheartened; and were it not for the magnitude of my task, would place myself and my family instead of this letter upon the ship and sail for Sydney . . . It is too distressing to dwell on.' The impossibility of carrying out his role as colonial officials had envisaged it was now perfectly evident to James. However, the make-up of his character precluded the possibility that he might abandon his position or 'his' country. Despite the 'trouble and death and danger' that he told William he was facing, and his observation that it seemed he was 'intended to fail – as no doubt I was in some quarters!', the Resident was determined to show he was made of sterner stuff – that he could be the equal of anyone placed in such circumstances. It was almost as though the more severe the situation, the more defiant and dogged he became. 'I shall not fail ultimately,' he declared boisterously to his brother, 'and I dare say my enemies will be richly confounded.'[77]

It was good fighting talk, but if James was indeed sincere in his triumphalism, it was at the expense of any realistic appraisal of his situation. With the fighting between Titore and Pomare having begun to spread into parts of the Bay of Islands, and with the Resident being excluded from the frantic diplomatic efforts by missionaries at least to contain if not extinguish the hostilities, James was reduced to the role of a spectator. Not only was he without the capacity to impose his will, but the regard he was held in was so low that few people consulted him, and practically no-one now sought him out as an arbiter of disputes. The Confederation of Chiefs, in which James had vested his hopes for the future government of New Zealand, was now recognized in Sydney as a constitutional failure,[78] and in New Zealand it had been abandoned by its constituents. It seemed that the Residency was hanging by the thinnest of threads, and that at any moment James could be recalled. His only saving grace was that the growing British settlements in the country required a British presence to represent them, and it was unlikely that anyone else at this moment would want the role.

---

[77] J. Busby to W. Busby, 7 May 1837, in *BFR* 3, 766.
[78] Bourke regarded it as not even useful convening to circulate information among the chiefs. See Colonial Secretary to J. Busby, 16 May 1837, in *BFR* 3, 768.

10

The Rattlesnake

As the Residency looked to be on the cusp of ruin, circumstances took an unexpected detour. On 26 May 1837, HMS *Rattlesnake* sailed into the Bay of Islands.[1] At the very moment when the future of the main European settlement in New Zealand appeared (to James, at least) to be in imminent danger of being engulfed by the conflagration of large-scale inter-tribal war, here was the most reassuring sight the Resident could have hoped for. As the twenty-eight-gun naval vessel dropped anchor, the immediate future of the country seemed to have pivoted in James's favour. The fighting in the region could now be suppressed (allowing for the missionaries to patch up some form of peace) and the Resident would exercise tangible power for as long as the ship was in the harbour.

However, this was no casual visit. As well as offering British settlers in the Bay of Islands temporary protection, Bourke had instructed the *Rattlesnake*'s captain, William Hobson, to report on the situation in the country, and how the best interests of Māori and settlers might be served.[2] This was a significant shift in British colonial policy on New Zealand. Up until this time, the Resident had been relied on to do the best he could to maintain some sort of order, and if the possibility ever arose, to apprehend escaped convicts or British subjects who had committed a crime in New Zealand and send them to Sydney to face justice. Stability and order among British subjects in the country had been the cornerstone of colonial policy on the country. Now, though, Bourke had augmented this policy, extending the umbrella of protection[3] both to settlers *and* to Māori in New Zealand. The implications of this – constitutionally, legally, militarily, and financially – were momentous, even if they had yet to be fully thought through. Effectively, Bourke was anticipating that the Empire would

---

[1] S. Priestley, 'Charting Some Port Phillip Myths', *Victorian Historical Journal* 87, no. 1 (2016): 163–6.
[2] R. Bourke to Glenelg, 9 September 1837, in *HRA* 1, vol. 19, 84.
[3] Ballantyne, *Entanglements of Empire*, 244.

henceforth be asserting a more formal trusteeship role over New Zealand[4] – one that would encompass the roughly 100,000 Māori as well the 600 or so settlers in the country.

And what would the Resident's role be in this new order? The fact that Hobson had been nominated to report on the prospects for New Zealand amounted to a declaration by Bourke of no confidence in James. If there was a single point from which the decline of the Residency could be traced, this was it. After four years in the country, during which time he furnished his superiors with detailed and usually pragmatic reports on the state of New Zealand, and what was required to maintain order in its main British settlement, James was now being effortlessly brushed aside in favour of a fresh view from an 'outsider'.

As was customary with visiting naval vessels, James went from shore to the *Rattlesnake* to meet its captain and officers. The Resident was accompanied by Marsden and Henry Williams, and in the afternoon, Hobson returned the courtesy by visiting James at Waitangi, before calling in on the missionaries at Paihia. Hobson delivered a letter to the Resident from Thomson (MacLeay's replacement as New South Wales's Colonial Secretary). In it, James was advised not to recommend to Hobson that he interfere in the inter-tribal wars, and that the *Rattlesnake*'s presence was solely to 'offer some appearance at least of protection to the British', while its captain made observations about New Zealand and reported these back to Bourke.[5]

Thomson also confirmed that as Glenelg's draft bill to extend certain powers to officials in territories such as New Zealand had not yet been presented to the House of Commons (and there was now little prospect of his being introduced), an additional £300 would be allocated to the Residency annually to pay for a constable, and for presents 'to conciliate' local chiefs. However, James was expressly barred from 'controlling British Subjects' in the country, and Thomson added that the Resident's future depended on the influence he was able to exercise demonstrably over the chiefs.[6]

Four days after arriving, Hobson travelled to Kerikeri – around eighteen kilometres northwest of Waitangi – with James and the Anglican missionary, the Reverend Alfred Brown.[7] There the captain continued to interview traders, leading Māori, missionaries, and anyone else of note as part of his instructions to observe and report on the state of the country. James soon returned to

---

[4] For the historical basis of this notion of colonial trusteeship, see M. P. Cowan and R. W. Shenton, 'The Invention of Development', in *Power of Development*, ed. J. Crush (London: Psychology Press, 1995), 34; J. Bentham, UCLMC, 1795, box 170, 182; J. S. Mill, *Considerations on Representative Government* (London: Parker, Son & Bourne, 1861), 322.
[5] E. D. Thomson to J. Busby, 16 May 1837, in *BFR* 3, 768.
[6] Ibid., 768–9.
[7] *The Letters and Journals of Samuel Marsden*, 528.

Waitangi while Hobson spent the rest of the following month sailing to various parts of the North Island to build up an impression of New Zealand.

Once back at his desk, James applied his mind to the policy predicament Hobson's visit had posed. The result was a 7,000-word letter to Thomson which James completed on 16 June. It was designed to be more detailed than the report that Hobson had been instructed to write, and would reach the Governor prior to Hobson completing his observations. The Resident's dispatch began with an unnecessarily intricate account of the conflict among Māori in the region, and noted that the presence of the *Rattlesnake* had helped deter the combatants from further fighting. James then conceded that the situation in Northland had deteriorated to the point that neither the £300 being offered for a possible constable to support him, nor the (now remote) prospect of Glenelg's Bill to empower officials such as himself was sufficient any longer to grapple with the challenges the region was facing. 'What is wanted', James made plain, 'is a paramount authority supported by a force adequate to secure the efficiencies of its measures.'[8]

It was Māori, in James's eyes, who were paying a catastrophic price for Britain allowing its settler population in New Zealand to grow without any corresponding regulations. He noted there had been a rapid depopulation among Māori, due to a variety of causes associated with contact with Europeans, and that should the present circumstances continue, New Zealand would be left 'destitute of a single aboriginal inhabitant'. In the wake of this apocalyptic warning, the Resident unfurled his plan which he believed 'would give as great a degree of peace and security to all classes of persons in this country as is enjoyed by the inhabitants of the majority . . . of civilized states', and that would avert the risks of intervention by a foreign power, or leaving 'the Natives to go on destroying each other', with Britain consequently left to deal with the 'accumulating anarchy'.[9] Drawing on the principle of trusteeship that Bourke had recently espoused,[10] James assumed the role of a de facto constitutional lawyer, proposing that Britain's role in New Zealand should be

> Founded upon the principle of a protecting state administering . . . the affairs of another state in trust for its inhabitants as sanctioned by the Treaty

---

[8] Marsden took a slightly different view, suggesting in 1830 that 'it would not be advisable to form at New Zealand a military establishment, as the soldiers would be too much exposed to temptation from the native women: a small armed King's vessel, with proper authority, would be the most likely to prevent much mischief, as she might visit all the harbours into which the European vessels enter'. S. Marsden, 2 August 1830, in *Historical Records of New Zealand* 1, 707–8.
[9] J. Busby to E. D. Thomson, 16 June 1837, in 'James Busby Official Letters to Various People', AML, MS 46, 28–35.
[10] Ballantyne, *Entanglements of Empire*, 244.

of Paris in the case of Great Britain and the Ionian Isles, and as applied, I believe, in several instances on the border of our Indian possessions.[11]

James was rejecting Old World imperial expansion in favour of an idealistic internationalism appropriated from French *philosophes*,[12] in which colonial possessions were temporary states until they were granted independence.

The reference to the Ionian islands related to the 1815 Congress of Vienna, which placed that territory under the amical protection of Britain. The principle was that the islands would be self-governing, democratic, and overseen by a British official who would act as guarantor of the system on behalf of the British government.[13] In New Zealand's case, James proposed that such an arrangement could be achieved via a treaty, and supported by a small garrison of imperial troops. Māori already had a flag which purportedly signified their independence, and had decades of contact with Britons. And according to James, they had also exercised some collective sovereignty in recent years. Considered cumulatively, the chiefs were therefore 'competent to become parties to a Treaty with a Foreign Government, and to avail themselves of Foreign assistance in reducing their country to order'.

The Resident then outlined his thoughts on how power and jurisdiction would be marked out in what would effectively become a British colony. Significantly, though, his cherished Confederation of Chiefs was relegated to a more symbolic role. He conceded that

> the present race of chiefs could not be entrusted with discretion in the adoption or rejection of any measure that might be submitted to them; moral principle, it if exists among them at all, being too weak to withstand the temptation of the slightest personal consideration.[14]

This was a breathtaking reversal in James's attitude towards the chiefs. For years, he had been advocating forcefully for them to act collectively as the sole sovereign authority in the country. Now though, he was effectively announcing that he had lost faith in their capacity and reliability to act in

---

[11] J. Busby to E. D. Thomson, 16 June 1837, in 'James Busby Official Letters to Various People', 28–35.

[12] L. S. Kaplan, 'The Treaty of Paris, 1783: A Historiographical Challenge', *The International History Review* 5, no. 3 (1983): 434.

[13] L. R. Schumacher, 'Greek Expectations: Britain and the Ionian Islands, 1815–1864', in *Imperial Expectations and Realities: El Dorados, Utopias and Dystopias*, ed. A. Varnava (Manchester: Manchester University Press, 2015), 47; H. Wheaton, *Elements of International Law* (London: Carey, Lea and Blanchard, 1916), 52–3.

[14] J. Busby to E. D. Thomson, 16 June 1837, in 'James Busby Official Letters to Various People', 28–35.

concord. On the issue of Māori sovereignty, which he had advocated with vigour until very recently, he had come around to a much more dismissive view. 'There is no dominion anywhere [among the chiefs] to rival that which would call the British Government to its aid,' he wrote. '[N]or is any Chief possessed . . . of any sovereignty or territorial rights in support of which he might induce others to join him in resisting the established power.'[15] As evidence of the need for Britain to exercise some form of trusteeship role over Māori, James cited the Declaration, according to which the King would 'continue to be a parent' to Māori, and 'would become their protector'. This sentiment and the language used, the Resident guilefully claimed, 'were their own', and not his.

In providing such an 'expert' analysis of the state of New Zealand, and a prescription for its future as part of the British Empire, James was angling for a job leading the country after it had been absorbed as one of Britain's colonial 'possessions'. Experience had taught James that the direct approach was the best way to gain a desired position. It was apparent that Bourke was looking for a solution to the increasingly problem-ridden situation in New Zealand, and relied on Hobson offering a fresh pair of eyes when reporting on the possibilities for the country. In response, James made an overt claim to play a central role in New Zealand if British policy was reconfigured.[16]

James's plan for a future government for New Zealand was no hastily assembled set of ideas drafted solely in an effort to counter the report Hobson had been commissioned to write. Rather, it seems the essence of the Resident's proposals had been devised at least a year earlier, and they were to form the basis of a report he planned to present personally to the Colonial Office and British politicians if he had been given permission by Bourke to travel to London.

Bourke could not respond to James's proposals until he had received the report that Hobson had been sent to New Zealand to prepare. This was completed on 8 August 1837, and by comparison to James's effort was meagre in content and originality. Hobson's portrayal of New Zealand overall was cursory, and his assessment of the country's political situation not much better. He noted that there was no collective government by the chiefs, despite the promises of the Declaration, and that if a meeting of chiefs was convened, 'bloodshed' would be the likely outcome. And in a further snub to James's vision for New Zealand, Hobson dryly asked '[h]ow, then, can it be expected that laws will be framed for the dispensation of justice, or the preservation of peace and good order, even if native judgment were sufficiently

---

[15] N. Wolloch, 'The Civilizing Process, Nature, and Stadial Theory', *Eighteenth-Century Studies* 44, no. 2 (2011): 245–59.

[16] J. Busby to E. D. Thomson, 16 June 1837, in 'James Busby Official Letters to Various People', 28–35.

matured, to enact such laws, or to carry them into execution?'[17] This rhetorical question was enough to end any hope of James's Confederation of Chiefs having the support of colonial officials. The Resident had admittedly expressed reservations about how the Confederation would function in the short term, but Hobson was entirely convinced that it was an utterly futile project.

The *Rattlesnake*'s captain recommended a trading-company model for New Zealand, of the sort that had already been replicated in other parts of the Empire. He proposed that factories (more in the vein of operations such as timber-felling than heavy industry) be established in certain locations in the country which had sizeable British settlements. Within these areas, British jurisdiction would apply, with the heads of individual factories serving as magistrates, and the overall managers in each area having the powers of a consul. He further recommended that a treaty be concluded with the relevant chiefs to confirm their recognition of this system.[18]

Hobson's report was unremarkable, lacking in anything innovative, and failed to address many of the more subtle challenges that James had tackled in his dispatch. However, Bourke was favourably disposed to it. He described Hobson's proposals as being 'of great value', and commended them to Glenelg. Bourke was also required to present James's report, which he not only failed to endorse, but dishonestly denounced, alleging that the Resident's suggestions 'would probably be found difficult to reconcile with some of the peculiar circumstances affecting the matter under consideration'.[19]

Bourke's appointment of Hobson to examine the 'difficult question'[20] of New Zealand was set against the backdrop of a shift in the culture, policies, and operations of the Colonial Office. In 1834, James Stephen, the Assistant Under-Secretary of State for the Colonies, had drafted a minute that outlined his view on the construction of colonial governments. He was not at all concerned that they resemble the Westminster model of parliamentary democracy – recognizing that a system of such intricacy, which was dependent on a large bureaucracy, was not often suited to the needs of fledgling colonies. Instead, he emphasized the pragmatic over the idealistic. Colonial administrations, he insisted, 'must be [a] matter of compromise and of adaptation to the particular conditions, character, wants and resources of the place'.[21] In New Zealand's case, the Residency had manifestly fallen short

---

[17] W. Hobson to R. Bourke, 8 August 1837, in *Correspondence with the Secretary of State Relative to New Zealand*, 10.
[18] Ibid., 10–11.
[19] R. Bourke to Glenelg, 9 September 1837, in *Correspondence with the Secretary of State Relative to New Zealand*, 8–9.
[20] Ibid., 8.
[21] J. Stephen to T. Spring-Rice, 30 June 1834, CO 323/50.

of adapting to the particular conditions of the country, and so a revised look at New Zealand's requirements was warranted.

The 'Stephen Doctrine' began to transform from proposition to policy in 1836, when he took over from Spring Rice to become Under-Secretary of State for the Colonies – a post he would hold for the next eleven years. The recommendations contained in Hobson's report were broadly in keeping with Stephen's insistence on accommodating the circumstances of a territory when considering further intervention.[22] Stephen may also have been inclined to support Hobson's proposals because he had developed a distaste for the sort of approach to influencing policies that James had employed. The Resident had previously relied on support from friendly politicians, and unannounced visitations to the Colonial Office, where he held casual discussions with officials about his plans. Stephen insisted that all communications be dealt with through a much more formal process, with full written records maintained of all meetings and decisions, and was disdainful of casual, private, and disordered contact of the sort James had depended on.[23] Stephen was determined that the earlier Colonial Office culture, which was focussed mainly on the broad and vague sweep of colonial policy, would be replaced by an approach that paid much more attention to detail. It would henceforth concern itself with the smallest tart as well as the largest pie, as Dickens partially parodied it.[24]

When Hobson's report (accompanied by Bourke's endorsement of it) reached London, Stephen requested that the Admiralty send its ships to New Zealand 'as frequently as possible' to help secure the safety of the country's inhabitants – both Māori and settler.[25] This was an interim measure while he endeavoured to convince Glenelg to adopt a new policy on New Zealand. The policy Stephen envisaged was still in embryonic form, but it would spell the end of the Residency by appointing a Consul to the country.[26] As for how James would take the news, Glenelg referred to a dispatch he had sent to the Resident in October 1835, in which the possibility of terminating his role had vaguely been alluded to.[27] It was a feeble justification as so many other dispatches had gone between London, Sydney, and the Bay of Islands in the intervening three years without mentioning the possibility of the Residency's

---

[22] J. Stephen, minute, 3 December 1838, CO 209/3
[23] W. E. Williams, 'The Colonial Office in the Thirties', *Australian Historical Studies* 2, no. 7 (1943): 148–9.
[24] C. Dickens, *Little Dorrit* (London: Bradbury and Evans, 1857), 75.
[25] J. Stephen to C. Wood, 15 August 1838, in *Correspondence with the Secretary of State Relative to New Zealand*, 19.
[26] Glenelg to G. Gipps, 1 December 1838, in *Correspondence with the Secretary of State Relative to New Zealand*, 19.
[27] Glenelg to R. Bourke, 28 October 1835, in *HRA* 1, vol. 18, 170–4.

cessation. And since Bourke had only recently granted additional funding to support the Residency,[28] James had more than a reasonable expectation that his role would continue. However, notice that it would be terminated was still more than a year away from reaching him, and so as far as he knew, it was still business as usual in New Zealand.

Except that little was 'usual' in the country's affairs. In August 1837, McDonnell unexpectedly wrote to Bourke, claiming full responsibility for bringing about an end to the tribal wars in the region. From reports he had received from Hobson, James, and various missionaries, Bourke had every reason to know that this claim was unwarranted. However, in order to further his campaign to oust the Resident, he sent a copy of McDonnell's letter to London, feigning the requirement for balance in reporting as the basis for doing so.[29]

Meanwhile, De Thierry was building up political momentum for his venture in New Zealand. He published a verbose explanation of his ambitions for the country in the Sydney press, followed by a series of articles that outlined the nature of the 'state' he hoped to form a soon as he left for New Zealand. Among the main points were his assumption of the role of 'Sovereign Chief' over his territory, with exclusive authority and jurisdiction over all those who lived in it, the equality of the races, a proposed justice system, with juries made up of settlers and Māori, and a monthly meeting of elected representatives of the territory, which would deliberate on matters 'connected with the happiness and prosperity of the community'.[30]

Officially, when it came to De Thierry's claims to sovereignty over parts of New Zealand, Bourke maintained the line that he 'could not recognize him in any manner'. Unofficially, though, the baron proved to be a minor but nevertheless useful additional tool in destabilizing the Residency, and to that end, Bourke made a point of forwarding some of De Thierry's statements to Glenelg. Ostensibly, this was purely for information purposes,[31] but Bourke knew that it would have added to the pressure on the British government at least to review the Resident's role. Even though the New South Wales Governor had already resigned and was just a matter of months from leaving the colony, such was his aversion to James and his position that he was determined to continue undermining him to the very last moment.

There were thus several developments which, depending on how they were assembled by James, could have been interpreted by him as ranging

---

[28] E. D. Thomson to J. Busby, 16 May 1837, in *BFR* 3, 768–9.
[29] R. Burke to Glenelg, 13 September 1837, in *HRA* 1, vol, 19, 90.
[30] These articles were dated 20 September 1837, and were published in Sydney a fortnight later. *The Australian*, 3 October 1837, 4.
[31] R. Burke to Glenelg, 25 October 1837, in *HRA* 1, vol, 19, 133.

from mildly irritating to career-ending. What muddied the waters, as far as he was concerned, was that the news was not universally negative. Without knowing that Bourke had sent De Thierry's ludicrous claims to the Colonial Office, thus giving them some semblance of credibility, James received a message from the duplicitous Governor in which he was reassured that there was not even the slightest degree of support for the baron's colonizing fantasies.[32] It was to be Bourke's final communication with the beleaguered Resident. On 5 October, the Governor's replacement – Sir George Gipps – was appointed (he arrived in Sydney on 23 February 1838). And not seeing any reason to wait for some sort of formal, ceremonial handover, Bourke sailed out Sydney on 5 December 1837.[33] James's nemesis was gone.

Just two and a half weeks earlier, a verdict in a Sydney court case had given the Resident added cause to believe that his fortunes were improving. In June 1837, a settler in the Bay of Islands, Edward Doyle, had been apprehended for burglary and the attempted murder of another settler, John Wright. Doyle had been sent to Sydney to be tried for his alleged crimes, even though they were committed in a territory that was beyond British jurisdiction.[34] The issue was further complicated by the fact that Doyle claimed he was not a British subject anyway, on the basis that he had been born in America. The New South Wales court overrode these technicalities, and on 18 November it sentenced Doyle to death for his crimes.[35]

The press saw this for what it was – a de facto extension of British law applying to settlers in territories over which Britain exerted no authority. 'The decision of the Court', the *Sydney Gazette* announced, 'shews that the Supreme Court of New South Wales has jurisdiction over all British subjects, resident in the various Islands in the South Seas.'[36] And in a rare move, the colonial authorities in Sydney attributed what it saw as an advance in regional order to James, citing his previous representations made to have British law apply to British subjects in New Zealand as the basis for the latest development.[37]

Closer to home, there were other reasons for James to feel optimistic as 1837 was coming to an end. On 19 November, he and Agnes welcomed another son into the world – 'a fine little fellow', he told Alexander. And on the political front, the great threat that James once believed De Thierry had posed

---

[32] Ibid.; R. Burke to J. Busby, 13 October 1837, in *BFR* 3, p. 840.
[33] *The Sydney Monitor*, 6 December 1837, 2.
[34] *The Australian*, 4 August 1837, 2.
[35] W. Rumbles, 'Spectre of Jurisdiction: Supreme Court of New South Wales and the British Subject in Aotearoa/New Zealand 1823–1841', in *Law Text Culture* 15 (2011): 218–19; *The Australian*, 21 November 1837, 2.
[36] *SGNSWA*, 25 November 1837, 2.
[37] *SGNSWA*, 14 December 1837, 2.

to New Zealand's sovereignty had now shrunk to its true proportion. In a jocular mood, he informed his brother the following month that 'the Baron has been on his territories for the last 7 or 8 weeks and though he still talks big, is selling rum by the gallon, it is even said by the bottle. He will be sovereign as far as the shadow of his hat covers.'[38]

Around 12 January 1838, news reached James of the landing of Bishop Jean Baptiste Pompallier at Hokianga. The French cleric had immediately found a handful of mainly Irish Catholic settlers who offered their support to him, and while the Protestant missionaries were outraged at his presence (some describing him as an anti-Christ),[39] the Resident seems not to have been concerned in the slightest, and did not even give news of the Bishop's arrival a mention in his reports to his Sydney superiors. He was aware of the risks of sectarian friction, and wisely rose above them, ignoring his personal preferences for the sake of political stability and social order. When the possibility of a visit to New Zealand by the Anglican Bishop William Broughton came to the Resident's attention, at the same period as Pompallier was expected in the Bay of Islands, James quipped that '[i]t should be a good joke if the two should come at the same time'.[40] His Presbyterian sensibilities were rising to the surface as the prospect of episcopal rivalry between the Catholics and Anglicans in particular looked more likely.

James's ecumenical stance was in keeping with his official role, but privately, he could display some ambivalence. Just a month earlier, he had mentioned to a relative that '[t]here is not one of the missionaries with whom in private I would not have been on the most cordial terms, nor can I conceive the least chance of an unpleasant feeling arising between myself and any of them, except through my public duty'.[41] Yet by the close of January 1838, there was an uncharacteristic bitterness in James's attitude towards a few of the local Anglican ministers. He had noticed that for the previous two Sundays, he had not been called on to do the readings during the church service, as had been the normal practice. On its own, this was hardly cause for concern, but he was then approached by some missionaries who said that Henry Williams wished to meet with him. This unexpected level of formality, with Williams apparently using intermediaries to arrange a meeting, piqued James's curiosity, although he still was not overly concerned. The meeting was arranged for a Monday, where the Resident expected an apology for being sidelined in church. Instead, he was astonished at Williams, whose 'manner was very

---

[38] J. Busby to A. Busby, 20 December 1837, in *BFR* 3, 853.
[39] A. N. Brown, *The Journals of A. N. Brown, C. M. S. Missionary Tauranga* (Tauranga: The Elms Trust, 1990), 39.
[40] J. Busby to A. Busby, 13 March 1838, in *BFR* 3, 873.
[41] J. Busby to A. Busby, 20 December 1837, in *BFR* 3, 854.

arrogant', and who instead of excusing himself for overlooking James's role in Sunday services, alleged that the Resident had insulted him. The issue was to do with James apparently complaining to others about his status not being sufficiently recognized in church. The two men patched up their differences, mainly because the Resident felt he was obliged to Williams for all the assistance the missionary had previously rendered to him. However, as James wrote to Alexander, 'on my part the reconciliation was only outward', and he told Williams this to his face. For the next several months, communications between the Resident and local missionaries ceased almost entirely.[42]

For most of that summer, and into the autumn of 1838, James was largely left alone by his Sydney superiors. As they waited for the new Governor to arrive, and then settle himself into the role and finally to acquaint himself with the innumerable issues that awaited his deliberations, correspondence with the Resident waned. James occupied himself with his garden, his family, and intermittently by sending letters to his siblings with advice on how they should manage their affairs. In May, though, he was suddenly jolted from this political calm by news that a British subject – Henry Biddle – had been murdered. Biddle was being transported by canoe from his home at Whirinaki by two Māori, who had got into an argument with him. After a short tussle, Biddle ended up overboard and most likely drowned.[43]

As soon as Biddle's body was discovered washed up on shore, the perpetrators were quickly identified: an adult named Kite and a youth aged about nine. James was acutely aware of the peril this event placed the region in. Crimes committed by one British subject against another were a more straightforward proposition, while in general, the Resident tended to avert his gaze from acts carried out between Māori. However, here, on the face of it, was a crime committed by Māori against a British subject. James had to contend not only with the potential for tensions being heightened as a result of the killing,[44] but also the murky jurisprudential issues it brought to the fore (made more complex by Kite's status as a slave in Māori society,[45] which made his possible punishment by settlers more tolerable to local Māori, and thus placed a greater burden on James to enact some punitive measures). From whichever angle he looked at it, there was no escaping the situation. The settlers expected justice, and Māori were attentive to what type of precedent the Resident's response might set.

---

[42] J. Busby to A. Busby, 26 January 1838, in *BFR* 3, 867.
[43] *Otago Witness*, 18 March 1882, 26; J. Busby to E. D. Thomson, 28 May 1838, in Despatches from British Resident 1833–1839, qMS-0344, ATL; N. Turner, Journal 1836–1846, A 1873, Mitchell Library, SLNSW, 116.
[44] J. Ashton, '"So Strange a Proceeding": Murder, Justice, and Empire in 1830s Hokianga', in *NZJH* 46, no. 2 (2012): 149.
[45] Ibid., 148–9.

Kite was handed over by local chiefs to the missionaries at Mangungu, who took him to Horeke, where he was held in custody. A group of twenty-seven settlers from Hokianga then carried out a rudimentary investigation, and determined that Kite had to be held accountable for committing murder. A request was then sent to Waitangi for the Resident to oversee Kite's trial – a request that proceeded only because it had been consented by local chiefs.[46]

Both settlers and chiefs attended the trial, held on 19 May at Mangungu. James acted as judge, but without the backing of any higher authority or within any established judicial system, while the settlers served at times as a de facto jury. The Resident's address to those present gives some indication of how he saw this 'trial':

> I stated to my country men who were assembled that I considered it to be a duty which each individual owed to the community to take part in the proceedings, and I admonished them to give the strictest attention to the evidence that they might be prepared to give their verdict with a clear conscience in the sight of God; as I should consider it my duty to apply to the Chiefs for the execution of the prisoner should two thirds of them agree in a verdict of guilty.[47]

In the end, 75 per cent of those present approved a guilty verdict. But whose justice was being carried out here? It was not British justice because British law did not apply in the country, and because the apparatus of the British trial system – with its qualified lawyers and judges – was absent. But neither was it traditional Māori justice, as guilt was voted on democratically, and without chiefs dominating the process. The answer was that it was a hybrid system, drawing on elements of both cultures, and importantly, relying on the mutual consent of Māori and European in order for justice to be done – in this case, in the form of a death sentence.

On 21 May, Kite was executed by being shot. The 'executioner' was a local chief whose community had been in dispute with Kite's. From the settlers' perspective, the matter had been closed, while from a Māori point of view, the killing of Kite conveniently also resolved the sense of grievance between the rival communities, with balance thus being restored to tribal relations in the area. The episode also dispelled to some extent the caricature of the Resident published in 1838 (and that has stuck with him to the present time) of 'a man-o-war without guns . . . [who] has authority to restrain disorderly

---

[46] Ibid., 150.
[47] J. Busby to E. D. Thomson, 28 May 1838, in *BFR* 3, 884.

conduct, but . . . not the means of putting it into execution'.[48] In every sense, the Kite trial revealed James's capacity to put his decisions into execution.

At first, there was mild bewilderment in Sydney at this irregular chain of events. The Attorney General reduced the episode to its bare elements, describing the Resident's account as 'a mere recital of the death of a British subject who was murdered at New Zealand by New Zealanders', and as a result, concluded that 'it would not be to the honour of the British Government to countenance so strange a proceeding'.[49] Gipps saw beyond the technical jurisprudential deficiencies of the trial, and appreciated the requirement for natural justice to be exercised in New Zealand, particularly in a case like this where James had obviously acted so efficiently, and – dare it be said – judiciously.[50] James, for his part, claimed that the matter was 'a triumph of order which persons unacquainted with New Zealand can ill appreciate'.[51]

Given the anticipation of New Zealand's annexation (or something along those lines) by Britain, James was slightly suspicious of the arrival, on 16 August 1838, of the French corvette *L'Heroine* at the Bay of Islands.[52] Its captain had been instructed simply to report in general terms on the state of the country,[53] but when Pompallier went on board to conduct a mass, the deeply ingrained British suspicions of French intentions returned. What infuriated James personally about Pompallier's visit to *L'Heroine* was that the Bishop had still not condescended to visit him. It was not until a month after mass was held on the French ship that Pompallier finally made his way to Waitangi to meet the Resident. Two days afterwards, on 24 September, James completed an assessment of recent events involving the Bishop and French ships in New Zealand waters and sent it to Sydney, hoping that it would influence Gipps to advocate for a firmer British presence in the country. James argued that there was 'every reason to believe' that the French intended to form a settlement in New Zealand. A chief who had befriended Pompallier informed the Resident that the French were offering to send troops to maintain security in some Māori settlements, and although James reacted with some skepticism to the claim, he could not dismiss it outright.[54] The truth was far from being this dramatic. There is no evidence that Pompallier sought any

---

[48] *The Monthly Supplement of the Penny Magazine of the Society for the Diffusion of Useful Knowledge* (London: Charles Knight & Co., September–October 1838): 418.
[49] F. Fisher, 18 September 1838, in *BFR* 3, 900.
[50] G. Gipps to Glenelg, 5 October 1838, in *HRA* 1, vol. 19, 602.
[51] J. Busby to E. D. Thomson, 9 November 1838, in *BFR* 3, 907.
[52] J. D. Lang, *New Zealand in 1839, or Four Letters to the Right Hon. Earl Durham* (London: Smith, Elder & Co., 1839), 93.
[53] R. McNab, *The Old Whaling Days: A History of Southern New Zealand from 1830 to 1840* (Wellington: Whitcombes and Tombs, 1913), 249–50.
[54] J. Busby to E. D. Thomson, 24 September 1838, in *BFR* 3, 898–9.

French military presence in the country, but clumsy translations and an innate British distrust of the French conspired to make James's assessment of the situation far more panicked than it needed to be. And on reflection, James admitted he had overreacted, and later confirmed to his superior in Sydney that the Bishop had no political objectives whatsoever.[55]

In October 1838, James received a copy of the report from the Select Committee of the House of Lords that had been appointed to investigate the possibility of regulating British subjects living in the country. The Committee did not make a firm recommendation for intervention, but did lend the Lords' support for the efforts that had already been undertaken that had 'effected the rapid Advancement of the religious and social Condition of the Aborigines of New Zealand . . . [and] their future Progress in Civilization'.[56] This was as good a signal as any to James that there was political support in London for his performance as Resident. However, the report determined that something needed to be done about the New Zealand question overall, although exactly what would be a decision left to the Colonial Secretary and his advisors in the Colonial Office.

Did James now sense that the Residency's days were numbered? It is telling that at this moment, his attention had suddenly swung sharply to his personal financial future – as though he was anticipating a time when he would not be in the employ of the British government. In one of his final letters of 1838, he told Alexander that he was busily engaged in land purchases, and commented that when these were complete, he would have sufficient land to hold stock 'that will be at least worth as much as my salary if not a great deal more'.[57] On 1 December, the decision on New Zealand's future status in relation to the Empire was reached in London, and although it would take several months to reach Sydney and Waitangi, it was in keeping with what James had most likely suspected. Glenelg announced to Gipps that a Consul would be appointed to New Zealand as soon as the appropriate person was selected. Glenelg assumed that James 'will have been in some measure prepared for a discontinuation of his present office', and suggested to Gipps that the Resident could be employed once more by the colonial administration in Sydney.[58] James had been completely ruled out of any future official role in New Zealand.

In late December 1838, it seemed that commercial and social activity in the whole of the Bay of Islands had come to a halt. A bout of influenza had swept

---

[55] J. Busby to E. D. Thomson, 10 November 1838, in *HRA* 1, vol. 19, 700.
[56] *Report from the Select Committee of the House of Lords, Appointed to Inquire into the Present State of the Islands of New Zealand*, iii.
[57] J. Busby to A. Busby, 16 November 1838, in *BFR* 3, 914–15.
[58] Glenelg to G. Gipps, 1 December 1838, in *HRA* 1, vol. 19, 690.

through the region, possibly having arrived on the *Elizabeth* (whose captain contracted it before reaching New Zealand, and on arrival, 'dropped down dead on the deck'). James and his family were all struck by the virus, and its reach in the area was 'all but universal'. Agnes was particularly ill and had to be bled as a drastic form of treatment, while James continued to attend to his official duties despite also being very sick.[59]

The epidemic passed swiftly, and the strain of the virus was comparatively mild. Within a few weeks, the Bay of Islands was back to normal, except that it was contending with one of its quietest seasons in years, with shipping dropping over 40 per cent from what it had been in 1836. The Resident attributed this decrease to the ongoing problems stemming from captains being unable to regulate their crews once they landed in New Zealand, and the ensuing desertions, which were as frequent as ever.[60] The implication was that British law was in urgent need of application in the region, but for once, James did not make this point explicitly, and neither did he propose any remedy.

The Resident had not changed his spots completely, though. Affronted by what he saw as an erroneous account of New Zealand by FitzRoy in his testimony before the 1838 Select Committee of the House of Lords, James assembled written evidence from various missionaries and then took the unusual step of writing directly to Glenelg, with a long-winded refutation of what FitzRoy had said. In a heated dispatch, James referred to FitzRoy's testimony as being 'false', 'injurious', and 'derogatory to my character', and provided twenty-seven pages of text – much of it rehearsing his career as Resident – to justify his case.[61] Gipps read this letter when it reached Sydney, before being sent on to London, and wrote to Glenelg saying that he could not comment on the matters it raised.[62]

Privately, James was even more livid over FitzRoy's condemnation of the Residency. In a letter to Alexander, he accused the captain of intriguing with members of the Committee and some missionaries to get the role of Resident for himself. He then disclosed what he could not make known to his superiors: his fear that if the testimony presented to the Committee was taken at face value, the British government 'would be quite justified in superseding me as soon as they can'. The anxiety James felt over this situation was palpable.[63]

Other slivers of intelligence were reaching James around this time that would have confirmed to him how precarious his position was becoming, even if some

---

[59] J. Busby to A. Busby, 3 January 1839, in *BFR* 3, 922–3.
[60] J. Busby to E. D. Thomson, 15 January 1839, in *BFR* 3, 925–6.
[61] J. Busby to Glenelg, 22 February 1839, in *BFR* 3, 936–43.
[62] G. Gipps to Glenelg, 21 March 1839, in *HRA* 1, vol 20, 66–7.
[63] J. Busby to A. Busby, 1 March 1839, in *BFR* 3, 944.

of the channels of information were convoluted. He heard from the missionaries John Hobbs and Richard Davis, for example, that the French government had advised its British counterpart that if there was a treaty between Britain and New Zealand, France would respect its provisions. On another occasion, James referred to meeting a Polish count who was visiting the country, and who (incorrectly) informed him that the New Zealand Association had been given tacit endorsement by the British government for its plans to settle parts of the country. And shortly afterwards, one recent immigrant from New South Wales advised James of the chance that the New South Wales Legislative Council would not be voting for a continuance of the Resident's salary from next year.[64] There was no immediate way that James could verify any of these accounts, but he could not ignore them completely either, especially as they came from unconnected sources, and all seemed to have as their common theme a significant change in British colonial policy on New Zealand.

It turned out, in the case of James's salary, that there was some basis to the bad news he had received. Thomson sent him a dispatch on 16 April, advising that expenditure was to be strictly limited for the following year to 'indispensable items'.[65] Gipps, however, had now given some consideration to the Residency, and told Glenelg that there had been 'very little advantage' in having a Resident in New Zealand, and that he would 'feel extremely happy' if New South Wales no longer had to pay the salary for the role.[66]

James was not privy to this information, however. A veil had been drawn by various colonial officials to conceal precisely what was in store for the Resident and New Zealand. He had an inkling, but it was not until mid-June that he received what he described as 'startling news'. Thomson had written to him, confirming that a Consul would be appointed to New Zealand with precisely the sorts of power James had lobbied for since 1833, and that 'there is no immediate prospect of a vacancy in any other situation which be likely to meet your wishes'.[67]

James now cut a lonely, isolated figure.[68] He knew that his role had not lived up to his own expectations, let alone those of his superiors, and much as he might have vaguely anticipated his Residency eventually coming to an end, reading directly in Thomson's dispatch that his career was to be terminated in the near future was a chilling experience. He quickly penned a letter to Alexander, sketching an outlandish scheme to export a shipload of wine from

---

[64] J. Busby to A. Busby, 9 April 1839, in *BFR* 3, 950–2.
[65] E. D. Thomson to J. Busby, 16 April 1839, in *BFR* 3, 955–6.
[66] G. Gipps to Glenelg, 21 March 1839, in *HRA* 1, vol 20, 67.
[67] J. Busby to A. Busby, 13 June 1839, in *BFR* 3, 966; E. D. Thomson to J. Busby, 30 May 1839, in *BFR* 3, 965.
[68] Lang, *New Zealand in 1839*, 11.

Malaga to Sydney to make a quick profit.[69] It was an improbable idea, which James may have committed to paper to convince himself more than anyone else that his enterprising spirit had not diminished in the years he had been employed as Resident. But it did little to dull his fury at having his future in New Zealand torn away from him. Of all those whom he felt had a hand in his decline, he singled out FitzRoy for special attention – even going so far as to inform Alexander that if the captain was made Consul to New Zealand, he would refuse to sell or let his house at Waitangi to him.

James's initial shock at his impending dismissal eventually subsided, and after composing himself, he wrote a stoic response to his Sydney superiors, but without conceding he was in any way responsible for his imminent downfall. He emphasized, for example, that he had not even heard of the particular dispatch (a copy of which had allegedly been sent to him previously) in which mention was made of his role coming to an end, but conceded that he was not surprised, given the scheming that had gone on behind his back over the past few years.[70] What the Resident now sought was permission to leave New Zealand in September to go to London, where he no doubt planned to plead his case before colonial officials and politicians. At the same time, James wrote to his father seeking a loan to establish himself in Sydney as a wine merchant, should the need arise. He was now facing a financial as well as career dilemma. Travelling to London to 'obtain justice' from the British government would be 'ruinous' to his finances, but might just save his career. On the other hand, if he accepted that there was little chance of him becoming the Consul to New Zealand (as all the official signs indicated) then his limited funds would best be diverted into a business.[71]

Drastic times called for drastic measures, and James's mind was working furiously on alternatives to the career that he had devoted nearly a decade to. He then landed on an idea that seemed to be perfect from whichever angle he viewed it. His inspiration may have had its paternity in Wakefield's scheme of systematic colonization that he had recently read about, as well as in an awareness of the rising value of the land he had purchased over the past several months. But whatever its origin, James's latest plan seemed to him to be flawless. In July 1839, he offered Alexander a share in 'the first public building in my future town – city it maybe'. James intended to turn the fields around Waitangi into a major settlement, which he would call Victoria. He had heard of similar towns being created in America, and was alert to the possibilities for profit that they could generate for landowners if successful.[72]

---

[69] J. Busby to A. Busby, 13 June 1839, in *BFR* 3, 967.
[70] J. Busby to E. D. Thomson, 8 July 1839, in *BFR* 3, 969–70.
[71] J. Busby to A. Busby, c. 9 July 1839, in *BFR* 3, 976–7.
[72] Ibid., 978.

Having roughly mapped out the position of the allotments, James decided to go to London and find someone suitably competent to handle sales in his absence. If he managed to secure the role of Consul, he would have ready-made capital (with a substantial financial interest in it). And if he did not secure the position, which was looking likely, the growth of the settler population in the region[73] would prove lucrative regardless.

Around the time that James was envisaging the city of Victoria arising from its epicentre at Waitangi, at the Colonial Office Stephen was putting the finishing touches to the instructions for James's replacement. At the start of the year, there had been no great urgency in London to remove the Resident. Officials would plod their way through the process until everything was in place, after which an orderly transition could be undertaken from Resident to Consul. However, Wakefield's renamed New Zealand Company was (rightly) fearful of the implications of a consular appointment for its land-trading business, and so accelerated its plans to found its own colony in New Zealand. In May, the Company sent the *Tory* – with senior Company agents – to the southern end of the North Island, where they would establish their base. The British government was by now resolutely opposed to Wakefield's actions, and so hastened its own plans for the prospective colony.[74]

On 13 August, it was Hobson (not FitzRoy as James had feared) who was appointed as British Consul to New Zealand.[75] The following day, Hobson was issued with a set of instructions by the Colonial Secretary, Lord Normanby (but drafted by Stephen), which among much else required the captain to secure a cession of sovereignty by means of a treaty – similar in essence to what James had proposed in June 1837. The British government's decision to intervene was based on the proliferation in New Zealand of settlers 'of bad or doubtful character' who 'were alternatively the authors and victims of every species of crime an outrage'.[76]

Although notice of Hobson's appointment did not reach New South Wales until December 1839, there was already a solid rumour in the colony that he was to be made Consul. On 3 August, the *Sydney Gazette* published a brief article, mentioning without qualification that the captain had been offered the post but had yet to make up his mind on accepting it.[77] When Alexander told

---

[73] P. Hudson, 'English Emigration to New Zealand, 1839–1850: Information Diffusion and Marketing a New World', in *The Economic History Review* 54, no. 4 (2001): 682.
[74] Wakefield, *Adventure in New Zealand*, 15–16; H. Labouchere to W. Hutt, 1 May 1839, in *GBPP 1840*, vol. 40, 26; also see J. Stephen, minute 10 October 1839, CO 209/4.
[75] Palmerston to W. Hobson, 13 August 1839, in *Correspondence with the Secretary of State Relative to New Zealand*, 36.
[76] Normanby to W. Hobson, 14 August 1839, *Correspondence with the Secretary of State Relative to New Zealand*, 37.
[77] *SGNSWA*, 3 August 1839, 2.

James about this appointment (even though it had not been made yet), the Resident was in no doubt that it was true, and accused Hobson of somehow having inserted the piece in the newspaper himself, 'to make him look an important person'. James also believed that the deal for Hobson's appointment had been stitched up by Bourke while he was still Governor – part of the conspiracy to oust James from his role.[78]

To make matters worse, James had come to realize that there was now no purpose in him going to London as long as Normanby remained as Colonial Secretary. And with the impending arrival of Hobson as Consul, James turned his thoughts once more to his own future, and toyed with the idea of offering the New Zealand Company half of the land he had allotted for Victoria, in the hope that the remaining half in his possession would increase four-fold in value. The only fly in the ointment, as he saw it, was if Hobson took on the role of investigating claims to ownership of land in New Zealand. '[H]e might soon find a flaw in the best title in the country.' At this time, James even considered buying a large area of land in Poverty Bay and starting a farm there – away from the potential meddling of the future consul.[79]

James was still smarting at being replaced by Hobson, but was beginning to see the decision as the result of plots and deceit in almost every direction rather than arising from any inherent failure of the Residency itself. The list of conspirators was substantial – extending from Bourke to Normanby, Hobson, and FitzRoy. And to this list, James added in September 1839 one of the most principled settlers in New Zealand: Henry Williams.

The reason for Williams becoming the latest target at whom the Resident unleashed his indignation was the reluctance by the missionary fully to back James's scheme for Victoria. Williams was not convinced about the suitability of its location, and when James began to seek subscriptions for the Victoria Institution – his scheme for a religious and educational academy that would be at the heart of the planned settlement[80] – Williams was not as forthcoming with cash as the Resident had hoped. Rather than Williams simply entertaining doubts about the scheme, James was convinced (completely without evidence) that the missionary harboured plans to build an alternative such institution at Paihia. He grumbled that Williams withdrew any support 'when he found I would not be a tool in his hands, but would take my office out of my hands as far as he could'.[81] And looking back on his career as it was approaching its end, James added that '[h]ad the Missionaries been my brothers . . . I could not have struggled more than I have done to

---

[78] J. Busby to A. Busby, 16 August 1839, in *BFR* 3, 1002.
[79] J. Busby to A. Busby, 24 August 1839, in *BFR* 3, 1003–4.
[80] *Sydney Herald*, 4 September 1839, 2.
[81] J. Busby to A. Busby, 5 September 1839, in *BFR* 3, 1007.

maintain a good opinion of them, nor could I have been more tender of their reputation'.[82]

The number of those whom James believed had militated against the Residency continued to grow. He alleged that Charles Baker – another Anglican missionary – had conspired to secure Hobson the post of Consul, and he further claimed that the respected English merchant James Clendon (who had taken on the role of American Consul in the country the previous year) had fallen under the corrupting influence of the missionaries.[83] The idea that so many people had turned against James as part of a great synchronized movement was totally misplaced, but at the same time, fully explicable. As the Residency descended into total redundancy, and episodes of serious lawlessness abruptly escalated in the final months of 1839, James found it impossible to attribute this collapse in any way to his own conduct. Surely someone as diligent and virtuous as he could not be presiding over the disintegration of his career? The only alternative explanation that came to him was that others had colluded against him.

James now devoted himself almost exclusively to Victoria. On 14 September, he confidently informed Alexander that he had 'no doubt that the sale of allotments will be so very successful'.[84] Indeed, he was so optimistic that he wrote how 'it would be wrong were I to quit the country without making some further acquisitions of land, as it will probably be out of my power to do so when I am come back'.[85] However, James was eager to have one more roll of the dice when it came to salvaging his Residency, and maybe even securing a position as Consul. He maintained his faith in the creation and growth of the Victoria settlement as the source of his future wealth, but also reiterated his plan to travel to London in order to 're-establish' himself in New Zealand. Once more, he misjudged the political climate. James was convinced that when he arrived in England, Parliament would reconvene a select committee on New Zealand if he lobbied for it, and that once underway, it would hear his evidence against FitzRoy.[86]

Such a belief – had it been made public – may well have had the opposite effect: confirming in the minds of colonial officials that James was entirely unsuited to further service in the government. It is possible, though, that he put this suggestion to paper – in the privacy of a letter to his brother – as a way of working through options in his mind. Most of his attention remained on

---

[82] Ibid., 1008.
[83] Ibid. B. Gawith, 'James Reddy Clendon, 1800–1872: Trade, Entrepreneurship and Empire' (MA thesis, Massey University, 2005), 83–6.
[84] J. Busby to A. Busby, 14 September 1839, in *BFR* 3, 1012.
[85] Ibid., 1013.
[86] Ibid.

establishing a future for himself and his family (including Alexander, whom he was encouraging to immigrate) in New Zealand, rather than challenging officials. He outlined to Alexander a scheme in which a 'firm' would be formed with agents in Sydney and London who would sell sections in Victoria to prospective settlers and speculators.[87]

James quickly began to fixate on the details of his planned settlement. Without a single lot yet being sold, he put 'a good deal of thought' into issues such as regulating the number of dwellings on each section, the provision for additional roads, having thoroughfares through private properties, and so forth. He was further encouraged by news in the Sydney press that Wakefield's Company was 'raising immigrants in great numbers for New Zealand'.[88] This sort of enthusiasm by settlers to move to the country would have given James the confirmation he needed that Victoria could indeed be a substantial success.

In mid-November, Alexander arrived in the Bay of Islands and moved into the Resident's house at Waitangi. By this time, James was preparing to relinquish his official role, and according to family tradition, he enjoyed his time with his brother without the burden of office which, until recently, had bore down on him relentlessly.[89] Alexander purchased a fifty-acre block of land adjacent to Paihia in the first week of 1840 – possibly to farm if he decided to remain in New Zealand – and around the same time, James finalized several major land purchases of his own, totalling around 50,000 acres.[90] For some of the purchases, James had formed a business partnership with the merchant Gilbert Mair. The pair acquired a forested block of land at Ngunguru, and paid for it in goods to the value of £494.[91] Mostly, though, James was the sole purchaser, and raced to amass sufficient territory to make his business ambitions viable.

---

[87] Ibid., 1014–15.
[88] W. Busby to J. Busby, 22 October 1839, in *BFR* 3, 1021.
[89] Oral history of Busby family, in *BFR* 3, 1024.
[90] G. Gipps to Russell, 16 August 1840, in *HRA* 1, vol. 19, 760.
[91] *BFR* 4, 2–3.

11

'Your Functions will Cease'

In the morning of 29 January 1840, the HMS *Herald* reached the Bay of Islands after a ten-day voyage from Sydney. As it dropped anchor in the harbour's placid waters, its principal passenger, William Hobson, got dressed and prepared himself to arrange the handover of authority from the Resident. Three year earlier, Hobson had been sent to New Zealand to undertake a cursory assessment of the country, and was now returning – almost in triumph – as British Consul, and Lieutenant-Governor over any territories where the chiefs ceded their sovereignty over British subjects to the Crown.[1]

The British government was acutely aware that the Consul would face many of the same sorts of difficulties in exercising his authority that had plagued the Resident, but it was now committed to giving Hobson all that it had denied James: a force of up to 100 men to ensure his will was followed in the country; authorization to establish a court to hear civil and criminal cases; and with the consent of the chiefs, to apply British law to British subjects in New Zealand.[2] Seven years of James urging for these very measures had finally paid off, but it was Hobson who would now receive the dividend of this lengthy lobbying. James could not have avoided being at least slightly embittered by this irony, but he had no say in the matter, and although he was no longer in the employ of the British government from this moment, he was determined to maintain his professional demeanour to the very end. He later wrote, 'Though my official character terminated on the arrival of Captain Hobson, I did not the less consider it to be my duty to aid him with my experience and influence, and . . . our relations were of the most unreserved and confidential character.'[3]

James was rowed out to meet Hobson on the ship, where they talked for almost two hours. The Resident was handed a letter written by Thomson,

---

[1] P. Moon, *Te Ara Ki Te Tiriti: The Path to the Treaty of Waitangi* (Auckland: David Ling, 2002), 74–123.
[2] Russell to G. Gipps, 26 September 1839, 4 December 1839, in *HRA* 1, vol. 19, 358–9; 409–11.
[3] J. Busby, *Remarks upon a Pamphlet Entitled 'The Taranaki Question'* (Auckland: Philip Kunst, 1860), 3.

which advised him in a perfunctory way that as of the time of Hobson's arrival in New Zealand, 'your functions will cease', and that all the paperwork associated with the Residency was to be handed over to the Consul. Later that afternoon, Hobson reported to Gipps, confirming that 'I this day relieved James Busby Esq. from the duty of Resident.'[4]

The following day, Hobson went on shore at Kororāreka (as opposed to the seat of James's authority at Waitangi) and read out a proclamation to an assembled crowd of settlers and Māori. It referred to his intention to establish 'a settled form of Civil Government' over British subjects in New Zealand, and to extend the boundaries of the New South Wales colony to include those parts of New Zealand where sovereignty was acquired in the name of the Queen. Hobson also declared that from that day, his rank was that of Lieutenant-Governor.[5] With this public announcement, James's career as a civil servant was over. However, if he was expecting that anything else Hobson had to say would have little relevance to him, he was mistaken. The Lieutenant-Governor made another proclamation that had the potential to shatter James's plans for the future. Hobson declared that the Crown would not recognize 'any titles to land in New Zealand which are not derived from or confirmed by Her Majesty'. To this end, the Lieutenant-Governor would establish a commission to investigate all land purchases by settlers, who would have to prove that they had paid a fair price for their acquisitions.[6]

With good reason, Gipps had been concerned with the propriety of land purchases that had taken place in New Zealand, and supported the examination of so-called titles, with a view to 'disallow all exorbitant claims'. However, when the policy was enacted, the Governor recorded how 'it occasioned much dissatisfaction among those purchasers or speculators; and . . . was loudly denounced by the parties interested as illegal and unjust'. Several of those affected petitioned the colonial government to challenge this decision, and five were admitted to present their pleas directly to the Legislative Council. One of those five was James, who 'claimed somewhat more than 50,000 acres of land, besides a Township or site of a Town in the Bay of Islands, which he valued at £30,000'.[7] Victoria – the site of the town Gipps was referring to – still existed only in James's imagination, but became suddenly less likely ever to materialize when Hobson chose a location across the bay to base his new administration.

In the meantime, James was drawn into the process of arranging the treaty that Hobson had been instructed to conclude with the chiefs. Hobson was

---

[4] E. D. Thomson to W. Hobson, 13 January 1840, in *BFR* 4, 10; W. Hobson to G. Gipps, 29 January 1840, in *BFR* 4, 1.
[5] *Parliamentary Papers Relating to the Colony of New Zealand* (1844), 25.
[6] Ibid., 26–7.
[7] G. Gipps to Russell, 16 August 1840, in *HRA* 1, vol. 19, 760.

aware of the political capital that James had accumulated, and so the invitations sent to local chiefs to discuss and sign the treaty were issued in James's name, the location of the meeting and signing would be at Waitangi, outside James's house, and Hobson was keen to negotiate with the Confederation that he believed still existed (James knew it was defunct, but chose not to inform his replacement of this fact).[8] Hobson was probably thinking that a body of chiefs that had already committed to one document with the British was more likely to do so a second time, and who was James to disabuse him of this belief?[9]

The day after Hobson's arrival, with the invitations on their way to their recipients, James's official role in New Zealand affairs concluded. The former Resident was now facing life in the country as a private individual, or so everyone – including himself – thought. Then, without warning, Hobson was struck by a severe illness (which remains undiagnosed) and on 1 February, was too unwell to see anyone, let alone work on the treaty's text.[10] The precise sequence of who did what next in relation to the preparation of the agreement is still uncertain.[11] However, James certainly played a role in its wording. The initial draft of the treaty was dictated by Hobson to his secretary, James Freeman, but on Hobson falling ill, Freeman and George Cooper (Hobson's treasurer) consulted James on the text. The former Resident made some significant adjustments to the agreement's second article, and then returned it to Hobson, who was recovering on the *Herald*.[12] Although the extent to which he influenced the wording of this seminal agreement in New Zealand history is open to debate,[13] in later years, James was adamant that his role had been central. His recollection of his involvement certainly gave the exaggerated impression that the treaty's text was largely his own work: 'The draft of the Treaty prepared by me was adopted by Capt. Hobson without any other alteration than a transposition of certain sentences, which did not in any degree affect the sense.'[14]

And it was not just in the composition of the treaty's text where James claimed credit. At its signing, he similarly put himself centre stage. Decades

---

[8] Orange, *The Treaty of Waitangi*, 35.
[9] W. Colenso, 'Day and Waste Book' MS76, AML; J. Busby to W. Colenso, 29 January 1840, in William Colenso papers, ATL MS Papers 4622.
[10] R. V. Trubuhovich, *Governor William Hobson: His Health Problems and Final Illness* (Auckland: RVT, 2015), 9–11.
[11] *He Whakaputanga Me Te Tiriti*, 344.
[12] Parkinson, *Preserved in the Archives of the Colony*, 22, 24, 30; R. Ross, 'Te Tiriti o Waitangi: Texts and Translations', *NZJH* 6, no. 2 (1972): 132–3.
[13] D. Loveridge, *'The Littlewood Treaty': An Appraisal of Texts and Interpretations* (Wellington: Treaty of Waitangi Research Unit, 2006), 14.
[14] Busby, *Remarks upon a Pamphlet Entitled 'The Taranaki Question'*, 3–4.

later, he quoted from a letter he had received from Hobson shortly after the initial signing, in which the Lieutenant-Governor asserted to James that

> without your aid in furthering the objects of the Commission with which I was charged . . . I should have experienced much difficulty in reconciling the minds of the natives, as well as the Europeans . . . to the changes I contemplated carrying into effect.[15]

In the years following the treaty's inception, James tended to elevate the magnitude of his role in the creation of the agreement roughly in proportion to the decline of his reputation in public. And there were other cases of the artistic licence he applied to the history of the treaty. He claimed, for example, that when he met with Hobson to discuss the final version of the text, Hobson was still interested in pursuing the option of the factory system for New Zealand – of the sort he had proposed in 1837. Again, in James's reconstruction of history, it was his expertise and foresight that prevented Hobson from making this error when preparing the treaty. James allegedly responded to Hobson by pointing out that when it came to the factory idea, 'however suitable the establishment might be for the gold and gems of Oriental commerce, it might prove rather difficult to collect the pig and potato merchants of New Zealand within the walls of a factory'.[16] James was at once heroic and sarcastic – saving the country from an unworkable agreement based on a flawed concept, and belittling the person who proposed it. However, in this instance, it looks as though James was being deliberately disingenuous. Yes, Hobson had proposed a factory system back in 1837, but in the intervening two years, the Colonial Office had formulated a simpler option for New Zealand. Hobson had been instructed on enacting this new approach in August 1839, and executed these instructions as required, with not even a thought given to his earlier and cursory suggestion of factories. It seems that long after the fact, James alleged otherwise, and then went one stage further, by misrepresenting what Hobson had meant in 1837 by a factory.

Another distortion relating to James's precise role in drafting the Treaty came from the *Herald's* disagreeable captain, Joseph Nias. He had clashed with the Resident and with Hobson at the end of January 1840,[17] and in July, when back in Sydney, had claimed that James and Hobson had argued about the Treaty's text, to the point where James had grabbed Hobson's draft

---

[15] W. Hobson, in ibid., 3.
[16] J. Busby in *BFR* 4, 18.
[17] *The Founding of New Zealand: The Journals of Felton Mathew*, ed. J. Rutherford (Dunedin: A. H. and A. W. Reed, 1940), 28–9.

and thrown it over the side of the ship.[18] The absence of any corroborating evidence for this allegation, along with the circumstances of the period which conflict with Nias's version of events, make his account dubious. However, it is indicative of the way in which reputations could be worn away by false rumour in small colonial societies, with little to check their spread. In September, Nias's allegation was finally put to rest, and James's honour restored, when Hobson wrote the former Resident a kind and fulsome endorsement of his character, and thanked him for all the assistance he had rendered when preparing the treaty.[19]

On 5 February 1840, Hobson returned to shore, where he met with James at his house. There, arrangements were finalized for the treaty to be presented to the chiefs who had been gathering for the occasion. Along with missionaries and others, this official party moved outside, where the treaty was read out in English and Māori to the audience. James then offered an assurance to the chiefs that the Lieutenant-Governor had not come to take their land, but to secure it for them, and explained the intention that all land acquired unfairly by Europeans would be returned to its previous Māori owners. At some stage during the proceedings, James was asked by a settler about his own purchases. James defended his recent acquisitions, but the question revealed an undercurrent of disquiet among some in the region about the extent of land that the former Resident had managed to accumulate.[20]

James's land purchases, and his part in proceedings relating to the treaty being signed on 6 February 1840, were of great importance to him. Yet when Hobson reported on the events at this time, his comments about James were confined to the single fact that the former Resident was present at the signing process, suggesting that James's actual contribution was peripheral.[21] However, despite the two men now having very different roles in the colony, their career trajectories were soon to intersect again. Hobson's Land Commission was about to be instituted to investigate land purchases in what was now nominally a British colony – a move which effectively put James's plans of on-selling sections at Victoria on hold. Given this stalemate in his only real business interest in New Zealand, James decided to leave the country with his family for a period. He had managed to sell a few allotments at Victoria for prices ranging from £24 to £65,[22] but with an effective freeze on further

---

[18] W. Busby to A. Busby, 16 July 1840, in *BFR* 4, 75.
[19] W. Hobson to J. Busby, 1 September 1840, in *BFR* 4, 80.
[20] W. Colenso, *The Authentic and Genuine History of the Signing of the Treaty of Waitangi* (Wellington: Govt. Printer, 1890), 17, 21; J. Belich, *Making Peoples: A History of the New Zealanders from Polynesian Settlement to the End of the Nineteenth Century* (Auckland: Allen Lane, 1996), 193.
[21] W. Hobson to G. Gipps, 5, 6 February 1840, in *Report from the Select Committee on New Zealand*, 145–7.
[22] *South Australian Record and Australasian Chronicle*, 18 April 1840, 4.

sales, on 25 March, the Busbys boarded the *Eleanor* for Sydney, reaching their destination on 6 April.[23] What is noticeable from this point is that the trail of material produced by James thins dramatically. Not only was the demand to produce official accounts now removed, but as the former Resident reunited with his siblings in New South Wales, there was similarly no longer any need for the sort of lengthy correspondence he had been in the habit of writing for the previous seven years.

On reaching Sydney, the family was almost immediately struck with disaster. James and Agnes's infant son, James junior, died in Darlinghurst just four days after arriving.[24] But as the death occurred in New South Wales, James was not compelled to correspond with anyone about it, and thus the cause of James junior's death is among the details that are now unknown. It would have been a harrowing subject for the family late in the summer of 1840, but like so much personal information not committed to paper, it was whittled away by time, and eventually vanished over subsequent generations.

Despite the paucity in extant material on James from 1840, it is nonetheless possible to detect a fairly abrupt change in his approach to life. Gone were the lengthy deliberations written over points of minimal importance. Gone too were the grand political stratagems and the vain efforts to acquire status through position and promotion. If his time in New Zealand had taught him anything, it was that frontier societies and the economies that propped them up were no respecters of rank. If James was to secure some level of financial security for his family in the colony, he now needed to put aside some of his earlier attitudes and take a more uncompromising approach to his new occupation – that of land trader and entrepreneur.

Before departing New Zealand, one of the projects James committed himself to was a business partnership with Gilbert Mair, which both men hoped would generate profits from land deals and timber processing. James gave Mair power of attorney (written in his typically verbose pseudo-legal style) over the business while he was in Sydney, and the two signed a memorandum detailing the nature of their partnership. They had paid roughly £500 for up to 50,000 acres of land in Ngunguru, and together with a third partner who joined the venture – John Lewington – had purchased a timber mill. Their plan was to export timber to New South Wales, with Mair managing the business, and James overseeing the operation as a silent partner.[25]

However, just as this earnest enterprise was getting under way, developments in Sydney were about to inflict enormous instability on New Zealand's nascent

---

[23] *Sydney Herald*, 8 April 1840, 2.
[24] *The Colonist*, 15 April 1840, 2.
[25] Power of Attorney, and Memorandum of Agreement, 10 March 1840, in *BFR* 4, 54–5; Harold Rodwell research papers on James Busby and Gilbert Mair, University of Auckland, MSS & Archives, A291, folder 1.

settler economy. The problem had started with William Wentworth – a Sydney speculator who claimed to have purchased around twenty million acres of land in the South Island for a meagre £200.[26] Gipps was rightly jittery about the implications of such dubious purchases. An individual buying almost a third of the country's territory for such a small sum not only raised serious questions about the validity of the purchase, but also had implications for how British sovereignty might extend in New Zealand – especially as Wentworth had advised some South Island chiefs not to sign the Treaty unless his purchase was first confirmed by British officials. Gipps's solution was to get the apparatus of the state involved. He withdrew his previous recommendation for Wentworth to have a seat on the New South Wales Legislative Council,[27] and sponsored a bill that would invalidate all large land purchases in New Zealand.[28]

A very worried James promptly wrote to Mair, informing him of the situation and the implications for their business. Reading this letter, Mair would have had good reason to be concerned. '[I]t seems beyond doubt that in law our titles are of no validity,' James told him prematurely. He encouraged Mair to proceed quickly with the construction of a sawmill, which he saw as the best way of potentially enhancing the validity of their purchase.[29]

James was acting as the Sydney agent for the timber business he had formed, and was initially confident that the market for timber spars in the colony would be a source for ongoing profit. However, this was not the only timber venture in the region, and in May, he discovered that two recent shipments of timber from other firms in New Zealand had arrived in Sydney, and that it was 'difficult to judge how their cargoes will affect the market'.[30] He had also secured a meeting with Gipps to discuss circumstances in New Zealand, and received further bleak news. He wrote to Mair to inform him that the Governor 'intended to treat us all as squatters and to claim all lands in the Queen's name'. By way of compensation, Gipps was considering an offer of 1,000 acres for every 10,000-acre block purchased. And for those who had purchased 100,000 acres, they would have just 5,000 acres returned. For the land-sharks, such an offer might have even looked attractive, but as James said to Mair, 'it will not do for us'.[31] The insecurity of land tenure, and a Sydney market that was beginning to be flooded with New Zealand timber, were the twin challenges James was now having to contend with.

To make matters worse, James was now finding people like Wentworth and Wakefield – both of whom he held in low regard for their dubious dealings

---

[26] *Historical Records of New Zealand South*, ed. R. Carrick (Dunedin: Otago Daily Times, 1903), 91.
[27] G. Gipps to Russell, 16 August 1840, in *HRA* 1, vol 20, 761–2.
[28] Ramsden, *Busby of Waitangi*, 257–8.
[29] J. Busby to G. Mair, *c*. March 1840, in *BFR* 4, 53.
[30] J. Busby to G. Mair, 6 May 1840, in *BFR* 4, 64.
[31] Ibid., 65.

in Māori land – as political bedfellows in the battle against Gipps's bill. What followed was a period of intense lobbying by James as he endeavoured to dissuade individual Legislative Councillors to back the bill. At the end of June, he addressed the Council in person, concluding his detailed assessment with a warning that Māori would come to regard the Crown as 'robbers' if such a revolutionary measure as Gipps was proposing was implemented.[32]

It was not until October that James again wrote to Mair. After complaining about the economic downturn in Sydney,[33] he advised that he intended to return to New Zealand and bring fifty head of cattle with him, in an effort to diversify his business activities. He also had ideas about how their timber could gain a share in an increasingly depressed Sydney market. James insisted that only the best-quality kauri be exported from Ngunguru, but conceded that Sydney builders were still unaware of the different woods they were milling, and by implication, would have to be educated about the benefits of the timber James and Mair were supplying.[34] James needed to return a profit soon, as he had spent £3,500 to set up the milling operation.[35]

At the end of the month, James managed to charter a 294-ton barque to take him and his cattle to the Tutukaka coast, where he planned to establish his farm. And there was encouraging news from London at this time. The Secretary of State for Colonies had raised concerns about Gipps's Land Titles Bill for New Zealand. For James, this was enough to renew his confidence in his plans to establish the town of Victoria. 'I am going to put other buildings there immediately,' he announced enthusiastically to Mair, before putting in his own order for timber so that construction could start as soon as he arrived.[36] On 22 November, James departed for New Zealand with his brother, John.[37] James had borrowed heavily to finance the cost of chartering the vessel, and for the accompanying forty-two labourers and farmers, and £700 worth of livestock and tools. The total cost was in excess of two years' salary for him, but this expenditure was essential if Victoria was to come into being.

But on reaching New Zealand, James was dealt two further cruel blows that devastated his plans. Firstly, he had sailed to Whangarei, where he intended to unload the livestock and farmhands who would establish his farm on his land. However, Hobson's investigations into land purchases had only recently begun, and so James was prohibited from landing workers and

---

[32] J. Busby, Address to Legislative Council, New South Wales, 30 June 1840, in *BFR* 4, 67–9; *New Zealand Gazette and Wellington Spectator*, 15 August 1840, 2.
[33] See N. G. Butlin, *Forming a Colonial Economy: Australia 1810–1850* (Cambridge: Cambridge University Press, 1994), 224.
[34] J. Busby to G. Mair, 8 October 1840, in *BFR* 4, 81–2.
[35] Busby, *The First Settlers in New Zealand and their Treatment by the Government*, 8.
[36] J. Busby to G. Mair, 24 October 1840, 4 November 1840, in *BFR* 4, 83.
[37] *The Australian*, 24 November 1840, 2.

animals on the land until his purchase had been confirmed. With no indication of how long it would take, this was a financial disaster. James was forced to return to the Bay of Islands, where he struggled to maintain his livestock on small landholdings. Within a few months, most of the animals had died.

The losses were enormous, but paled in comparison with the second calamity. Within weeks of the treaty's first signing, Hobson had reached the conclusion that the Bay of Islands was not the best location for the country's capital, and by October 1840, he had confirmed his preference for a site on the Waitemata Harbour, which he named Auckland.[38] With the seat of government shifting 200 kilometres to the south, Waitangi (and the planned town of Victoria) was relegated from being adjacent to the seat of government to being a remote settlement with few prospects for growth. From late 1840, trade began to wither in the Bay of Islands[39] as Auckland became the country's commercial entrepot.

Over the following months, James's financial circumstances quickly descended into crisis, stemming primarily from the vexed issue of land ownership. The prohibition on farming his land at Whangarei was quickly followed by an instruction from Thomson to Hobson, arbitrarily asserting that 150 acres of land around Waitangi that had been in James's ownership was now effectively Crown land.[40] And worse was to come. The recently appointed Land Commissioners were taking a vigorous and meticulous approach to their assignment. The combination of pedantry and power was a potentially toxic recipe for managing the commercial and cultural intricacies of land transactions – many of which dated back several years. On 30 December 1840, the colonial government gave notice of an intention to review James's acquisition of various parcels of land, and that the Crown would reserve some of the land around Waitangi for its own use.[41] As William Swainson, the country's second Attorney General, later observed, this sort of draconian measure was 'almost universally regarded by the claimants as an act of general confiscation', which in many instances is exactly what it was.[42]

The only good news James received in the period came from Sydney, with the announcement that Agnes had given birth to a boy, William, on 19 January 1841.[43] Apart from this, James was back in the familiar position of trying to hurdle obstacles that were frustrating his plans. In February, Willoughby Shortland, Hobson's conniving Colonial Secretary, assured James that despite

---

[38] W. Hobson to Russell, 10 November 1840, in R. A. A. Sherrin and J. H. Wallace, *Early History of New Zealand* (Auckland: H. Brett, 1890), 533.
[39] O. Wilson, *Kororareka, and Other Essays* (Dunedin: John McIndoe, 1990), 110.
[40] E. D. Thomson to W. Hobson, 18 November 1840, in *BFR* 4, 86.
[41] *New Zealand Gazette Extraordinary*, no. 1, 30 December 1840, AML, ref. 1949.16.1.
[42] W. Swainson, *New Zealand and its Colonisation* (London: Smith, Elder & Co., 1859), 89–90.
[43] *Sydney Herald*, 20 January 1841, 3.

the government having reserved some of his land at Waitangi for 'Public Purposes' (which amounted to appropriation), there was nothing for him to worry about when it came to the subsequent investigation into the validity of his title to the land.[44] Yet to assert that a claim to land would be unaffected despite the Crown seizing some of the land in question was a contradiction that either did not occur to or did not bother the Colonial Secretary. And to add indignity to injustice, James ended up having to pay a fee for each block of land he had purchased that the government planned to investigate – a total of twelve fees.

There was also a broader issue at stake which James was fighting for (and continued to do so in the following two decades). The position of the British government now was that 'uncivilized' people only exercised limited dominion over their lands, and therefore could not claim individual ownership of any land (and thus were in no position to be able to sell land).[45] James, however, was adamant that Māori had possessed a degree of sovereignty and agency by the 1830s that enabled them to trade in land – something he believed the Declaration of Independence had confirmed. He regarded the principles by which Hobson's Land Commissioners operated as 'repugnant', and was convinced that the whole course of government policy towards Māori land was essentially unjust, to both Māori and most settler purchasers.[46]

Without being able to sell or in some cases even use his land, James was forced to return to New South Wales in May 1841, partly to raise funds in the absence of any income from his planned New Zealand ventures, and partly to see if he could make some progress politically to secure his land purchases. On arriving in Sydney on 9 June,[47] he spent some time with his family, whom he found to be 'perfectly well', and then tried to get an impression of the economic situation in the colony. What he found was distressing. 'Mercantile affairs are still in a very bad state here', he wrote to Mair, 'and there is I fear no chance of the cargo of timber realising as much as will pay the freight.'[48]

After a month of scouring Sydney for buyers, James had failed to sell the spars he had imported from New Zealand. The situation was so dire that he had to borrow £200 just to meet the shortfall in costs, and he admitted that he was finding it all 'very difficult to manage', although he was still optimistic that the situation would improve in a few months.[49] This hoped-for change in circumstances did not eventuate, however, and by the end of August, James

---

[44] W. Shortland to J. Busby, 9 February 1841, in *BFR* 4, 6.
[45] *Papers Relative to the Affairs of New Zealand* (London: House of Commons, 1845), 3.
[46] J. Busby, *Speech Delivered to the Provincial Council of Auckland* (Auckland: n.p., 1853), 1–14.
[47] *Sydney Monitor and Commercial Advertiser*, 11 June 1841, 3.
[48] J. Busby to G. Mair, *c.* 13 June 1841, in *BFR* 4, 11–12.
[49] J. Busby to G. Mair, 22 July 1841, in *BFR* 4, 13.

had only managed to sell £100 of goods that he and Mair had shipped from New Zealand, while incurring a £400 debt in the process.[50]

When the options for making more money (including the possibility of exporting sulphur to New Zealand) were exhausted, James left Sydney and arrived in the Bay of Islands on 17 November. All he could hope for now was to salvage something of the land he had purchased and the businesses he was involved in. Once back at Waitangi, though, James's prospects looked to be even more dismal than when he had left. His land purchases still had not even been assessed by the Land Commissioners, he was desperately short of funds, and his garden – into which he had put so much effort – had not been tended during his absence and was completely overrun with weeds.[51]

In December 1841, James's name appeared on a notice by the New Zealand Banking Company, which was considering shifting its headquarters from Kororāreka to Auckland. James was one of the bank's directors (along with Mair, Clendon, Edward Williams, and others), and moved this motion (probably accepting the inevitability of the shift)[52] supporting the bank's relocation, which was duly passed. Following the shift, James resigned as director, mainly because of the impracticality of continuing with his duties while living in the Bay of Islands.[53] He may have wished to relocate to Auckland too, but as long as the status of his land remained frozen, he had no alternative but to wait until a decision on his purchases had been made by the government.

In the meantime, James and his family carved out a basic existence for themselves in Victoria. There were occasional variations to their routine, but whether it be responding to a request for more evidence about his purchases from the Land Commissioners, or welcoming visitors, such as Bishop George Selwyn, who arrived in June,[54] these were only temporary distractions. Even news of Hobson's death in September 1842 (preceded by notice that James's mother, Sarah, had died the previous month)[55] was not enough to interrupt the monotony of life in the Bay of Islands for the Busbys.

It was not just James and the remaining settlers in the region who were affected by the shift of the capital to Auckland. Local Māori also experienced the effects of the contraction of commerce, and one hapū leader in particular – Hone Heke, the Te Matarahurahu chief – interpreted the founding of Auckland

---

[50] J. Busby to G. Mair, 27 August 1841, in *BFR* 4, 17.
[51] J. Busby to W. Busby, 19 January 1842, in *BFR* 4, 2–3.
[52] *New Zealand Herald and Auckland Gazette*, 1 January 1842, 1; H. Carleton, *The Life of Henry Williams: Archdeacon of Waimate* 2 (Auckland: Upton & Co., 1877), 48.
[53] *Auckland Times*, 15 September 1842, 3.
[54] H. W. Tucker, *Memoir of the Life and Episcopate of George Augustus Selwyn* 1 (London: William Wells Gardner, 1879), 124.
[55] *Sydney Morning Herald*, 19 August 1842, 3.

as the colony's capital as an act of supreme betrayal by the British. Heke had been the first chief to sign the treaty, and was also a signatory to the Declaration of Independence. To that extent, he had committed himself to the cause of the British in the country. Now, though, he felt that this was not being reciprocated. Dissatisfaction among some Māori in the region was growing, making for a potentially volatile mix with the existing economic depression in the area. Henry Williams was anxious about the threat this posed to peace and order, and wrote to James, expressing his 'deep regret at the present state of New Zealand'.[56]

When it came to James's land acquisitions, though, there was no dissent from Heke – who, in the case of many of the parcels of land purchased by James, had been the previous the owner. Henry Williams later made this clear, and as a disinterested party, his testimony is of considerable value. When the Land Commissioners questioned Heke about the lands he had sold to James, the chief was 'very indignant'. Williams recorded Heke's words to these officials: 'I told you before that there was no fraud in it, the land is Mr Busby's, we received the price, and were satisfied with it.'[57]

The stress James was experiencing over the ongoing uncertainty over the title to his land was added to at the beginning of 1843, when the economy experienced a sharp downturn due to the collapse of the Bank of Australia.[58] In New South Wales, the Busbys, along with thousands of others, were affected by the failure. The bank was calling in loans, and William and Alexander attempted – in vain – to sell their livestock to meet the demands. 'The claims upon us are urgent', they wrote to the bank's directors on 30 January 1843, and even with a forced sale of their properties, they would still have insufficient funds to pay off their loans.[59] With the family struggling financially in New South Wales, James decided to go to their assistance and arrived in Sydney on 7 May 1843.[60]

While James was in Sydney, the New Zealand Company attempted forcibly to move Māori from land it claimed to have bought in Wairau Valley, in the northern South Island. The ensuing confrontation – on 17 June 1843 – resulted in four Māori and twenty-two British being killed.[61] When news of the Wairau Massacre, as it became known,[62] reached Sydney, James at once offered his

---

[56] H. Williams to J. Busby, in H. Williams, *Plain Facts Relative to the Late War in the Northern District of New Zealand* (Auckland: Philip Kunst, 1847), 10.
[57] Ibid., 30.
[58] *Sydney Morning Herald*, 2 March 1843, 2.
[59] A and W. Busby to Directors, Bank of Australia, 30 January 1843, in *BFR* 4, 1235–6.
[60] *Sydney Morning Herald*, 8 May 1843, 2.
[61] M. Belgrave, *Historical Frictions: Maori Claims and Reinvented Histories* (Auckland: Auckland University Press, 2005), 142–3.
[62] G. W. Rusden, *History of New Zealand* 1 (London: Chapman and Hall, 1883), 332.

services to Gipps to help mediate between the parties. And as he was planning to return to New Zealand in a matter of days, the timing seemed ideal. However, the Governor responded by arguing that the matter was out of his jurisdiction, and turned down the offer.[63] In response, the *Sydney Morning Herald* cast Gipps as being 'cold' and 'heartless', and argued that in rejecting James's offer, he had 'lost an opportunity of affording valuable assistance in a critical and alarming emergency'.[64] This uncharacteristic endorsement of the former Resident did not last long, though. Two days later, the same newspaper did an about-face, accusing James of offering his assistance in the crisis at Wairau was as a result of his guilty conscience pricking him.[65]

In a response to this article, James openly admitted he had a vested interest in his proposed mission, but it was not as tawdry as the journalists had insinuated. Rather, he was acutely aware of the potential for a much wider conflagration if the matter was mishandled. He warned that he had 'received an intimation, couched in no doubtful terms, that should it turn out to be the intention of the British government to take possession of their [Māori] lands, they have been betrayed by us, and we shall be the first victims of their revenge'.[66] With this foreboding prophecy sent to the newspaper for publication, James left for New Zealand on 22 July 1843.[67]

Once back in New Zealand, he sent copies of his correspondence with Gipps on the Wairau Affray to the *Auckland Chronicle and New Zealand Colonist*, which subsequently published it.[68] There was clearly still some ember of political ambition in James mind that could not easily be extinguished. To a degree, he had yet to come to terms fully with the fact that he was 'merely' a private settler now, with no official role or the sort of status he had previously possessed. And this lack of influence was dramatically brought home to him when the newspaper turned on him. Just over a week later, it labelled James's offer to help calm the tension in Wairau as 'officious interference [sic]', 'silly', 'mischievous', and 'rediculous [sic]'.[69]

Incensed at this barrage of abuse, James replied, condemning the newspaper for its 'profaneness', and expressing his intention to cancel his subscription. The response was a prolonged mocking of the former Resident – proof, if any was needed, that whatever esteem he was once held in had long since been shed. James's criticism was cited by the newspaper as 'proof of the very extraordinary obliquity of mental vision by which some men are

---

[63] Correspondence between J. Busby and G. Gipps, in *Sydney Morning Herald*, 17–19 July 1843, 3.
[64] *Sydney Morning Herald*, 20 July 1843, 2.
[65] Ibid., 22 July 1843, 2.
[66] Ibid., 24 July 1843, 2–3.
[67] *Colonial Observer*, 26 July 1843, 1188.
[68] *Auckland Chronicle and New Zealand Colonist*, 12 August 1843, 3.
[69] *Auckland Chronicle and New Zealand Colonist*, 23 August 1843, 2.

affected', and went on to 'humbly beg Mr Busby's pardon'. It was wrong, the nameless journalist continued, to criticize someone of such 'eminence', and concluded with overwrought sarcasm: 'We kiss Mr Busby's shoe ties in an apology of any length he pleases to imagine, and regret exceedingly that our gazette was displeasing to him.'[70]

A bruised ego was easier for James to deal with, though, than a battered budget. Financially, his partnership with Mair was the best prospect he had in the foreseeable future to earn some much-needed funds. In October, he travelled to Whangarei, to inspect the timber business the two men had founded, and returned to Victoria at the beginning of November. On reaching his home, though, he was confronted with yet more bad news. Most of his lambs had been killed in a recent storm, and many of those that had survived, as well as the majority of his sheep, had been savaged by dogs. There was also a formal notice awaiting him which advised that he would be awarded a total of just 2560 acres of land by the Land Commission – roughly 5 per cent of what he had purchased. And on top of this, James had learned that a replacement Governor had been selected following Hobson's death in September the previous year, and was due to arrive in the country shortly. It was Robert FitzRoy – one of those James had held principally responsible in the late 1830s for conspiring against him when he was Resident. Yet none of this news was as immediately challenging as the dramatically plummeting market for goods in New Zealand and New South Wales. James informed Mair that there was no demand for timber, and that overall, trade was 'in a miserable state. In fact, there is no trade.' He had experimented with trying to sell animal skins, kauri gum, and even tobacco, but the buyers were simply not there.[71]

On the land front, at the end of the year it looked as though there could be a breakthrough in James having his purchases confirmed. The Land Commissioners decided that for a claim to be considered, they would need the deeds to confirm the validity or otherwise of the purchase. Although this seemed like an entirely reasonable request, James said he 'smelt a rat'. His fear was that once the documentation relating to his acquisitions was in the government's hands, there would be little he could do to wrestle it from them. This suspicion was justified when 'it leaked out that the motive of this unusual haste was the intention of the Governor to invite Captain Wakefield [of the New Zealand Company] to settle his Nelson colony on my land'. For James's act of defiance in refusing to hand over his purchase deeds, the Land Commissioners responded by punitively confiscating a portion of land he owned near Whangarei.

---

[70] *Auckland Chronicle and New Zealand Colonist*, 6 December 1843, 2.
[71] J. Busby to G. Mair, 8 November 1843, in *BFR* 4, 1245–7.

For his part, FitzRoy had also been concerned with the land issue, and prior to leaving for New Zealand, he asked Stanley 'To whom should land now belong, which has been validly purchased from New Zealand natives, but which, exceeding a certain specified quantity, cannot be held, by existing laws, by the original purchaser or his representative?' Stanley's answer was the worst possible pronouncement for those hundreds of settlers in a similar position to James: 'the consequence seems immediately to follow, that the property in the excess is vested in the Sovereign, as representing and protecting the interests of society at large. In other words, such land would become available for the purposes of sale and settlement.'[72]

One settler who missed meeting the new Governor on his arrival at Auckland was the land speculator and trader John Logan Campbell. Campbell was one of those with whom James had previously, and unsuccessfully, conducted some business, and was in the Bay of Islands at the end of 1843 to recover a long-overdue trade debt from James.[73] He 'came up here in a great fright, wishing me to give them power of attorney over my property', James hurriedly informed Mair. Campbell had heard a rumour that a bank was about to foreclose on James's land at Victoria, and so had rushed there to secure himself as a creditor. James was able to show him a letter from the bank confirming that there were no such plans, and so Campbell left feeling slightly more reassured. However, James's success in placating Campbell was partly bluff. Privately he was fearful of what the bank might do at any moment, and admitted that the gradual accumulation of debts was enormously 'distressing' to him.[74]

The anxiety continued to eat away at James, compelling him finally to visit Auckland in January 1844 in an effort to extract himself from the worst of his financial entanglements. On arrival, he was confronted with the news that Campbell and the bank were in the process of taking legal proceedings against him over his debt. James urged Mair to do whatever he could to raise some funds to cover the overdue loan. Mair's response to this letter is lost, but James's reply suggests that their business partnership was heading towards the rocks: 'It is impossible you can be acting under your own sense of what is right and just,' he told Mair, adding that 'I shall of course pay no attention to your threat.' As a business collapse approached, the pressure seemed to have brought out the worst in Mair.[75]

---

[72] R. FitzRoy to Stanley, 16 May 1843, and Stanley to R. FitzRoy, 26 June 1843, in W. Brodie, *Remarks on the Past and Present State of New Zealand* (London: Whittaker & Co., 1845), 44–5.
[73] R. C. J. Stone, *Young Logan Campbell* (Auckland: Auckland University Press, 1982), 116.
[74] J. Busby to G. Mair, 25 December 1843, in *BFR* 4, 1269.
[75] J. Busby to G. Mair, 27 January, 12 February 1844, and c. 6 March 1844, in *BFR* 4, 1269–71.

Four months later, James's patience over the work of the Land Commissioners yielded him a small reward. In May, FitzRoy confirmed James's claim of 2090 acres (which incorporated part of the territory for the floundering Victoria project), but it proved to be too little, too late. The settler population in the Bay of Islands had stagnated at about 540 people, and showed no signs of growing, meaning that there was correspondingly no demand for the lots James had mapped out in Victoria. Auckland's settler population, in contrast, had already reached 2,800 and was growing rapidly.[76] The future prospects of Victoria seemed doomed.

James's more immediate concern at this time, however, was with how he would pay some of his outstanding debts. The bank was claiming £1424 from him, and was pressing him to make some prompt contribution towards this. On paper, at least, the situation was not as bad as it appeared because James was owed money by various parties. However, chasing loans and enforcing payments was extremely difficult, so he opted for negotiating with the bank – agreeing to sell his sheep and cattle, managing his other business interests, and collecting outstanding loans, with a view to repaying £250 every three months.[77] At the same time, he would work on getting one of his major debtors – William Mayhew – to repay him. Mayhew was an American merchant who had also been a director of the New Zealand Banking Company, and was serving as American Vice-Consul to New Zealand, but by this time was similarly heavily in debt.[78] The difficulty was that in such a depressed economy, with few people able to repay their debts, the best that those in James's situation could do was to throw themselves at the mercy of the banks and hope for clemency.

---

[76] *Blue Book of Statistics* (Auckland: Council Office, Colony of New Zealand, 1844), ref. IA 12 06, ANZ, 122–3.
[77] Details in *BFR* 4, 1277.
[78] J. Druett, 'The Salem Connection: American Contacts with Early Colonial New Zealand', *JNZS* 8 (2009): 181.

12

'Satan Rules'

Mayhew saw the walls closing in on him financially, and decided the best way to deal with his debts was to flee New Zealand, which he did in April 1844. This suddenly left James in a much worse financial position, and so he rushed to Auckland to make whatever frantic arrangements he could with the bank to stave off bankruptcy. The resulting deal involved him handing over to the bank all his goods (250 sheep, twenty-five tons of kauri gum, and all his cattle) so that he could retain possession of his land. The bank, for its part, only left James with his land for the moment because its ownership had yet to be determined by the government, and so its value as security for the debt James owed the bank was effectively nullified.

When James returned to Waitangi, the bank's agent was still on his property, scouring the farm for any assets that might serve as collateral for his loan, and packing up many of the items belonging to the Busbys to send to Auckland for immediate sale. James and Agnes together managed to put a stop to the agent's activities, and James then wrote immediately to the bank's Auckland directors, urging that the agent cooperate with him to allow the gum and livestock to be sold privately, which James believed would give him a better price than a 'fire sale' which the bank was planning.[1]

James now began supplying a local shopkeeper with a small but regular flow of goods for sale. His hope was that he would gradually chip away at his loan to the bank, to the point where he would be unencumbered. The single biggest asset that he wished to sell was his supply of gum, but his plans to ship it to England floundered when he failed to secure a vessel from Sydney to undertake the journey. Although James did not mention it, the problem almost certainly stemmed from the fact that he was unable to pay the ship's master up front for the cost of transporting his gum. Then, just as the door closed on this opportunity, another one opened. There was a whaling ship in the Bay of Islands that was due to depart for America, and which James

---

[1] J. Busby to Directors, New Zealand Banking Company, May 1844, in *BFR* 4, 1278.

discovered on enquiring had space for his gum. America was one of the major markets for gum at this time,[2] and James was hopeful that he could sell his product there and stave off his creditors in the process.[3]

On 6 June, James boarded the whaler with his cargo of gum, and began his journey to Salem, Massachusetts. His total debt to the bank stood at £1640, but while he was away from the country, the bank's agent continued to sell James's assets, raising £1744 by the end of 1844. Yet, despite having recovered all that was owed to it, plus an additional £104, the bank continued to sell property belonging to James and his family, taking advantage of his absence from the country to act with impunity.

James had no difficulty in finding a buyer for his gum in Salem, after which he went to Boston, where he intended to meet Supreme Court Associate Justice Joseph Story. Story was renowned for his constitutional and jurisprudential expertise[4] – a fact that James later reminded people of when citing him as an authority on his land problems.[5] He presented the jurist with a summary of his career and land purchases, and promised to send him the full bundle of supporting documents when he returned to New Zealand. James later wrote that Story displayed 'the greatest possible interest' in the status of his land, and noted his determination that '[t]he Government will find it necessary in the long run to acknowledge all your [James's] titles which are undisputed by the Natives'.[6]

Armed with what he felt was an iron-clad legal opinion, James left on the next available ship to England, reaching London in September 1844. In addition to Story's cursory assessment of his circumstances, James also had with him a letter from the Wesleyan missionary, the Reverend John Hobbs, who had been in New Zealand since James's Residency had commenced.[7] The letter was addressed to the Wesleyan Missionary Society, and praised James as 'a Christian gentleman of great uprightness and integrity of character', while claiming that the 'Native estimation of his character is of the highest kind'. It is likely that James solicited this letter from Hobbs, as it also recommended James for 'some office which will allow him to use that talent with which he is happily endued for the establishment of Christianity and good order in this distracted country'.[8]

---

[2] M. Fadiman, 'Kauri (Agathis Australis) Ethnobotany: Identity, Conservation and Connection in New Zealand', *The Florida Geographer* 41 (2010): 4–21.
[3] J. Busby to Directors, New Zealand Banking Company, May 1844, in *BFR* 4, 1281.
[4] M. Hoeflich, 'The Americanization of British Legal Education in the Nineteenth Century', *The Journal of Legal History* 8, no. 3 (1987): 250.
[5] Busby, *The First Settlers in New Zealand*, 13.
[6] Ibid., 14.
[7] J. Busby to J. Hobbs, 20 January 1843, in Auckland Museum Library, MS46, box 4, folder 15, n.p.
[8] T. Hobbs to Secretary, Wesleyan Missionary Society, 1844, in *BFR* 4, 1288.

Around the time James reached London, the security situation in the Bay of Islands was deteriorating, principally as a result of Heke's provocations. In July, Heke had dispatched some of his men to fell the British flagstaff at Maiki Hill, at Kororāreka. The action may have been largely symbolic, but Bishop Selwyn, who was in Paihia at the time, later described how he 'shuddered' at the gesture, which was 'so full of presage of evil for the future'.[9] Within four months, Henry Williams was warning that the ability of the colonial government to maintain peace in the region was diminishing rapidly.[10] It seemed only a matter of time before the first full military confrontation between Māori and the Crown broke out. News of the heightening tensions appeared in the Australian press from September,[11] but there was a delay of several months even before the first hints at trouble reached London. As the danger to Agnes and the children escalated, George stepped in and evacuated them to New South Wales. He paid for their fares, and planned for them to stay with Catherine initially when they reached the sanctuary of Sydney.[12] It was not until 3 April 1845 (after Heke had sacked Kororāreka in an early-morning raid on 11 March) that Agnes and the four children finally reached the safety of New South Wales.[13]

Still unaware of the risks his family had faced, James had been busy in London endeavouring to shore up his claim to the land he had purchased in New Zealand. In the course of seeking political allies to assist his cause, he formed what would become a lasting friendship with the MP John Colquhoun, who was an active supporter of the Church Missionary Society.[14] The Edinburgh-born politician took a strong interest in the role of Wakefield in the colony, and the damage that his Company had inflicted on Māori land rights. However, one MP, like one legal opinion, counted for little in James's struggle to get his grievances heard.

Although being remote from New Zealand left James in the dark about developments taking place there until several months after the fact, it did bring him one advantage: through his political contacts, he was privy to the latest developments in London affecting the colony. One of these involved FitzRoy's recall as Governor.[15] The New Zealand Company had been militating against FitzRoy, and through its lobbying prowess had managed to convince

---

[9] G. Selwyn, in T. L. Buick, *New Zealand's First War* (Wellington: Govt. Printer, 1926), 39.
[10] Williams, *Plain Facts Relative to the Late War in New Zealand*, 11.
[11] *Colonial Times*, 24 September 1844, 2.
[12] *BFR* 4, 1293.
[13] W. Busby to G. Busby, 11 April 1845, in *BFR* 4, 1903.
[14] *The General Baptist Repository and Missionary Observer* 5 (London: Sherwood, Gilbert, and Piper, 1843), 220.
[15] Busby, *The First Settlers in New Zealand*, 26.

the British government that he was a liability.[16] The rumour of his recall began circulating in London in March 1845[17] – seven months before FitzRoy was officially informed of the decision. James was gratified by this development, not so much for the fact of the incumbent's departure as much as the nomination for his replacement: Sir George Grey. '[T]he affairs of New Zealand were at last to be entrusted to a man of experience',[18] was James's relieved response.

James now plunged into another of his letter-writing bouts. He wrote to Stanley outlining the current circumstances in New Zealand, but did not even receive the courtesy of a reply. He then started dispatching letters to other politicians, in which he argued that the war launched by Heke 'was one of principle throughout', and had been provoked by the government.[19] He informed George Hope (the West Lothian-born Under-Secretary of State for War and the Colonies) that he had been at Heke's baptism, and claimed that the chief was now 'only doing the duty of a patriot'. According to James's assessment, Heke and those Māori who were joining the war against the Crown had been provoked by the colony's government, having effectively gone into competition with the avaricious New Zealand Company, and by its actions, breaching the Treaty of Waitangi in the process.[20] In February and March 1845, much of the correspondence James had sent to politicians and officials was tabled before the House of Commons, and his principal arguments were debated in mid-June.[21] These exchanges in Parliament amounted to little more than an airing of views, but they were sufficient to prompt Stanley to act, instructing Grey to attend to James's concerns over the unresolved land claims.

James's tactic when pleading for his rights had now changed, which may have helped his cause. His previous approach, which had been didactic, with overblown accounts of his career and references to obscure constitutional precedents in other countries, was largely absent. Now he was requesting that his land issue be resolved on the basis that it was the right thing to do, and that he had not acted for personal gain when serving the Crown. He noted how he had 'given the fifteen best years of my life to the public service under the Colonial Department', and that he had deliberately avoided opportunities to profit from his position.[22]

---

[16] G. W. Hope, in House of Commons, in *British Hansard*, 30 May 1845, 1088–9.
[17] Moon, *FitzRoy: Governor in Crisis*, 233.
[18] Busby, *The First Settlers in New Zealand*, 26.
[19] J. Busby to W. Busby, c. February 1845, cited by C. Buller, in *British Hansard*, 17 June 1845, 692.
[20] J. Busby to G. W. Hope, 17 January 1845, in *GBPP, Accounts and Papers* 33 (London: House of Commons, 1845), 14–16.
[21] *Journals of the House of Commons* 100 (London: House of Commons, 1845), 13, 100.
[22] J. Busby to Stanley, 1 July 1845, in *BFR* 4, 1906.

On 1 July, James followed this up with another submission to the Secretary of State for Colonies, which similarly relied on an appeal to natural justice rather than any specific legal obligation. 'I have resided nearly 11 years in New Zealand, which is the birthplace of my children', he informed Stanley, 'and I see no other prospect for them or myself than a permanent residence there'.[23] Four weeks later, having probably taken James's arguments into consideration, Stanley instructed Grey to recognize land sales that FitzRoy had sanctioned.[24]

James knew none of this at the time, though. In the winter of 1845, he had a great deal of time to reflect on the success of this visit to London. Since he had left New Zealand more than a year earlier, he had befriended one or two MPs of comparatively little influence, had obtained the cursory opinion of an American jurist which he does not seemed to have relied on much (probably as he intended to wait until he had furnished Justice Story with all the relevant documentation relating to his land situation), and had received little in the way of response from Stanley to his pleas for his land purchases to be validated by the Crown.

Sensing that not much more that could be achieved in England, on 7 July 1845 James sailed from Deal, in Kent,[25] bound initially for Boston. Since his previous visit to America, he had assembled a collection of documents to deliver to Story. His hope was that the Justice would provide a comprehensive written opinion that would convince the colonial authorities in New Zealand that they had acted unjustly when examining his land purchases. However, this plan came to nothing as Story died on 10 September, and James did not reach America until four days later. With no purpose now to remain in America, James sailed to Australia, arriving in Sydney on 9 November.[26] He was soon reunited with his family, and his joy at that moment was palpable. 'Willy is grown a great lad during my absence, and has much improved in his reading and writing and arithmetic,' he wrote. 'He spends a part of every day reading to my father, whose sight and hearing are nearly gone. I must say, the exercise has developed his voice, which is about to break, and from a childish treble may suddenly become the tones of a fullgrown [sic] man. He can roar like a lion on occasions.'[27]

However, James had no intention of spending any more time than was absolutely necessary in Australia. As much as he relished being with his wife and children again, after more than a year's absence, he was eager to return

---

[23] Ibid., 1908.
[24] *Copy of Correspondence Relative to a Proposal for a Grant of a Proprietary Government to the New Zealand Company* (London: House of Commons, 1845), 7.
[25] *The Australian*, 11 November 1845, 2.
[26] Ibid.
[27] J. Busby to G. Busby, December 1845, in *BFR* 4, 1910.

home as soon as possible. He planned to go alone, leaving the rest of the family with George. The situation in Northland, according to the latest newspaper reports, was still extremely volatile. '[T]he settlers are on a volcano', one journalist had recently warned in reference to the conflict in New Zealand, 'which may . . . in a few short months burst forth, desolating the whole colony with war and bloodshed.'[28]

James arrived in Auckland on 1 January 1846, and straight away headed north to Waitangi. As he approached his home, he was confronted with a very different scene from that which he recalled when he had last seen it in mid-1844. British troops were encamped on his lawn, while their officers had occupied his house. Four days later, he wrote to William, lamenting that his garden 'was in a dreadful state from the trampling of men and horses everywhere'. When James approached some of the troops asking for an explanation, he was told 'it was the Commandant's orders'. His response was unequivocal. 'I got rid of them immediately,' he noted. James was clearly furious at how the government had disregarded his property. The troops did withdraw, as he demanded, but he was annoyed by the whole situation, and put it to William: 'when has it become necessary for a man to announce his entry into his own house to those who occupy it without permission in his absence?'[29]

James's agitation at the cavalier attitude of the soldiers towards his property was tempered by the fact that there had been some progress with his plans for the town of Victoria. Clendon informed him that thirty-three allotments had been purchased, which was very encouraging given that the area was going through the closing stages of a war. However, no buildings had yet appeared on the sections that had been sold, which James attributed to the high cost of timber, and the fact that the land's legal status had yet to be solved. But there was hope in the form of the new Governor, Grey, who had arrived in New Zealand on 14 December 1845.[30] James was convinced that he would 'make short work of the difficulties'.[31]

The former Resident was indignant, though, at the bank to which he had previously owed money. Although its representatives had assured him that they would await the sale of his gum in America before seizing any of his possessions, he discovered that 'they have stripped me of practically all I possess. All is gone, sacrificed for a tithe of its value.'[32] The bank's rapacious debt collecting, along with the ongoing uncertainty of his land titles and the

---

[28] *Geelong Advertiser and Squatters' Advocate*, 15 November 1845, 1.
[29] J. Busby to W. Busby, 5 January 1846, in *BFR* 4, 1912.
[30] *New Zealand Spectator and Cook's Strait Guardian*, 6 December 1845, 3.
[31] J. Busby to W. Busby, 5 January 1846, in *BFR* 4, 1912.
[32] Ibid., 1913.

dilapidated state of his garden, farm, and house, forced James to return to Auckland in the hope of rectifying some of these problems. In February he met with directors of the bank, and ended up threatening them with legal action if they did not indemnify him for the losses they had unlawfully inflicted on him through their over-zealous debt recovery. Shortly after this meeting, he was informed that Captain William Lewington, who had been working at the timber mill at Ngunguru, had abandoned the location out of fear of the war in the north expanding to that area. This was another setback to his business interests, but James was powerless at this stage to do anything about it, other than wait until his title to the land there was confirmed, after which he could use it as security to borrow to invest in the site.

With Auckland hosting several settler families who had fled the fighting in Northland, now was the worst possible time for James to attempt to sell sections at Victoria. But with his available funds just about dried up, he resorted to advertising an auction at Auckland, at which lots at Victoria would be offered. He even promised to purchasers who wanted to settle immediately that he could offer them temporary accommodation in the Bay of Islands, and that the government had confirmed his title to the land.[33] The auction seems to have been one in which prospective buyers put an offer on a lot at the offices of the *New Zealander* newspaper,[34] but after a month of advertising, there appeared to be no resulting sales.

James remained optimistic, though, that the Victoria lots would sell, particularly as the war in the region had been brought to a conclusion by January.[35] Indeed, he regarded the location as being sufficiently secure that he brought his family back from Australia so that they could resume their lives at Waitangi. Agnes and the children arrived in Auckland on 11 April,[36] where James met them, and from where they travelled together to their home. However, plans for the adjacent settlement of Victoria continued to stagnate. The following month, James decided to break the deadlock in the status of his land by addressing his concerns directly with Grey. He wrote to the Governor, offering unconditionally any amount of land that might be required at Victoria for public purposes, including government buildings, and that Victoria was a superior location to Kororāreka, and therefore its development should be favoured by the government.[37]

When Kororāreka's residents discovered the contents of James's letter, they accused him of 'feathering his own nest'. The government, for its part,

---

[33] *New Zealander*, 21 February 1846, 1.
[34] Ibid., 21 March 1846, 4.
[35] Williams, *Plain Facts Relative to the Late War*, 23.
[36] *The Maitland Mercury and Hunter River General Advertiser*, 25 March 1836, 3.
[37] J. Busby to G. Grey, 18 May 1846, in *BFR* 4, 1918–19.

saw no advantage at all in moving any of its offices or departments away from the capital to anywhere in the Bay of Islands anyway, and so that particular scheme hit a dead end.[38]

All of these issues were overshadowed, though, by the economic state of Northland. It had been five months since the war had ended, yet the restoration of peace in the region had not coincided with a return to previous levels of trade. This had the effect of making Victoria even less appealing to would-be buyers, thus undermining the single main plank in James's hope for reviving his financial fortunes.

In the midst of struggling to see any way out of this regional economic torpor, James received news in connection with the court action he had initiated against the bank that had sold his assets while he was overseas. The verdict delivered by the judge confirmed that James had been unjustly treated by the bank, which had 'sacrificed all his property for a third of its value', even going as far as taking bottles of wine and some soap from his house to sell for next to nothing. It also emerged that the bank seemed to have singled out James (for whatever reason) and had not pursued any of its other debtors to anywhere near the same degree. Worse still, the judge noted that the bank's agents who had been selling James's assets had used some of the money raised to pay the debts of other, unconnected parties.

The bank had assured James prior to his departure to America and England that it would leave his assets in the Bay of Islands unmolested until he had attempted to sell his gum. The judgment recorded that this agreement had been 'utterly violated' by the bank, and on the basis of this, and the fact that the money he received for the gum in America covered the entirety of his debt, the accrued interest, and any sundry expenses, the court awarded James £820 – but this was still insufficient to cover the losses the bank had inflicted.

The Busbys continued to eke out an existence at Waitangi at this time. James re-established part of his garden, Agnes attended to the education of the children, and outwardly the family must have appeared much like any other in the region. But the financial burden under which the Busbys existed, along with the fast-fading hopes that Victoria would ever come to life as a settlement, had a corrosive effect on James. His money problems were not solely or even principally his fault, as far as he was concerned. Rather, they emanated from the great injustice of his land purchases not being confirmed by the Crown. It was over six years since Hobson had announced that all land purchases made by settlers were to be investigated by the colonial government, and then confirmed if found to be legitimate. Yet in the very place where the treaty that gave the Crown that authority was first signed,

---

[38] Colonial Secretary to J. Busby, c. 18 May 1846, in *BFR* 4, 1920.

James's right to his land remained suspended in an administrative limbo. He had provided evidence of its fair purchase, and the original Māori vendors had supported the validity of James's claim to the land. What more could the former Resident do?

One answer was to confront the Governor directly. The opportunity for this arose in early 1847, when Grey visited the Bay of Islands. He arrived on 10 January, along with 80 troops from the 65th Regiment, landing at Kororāreka.[39] The troops were part of a standing force in the area – stationed to quash any thought among Heke's followers of reviving their rebellion.[40] Whether James even got a chance to raise his grievance with the Governor is not known. However, James was quickly put on the back foot during the meeting, with the Governor provocatively asking why, during the recent war in the region, 'it should be that all the natives "against us", should be the people of the Church Mission, while all "our friends" are the Wesleyans and Roman Catholics'. James raised the issue with Henry Williams, and the two agreed that James would correct Grey's misunderstanding of the conflict by giving him a thorough account of the war. However, when James approached him the next morning, the Governor 'declined entering into this enquiry'.[41] If James had presumed that he was due even the faintest vestiges of respect from the Governor for his former role as the country's Resident, this encounter quickly disabused him of such a hope.

There was an infinitely harsher setback for James and Agnes a month later, when their four-year-old daughter, Agnes, died.[42] In a letter to George written shortly after the funeral, a distraught James conveyed something of the grief he was experiencing: 'You will . . . have heard our melancholy news. Our child passed from our keeping . . . into the Loving hands of the Father of us all. We have placed her little body in the churchyard at Paihia.' These lines are heavy in pathos. It was a tragedy that James struggled to contain himself over. Young Agnes had succumbed to whooping cough, along with several other children in the Bay of Islands who had contracted the contagious bacteria. '[A]ll this sorrow and suffering was caused by the captain of one of the American ships,' James concluded, needing to find someone to blame for his daughter's death. But attributing blame did nothing to lessen the despair. '[W]ith the younger children, such as our dear little one,' he explained to his brother, 'although the cough was almost gone, they could not regain their strength, and a sort of wasting overtook them, and weakness.'[43]

---

[39] Ibid., 9 January 1847, 3.
[40] J. Rutherford, *Sir George Grey: A Study in Colonial Government* (London: Cassell, 1961), 92–3.
[41] Carleton, *The Life of Henry Williams* 2, xvii.
[42] Agnes jnr died on 16 February 1847. *New Zealander*, 27 February 1847, 2.
[43] J. Busby to G. Busby, 9 March 1847, in *BFR* 4, 1951.

A sure sign of the gradual decline in the Bay of Islands from its former prominence was the reduction in the region's postal service. As the settler population continued to drain southwards to Auckland, by 1847, most of the main communities on the perimeter of the Bay as well as in the hinterland were shrinking. In July, James wrote to the Colonial Secretary in Auckland, highlighting the inconvenience of the cutbacks in the mail service, and illustrated his point with the example of a ship that had recently arrived in the Bay of Islands. It was carrying correspondence 'of great importance to me', James explained, but the vessel was not now allowed to unload its mail. Consequently, the letters in question had to go to Auckland and took a further twenty-three days to reach the Bay of Islands. And to add cost to frustration, James had to pay double the postage for this extra unnecessary handling. The government acceded to his request, and a month later, authorized that mail coming from Australia addressed to residents in the Bay of Islands could be delivered directly at Russell.[44]

This small bureaucratic victory was eclipsed, however, by a vaguely sinister allegation levelled against James in the same week. He had been accused by a trader in Auckland of arming Māori in a part of the country that the government still regarded as volatile. The charge was not as treasonous as it sounded, though. James was simply selling tools which included hatchets and tomahawks. He suggested that far from presenting a danger to peace in the region, such tools were used by local Māori for clearing land, and the extension of agricultural ventures. No action was taken against him as he had breached no law,[45] but James must have felt irritated by this level of official pettiness in even considering the allegation. The government apparently had the means to investigate trivial aspects of his business, but not to resolve the long-standing issue of his title to the land he had acquired.

While his aspiration for the future of Victoria had not quite been extinguished yet, James was more pragmatic when it came to some of his other land holdings. The block he had purchased at Ngunguru had been lying unused since the collapse of the sawmilling business there three years earlier, and the government had still to investigate his acquisition of it. He understood that he had capital tied up in what was effectively a worthless asset, and so devised what he thought was an elegant solution to this dilemma. In September, he proposed to the Governor that the Crown take the titles to the land in return for reimbursing him for the price he had originally paid for it. It was a good solution as far as James was concerned but, perhaps concerned about setting a precedent, Grey failed to rise to the bait, and the idea was rejected.[46]

---

[44] J. Busby to Colonial Secretary, 2 July 1847, in *BFR* 4, 1953.
[45] J. Busby to Colonial Secretary, 6 July 1847, in *BFR* 4, 1953–5.
[46] J. Busby, in *BFR* 4, 1946.

The following month, however, Grey wrote to James with what was, in principle, a very similar proposal. The issue arose out of the need for colonial troops to have a base in the Bay of Islands. The Governor suggested that some of the land set aside for Victoria would be suitable for the purpose. The terms of the mooted deal were straightforward, as James noted: 'I would give up to the Government gratuitously one half of all my land, with an equal share of advantages of water frontage and arable land; or, on the same conditions, I would give the whole of it, with the exception of 1000 acres, at 2s. 6d. an acre.'[47] This potential deal was important to James financially, but it was also of symbolic consequence. He had finally surrendered any remaining ambitions for Victoria to evolve into a township, and now saw it as an asset to be disposed of for whatever its salvage value was.

Privately, James was disillusioned by the developments that had led him to this point. He saw Grey as a man without scruples, citing the ordinance the Governor introduced which imposed a £100 fine on any settler either living on or making use of land that had not been confirmed to them by a Crown grant.[48] He also regarded Grey as dishonest, and unjust to Māori.[49] But whatever his personal views, James was obliged to heed to circumstances. Accordingly, at the end of January 1848, James placed an advertisement in the *Daily Southern Cross* in an attempt to dispose of most of Victoria.[50]

A fortnight after the advertisement appeared for the sale of Victoria (and with no buyers in sight), a lengthy letter written by James to the editor of the *Daily Southern Cross* was published. James, who signed the letter only as 'The Correspondent', used this opportunity to avenge what he felt was the forced sale of his beloved Victoria (which was still being advertised two months later).[51] As with so many of his other public pronouncements, it was wordy, and contained detail that was largely superfluous to the main point. However, James furnished readers with histories and minutiae because he presumed that for some, this would be the first they were aware of the issue he was raising, and so they deserved to be sufficiently informed.

'The heart of every thinking man must sicken', James suggested to the newspaper's readers, 'in contemplation of the blood which has been shed, the treasure expended, and the sorrow occasioned' by the fighting with Māori that had occurred so far as a consequence of the 'rashness' of Grey's governorship. Grey 'seemed to bring into New Zealand along with him an angry feeling towards the maories [sic] . . . [and] urged the necessity of

---

[47] Busby, *The First Settlers in New Zealand*, 34–5.
[48] This was a reference to s.1 of the Native Land Purchase Ordinance 1846.
[49] J. Busby to J. Colquhoun, 10 January 1848, in *BFR* 4, 1931–5.
[50] *Daily Southern Cross*, 29 January 1848, 1.
[51] *New Zealander*, 15 November 1848, 1.

drawing the sword against them'. James's tirade against the Governor was now gathering force: 'Grey has not turned out the man that was expected. *He has moreover kept his arrows flying about in the dark*, and his victims have been struck before they were even aware of having been aimed at.'[52] The reference to victims clearly included himself.

Despite such a public assault on the integrity of the Governor, officials in Auckland ignored the affront and continued to deal with the issues arriving on their desks, including James's proposal that some of his land at Waitangi be used for accommodating British troops stationed in the region. On 25 March the Colonial Secretary responded to this suggestion, informing James that the government would offer him £3,000 for all his land at Waitangi, provided that he could 'convey a clear and valid title'.[53] This was as plain a case as any of the government's right hand not knowing what its left hand was doing. The stumbling block all along to James selling his land was precisely that the government had not issued him with the title he sought.

The trail of documents on James's life narrows even further from 1848. Most of his correspondence with his siblings has disappeared, while the daily routine of what was largely a subsistence living left little time for the sort of heavy writing schedule he had once been accustomed to. He was occasionally the subject of scorn in the press,[54] but these tended to be passing comments, and probably of only peripheral interest to most readers at this time. As a public figure, James was known principally for events that had transpired years earlier, and had since slipped largely into obscurity. Part of this was of his own making. It is telling that his most recent foray into public debate – in February 1848 – was in the form of a letter to a newspaper to which he refused to put his name.[55] And for over a year afterwards, James maintained a very low public profile.

He was shaken out of this silence, though, in August 1849, when he experienced another consequence of government inaction in the area of land titles. A Māori he was acquainted with had just returned to the Bay of Islands from a visit to the south, and informed James that nineteen Europeans were on his land at Ngunguru, felling trees and milling the timber. The injustice of the situation was intolerable. Not only was James forbidden to undertake any commercial activity on the land until its ownership had been officially settled, but now there were others profiting from the timber on the territory in question, which appeared to be perfectly legal. James wrote immediately to Grey about this matter, and received a reply from the Attorney General, Frederick Whitaker,

---

[52] J. Busby, in *Daily Southern Cross*, 12 February 1848, 3.
[53] Colonial Secretary to J. Busby, 25 March 1848, in *BFR* 4, 1985.
[54] As examples, see *Nelson Examiner and New Zealand Chronicle*, 10 June 1848, 2, 1 July 1848, 2.
[55] J. Busby, in *Daily Southern Cross*, 12 February 1848, 3.

whom James regarded with good reason as being corrupt.[56] Whitaker coldly rejected the concerns raised, on the basis that James could not 'be recognised as having any claim to the land'. James immediately replied, insisting that those extracting timber from his land at Ngunguru be prosecuted under the provisions of the Native Land Purchase Ordinance.[57] However, as they were simply taking assets (timber) from the land without claiming to own it, the Ordinance did not apply to them.[58] Whitaker's position was correct in law, but he must have been very aware of how unjust it was in practice.

At the start of 1849, James was still without a title to his land at Ngunguru, and was lumbered with Victoria, which remained unsold. Because of uncertainty surrounding his titles, he decided to lease Victoria as pasture land for up to three years,[59] but even in this, he was unsuccessful. The location's remoteness, and the relatively plentiful availability of other land in the region, meant that the demand for grazing pastures at Victoria was negligible.[60]

James still had monies owed to him, including from his former partner, Mair. In January 1850, James geared himself up for a battle to recover the debt, writing to Mair's solicitor, Frederick Merriman. As James acknowledged, the matter would perhaps better have been handled if he had hired a lawyer, but as he explained to Merriman, the last time he had done this to recover the debt Mair owed him, Mair filed a defence and the matter was left unresolved, with James having to pay £14 for his solicitor. He was adamant that he would not make the same mistake again.

Mair was not necessarily avoiding his obligations entirely when it came to how he managed his debts, but James did not see it that way. James was under the impression that Mair had settled his outstanding debts with everyone else, but not him. Mair offered James some sections in Auckland in lieu of a cash payment, but James felt he would be being short-changed in such a deal. He explained to Merriman that had Mair 'been the best beloved brother I had, I could not have exercised more liberality and forbearance towards him than I had done, and the reward I got was to be used just as badly as he could have used me'.[61]

It seems that Merriman forwarded this letter to Mair's mother, who was serving as a de facto representative for her son in some of his business matters. She then passed it on to him, and he replied to her, addressing its contents. 'I have never had it in my power to give him cash, and he would take

---

[56] J. Busby, *Illustrations of the System called Responsible Government* (Auckland: W. C. Wilson, 1860), 18–19.
[57] s.1 of the Native Land Purchase Ordinance 1846.
[58] J. Busby to Attorney General, August 1849, in *BFR* 4, 2083.
[59] *Daily Southern Cross*, 20 January 1849, 1.
[60] *New Zealand Spectator and Cook's Strait Guardian*, 26 September 1849, 4.
[61] J. Busby to F. Merriman, 3 January 1850, in *BFR* 4, 2009–10.

nothing else,' Mair moaned to his mother. The challenge for Mair was that James would only accept cash to settle the debt. 'I could not give him what I had not got,' Mair continued; 'I have no cattle, no property of any kind and no prospect of doing so; not even the expenses he speaks of can I command money to pay . . . The only satisfaction he can get from me is to sell me off – that is, out of the little furniture and wearing apparel – and put me in jail.'[62] It was a difficult and sorry situation for Mair, but so too was it for James, with the financial welfare of his family at stake.

The root cause of this debt chasing in the colony among numerous financially interconnected parties was the intransigence of the Grey administration over the issue of resolving land titles. Grey's manipulation of the land issue had a more serious consequence for another long-standing settler: Henry Williams, who 'was sacrificed to a political combination, which included the New Zealand Company; Lord Grey, their patron; Governor Grey, Bishop Selwyn, and the Church Mission Society'.[63] It was a conspiracy of the powerful, whose individual motives coincided in the persecution of Williams over his land purchase at Paihia, and the subsequent usurpation of that land, even though his title had been confirmed during FitzRoy's governorship. The fact that Grey was prepared to overturn what had been legally declared (after full investigation) to be a valid title made the security of land tenure in general that much more uncertain. It also signalled the power of political influence over what ought to have been a matter free from such interference. In addition to losing his land Williams was dismissed from the Church Missionary Society on bases that were entirely unwarrantable.

James wrote to the Earl of Chichester, expressing his indignation over this deep injustice. 'Could any punishment', he asked, 'be more severe than to be thus cast off as if unworthy longer to continue . . . with that Christian Society whose servant he had been for so many years'?[64] This was James's deeply felt view on Williams's appalling treatment by both secular and Church authorities. But there was more to James's outrage than the maltreatment of a long-standing friend. Williams was another 'old settler', a class of migrant which was increasingly the subject of popular vilification. (One British officer in the colony condemned them as 'a clique of Land Sharks', and 'noxious vermin').[65] Williams's plight was a warning that others who earned the Governor's displeasure could face similarly stark consequences.

However, James had never been one to cower in the face of larger threats. He drafted a letter of appreciation for Williams, and then travelled around the

---

[62] G. Mair, undated, 1850, in *BFR* 4, 2010.
[63] Carleton, *The Life of Henry Williams* 2, 161.
[64] J. Busby to Chichester, undated 1850, in *BFR* 4, 2013.
[65] A. W. D. Best, in *The Journal of Ensign Best, 1837–1843*, ed. N. M. Taylor (Wellington: R. E. Owen, 1966), 322.

Bay of Islands seeking signatures to add to it. He found that both Māori and settlers were keen to put their names to the document, as there was a general feeling of regret at the imminent departure of the missionary and his family, and anger over the reason for it.

On the morning of 31 May 1850, James took a boat from Waitangi to the church at Russell in heavy rain to bid farewell to the Williams (who were effectively being exiled to the farm of one of their sons at Pakaraka, around seventeen kilometres inland) and to present this letter to them. In front of the congregation, deeply saddened by Williams's dismissal, James arose and read out the letter of appreciation to the missionary. As the former Resident began to speak, Marianne recalled how '[h]is voice faultered [sic], and he frequently stopped', while one of the men present 'cried like a child, and went out of the room several times'. It is the knowledge of these scenes that give such poignancy to the text which James struggled to deliver to Williams:

> Astonished and grieved at the unexpected termination of your valuable labours to us, we cannot allow you to leave . . . without the expression of our deep sympathy with you, and our strong sense of the value of those exertions which . . . have exercised so beneficial an interest upon the country around us during the last . . . 27 years . . . [O]ur affectionate interest will accompany you to the sphere of your future ministrations, with heartfelt prayer that the best blessings may attend you and your . . . family.[66]

When James finished reading the address, he sat down, feelingly deeply despondent. Such was the sombre atmosphere that when the normally voluble Williams rose to respond to James's message, 'it was long before he could speak. There was a long, deep pause; we all sat and looked at each other, or on the ground.'[67]

Towards the end of the year, James published *A Vindication of the Character and Proceedings of Archdeacon Henry Williams*, as part of a volume of correspondence addressed to Chichester.[68] It surveyed in detail the machinations of the Governor, and what James regarded as the despicable treatment Williams had suffered as a result. It was surprisingly well received, with one journalist recommending readers acquire a copy in order to obtain an insight into the issue from Williams's perspective, written by 'one of the most able, temperate, and influential of the Archdeacon's defenders'.[69]

---

[66] Address by J. Busby, 31 May 1850, in *Daily Southern Cross*, 18 June 1850, 4.
[67] M. Williams, in Carleton, *The Life of Henry Williams*, 2, 239.
[68] J. Busby, *Letter to the Right Hon. the Earl of Chichester, President of the Church Missionary Society* (Auckland: Williamson and Wilson, 1850).
[69] *New Zealander*, 13 November 1850, 5.

Three months after Williams's dismissal, there was some movement in another area of interest for James. Mair's lawyer had finally begun to look into the debt his client owed to James. He wrote to Mair on 28 August, outlining in some detail the situation as it stood, and the threat James had made to take Mair to court if the outstanding debt was not paid in full, with interest. Merriman subsequently quibbled with James's solicitor, William Donnelly, over the quantum, but it was a hopeless case to defend, and Mair eventually managed to secure some cash which was paid to his former friend and current creditor.[70]

By 1852, the settlement of Mair's debt, together with farming, and trading in just about any good that would turn a profit, had staved off bankruptcy for James. However, the struggle for survival was far from over, and the status of his land continued to be held in abeyance. What James was increasingly hankering for, though, was a different sort of commodity: influence. It was now twelve years since his Residency had ended, and whatever prestige and leverage he had derived from that role had long since expired. From the moment that New Zealand had become a British colony, the Governors had exercised power in the country in an autocratic fashion. However, officials and politicians in London were keen for New Zealand to move to much greater self-government,[71] and as plans were put in place for this, James was attracted by the possibility of returning to politics.

Under Grey's 1851 Provincial Councils Ordinance, a series of electoral districts were created in every province which would return elected members to participate in the country's Legislative Council.[72] The Bay of Islands was one of six electoral districts comprising the Auckland Province, and it was in that district that James naturally saw his best chances of being elected. On 20 August 1852, nominations were put forward for candidates. James was proposed by Captain William Butler, a retired whaler living in Mangonui, and William White, the Resident Magistrate.

James's announcement of his candidacy was made in a shrewd manner, through the press. He published a letter in the *New Zealander* in June 1852, in which he explained that because he had declined roles in the administrations of Hobson and FitzRoy, voters could be forgiven for thinking that he would be disinclined to serve on the Provincial Council that was about to be formed. However, this was 'by no means the case'. Then came the posturing. James

---

[70] Correspondence between F. Merriman and W. Donnelly, undated, in *BFR* 4, 2028–30.

[71] P. A. Joseph, 'Foundations of the Constitution', *Canterbury Law Review* 4 (1989): 60–1.

[72] *Provincial Councils Ordinance*, 1851, ss. 1–3; G. Grey to Grey, 30 August 1851, in *The New Zealand Constitution Act [1852]: Together with Correspondence between the Secretary of State for the Colonies and the Governor-in-Chief of New Zealand in Explanation Thereof* (Wellington: New Zealand Government, 1853), 33–45.

decided to put himself forward almost as the reluctant candidate who was being dragged into politics by popular demand. He went on to inform potential voters that he did not intend to stand 'to gratify personal feelings', and that there were few others who had better knowledge of the important issues in the region than him, or who were 'more interested in promoting its prosperity'.[73]

On 28 August, three days after the election was held, the preliminary results were released. Of the three candidates standing in the Bay of Islands, George Clarke received forty-three votes, Charles Waitford ten, and James just six.[74] When the final results were tallied a few weeks later, though, the margin was much tighter. Clarke reached fifty-one, James got forty-six, and Waitford obtained thirteen.[75]

James had failed to secure a seat but his keenness to enter local politics was undiminished. In April 1853, he again offered himself as a candidate for the Auckland Provincial Council.[76] With his reputation, his standing in the community (he had been appointed magistrate for the Bay of Islands on 7 March 1853),[77] and the closeness of the election result the previous year, he was hopeful that a victory was in reach. Three months later, the elections were held, and James, along with Clarke, was successful (although as they were the only candidates of the two posts, the outcome was a formality).[78]

Of the letters James wrote to his family at this time, only one to Alexander has survived. In it, James confided how he had been 'besieged with individuals' enlisting his help with their land claims, and disturbingly, that 'the Government has not been above trying to buy me off with offers which it is impossible for me to accept'. He was now face to face with the corruption that was at the core of the Grey government. The deal he was covertly offered was that if he ignored the pleas of other claimants to have their land purchases confirmed by the Crown, he stood a much better chance of his own acquisitions finally being awarded the titles he had been pursuing fervently for over a decade. But he was not to be tempted. As he told Alexander:

> The more I see of people in authority here [Auckland], the more I wonder whether they have been visited with some fell disease of the brain which eats away all sense of moral obligations. Satan rules in this distressed land, his myrmidons are everywhere, with Governor Grey at their head.[79]

---

[73] *New Zealander*, 3 July 1852, 1.
[74] *New Zealander*, 28 August 1852, 2.
[75] *New Zealander*, 11 September 1852, 2.
[76] J. Busby, 12 April 1853, in *New Zealander*, 18 May 1853, 2.
[77] *New Zealander*, 6 April 1853, 5.
[78] Gazetted 14 July 1854, in *New Zealander*, 7 September 1853, 3.
[79] J. Busby to A. Busby, 21 July 1853, in *BFR* 4, 2045.

While constitutional changes heralded a new political era for the colony from 1853, they also threatened one of its more established institutions: the New Zealand Company. Under the 1852 New Zealand Constitution Act, the newly instituted General Assembly assumed power over Crown waste lands in the country (some of which were claimed by the Company), and the Governor was granted much greater authority over the affairs of the Company, which was by now heavily indebted. However, while the demise of the Company was looking increasingly certain, the principles on which it had been based were not as easily abandoned. The idea of systematic colonization appealed to the government because it would bring in much-needed labour and capital. Therefore, Grey effectively enacted programmes similar to those of Wakefield's – in concept if not in scale – in a bid to boost the colony's economy and population.

One of these small-scale settlement schemes involved around 50,000 acres of land at Waipu, near Whangarei, which included some of the territory James had previously purchased, and for which he was still waiting for resolution on its title. Unknown to James, though, in October 1851 Grey had offered a grant of this supposedly 'Crown land' to a group under the leadership of a Presbyterian minister, Norman McLeod.[80] McLeod had initially taken his flock from the Highlands of Scotland to Nova Scotia. However, when that settlement proved to be economically unfeasible, they moved to Australia, where they discovered that the land was unaffordable for them. Grey's offer was more than alluring enough for them to migrate to New Zealand, which they did over a period of several years, starting in September 1853, when the schooner *Margaret* arrived in Auckland, laden with the first batch of these migrants destined for Waipu.[81]

Even by his own standards, Grey had pushed the boundaries of impropriety. With the full knowledge that title to the land in question had yet to be settled, and despite his awareness of James's habitual rectitude in his dealings, the Governor had gone ahead with this unethical transaction. The Presbyterian purchasers were an innocent party, and James was the luckless victim. A chain of correspondence ensued between James and the Colonial Secretary, Andrew Sinclair, who had become something of an apologist for Grey, as well as a beneficiary of his growing web of corruption.[82] These letters were

---

[80] G. Grey to N. McLeod, 1 October 1851, in *Forbes Eadie Scrapbook*, National Library of New Zealand, Ref: MSY-5842, *c.* 1940, 64; N. Robinson, *To the Ends of the Earth: Norman McLeod and the Highlanders' Migration to Nova Scotia and New Zealand* (Auckland: HarperCollins, 1997), 18ff.
[81] M. Molloy, *Those Who Speak to the Heart: The Nova Scotian Scots at Waipu, 1854–1920* (Palmerston North: Dunmore Press, 1991), 43; *New Zealander*, 14 September 1853, 2.
[82] As an example, see C. Partridge, *Calumny Refuted, the Colonists Vindicated, and the Right Horse Saddled* (Auckland: Creighton and Scales, 1864), 38.

subsequently published in the *Daily Southern Cross*, offering the public an insight into how the government handled such matters: in a manner that was both cavalier and contemptuous.

James pointed out to Sinclair that Māori in Whangarei were in a state of 'great excitement' over rumours that the land they had sold to James was being sold to someone else. He then advised that he had been in contact with the Scottish buyers, and presumably had put his case for the illegality of the sale to them (although given that the Governor had personally stitched the deal together, the concerns of an apparently disgruntled settler would not have been given too much credence). James was adamant that he would 'take advantage of the first occasion which may arise for trying the validity of my . . . title before the Supreme Court'.[83]

Reference to court action opened up the opportunity for Sinclair to respond with a (simple) legal argument: because the Crown had not yet confirmed the validity of the title, it could not become a party to any legal challenge.[84] James partially conceded the point, but in his reply he again warned of growing Māori agitation over the Crown's failure to confirm his title. He then turned from threatening a court case to a more conciliatory approach, proposing that the Chief Justice, William Martin, act as arbiter in the dispute. Sinclair declined the suggestion outright.[85]

The Crown had failed to follow its own prescribed process when it came to investigating and confirming titles, but what James discovered had been occurring behind the scenes was much more insidious. A junior chief from the Waipu district – Poukoura – had been visiting Auckland at the time that Grey was plotting to divest James of his land. The Governor arranged a meeting with the chief, and explained that the Crown wished to acquire the land at Waipu. (James later interviewed Poukoura about this encounter and recorded the details of what took place.) Poukoura responded to Grey's suggestion, saying 'O Governor, the men of Wangarei will not sell that land to you, for they sold it many years ago to Mr Busby.'[86] Grey then tried to induce Poukoura to change his mind by offering him money to sign the land over to the Crown, but the chief remained adamant that it belonged to James. Seeing he was getting nowhere, Grey dismissed Poukoura, calling him 'a child', and advising him that he would send John Johnson, the District Land Commissioner, to Waipu to secure the territory for the Crown. Poukoura's parting words to Grey were 'O Governor, I now perceive you are a robber of land.'[87]

---

[83] J. Busby to A. Sinclair, 4 January 1854, in *Daily Southern Cross*, 10 February 1854, 3.
[84] A. Sinclair to J. Busby, 20 January 1854, in *Daily Southern Cross*, 10 February 1854, 3.
[85] J. Busby to A. Sinclair, 24 January 1854, and A. Sinclair to J. Busby, 31 January 1854, in *Daily Southern Cross*, 10 February 1854, 3.
[86] Poukoura, cited in Busby, *Our Colonial Empire and the Case of New Zealand*, 145–6.
[87] Ibid., 146.

Johnson promptly went to Waipu, and managed to find a member of the local hapū who was prepared – on being paid £200 – to agree to Grey's terms. However, when news of this offer spread through the hapū, its other members were filled with 'the greatest astonishment and indignation'. According to James, '[t]hey looked upon it as some treacherous scheme to entrap them, the nature of which they were unable to unravel'. The money was returned to the government with a message that the land was not theirs to sell. Grey would not be deterred, though, and offered the hapū up to £4,000 to sell the land, but its leaders wanted firm assurances that James would not be prejudicially affected by any transaction they were involved in with the Crown.[88]

Eventually, though, the influx of an increasing number of migrants, to whom the government sold sections, was the method by which James's land was wrenched from him. Within a few years, the settlement at Waipu presented 'every indication of a contented and thriving community', with some of the settlers already having accumulated enough capital to enable them to purchase additional land.[89] Understandably, James was infuriated by the underhand tactics the government had used to confiscate his land. However, not since the formation of the colony had he been in a better position to fight back. He was now a member of the Provincial Council, and so was part of the apparatus of government, albeit a very minor part. Having spent more than a decade battling the state from the outside, now he was within its walls, and ready to fight for his rights.

On 9 November 1853, James stood before his fellow Provincial Councillors in Auckland and tabled a motion which he then spoke to. It was described (with only slight exaggeration) by one newspaper as the 'Impeachment of Governor Grey'.[90] The motion James put before the Council urged that all the ordinances and regulations affecting land ownership that were 'repugnant to the laws of England' be expunged. It also pleaded for full compensation to be paid to those whose titles to land had not been confirmed by the Crown. James favoured the convening of a select committee for these purposes, which would allow for evidence to be received from affected parties, no doubt including himself.[91]

With the motion tabled, James then delivered a lengthy address to the Council, detailing the reasons behind it. This was no issue of abstract principle, party loyalty, or individual conscience, he told his audience. Instead, it was a

---

[88] Ibid., 146; *Daily Southern Cross*, 10 February 1854, 3; J. Buller, *The Maori War: A Lecture* (Auckland: Charles Williamson, 1869), 6.
[89] *Voices from Auckland, New Zealand* (London: Alex. F. Ridgway & Sons, 1862), 47–8; W. Swainson, *New Zealand and its Colonization* (London: Smith, Elder & Co, 1859), 202–3.
[90] *Daily Southern Cross*, 15 November 1853, 2.
[91] Busby, *A Speech Delivered in the Provincial Council of Auckland*, ii.

concern that went 'to the foundation of our existence as a community'. The current regime that determined land tenure in New Zealand, he suggested, was the product of 'illegal and unjust acts of ignorant or self-willed men'. This was strong language, and he continued in a similar vein, accusing those responsible for the current regulations of having been 'perverted by the power with which they were entrusted'. Having summarized the Crown's transgressions against natural justice, James argued that 'all this is so monstrous that it is difficult, even with the evidence before our eyes, to believe that such things can be'.[92]

The conclusion to this address contained the comment that excited the press the most. '[I]f providence had placed me in such a situation as to make it possible for me to impeach Sir George Grey,' he told the surprised audience, 'I do not believe I could have slept quietly without impeaching him.'[93] With the evidence and precedent he had alluded to in his speech, James's request for a select committee investigation was no hastily conceived political manoeuvre or irrational outburst that could easily be dismissed as unwarranted. Certainly, the newspapers took his proposal seriously. James's speech was described by the *Daily Southern Cross* as presenting 'a painful picture of the local misgovernment of New Zealand'. The central concern, as the press rightly saw the matter, was 'the violation of national faith, the invasion of private rights, the spoliation of private property, and the secret and systematic defamation of private character by Governor Grey'.[94]

The suggestion that a select committee investigate the government's land policies was an astute move by James. If his allegations were without foundation, Grey's cause would be strengthened enormously by an enquiry. However, 'every possible influence' and 'every available means' were adopted by Grey's supporters to smother any chance of the select committee being convened, and they were successful.[95] The Provincial Council voted by a margin of twelve to eight to reject James's motion. On 30 November, in a futile bid to reverse the decision, James wrote to the Secretary of State for the Colonies, reiterating the purpose of his motion and supporting it with evidence,[96] but it was no use. James had been robbed of a chance for justice.

Perhaps the only consolation James could draw from this otherwise exhausting and ultimately fruitless episode came from the announcement that Grey's tenure as Governor was coming to an end. In early 1854, Grey left

---

[92] Ibid., 2–3.
[93] Ibid., 14.
[94] *Daily Southern Cross*, 15 November 1853, 2.
[95] Ibid.
[96] J. Busby to Duke of Newcastle, 30 November 1853, in Busby, *A Speech Delivered in the Provincial Council of Auckland*, i.

to take up the governorship of Cape Colony in South Africa. His departure coincided with an outbreak of measles among Māori in the Auckland region, which was seen by many of them as a bad omen.[97] Certainly, for James, the Governor's actions had plagued his life for the past eight years, not only by ravaging his financial position, but also by pitting him against officials and politicians, and there was still no resolution to his land issues in sight.

---

[97] Rusden, *History of New Zealand* 1, 542.

13

The Ink-blotter

With Grey gone, James may have felt some momentary respite, but the difficulties over the status of his land lingered. He had mounted a formidable assault in the Provincial Council on the corruption of the Grey administration, and had supported his case with compelling evidence. But his motion had failed to win a majority, and having effectively fired all his ammunition in this unsuccessful bid to get Grey's venal land policies investigated, for the moment James was a spent political force. If he had won the motion, his political stock would have risen substantially, but as it was, his failure left him with few allies, and no further along the route to securing his land purchases.

One of the aspects of the case that worked against him was his refusal to hand over to the land commissioners any of the documentation relating to his acquisition of the sections under dispute. His rationale was that the entire process established by Grey was designed principally to deny settler rights to land they had acquired from Māori, and then vest that land with the Crown. James asserted that his purchase was valid under the rules as they applied prior to 1840, and that the Māori leaders from whom he had acquired the land were to prepared to tell anyone who enquired that they were satisfied with the price they had received (and were willing to testify to that effect).[1] Subsequent changes in regulations and policies may have turned the law into an ass in James's mind, but it was the law nonetheless, and his defiance of its provisions made him look like he was bumbling in the way he attempted to preserve his rights.

Resolving the issue of titles had become suddenly more acute with the application by a settler, Duncan McKenzie, to purchase a block of land in Waipu from the Crown – part of the territory James asserted ownership over. James placed an advertisement in the press which he entitled 'Caution'. It notified

---

[1] J. Busby, *Rebellions of the Maori Traced to their True Origin* (London: Strangeways & Walden, 1865), 38.

readers that an application to buy part of his land had been received by the government, and in his best legalese, James warned that 'whereas all the land comprised within the boundaries specified . . . is my property . . . no person has any lawful authority to interfere therewith without my permission. The said Duncan McKenzie [and] all other parties are hereby cautioned and warned not to interfere with or intrude upon the said land.'[2] The prose style deliberately suggested that purchasing the land in question would be an illegal act, but the fact that the Crown was arranging the very transaction that James was objecting to thwarted his implicit threat. It was another futile effort by James to swim against the tide of government policy.

Grey's interim replacement was Colonel Robert Wynyard, who assumed the role of Acting Governor on 3 January 1854, and held it until September the following year. On the day after Wynyard formally took on his position, James wrote to him, blaming Grey for nearly reigniting war in the Bay of Islands, and for continually refusing to act justly in confirming titles to land that had been legitimately acquired by settlers. He then outlined the more recent sequence of events in which the former governor had laboured hard in essence to bribe Māori in the Waipu region, noting that '[i]t took him [Grey] 18 months before he could succeed in overcoming their repugnance to receive money for land which they told him belonged not to them but to me'. James also revealed that local chiefs had been falsely advised by the District Land Commissioner that compensation had been paid to him for the land, and that he was satisfied with the amount he had received.[3] James described this as 'a humiliating page in British history',[4] but for the government, it was serving a greater good, and however distasteful such means were, they justified the ends in the minds of officials.

It looks as though James's approach was to draw attention to the worst excesses of the government's dealings with his land in the hope that Wynyard would wish to distance himself from the corruption of his predecessor. It may have been an appeal to Wynyard's sense of propriety, but regardless of what the Acting Governor felt privately, he was aware of the risk of setting a precedent by undoing a Crown purchase. It could upset other titles (including those acquired by the New Zealand Company) and potentially destabilize the economy and society of the colony. Although Grey had acted reprehensibly, upholding the Crown's misappropriation of James's land at Waipu was a small concession to make in order to secure stability for the country.

Some cheer for James amidst his ongoing battle with the government's land policies came with the marriage of his only daughter, Sarah, to John

---

[2] J. Busby, in *Daily Southern Cross*, 6 January 1854, 1.
[3] J. Busby to R. Wynyard, 4 January 1854, in *BFR* 4, 2068.
[4] Busby, *Rebellions of the Maori Traced to their True Origin*, 5.

Williams (fifth son of Henry, who conducted the wedding service) on 3 May 1854.[5] This shored up what was already a strengthening relationship between James and Henry, both of whom were struggling to assert ownership over land they had previously purchased.[6] Whatever joy James experienced at his daughter's marriage was short-lived, though. A notice from the Surveyor-General in the *New Zealand Government Gazette* on 6 June advised that a block of land at Ruakaka was up for sale. The section included the northern part of James's Waipu purchase, and he was naturally incensed at this latest effort by the government to deprive him of his property.

The announcement was worse than it seemed, however. While in Auckland, James heard a rumour that two settlers – McKenzie and a fellow Scot, MacKay – had already secretly purchased the block, thus making the *Gazette* notice an administrative measure designed to give the deal a façade of legality. James responded by publishing a statement in the *Daily Southern Cross*, warning the two purchasers by name that the land in question was not the government's to sell, and that the issue of its title was to be the focus of impending legal proceedings.[7] Again, though, James's bluster came up against the greater authority and resources of the Crown, and the purchase went ahead.[8]

One of the unintended consequences of the government's offer to purchase land from Māori that they had already sold to settlers occurred in the Bay of Islands on 27 June. A local resident recorded how that morning, 'the usual quietness of Kororareka was strangely varied by the sudden appearance of a gay flotilla of canoes, thronged with some hundreds of half-armed natives'. This small armada had arrived 'to demand a second payment for the whole extent of the township'. The reason for this demand was that news had spread through Māori communities in the region about the government paying chiefs for land they had already disposed of, and others were keen to capitalize on this.[9]

As the pressure mounted on James, he opted for the now-familiar tactic of addressing his concerns to someone high up in government circles, and there was no-one higher than the British Prime Minister, to whom he wrote on Boxing Day 1854. He wanted to alert the Prime Minister to the 'peculiar circumstances' of his land status, and subsequent misrepresentations on the matter made by Grey. As James saw it, not to go to the highest echelon of imperial power would be 'a dereliction of duty'.[10] What he failed to appreciate,

---

[5] *The Early Journals of Henry Williams*, 479.
[6] In February 1854, Henry Williams wrote a letter (anonymously) to the press, supporting the land claims of 'old settlers' such as James. See *Daily Southern Cross*, 7 February 1854, 3.
[7] J. Busby, *Daily Southern Cross*, 30 June 1854, 4.
[8] Molloy, *Those Who Speak to the Heart*, 158–61.
[9] *Daily Southern Cross*, 21 July 1854, 2.
[10] J. Busby to Earl of Aberdeen, 26 December 1854, in *Daily Southern Cross*, 5 January 1855, 2.

however, when writing this letter, was a sense of proportion. His myopic view of politics excluded any consideration that perhaps the Prime Minister of the most powerful nation on earth at this time might not be particularly interested, or might not have the time to consider a dispute over a comparatively small land purchase in a remote colony. Furthermore, James ought to have realized that with a fully fledged representative government in New Zealand, it would have to take a transgression on a massive scale for politicians in London (let alone the Prime Minister) to sit up and take note. James's problems with his titles were nowhere close to such scale and severity.

Also in December, James had issued proceedings in the Supreme Court against McKenzie, challenging the latter's purchase of the disputed section. There was little personal animosity between the two men, and McKenzie had even suggested that court action was the best means to resolve the issue once and for all. 'We had better make this a test case,' he had told James in late 1854. 'I wish to do the right thing, and so do you. I shall settle on the land and you can prosecute me, and we'll see what the Government has to say about it and the court.'[11] However, McKenzie soon grew more concerned than his initial statement indicated, and on 13 December he sent a copy of the Supreme Court summons to the Colonial Secretary, along with a request that the government take whatever steps were necessary to defend his title. The reply from the Colonial Secretary was that 'the Government cannot interfere in this case'.[12] Such nonchalance concealed underlying 'alarm and anxiety' among some settlers in the colony, due to 'official incapacity' and 'Imperial misrule' in a country that had been 'so cruelly abused' by its government.

Public interest in James's court case grew in early 1855. Although the action had been brought against another settler, most people realized that the defendant was a proxy for the Crown, and that the implications of the outcome could affect the titles of many other colonists. The stakes were thus as high for the state as they were for James. The summary of the matter produced by the press at this point threw light on some of the implications of the forthcoming case. 'It has hitherto been erroneously supposed that when the Government sell land, they guarantee title,' one journalist wrote, before observing that this was a mistaken belief, and 'that purchasers, under Crown title, must either brave a lawsuit, or trust to their own good broadswords for defence'.[13]

As the hearing neared, James was suddenly drawn into another case, in which he was the defendant. The plaintiff, Henry Snowden, was seeking £500

---

[11] D. McKenzie to J. Busby, c. November 1854, in *BFR* 4, 2096.
[12] Colonial Secretary to D. McKenzie, 28 December 1854, in *BFR* 4, 2096.
[13] *Daily Southern Cross*, 19 January 1855, 2.

from James for (among other things) false imprisonment. In February the previous year, Snowden had purchased around six tons of kauri gum from two Māori vendors, and shipped it from Kerikeri to Auckland to sell. On returning to Northland, though, he was summoned by the police and charged with illegally taking gum belonging to James. At the ensuing hearing into the matter, Snowden alleged that James had interfered throughout – from challenging procedures to undertaking translations of evidence given by Māori witnesses. Snowden was then held in custody for two days, which led to his accusation against James for wrongful imprisonment.[14]

In his summing up, the judge (Chief Justice William Martin) advised the jury that although Snowdon had not committed a felony, there was probable cause for James to think otherwise at the time. For the jury to find against James, they would have to be convinced that he was disingenuous and actuated by 'evil feelings'. In under two hours, the jury returned, and against the Chief Justice's guidance, found against James, and awarded Snowden £200 in damages.[15]

To James, this was a bitter setback. The verdict implied that his motives were 'evil' and vexatious, and that he had interfered with the hearing conducted by the magistrate who had investigated Snowden's activities. The fact that the jury also seemed to favour the testimony of a person with a dubious background (which Snowden certainly possessed) over the word of the former Resident was even more galling to James. And the final insult was the hefty damages he was now obliged to pay to a person whom he regarded as a criminal.

James then had to turn his attention immediately to the next case: his action against McKenzie. Singleton Rochfort was the solicitor appearing for James, and opened by emphasizing that the matter before the court boiled down to one of land ownership. The particular block in question was eighty acres at One Tree Point, on the south head of Whangarei Harbour – the site McKenzie asserted ownership of by virtue of having purchased it from the Crown.

In giving evidence, James noted that twenty-three Māori chiefs had signed the memorial in 1839 transferring ownership of the site to him, including one chief not from the region, but who had an ancestor buried on the land. The translation of James's memorial with the chiefs was deemed to be correct by a court-approved interpreter, following which a succession of chiefs who had been signatories of the land sale to James testified before the court that the transaction was legitimate and that they continued to uphold it.[16]

---

[14] *New Zealander*, 9 June 1855, p. 5.
[15] Ibid.
[16] E. Toenga, in *New Zealander*, 9 June 1855, 7.

The evidence in favour of James's right to the land looked solid. Rochfort reminded the jury that their role was to stick to the evidence and not to delve into the murky area of legislation and politics. The three questions for them to deliberate on, he proposed, were whether James had fairly purchased the land from its Māori owners; whether One Tree Point was part of that purchase; and whether James had subsequently sold any portion of that land. If the decision did not go in his client's favour, Rochfort announced he would take the matter to the next appellant tier: the Privy Council.

The judge presiding over the case then clarified for the jury the principal matter they were charged with deciding on: 'whether effect was to be given to the fundamental law of the Colony . . . by which every colonist must be bound'. Rochford immediately sprung to his feet and challenged the judge, claiming that the jury was being unduly influenced, and threatened to move for a new trial on the grounds of misdirection. However, the judge was not to be so easily quelled, and proceeded to raise doubts about the value of the testimony provided by the Māori vendors on the basis that it was around fifteen years since the transaction, and that there may have been dissenting parties whose voices were not heard in court.

The central point in the judge's direction to the jury, however, involved the application of the law. Referring to an 1841 ordinance, he observed that all title in the colony existed only if confirmed by the Crown.[17] 'It is incumbent therefore on the plaintiff', he continued, 'to show some proof that his alleged title to the piece of land now in possession of the defendant has been allowed by the Crown.' It was a damning statement. And as an added measure of ill-will, the judge implied that James had acquired the land in question dishonestly.[18] Rochfort was incensed at this turn of events, and after challenging the judge at least twice, had to be prevented – for the sake of his own career – from further interjections by a colleague who pleaded with him to remain quiet and seated (Rochfort was later censored for his outburst). Given such a clear direction, it took the jury just a few minutes to return a verdict in favour of McKenzie. The law prevailed, but justice had not been served in the process, certainly as far as James was concerned anyway.[19] On 26 June 1855, James gave warning through a newspaper advertisement that he intended to appeal the decision against him to the Privy Council, and that anyone occupying his land without his permission would be regarded as a trespasser.[20]

---

[17] New South Wales Act, 4 Vict., No. 7, Repealed, s.2.
[18] *Daily Southern Cross*, 15 June 1855, 3.
[19] *New Zealander*, 9 June 1855, 7; 13 June 1855, 2.
[20] *New Zealander*, 7 July 1855, 4.

An appeal to the Privy Council – the highest court in the Empire – was a vastly more costly, lengthier, and strenuous undertaking than a hearing in the Supreme Court in Auckland. Even if he was successful in having his case heard, it could be years before a judgment was reached, with no certainty that the law lords would decide in his favour. James therefore abandoned this option in favour of appealing the Supreme Court decision on the basis that the verdict was contrary to the evidence, the jury were misdirected, and the judge had made prejudicial statements during the case. There was also the intriguing issue of whether an ordinance (which the judge had used as an authority in his summing up) had the same status as a law. The appeal was heard on 31 October, with the judge rejecting these points and upholding the original judgment against James.[21]

However, even before the appeal was heard, James had calculated that there was a chance to alter the colony's unjust (as he saw it) land legislation if he became a law-maker himself by being elected to the House of Representatives. Accordingly, on 10 September 1855, he announced that he would be putting his name forward for the forthcoming general election – a two-month-long period of voting that was due to commence at the end of October – around the same time as his appeal hearing was scheduled for.[22] It is possible that the arrival in New Zealand of the new Governor – Thomas Gore Browne – four days earlier may have been a consideration in James's decision to stand for Parliament. Browne was regarded as the sort of person who was conscientious and determined. 'Naturally simple and retiring,' a later colonial secretary wrote, 'he was quick, intelligent, and had great moral courage', and was 'endowed with "that chastity of honour which feels a stain like a wound"'.[23]

James failed in his bid to get elected to the House of Representatives, though.[24] Coming on the tail of his defeat in court, this was a substantial blow to his ambitions to retain his land, and to have a political career. He now turned his attention back to his financial situation. He owned land he was unable to use or sell, he was based in Waitangi (which by now had been reduced to a remote rural outpost), and he was without regular full-time employment. Moreover, what little agricultural output he managed to produce for sale was affected by a slump in prices in the middle of the decade.[25] Surrendering to circumstances was not something James even contemplated, however. There

---

[21] *Daily Southern Cross*, 2 November 1855, 3.
[22] *Daily Southern Cross*, 5 October 1855, 4.
[23] W. Gisborne, *New Zealand Rulers and Statesmen from 1840 to 1897* (London: Sampson, Low, and Marston, 1897), 83–4.
[24] *New Zealander*, 14 November 1855, 2.
[25] V. Wood, T. Brooking, and P. Perry, 'Pastoralism and Politics: Reinterpreting Contests for Territory in Auckland Province, New Zealand, 1853–1864', *Journal of Historical Geography* 34, no. 2 (2008): 229.

is evidence that – having failed in court – he was now resorting to other means to uphold his land claims. Operating on Cromwell's principle that 'necessity hath no law', James appears to have lobbied Māori on his land at One Tree Point to obstruct McKenzie. McKenzie complained in early 1856 that '[t]he Natives of the Wangarei Tribes would neither take employment with me to plough the land, nor sell me potatoes, nor flax, nor any other commodity whatever'.[26] James's hand was clearly at work here, frustrating McKenzie in the hope that it would eventually drive the court-confirmed owner off the land that James still believed was his.

The shambles surrounding the status of land that had been acquired by some settlers required a final resolution, and Browne took it upon himself to do this, thus hopefully bringing to an end to the sorts of situations that had led to James taking court action. The result was the Land Claims Settlement Act, which was passed in August 1856,[27] but which proved to be far from the panacea that James and others had hoped for. On obtaining a copy of the Bill three months earlier, James had become concerned with the 'arbitrary powers' the proposed legislation would vest in the Land Claims Commissioner (who would be charged with determining the validity of titles).

On 1 August, James addressed the House of Representatives on the proposed legislation, having been granted special permission to do so. He opened his speech with an attack on the select committee process that had preceded the final reading of the Bill in the House. He informed members that 'it is impossible' to understand the significance of the Bill before them without taking into account the evidence presented to the select committee. The problem, though, was that this evidence had not been printed and so was not available to the members to consider.[28]

On the substance of the proposed legislation, James was direct in his language. '[T]he enactments of this bill', he informed the House, 'amount . . . to a virtual confiscation of the property of the original settlers . . . It is . . . a Bill of Pains and Penalties.' From here, he indulged in melodramatic metaphors in the hope of swaying the opinion of the Members present: 'The persons whose interests are affected by this Bill ask you for bread, and you offer them a stone . . . They complain to you that they have been chastised with whips, and you threaten to chastise them with scorpions.'[29]

The next issue he addressed was the block he had purchased south of Whangarei, noting that the current Bill – if passed into law – would deprive

---

[26] D. McKenzie, in *BFR* 4, 2136–7.
[27] Land Claims Settlement Act, 1856.
[28] Busby, *The First Settlers in New Zealand*, 7.
[29] Ibid., 8.

him of the land and of any compensation for the loss. He pointed out that he had previously offered it to the Crown in return for the price he had originally paid for it, but that Grey preferred 'seizing upon my land without any recognition of my rights'. James also mentioned the fact that he had refused to hand over some of the documentation relating to his purchase. This had been regarded 'as a high crime' by some officials, but as it turned out, it was Grey's intention to take James's title, appropriate his land, and use it to settle some of the New Zealand Company residents in Nelson.[30] James's decision to retain the documents connected with his purchases was all that had prevented Grey from nullifying James's claims completely.

Speaking before the House also afforded James the opportunity to address (and make more widely known) the treatment he had received during his select committee submission. When he had detailed the damages and persecution he had suffered, as well as the 'bad faith and injustice of the Government', the smug response he received from one member on the committee epitomized precisely the indifference to justice that he had been up against: '[i]t is said that every man in the course of his life must eat a peck of dirt; and every man also must submit to a great deal of injustice.'[31]

The closing segment of James's carefully constructed address (which lasted more than two hours)[32] was calculated to appeal to the more elevated values of the politicians comprising his audience:

> I shall oppose the injustice which this Bill would work, as I have always, at the sacrifice of my own private interests, opposed the unjust measures of the Government in dealing with this question. I hold it to be the highest duty to which a citizen could be called; to oppose, by such means as a good citizen and a Christian might use, the unlawful and unjust acts of persons in power.[33]

James's speech was, according to one reporter, 'the bright coloured patch upon a sorry garment . . . [but] notwithstanding its intrinsic excellence, was so far unappreciated as to leave him in a minority'.[34] Despite its 'excellence' James had failed in his sole objective, and fifteen days later, the Bill was passed into law.

One aspect that emerged from of the press coverage of James's address to the House in August 1856 was the revelation that he was an accomplished

---

[30] Ibid., 35, 37–8.
[31] Ibid., 48.
[32] *New Zealander*, 2 August 1856, 2.
[33] Busby, *The First Settlers in New Zealand*, 49.
[34] *Daily Southern Cross*, 19 December 1856, 2.

and engaging public speaker – something that cannot necessarily be discerned from the text of his speech alone. James was alert to the praise he received, and decided to deliver a public lecture, so that a wider audience could share his insights into the country and its progress. Earning a living at Waitangi was his priority, but he announced in February 1857 that he planned to give a lecture on 'Colonies & Colonization' at the Mechanics Institute Hall in Auckland on the twenty-third of the month. However, as he surveyed the scale of his material, he realized he would need to deliver two lectures to cover all the topics he wished to address. He therefore planned a second part to be given a week later.[35] The first lecture was not well attended as there was another event on in Auckland the same evening, and his follow-up address had to be postponed due to a summer storm that battered the city. It was rescheduled for 6 March, but that also had to be postponed as James was unable to get to Auckland on that date.

In the meantime, James was about to confront a more personal blow. On Monday 10 May, John, the family's ninety-two-year-old patriarch, died at his Hunter River estate.[36] The slowness of communications meant that only two of his children – William and Alexander – were able to attend the funeral, with news of the death reaching James at Waitangi weeks later.[37] Although James and his father had long since overcome their more intense differences, this had been possible partly because of the estrangement brought about by living in separate countries. James's response to his father's death has not survived, but given John's great age, it would have been neither completely unexpected, nor laden with the sort of sadness that the death of a child brought – a type of tragedy which James was painfully familiar with.

It was not until June, when he was in Auckland on business, that James hastily organized the second part of his public address.[38] In the chilly but crowded hall on the twenty-seventh of the month, James commenced his lecture by reviewing the content of his February talk. He had conducted 'a rapid survey of the Colonies of the ancient world, as well as of those of modern times', which extended to the reasons why they were settled, their political and social structures, and their economic organization, and compared these to New Zealand in the 1850s.[39] He then offered what was, for the time, a conventional rendering of the colony's history. Prior to European arrival, Māori had experienced a 'total absence of all authority to restrain their unbridled passions . . . [and] war, with all its revolting circumstances, scarcely

---

[35] *New Zealander*, 18 February 1857, 2.
[36] *The Maitland Mercury and Hunter Valley General Advertiser*, 23 May 1857, 3.
[37] *BFR* 4, 2150–1.
[38] *New Zealander*, 14 March 1857, 2.
[39] Busby, *Colonies and Colonization*, 1.

ever ceased amongst them', he told his audience. Missionary activity gradually stemmed this evil, and was followed by the appointment of a Resident, then the signing of the Treaty of Waitangi, the arrival of the New Zealand Company, and the introduction of representative government.

It was the current system of government, however, that James railed against. He accused it of being overly complex, incompetent, and corrupt, and suggested that the success of settlers depended on their personal qualities rather than anything the government could do for them.[40] Then, after a lengthy and remarkably informed economic analysis of the state of the country, he turned to the topic of the colony's Māori population, and concluded with a note of warning. On the issue of the treaty, he cautioned that the government's view of it as being less than binding was leading to a growing political and even social gap between Māori and settler, and that 'sooner or later retribution will follow in the footsteps of injustice. Wrong never brings forth right, and gain unjustly acquired is productive of loss in the end.'[41]

There was widespread praise for James's speech, with one observer writing how the lecture was knowledgeable, and 'afforded much satisfaction'.[42] One of the few mixed views came from the *Auckland Examiner*, which started in a kindly tone, describing James's face as 'full of expression; sometimes hard and eager; always intellectual and striking', and asserted that no politician in the country looked 'more like a gentleman'. He would have appreciated this, but that was as far as the compliments went. Thereafter, the article began to pick apart aspects of the lecture. James's words may have been 'well chosen', and his arguments 'logical', but 'the manner of his discourse was not equal to its matter. Nor did his person altogether satisfy me. In the restless, uneasy glances of his eye, I read disappointment of ambition, and a mind ill at ease . . . he seldom smiles, and when he does, it is more in Cynic than Socratic fashion'.[43]

James, though, was largely satisfied with his address, and published the text of the lecture a few months later. Whether any of the audience, or those who subsequently read the published version, took his predictions on the risk of alienating Māori land seriously is unknown, but it was the sort of insight that was free of ulterior political motive, and based on over two decades' experience in the country. To a colony that was recovering in prosperity, and beginning to enjoy increased immigration matched with more agricultural land becoming available to meet this growing demand, James's speech was voice-in-the-wilderness material. It would be little wonder, then, if few people were inclined to heed its prophetic warning.

---

[40] Ibid., 8–10.
[41] Ibid., 2-67.
[42] *Daily Southern Cross*, 26 June 1857, 3.
[43] *Auckland Examiner*, 7 January 1858, in *BFR* 4, 2160.

Three days after delivering his speech, James announced that he would be putting his name forward for election as superintendent of the Auckland Provincial Council. Superintendents had the power to convene Councils, and together with their Councils were an important branch of government.[44] In his bid for election, James cited his thirty-four years of colonial experience, his lack of personal motives in pursuing the role, and his opposition to the partisan influence of political parties as the reasons why voters ought to choose him.[45] Two candidates were up against him: the incumbent, the newspaper proprietor John Williamson; and the Auckland surgeon, Samuel Stratford.[46] Williamson was victorious,[47] and James was left nursing yet another failed attempt to win popular support for public office.

However, before the results were announced, James decided to write an open letter to the Governor, addressing the deficiencies of the current system of government in the colony, as he saw them. Sent on 15 July 1857, it commenced by examining the extent to which New Zealand was truly politically autonomous, before detailing perceived shortcomings arising from the entanglement of various branches of government. Many of the points raised were worthy of further consideration, but James's substantial letter was composed under the delusion that it might contribute to a reform of the system of government. He continued to believe naively in the capacity of a good idea to influence situations despite the myriad of political considerations that tended to prop up the status quo.

Publication of the letter to Browne gave it a wider audience, but also flushed out some of James's detractors. One of these was the editor of the *New Zealander*, who alleged James had a reputation as an 'ink-blotter', and 'a litigant and unsatisfied old-land claimant' who had been at odds with every government in the colony. James's letter was said to have diminished his reputation 'as a politician, a logician, a statistician, or as one who judges others as he would be judged himself', and was riddled with misleading information.[48] The Auckland merchant George Vaile leapt to James's defence, arguing that the former Resident's character was the best riposte to such attacks, and accusing the press of trying to ruin James's reputation for political purposes.[49]

In September 1857, the Attorney General announced that under the provisions of the Land Claims Settlement Act (which James had opposed so trenchantly during its passage the previous year), anyone wishing to settle

---

[44] *The Cyclopedia of New Zealand* (Wellington: Cyclopedia Company Limited, 1897), 210–11.
[45] J. Busby, in *Daily Southern Cross*, 3 July 1857, 2.
[46] *Nelson Examiner and New Zealand Chronicle*, 22 July 1857, 2.
[47] A. Cox, *Men of Mark of New Zealand* (Christchurch: Whitcombe and Tombs, 1886), 143.
[48] *New Zealander*, 14 October 1857, 2.
[49] *New Zealander*, 30 October 1857, 3.

title to their land would be required to produce evidence of their purchase for the land commissioners to assess. This sounded fair, and the optimistically minded might have been inclined to hope that resolution at last was at hand. But there was a sting in the small print. If those who had claims to land did not hand over their purchase documentation to the commissioner on request, their claims could be declared null and void, and the Crown could end up asserting ownership over the disputed territories.

On 25 September, James met with the Land Commissioner, Francis Dillon Bell, at Waitangi, to discuss 3,264 acres of land that James had bought. Disputes soon arose between the two men over surveys, titles, and land allocated for native reserves.[50] They were compounded by James's refusal to hand over any documentation relating to his land purchases. The Act did not offer a lasting solution to the title conundrum in such circumstances, and so James was destined to endure more financial and emotional hardship in his ever-lengthening battle to seek justice. And as an act of protest at this denial of his titles to his land, he wrote to the Governor, advising that he was resigning from his role as a Justice of the Peace, and published this letter in a newspaper to publicize his plight.[51]

James's public act of flaunting his principles coincided with his campaign to be re-elected as a member of the Auckland Provincial Council. The election took place on 1 October, and through a show of hands by voters (all twelve of them), James and one other (John Bedggood) were returned to the Provincial Council. However, the unsuccessful candidate, Henry Hickton, refused to recognize the result, and served James with a protest note, claiming that the election had been conducted too informally to be valid. When the final results were added up, though, Hickton was placed a distant third, and the protest was subsequently ignored.[52]

James's victory in the election was soured by the fact that he had been unsuccessful in securing the role of superintendent of the Province. Rather than respecting the will of the voters, though, he decided to launch a rearguard action in response to what he saw as an injustice. On 2 December, the incumbent superintendent was served with a notice that James intended to impeach him, on the grounds that he had permitted funds to be spent in the province without the authority of an appropriation act (such an act had not been passed by the previous council due to a deadlock having been reached, allegedly as a consequence of James's earlier chicanery). Now, James was being accused publicly of 'perversity, ignorance and folly' for his 'illogical and disingenuous indictment' of the superintendent.

---

[50] Busby, *Rebellions of the Maori Traced to their True Origin*, 35.
[51] J. Busby to T. G. Browne, 24 September 1857, in *Daily Southern Cross*, 9 October 1857, 3.
[52] *New Zealander*, 17 October 1857, 3.

While the letter of the law may not have been complied with due to an administrative impasse, its spirit was, which made the impeachment seem unreasonable on the face of it. Moreover, there had certainly been no apparent irregularities in spending that had warranted this unprecedented gesture by James. James's petty action was that of someone impatient for revenge over a slight to his perceived status and authority. And as it turned out, insisting that the law be strictly adhered to was an unwise tactic for James to pursue. The press threw James's sanctimony and pedantry straight back in his face. '[F]or his own private interests', one journalist asserted, 'he is himself at this very moment refusing to obey one of the laws of this country.' This was a reference to James's reluctance to submit to the demands of the Land Commissioner when it came to handing over documents relating to his purchase of land at Waitangi.[53]

James had learned that in the normal course of events, it was preferable to disregard criticism from the press, but there was nothing normal in these allegations. 'I do not consider it a trifle to be charged with the violation of the law,' he responded angrily in a letter published on 11 December in the *Daily Southern Cross* (the rival paper to the *New Zealander*, which had made the accusations against him). Having explained that he had not, in fact, broken any law, James then went on the offensive, recklessly claiming that the superintendent had acted illegally 'in taking unlawfully upwards of £26,000 of . . . public money, and spending it upon objects which he and his supporters choose to declare to be for the good of the Province; while others think they see sufficient evidence . . . that the money was spent in order to . . . serve their own selfish interests'.[54]

Such outlandish accusations did not just disappear in the ether after they were made. Instead, they had the effect of further alienating James from those who wielded political power in the province. Within a fortnight, the *Auckland Examiner* published a lengthy and often rambling attack on James. He was depicted as being 'crotchety and selfish', and was accused of profiting throughout the entire period of his Residency while doing practically nothing to benefit the country. On the contrary, the article claimed that he was 'never known to give Natives the price of a turnip or so much as a fig of tobacco', and now had a reputation among other provincial councillors for 'apathetic listlessness'. The writer went on, damning James for being 'a mean man', and for having committed fraud – using the funds allocated to him in the 1830s for gifts for Māori to improve his own financial circumstances.[55]

---

[53] *New Zealander*, 9 December 1857, 3.
[54] *Daily Southern Cross*, 11 December 1857, 3.
[55] *Auckland Examiner*, 7 January 1858, in *BFR* 4, 2159–61.

The response James published to these scurrilous allegations was unexpectedly gracious. 'I do not quarrel with you for introducing a sketch of my character', he replied, and even agreed that there was some basis for him being seen as crotchety and selfish, especially considering that his claims for the land he had purchased had been repeatedly disregarded by the government. However, the accusations about his Residency were manifestly false, and James made sure readers knew this. He labelled them as being 'as unmixed a tissue of misrepresentation as could have been woven together', and then challenged the newspaper to cite the sources of its account of his Residency. This was followed by a lengthy narrative of his time as Resident, which was heavily laden with detail – all of which he offered to provide evidence for verification if requested.[56] Wisely, James avoided the temptation to be drawn further into an extended tit-for-tat exchange with the newspaper. Regardless of how offended he was with these attacks on his character, rebuttals only led to further taunts from the press, so having defended himself with some dignity, he left that subsequent charges against him unanswered.

For the first five months of 1858, James only attended Auckland's Provincial Council intermittently. The journey from Waitangi was long and costly, and when he made it, he usually tried to tie in selling goods in Auckland with participation in his representative role. It would be easy to see some sort of equilibrium having been reached in Busby's life, but that would be to ignore the interminable stress with which people in James's situation were burdened. The ongoing insecurity over land tenure weighed heavily on many of the old settlers.

The case of James Lowden brought to the public's attention the extent of anxiety that those dealing with the Crown's land commissioners had to contend with. Lowden had arrived in New Zealand in the 1830s,[57] and had eventually acquired some land, as had most other settlers in that generation, from Māori vendors. However, Lowden had also spent years struggling to have his purchases validated, and eventually, the stress he endured became unbearable. In May 1858, Lowden was found dead in an unfinished building in Khyber Pass in Auckland. The inquest into his death found that he had committed suicide by cutting his throat, 'whilst in state of temporary insanity'.[58] James was familiar with Lowden's circumstances and published a letter in the press to enable the public to get an insight into the human cost of the government's land policies:

James Lowden was one of the oldest settlers in New Zealand . . . but it was his misfortune – as it has been the misfortune of many others – that

---

[56] J. Busby, in *Auckland Examiner*, 17 January 1858, in A. D. W. Busby, vol. *BFR* 4, 2161–4.
[57] Polack, *New Zealand* 2, 436.
[58] *Daily Southern Cross*, 28 May 1858, 3.

he purchased a piece of land in New Zealand, and that the Government did to him as they did to many others – they deprived him of his land. They sold the land and put the money into the Treasury. Query – was it lawful to put it into the treasury? Is it lawful to keep it there? Is it not the price of blood?[59]

Charles Davis, a government interpreter, responded to James's letter by fully endorsing its contents. Davis had been a close friend of Lowden, and suggested that the latter's suicide could be traced 'to the treatment he [Lowden] received from various Civil . . . dignitaries who despoiled him of his land'.[60]

Such tragedies, as far as legislators were concerned, were the price to pay for progress in the area of land 'reform' in the colony. The old settlers were indeed getting older. Lowden was fifty-six when he took his life – the same age as James – and their numbers were insignificant in electoral terms. Evidence of the disregard shown by the government to those who were still clinging to the right to own the land that they had purchased came the following month, when the Land Claims Settlement Extension Act was passed. It was an even more draconian statute than its 1856 predecessor, in that it gave the government still greater powers to seize land from settlers with almost no checks or balances in the process.[61] James characterized this legislation as 'evil'. It threatened to undermine the provisions of the Treaty, and to deny 'honest men' the land they were entitled to.[62]

On 31 May, James brought an action in the Supreme Court against Whitaker, the Attorney-General. The incessant issue of land ownership was at the heart of the case. As one court reporter perceptively commented, 'there is some inherent charm about *land* which has a tendency to make men more tenacious of their real or supposed rights in it than any other species of property they possess'.[63] James claimed that he was being forced by Whitaker to hand over the written records of his purchases to the land commissioners, and that if he refused, he was being threatened with the dispossession of his land. James was seeking the comparatively small sum of £5,000 damages, and hoped the court's decision would be in his favour, and thus serve as a step towards him eventually securing his title. Whitaker was represented by Merriman, who provided a lengthy argument demonstrating that while there may have been some factual bases to James's claim, they were irrelevant in

---

[59] *Daily Southern Cross*, 1 June 1858, 3.
[60] *Daily Southern Cross*, 11 June 1858, 3.
[61] ss. 5, 6, 7, Land Claims Settlement Extension Act, 1858.
[62] J. Busby to A. Busby, 27 June 1858, in *BFR* 4, 2172.
[63] *New Zealander*, 2 June 1858, 2.

this context. James was representing himself in court, with all the perils that entailed.

The case was heard before Chief Justice George Arney, who advised the plaintiff and defendant that as he had developed a clear opinion on the case, it was his duty to express that opinion straight away, 'rather than to keep the parties in suspense, while a written judgment was in preparation'. After working his way through the arguments presented and the precedents cited in the case, he found for the defendant.[64] Shortly after this verdict, James returned to Waitangi. His future now appeared empty of any hope. As he saw it, he had been defeated not only by the Attorney-General and the Chief Justice, but also by the law itself. As long as such obstacles lay in front of him, he was restricted to making a meagre living as a merchant, while his lands remained untended and profitless.

---

[64] Ibid.

14

Colossal

Back at Waitangi (which he now defiantly insisted on calling Victoria), James delved into his substantial archive of official documents to select material for another letter he planned to write to the Governor. What he labelled his 'comprehensive view' of the actions of two of Browne's predecessors (FitzRoy and Grey) formed the substance of the letter (which he completed in February 1859). However, James commenced it not by addressing his own considerable grievances, but those of Esther Smithson, who had similarly suffered from Grey's underhand proceedings on the land issue, which James condemned as 'an outrage on public morality'.[1] James referred to the Smithson case – which was already familiar to the public – as a sort of proxy for his own legal battles. By citing it, he could engage in another bombardment of the government without facing accusations of any directed vested interest.

The remainder of the thirty-page letter, which James later published, was an extended denunciation of Grey, in which the former Governor was frequently damned by his own words. James had foraged through years of official reports and correspondence to build a case that was strong on evidence, even if its construction was at times a bit flimsy. But there was, nonetheless, some overall structure to the work. The bulk of the letter surveyed previous government decisions and legislation, before concluding with reference to the cases of Smithson, another old settler in a similar situation, and Lowden, who had recently committed suicide. The treatment these individuals had received from Grey in particular was 'equally deplorable', and in James's view, justified the formation of a judicial tribunal to explore the possibility of compensation for the affected parties.[2] James followed up his letter to Browne by raising in the Provincial Council the deficient aspects of

---

[1] J. Busby, *The Pre-Emption Land Question: A Comprehensive View of the Proceedings of Governors FitzRoy and Grey . . . in a Letter Addressed to Governor Gore Browne* (Auckland: Richardson and Sansom, 1859), 4.
[2] Ibid., 29–31.

the government's land policies, using Smithson's experience as a case study in injustice. However, the press again turned on him. He was judged by journalists to have failed to provide sufficient evidence to support his claims against the government, with one paper concluding that there remained a 'very embarrassing discrepancy between his warm rhetorical figures and the cold official facts'.[3]

On 12 June 1859, in what looked like a change of tack, James wrote to Bell, seeking compensation from the government for a stretch of land that comprised part of his Ngunguru purchase.[4] James was applying for this under the provisions of the Land Claims Settlement Extension Act, which had been passed the previous year. The relevant section of the Act allowed for the possibility that if there were difficulties in a claimant 'obtaining quiet possession of land to which he may be really entitled' as a result of delays or acts of the government, the commissioners could offer either monetary compensation or Crown land of an equal value in the same province.[5]

What brought about this change by which James was now considering disposing of the Ngunguru block? Most likely it was a financial consideration. He had purchased the land specifically for its timber resources. In the intervening years, loggers had entered his land and felled and sold much of the timber on it, without James receiving any revenue from this at all. The best he could salvage from the situation now was to get some compensation for the land from the government. For his part, Bell received James's application and then did nothing. Years of publicly attacking politicians and officials over land laws hardly endeared James to them. Consequently, when it came to his application for compensation, the paperwork languished unattended somewhere in Bell's office.

However, James did not rely solely on the cooperation of the land commissioners to advance his cause. In September he opened up a new front, with the Supreme Court serving as the battleground. On the face of it, the action that James decided to bring to the Court was a simple one. It aimed to recover a parcel of his land that had been sold to another settler, Titus White (whose name in many ways seemed symbolic in the context of this case). However, all was not as it outwardly appeared. In fact, the entire case was a contrivance that had been engineered by James and his lawyer (with White as a co-conspirator) in an effort to get the 1841 Land Claims Ordinance referred to the Privy Council for a determination of its legality. James had previously attempted to pursue a case (against McKenzie) for the same purpose, but

---

[3] *New Zealander*, 5 February 1859, 3; 2 March 1859, 3.
[4] J. Busby to F. D. Bell, 12 June 1859, in *BFR* 4, 2190.
[5] s. 3, Land Claims Settlement Extension Act, 1858.

had failed. This new action involving White was concocted to maximize the chances of getting the Ordinance's legality decided by the Privy Council.

James used a series of personal contacts as part of his conspiracy. Titus's brother was John White, the interpreter who had been a witness for James in his case against McKenzie. Titus was also the nephew of William White – the person who had nominated James for election to the Provincial Council in 1852. There was obviously a high degree of trust among these men for Titus to agree to play the part of defendant in the ruse that James and his lawyer (Rochfort) were preparing. In fact, Rochfort was most likely at the heart of this scheme, drawing on his legal knowledge to identify a possible loophole in the court system that would allow the plan to be put into effect.

The plot began with James giving a sum of money to White to purchase the relevant section being auctioned by the Crown. The section in question was a portion of the land that James had bought in 1839, and which the government had subsequently appropriated without paying him compensation.[6] Once White had received title to the land, James and Rochfort set about planning to sue him. The extent of collusion was made fully apparent by the fact that Rochfort prepared the pleadings and acted as lawyer for both parties. James's argument was described in the press as 'one of the most colossal legal statements ever placed before a Court of Justice'.[7] Standing in front of Arney, he read his statement before the court, which took several days (something that was compensated for only by the fact that White advanced no contrary argument whatsoever).[8]

What also singled out this massive submission was the audacious sweep of constitutional history it contained – spanning thousands of years and several countries. Ironically, in an effort to assemble precedent and arguments from such an unrealistically wide scope of sources, James's statement was thin on relevant legal detail despite being dense in content. There were references made to the Roman legions that invaded ancient Britain, to Julius Caesar, Abraham and Isaac,[9] the Ottoman Empire, North American Indians, James I, Edward the Confessor, the East India Company, the 'Kingdom of Jamba', the Treaty of Utrecht, and ancient Greece, among much else.[10] And from each such historical reference, some usually opaque legal principle was extracted

---

[6] The legal dimensions of the case are examined in N. Fletcher and S. Elias, 'A Collusive Suit to "Confound the Rights of Property through the Length and Breadth of the Colony"?: *Busby v White* (1859)', *Victoria University of Wellington Law Review* 41 (2010): 584.
[7] *New Zealander*, 17 December 1859, 6.
[8] J. Finn, 'Symbol and Myth: Magna Carta in Legal and Public Discourse about Law and Rights in New Zealand, 1840–1940', in *Magna Carta and New Zealand: History, Politics and Law in Aotearoa*, eds. S. Winder and C. Jones (Cham: Palgrave Macmillan, 2017), 92–3.
[9] *Daily Southern Cross*, 30 September 1859, 6.
[10] *Daily Southern Cross*, 14 October 1859, 5; 1 November 1859, 6.

for James to strengthen his case. At the conclusion of his statement, he expressed his 'sense of deep obligation for the extreme courtesy' which the judge had extended to him,[11] although it was more an example of patience and forbearance on Arney's behalf. In fact, the judge had been quietly 'irritated'[12] by the obscure legal precedents James and Rochfort had built their case on.

In the end, it all proved to be a wasted effort. Arney refused to make a determination on James's action. Not only was it collusive (which in this instance effectively denied the court the chance to hear the defendant's case), but the legality of the 1841 Land Claims Ordinance was not anywhere near as questionable as James had argued. Arney concluded that his observations on James's case had been made 'in vindication of the Court [more] than to rebuke the plaintiff. For this is probably a case in which the plaintiff has been led by a persevering pursuit of one idea, and a conscious conviction of one principle, to adopt a course which upon any other question he would be the first to condemn.'[13]

James did not accept the court's decision, and he was bothered that use of the term 'collusion' to describe his case might somehow bring into question his reputation. 'I went into Court without any misgivings upon the propriety of the proceedings,' he wrote in a letter to the press on 20 December. 'I considered it as a friendly suit, of the same nature as those which . . . are frequently brought into the . . . Courts of Westminster.' James's defence was simply that he was unaware of what precisely constituted collusion 'till it was explained to me by the Chief Justice, from the bench'.[14] Unusually, the fight seemed to be missing in James's tone. Instead of defiant justification, there was an almost apologetic concession.

There was very good reason for James being untypically subdued at this time. A disaster had befallen the family the previous month, and he was still coming to terms with it as the court action ground to a dissatisfying end. The event involved James's two sons – George and William – who had set out one morning on a boat to go duck-shooting on the Waitangi River. A short time later, James had heard a shot fired as he was riding on his horse to visit Henry Williams at Pakaraka, and thought little of it, assuming that his boys had fired at some prey. However, the sound was actually the gun's charge exploding at the cap as a result of George dropping the weapon as he reached for it.

The explosion lacerated his wrist 'in a fearful manner'. William frantically tore a strip off his shirt to use as an improvised bandage, and then rowed almost a

---

[11] J. Busby, in *New Zealander*, 24 December 1859, 3.
[12] Fletcher and Elias, 'A Collusive Suit', 594.
[13] Cited in *Daily Southern Cross*, 27 December 1859, 2.
[14] Ibid.

kilometre to the nearest house to raise the alarm and seek assistance. While George was being attended to, messengers were urgently dispatched to fetch James and the local doctor, but 'it was evident from the first that human skill could be of no avail'. Over the next four days, George's grip on life progressively weakened, and on the morning of Saturday 5 November 1859, 'mortification . . . set in', and 'death put an end to his sufferings'. But the sufferings of James and the rest of the family were only mounting. They were plunged into the deepest possible grief, and even Henry Williams, who had long experience at conducting funerals, 'was so much moved as to be hardly able to go through the service'.[15]

Throughout the region, people offered their sympathies to the Busbys, but once the funeral was over, the family was left alone to nurse their grief. James remained at Waitangi for a few weeks, but then returned to Auckland, perhaps in part to bury his sorrow by submerging himself once more in the political fray. What he had not expected, though, was a reply from Bell to the proposal he had put to him six months earlier about his Ngunguru purchase. The two men met on 19 December, most likely in Bell's office, after which the Land Commissioner put the substance of the discussion in a letter to James, at the latter's request. Bell made it clear that he could make no award in the case until he surveyed the land. On the central issue of the payment for the land, James had sought compensation equivalent to three times the value of the goods he had traded for it. The law, as Bell rightly pointed out, did not provide for this.[16] At least, though, this was a small sign of movement – sufficient to give James some crumbs of hope. There was still no offer of an amount of compensation anywhere near what James would regard as acceptable, but hope for the prospect of a resolution – however faint or distant – was there.

Keen to capitalize on what he interpreted as the beginnings of a sea-change on government attitudes to old land claims such as his, in mid-February 1860 James introduced to the Auckland Provincial Council a bill that would 'enable persons who consider themselves to have been aggrieved by any act or omission of the Government . . . to institute proceedings for the recovery of compensation'.[17] The reception to this initiative from some quarters was biting. 'Just . . . as we were beginning to hug a faint hope that the worst was over, and that these multifarious demands were getting paid off,' one newspaper editor wrote, 'an apparition arises, so novel and portentous, that but for the amusement it affords, it would go far to frighten us out of all propriety . . . The Bill . . . is really such a capital joke.'[18] It was a joke that soon ended, though. A

---

[15] *Daily Southern Cross*, 11 November 1859, 3.
[16] F. D. Bell to J. Busby, 19 December 1859, in *BFR* 4, 2196–7.
[17] Equitable Compensation Bill, 1860; *New Zealander*, 15 February 1860, 2.
[18] *New Zealander*, 22 February 1860, 2.

fortnight after its introduction, the Bill was voted down by the Provincial Council.[19] James had not miscalculated the mood of the council (the Bill was defeated by a vote of eighteen to twelve – hardly a landslide), but he had been overly ambitious in his hope that his political colleagues would turn, en masse, to support his private grievances. He had delivered an earnest address in support of this proposed statute, but it was essentially the same as his other 'multitudinous speeches' against what he termed as the 'Felon Governments'. Bombast aside, the problem with the Bill was that it far exceeded the legislative powers of the Provincial Council, and so was doomed regardless of the merits or otherwise of its content. Midway through the debate, James realized this, and proposed to send it to committee for amendment, but it was too late.[20]

Two months later, still anticipating that good fortune was about to turn his way, James penned another letter to the Secretary of State for the Colonies, repeating the theme of injustices committed by the colonial government against those who had purchased land in New Zealand prior to 1840. He cited 'incontestable evidence' supporting his case, and accused the former Grey administration of acting 'contrary to law, and contrary to right'.[21] Raging against a governor who had already departed was a vain undertaking, as was expecting the Secretary of State to act on this letter and interfere in domestic political affairs. But the fact that James published this appeal suggests that his motives were focussed more on shaping local popular opinion than on trying to get London to intervene. In particular, it is likely that James hoped that his letter would build on the momentum he believed was gathering within New Zealand to address finally the status of land such as his.

When surveying history, it can be all too easy to see patterns of cause and effect. However, such views are often only possible with hindsight. At the start of 1860, few settlers would have anticipated that one of dozens of land purchases that the government was involved in would soon trigger a major war in the country. The genesis of the conflict involved the 600-acre Pekapeka block in Waitara, which was acquired by Browne (despite misgivings about the rights of the Māori vendor to sell it, and despite explicit opposition to the sale by the most senior chief in the region, Wiremu Kingi).[22] Kingi's preferred expression of opposition to the government's encroachment on his ancestral territory was to interfere with the surveying of the land. This passive resistance

---

[19] *New Zealander*, 29 February 1860, 3.
[20] *New Zealander*, 3 March 1860, 3.
[21] J. Busby, *The Right of a British Colonist to the Protection of the Queen and Parliament of England Against the Illegal and Unjust Acts of a Colonial Legislature or Government; A Letter to His Grace the Duke of Newcastle* (Auckland: Philip Kunst, 1860), 9.
[22] Also known by his earlier name of Te Rangitake.

was met by active hostility, in the form of an assault by Crown forces, which Browne hoped would enable the purchase to be concluded, and at the same time, to reduce Kingi's power, and to deter any other Māori who might be considering a similar response to what were effectively enforced land acquisitions.[23]

Looking on at these events, James appealed to Ngapuhi leaders to maintain their neutrality as the fighting raged 600 kilometres to the south. '[I]f an ulcer breaks out on the joint of the little finger, it gives disturbance to the whole body,' he wrote to the chiefs. And to some of the younger men of the tribe, he cautioned that 'evil will come upon you if you do not turn from your folly. I counsel you, as an old friend, to cast away that folly and let the land be in peace.'[24] There was little chance anyway of Ngapuhi suddenly joining the Taranaki tribes in their fight against the Crown,[25] but if nothing else, this letter enabled James to position himself (in his mind at least) as a sort of patron or emissary when it came to Northland's Māori population.

Dispensing sage advice was one thing, but acting prudently proved more challenging for James at times. On 22 August 1860, he published yet another letter[26] (this one addressed nominally to Browne but written mainly for public consumption) which addressed the familiar gripes that he had long been highlighting. He laboriously detailed laws that were unjust, processes that were deficient, and evidence that had been ignored by politicians in favour of political expediency.

However, tucked away in this otherwise predictable denunciation of the government was a passage that contained an extremely serious allegation against John Williamson, the Superintendent of Auckland's Provincial Council. Williamson, whose role included administering waste lands in the province,[27] had purchased the block of land for £196, and subsequently arranged for its sale to the Crown, for which he received £1372 in compensation – roughly seven times what he had paid for it, without even having undertaken any improvements. By any measure, this had an odour of corruption about it. James then went on to detail the process by which Williamson had thus enriched himself in this deal, and the fact that there was no possible way that the price he received for the land reflected its true value.[28]

---

[23] J. Stenhouse, 'Churches, State and the New Zealand Wars: 1860–1872', *Journal of Law and Religion* 13, no. 2 (1998): 490–1.
[24] J. Busby, 20 June 1860, in *BFR* 4, 2202.
[25] T. G. Browne to Duke of Newcastle, 26 August 1860, in *Papers Relating to the Recent Disturbances in New Zealand, 1859–1861* (London: House of Commons, 1861), 97–8.
[26] *New Zealander*, 22 August 1860, 2.
[27] As defined in the Waste Land Act 1854.
[28] J. Busby, *Illustrations of the System Called Responsible Government. In a Letter to His Excellency, Colonel Gore Browne* (Auckland: W. C. Wilson, 1860), 24–6.

Three weeks after the letter's publication, James received notice from the law firm Merriman and Jackson that he would face criminal proceedings for libelling their client, Williamson. They emphasized that Williamson had decided on this course of action 'to refute calumny, and not to inflict punishment', and that they wished for the matter to be dealt with 'in the manner least offensive' to James personally.[29] James was used to the oleaginous approach of lawyers, and responded in kind on 19 September, thanking them for their 'desire to gild the pill you are preparing for me', and acknowledged receipt of the writ without indicating the name of his own solicitor.[30] Shortly after the letter arrived from Williamson's lawyers, James confided in Hugh Carleton, a long-standing friend, and more recently a relation through marriage. James was fearful of the cost of hiring a lawyer, but knew he might need to regardless. He initially considered Frederick Brookfield as a possible advocate, but on reflection, regarded him as unimpressive. He therefore sought Carleton's opinion '<u>very confidentially</u>' on who would be the best person to represent him.[31] No clear choice was forthcoming, and eventually James decided that his case would be best served if he represented himself, but with the assistance of the solicitor Robert Wynn.

On 14 November, James found himself yet again appearing before Chief Justice Arney in the Supreme Court, but this time as a defendant. Williamson's solicitors noted that their client had been accused of gross misconduct in his role as Superintendent, and that if the allegation were true, he would be disqualified from holding his role. Williamson naturally rejected James's claims, and presented supporting affidavits from William Richmond, the Colonial Treasurer, Frederick Whitaker, the Attorney General, and Daniel Pollen, the Commissioner of Crown Lands.[32] Testimony from such a formidable group revealed the strength of the group James was up against.

Williamson's counsel argued that the comments in James's publication 'far exceeded the ordinary license of criticism allowed in reference to the conduct of public men', and pointed out that Williamson only sought to clear his name from these 'unjust aspersions'. To avoid a protracted tussle in court, the plaintiff's solicitor merely sought James's retraction of the allegations that his client regarded as libellous. Arney concurred with this proposed course of action, and granted James the choice of either justifying or retracting his comments against Williamson.[33] James was also privately informed by

---

[29] Merriman & Jackson to J. Busby, 14 September 1860, in *Daily Southern Cross*, 14 December 1860, 3.
[30] J. Busby to Merriman & Jackson, 19 September 1860, in ibid.
[31] J. Busby to H. Carleton, 19 September 1860, in *BFR* 4, 2207.
[32] *New Zealander*, 1 December 1860, 7.
[33] Ibid.

Merriman in a letter sent on 5 December that Williamson considered the affidavits to be sufficient response to the accusations of corruption, and that it was in everyone's best interests to lest the matter rest there.[34]

It must have been a tempting offer. Having some of the colony's most senior politicians lined up against him should have given James cause to assess the value in continuing with his defence. There would be no damages awarded against him, and he could walk away satisfied in the knowledge that he had drawn the nation's attention to a case of corruption at the highest levels of provincial government. At times like this, surely pragmatism would rise above principle? Two days later, after serious consideration, James responded to this offer, stubbornly adhering to his accusation, and refusing to acquiesce. 'To do so', he replied, 'would be a betrayal of the cause of truth, of which no consideration of expediency or of personal inconvenience would induce me to be guilty.'[35] And if that did not frustrate the plaintiff enough, James sent a copy of all the correspondence between him and Merriman to the *Daily Southern Cross*, which happily published it.

The case spilled over into 1861, and on 28 January, the judge tried to encourage the parties to settle. He conceded that every citizen had the right to criticize politicians, but made it clear that James's allegation was that Williamson had violated the law intentionally. On the face of it, the allegations would oblige Arney to send the case to a jury trial, but to avoid that, he proposed a middle course. It was clear that James was not motivated by malice, and that a full trial would not only impose serious expenses on those involved, but would also heighten the animosity between the plaintiff and defendant. Arney urged that some accommodation between the parties be made before the case went any further.[36] James refused to relent, and on 8 March, a jury was empanelled, and the case got under way.

Early in the evening of Tuesday 12 March, the jury returned to court, with the foreman, John Logan Campbell, announcing a verdict of not guilty, and finding for James, on the grounds that 'illegal action' by Williamson had been proved, albeit without base motives. The jury also determined that James's comments that had led to the case 'were justifiable on the broad ground of public criticism, and that no malice has been proved on the part of the Defendant'. It was not a universally popular verdict, with one journalist commenting that James was 'a consistent opponent of free institutions in this Colony', and that in this 'latest crusade, he had not added to his laurels'.[37] James was euphoric at the verdict, and immediately announced that he would

---

[34] F. Merriman to J. Busby, 5 December 1860, in *Daily Southern Cross*, 14 December 1860, 3.
[35] J. Busby to F. Merriman, in ibid.
[36] *Daily Southern Cross*, 8 February 1861, 3.
[37] *New Zealander*, 16 March 1861, 3.

be putting forward his name as a candidate for the superintendent of the Auckland Province,[38] thus hoping to displace Williamson, and make his triumph over him complete.

A month before the verdict in the libel trial was delivered, the general election had taken place, with James and Carleton both contesting the Bay of Islands seat for the House of Representatives.[39] Because of his preoccupation with the libel trial, James had maintained a low profile in the electorate, undertaking no canvassing or other activities to improve his chances of success. In contrast, Carleton remained in the area, 'where he "worked" incessantly . . . appealing, pleading, promising, and even praying for votes'. For all his efforts, and for all James's corresponding torpidity in the campaign, Carleton won by just one vote.

Despite the margin, it was a win nonetheless – until an anomaly was uncovered. It turned out that two people by the name of George Scott had voted in the electorate. They were father and son, with Scott senior voting for James and Scott junior for Carleton. The problem was that the son's vote should not have been allowed as he was not on the electoral roll. As soon as this unauthorized vote was discovered the Returning Officer was notified, but he decided that he had no legal authority to change the initial result.[40] James's own feelings on the dubious result are not known, but it is a little surprising that it was a group of supporters, rather than James himself, which led the charge to have the vote annulled. Several voters signed a petition addressed to the Clerk of the House and the Examiner of Election Bonds, demanding that the unauthorized vote for Carleton be struck off, and that either the entire election in the district be declared void (and another one be held), or that James be appointed the Member for the Bay of Islands (which was illogical, as cancelling Scott junior's vote would deliver a tie rather than a majority in favour of James).

On 13 June, the petitioners received a reply from John Cracroft Wilson, the recently elected Member for Christchurch, who had been appointed to convene a Standing Order committee on the matter. He had discovered an anomaly in the petitioners' appeal (they had not sent a copy to the affected candidate) and on that flimsy basis, the petition was deemed to have failed to comply with Standing Orders.[41] Carleton thus retained the seat, and James's hopes of entering Parliament were dashed. The letter of the law may have triumphed on this occasion, but at least one newspaper editor was incensed

---

[38] *Daily Southern Cross*, 19 March 1861, 2.
[39] *New Zealand Parliamentary Record, 1840–1949*, ed. G. Scholefield (Wellington: Govt Printer, 1950), 99.
[40] *New Zealander*, 15 June 1861, 3.
[41] J. C. Wilson, 13 June 1861, in ibid.

with the breach of its spirit. He described Carleton's majority as a 'fictitious' one, and that 'he occupies a seat to which he is not . . . entitled:– we know that there are some "third-rate" men whose "coarser" conscience would not permit them to sit easily under such circumstances'.[42]

The run of controversies continued, and there seemed to be no let-up for James. In May 1861, he fell into dispute with another long-standing settler – George Clarke. This arose following the publication the previous year of James's pamphlet *Remarks Upon a Pamphlet Entitled 'The Taranaki Question', by Sir William Martin*. Martin – the former Chief Justice in the colony – had argued that '[t]he land occupied by a Native Community is the property of the whole Community', and that once an individual from the group ceased to use a particular portion of that land, that portion would revert back to the community's ownership.[43] James's response, in the form of his pamphlet, emphasized his own long career in the country as the basis for his authority on the subject, and then queried Martin's stance on Māori land, stating that 'so far as we can trace their history, there is no evidence of the New Zealanders [Māori] ever having possessed any rights', including a property right to land as understood in English law.[44] James also stressed that his knowledge of Māori society 'dates back to a period at which I had better opportunities of judging them in their aboriginal condition than Sir William Martin could have, after they had imbibed the ideas of property which are held by civilized men'.[45]

Clarke then stepped into the debate. In an article he wrote dealing with James's critique of Martin, published in the *New Zealander* in May 1861, he reminded readers that he had lived in the country for more than a decade before James's arrival, that he was 'consulted upon and took a deep interest in the Treaty of Waitangi', and had held the role of Protector of Aborigines at the time when land claims in the colony began to be investigated by the government. With his 'superior' pedigree of experience, Clarke set about trying to demolish James's position on the land issue. He started off with a corrosive criticism of the former Resident's comparative isolation in the country in the 1830s, depicting James as having been 'hemmed up in the shank end of New Zealand', before claiming that he had 'a very imperfect knowledge' of the Māori language.

James's denial that Māori possessed property rights prior to the treaty was the next matter on Clarke's agenda, and his response tackled it with great efficiency and effectiveness: 'I should have liked to have seen Mr Busby going into a New Zealand forest BEFORE the Treaty . . . and attempting to cut down

---

[42] Ibid.
[43] W. Martin, *The Taranaki Question* (Auckland: Philip Kunst, 1860), 1–2.
[44] Busby, *Remarks Upon a Pamphlet Entitled 'The Taranaki Question', by Sir William Martin*, 5.
[45] J. Busby, in *New Zealander*, 29 May 1861, 3.

a tree or catch a pig belonging to the natives. He knows full well that he dared not have done so, because it would have been infringing on their rights and privileges.'[46] This reference to rights and privileges echoed the phrase in the treaty's third article, and was a veiled taunt at James, who had often claimed to have played such a central role in drafting the agreement.

Clarke also pointed out that James's view that Māori traditionally did not have rights to their land was problematic as the former Resident relied entirely on those rights having existed to support his own claims that he had bought land from various Māori vendors fairly. After all, how could he attempt to uphold the reliability of his purchases from Māori while simultaneously denying, in a sense, that it was explicitly their land to sell in the first place? Clarke argued that James's pamphlet was 'burdened with mistakes from beginning to end',[47] and was a wholly inadequate counter to Martin's work.

Clarke's attack was one too many. James needed a more reliable means of making himself heard publicly, and the same month, he did this by going to the extraordinary effort of founding his own newspaper – *The Aucklander* – which one reader observed 'launches thunder at both Provincial and General Governments'.[48] Thunder maybe, but noticeably, no lightning. James was able to use the newspaper to convey his anger over the wrongs he felt encircled by, but it was ineffective as a means of remedying them. Moreover, the appetite for articles about the intricacies of government land policies was quickly satiated, and in the face of a rapidly declining readership, the last edition of *The Aucklander*, printed by James Hosking in High Street in Auckland, rolled of the press on 11 April 1863.[49] The paper was barely profitable, and although it carried roughly the same amount of advertising as other newspapers at the time, the absence of a reporting staff meant that it often relied on reproducing stories that had already been printed elsewhere.

It would be wrong, though, to assume that James's anger had completely embittered him, and that he was using any means within his reach to try to strike back at his growing list of opponents. Yes, his indignation over the injustices he felt he had endured for more than two decades (and the enormous financial burden these had placed on him and his family) was as strong as ever, but he did not allow this to contaminate his entire outlook on life. In August 1861, for example, in the midst of his newspaper campaign against the government, he joined the government committee established to

---

[46] G. Clarke, in ibid.
[47] Ibid.
[48] *Hawkes Bay Herald*, 1 June 1861, 3.
[49] G. M. Main, *The Newspaper Press of Auckland* (Auckland: New Zealand Herald, 1891), 3; P. Legel, *Heritage Auckland Newspapers* (Auckland: Auckland Museum Library, 2015), 1. J. Busby, Personal collection of *The Aucklander*, in Journals and Newspapers, Auckland Museum Library.

plan and run the 1862 International Exhibition in Auckland.[50] James was never against the fundamental system of government in the colony (even if he despised some of its leaders and saw aspects of its apparatus as failing or corrupt).

Of course, the tireless fighting for his rights did not endear James to many of his colleagues in the Provincial Council or elsewhere. His numerous complaints and demands for justice that appeared in the newspapers, or that were made in the political arena, are notable for how seldom they were followed with statements of support from others. There were by now only handful of politicians or public figures who had been in New Zealand since the 1830s, and of that small pool, few were evidently prepared to back James in what must have seemed to many people increasingly a matter of personal obsession rather than public interest.

In August 1861, James again drew on his almost inexhaustible reservoir of energy and ideas to launch a new offensive against the government. This time, he presented a petition to Parliament complaining about the conduct of Bell when investigating his titles, and sought an opportunity to address the House to air his concerns. Efforts were made by some members to quash the petition on the basis of petty procedural irregularities, but these failed, and it was referred to a committee, which James appeared before on 29 August.[51]

When the committee finally reported, its decision predictably went against James. His allegations were found to be unproven, with the small concession that the language Bell used when dealing with James was unsuitable. Bell disputed this, claiming that 'I was really mild and gentle towards . . . [James], and that the provocation I received was very great.' He cited a written statement James had made, which referred to him as being less respectable than a highwayman, which produced laughter from the House.[52] Bell also saw the funny side of such a preposterous accusation, and the matter ended in James being ridiculed in Parliament, not by scorn but by mirth.

The press was scathing of James's latest effort at seeking acknowledgement for the wrongs he had endured.[53] He complained that the articles in question were a 'gross . . . attempt to mislead the public in reference to what took place',[54] but it was a lost cause trying to correct the statements in a newspaper that was openly hostile to him, and he wisely let the matter fizzle out. As the date for the election for the superintendent of the Auckland Provincial Council

---

[50] *Daily Southern Cross*, 16 August 1861, 1.
[51] *New Zealand Parliamentary Debates [NZPD] 1861–1863*, Session 1861, Wellington, 1886, 322–3, 351.
[52] *NZPD 1861–1863*, Session 1861, 374–5.
[53] *New Zealander*, 14 September 1861, 2.
[54] J. Busby in *New Zealander*, 21 September 1861, 3.

drew closer, the *Daily Southern Cross* reviewed the forthcoming contest between James and Williamson, describing the incumbent as brimming with confidence that he would be re-elected. James, in contrast, had barely campaigned, and was characterized variously as 'the acquitted libeller', the 'denouncer of responsible government and responsible ministers', and someone who was 'constantly blundering and tripping over every little stumbling block in his path, high in principle, but . . . reckless in assertion'. James had been reduced to a caricature – the sort of depiction from which it is difficult to escape. He was said to have 'done his utmost to degrade the position of public men in New Zealand',[55] and as such, came across as someone with very little to contribute to the role. Probably predictably, he failed to be elected as Superintendent, which signified another door closing on his struggle to resolve the status of his land.[56]

In February 1862, James turned sixty, and was regarded by many in Auckland's political circles almost as something of an elder statesman. His age, his nearly three decades in the colony, and his normally gentlemanly demeanour gave this impression, but it was never the complete image. His embitterment over his treatment by successive governments could not be concealed, and he was regarded as 'prejudiced' because of that.[57] And occasionally, he could not help but lapse into a more argumentative state. During one debate in the Provincial Council, a reporter recorded how 'such an opportunity for throwing mud at the Superintendent . . . could not of course be passed over by Mr Busby, but unfortunately for this gentlemen he mixes so much intemperance with the said mud that its adhesive qualities are lost, and the only effect it has is to dirty his own fingers'.[58] If character is destiny,[59] then an ascent into graceful old age was not a path James was ordained to take.

It was not just the long-lingering grievances, though, that were animating James's mind. New ideas could occupy his thoughts with nearly as much force. In one example, on 21 February 1862, he tabled a motion in the Provincial Council that he be appointed to head a committee that would petition the Queen for Auckland to be granted a separate government and legislature. Part of the motive for this was the imminent shift of the colony's capital to Wellington, around 650 kilometres to the south of Auckland.[60] He saw political power moving, along with the capital, away from Auckland, and

---

[55] *Daily Southern Cross*, 17 September 1861, 3.
[56] *New Zealander*, 4 December 1861, 6.
[57] *New Zealander*, 18 January 1862, 5.
[58] *New Zealander*, 22 January 1862, 7.
[59] R. G. Geldard, *Remembering Heraclitus* (New York: Lindisfarne Books, 2000), 85.
[60] *New Zealander*, 26 February 1862, 5.

like many others, he was concerned that specifically Auckland issues might henceforth get less attention from the government as a result.

James cut something of a politically isolated figure at this time. When explaining his reasons for favouring Auckland's political separation from the rest of the country, he was 'almost the sole performer', and when he spoke,

> [n]obody attempted to controvert his platitudes, to expose the miserable narrowness of his views or the absurdity of his arguments; Mr Busby is a 'privileged' person now; men shake their heads compassionately, and resign themselves to being bored . . . no member replied to him or appeared disposed to interfere with his harmless pleasure.[61]

To some, he was little more than a quaint anomaly – a throw-back to an earlier age in New Zealand's colonial history whose concerns and ideas were increasingly out of touch. To others, though, he was a more unpleasant, even abrasive personality. In April 1862, an anonymous letter-writer to a newspaper branded James as a person who 'wantonly, and at times coarsely . . . attacks every body that gives him the least opposition'.[62] Certainly, few politicians at this time could rival James for his sharp tongue, his verbose harangues, and his sometimes seemingly impulsive lurches towards idiosyncratic policy positions.

When he considered that his reputation was sufficiently impugned, James was swift to resort to legal action in the hope that he could restore it. There was something slightly infantile about his propensity to sue in response to assaults on his character (be they real or imagined). It betrayed a vulnerable side to his outwardly usually brusque and solemn persona. In June 1862, he lined up Bell in his sights for a libel action. Shunning a lawyer, presumably because of cost, James chose to represent himself. Arney would preside over the case, and Bell would be represented by Whitaker.

The case revolved around comments Bell had made about James's letter to the Secretary of State for Colonies in September 1860. Bell had written that James's letter contained 'extravagant misstatements', and that the former Resident lacked 'reason or common sense'. James was seeking damages of £5,000, but he was also hoping to use the trial as a means of illuminating what he saw as the unjust stance of the government towards him. In his statement to the court, James noted (for public consumption more than on any legal basis) that the government's actions bore 'more resemblance to those of a society of gamblers intent upon securing a large stake for themselves'. And in

---

[61] *New Zealander*, 12 March 1862, 3.
[62] *New Zealander*, 26 April 1862, 3.

another flourish of exaggeration, he claimed (using a phrase he had initially penned in 1858) that no government in history had done as much 'to corrupt and debauch the people' as had the current regime in New Zealand.[63] Bell's defence was twofold: that his comment about James had not been published, and that when he had made his assessment of James's letter, he had done so in his capacity as land claims commissioner, and so it was a reasonable and even necessary summation to make, given his requirements of his role.

James saw himself as something of a veteran court campaigner by this stage, and judging by the confident, almost strident statements he made during the opening stages of the case, he regarded himself as the equal of any professional advocate, with the added advantage of knowing the intricacies of his long history of conflict with the government to an extent that no lawyer could hope to match. In addition to his confidence as he marched into court, there is a vague sense that emerges – like a silhouette in the fog – that on some level, James enjoyed these appearances. They offered him a public forum – closely reported in newspapers – where he could throw light on his grievances, and brandish his oratorical and legal skills. It was as though he was once again compensating (as he had done so often throughout his adult life) for some deeply rooted sense of inadequacy. He was not a lawyer, he had no formal qualifications, and he had long since been discarded by the Empire's bureaucratic apparatus. Court, however, enabled him to be at the centre of the nation's life once more – somewhere where he could rely on what he perceived to be his superior intellectual abilities to defeat lawyers and judges. Perhaps in some way the contest, as much as its outcome, was what mattered to him.

James had been deeply wounded by Bell's comments, to the extent that the judge assured him that his character was 'unimpeached and unsullied', and on one occasion, comforted James as though he was reassuring a child, telling him that 'I take it for granted that the highest personal respect is paid to your position in society and elsewhere. No one disputes that.' At the same time Arney made it abundantly clear to James that the jury could only award damages for material losses arising from Bell's allegedly defamatory comments. Only if the libel had directly led to James losing title to his land would damages be in order. From here, it was evident that James had practically no chance of winning the case. He continued with an attempt at cross-examining Bell, but the judge soon brought this to an end, advising that the libel had not been proved. However, the judge allowed for the case to be nonsuited, which gave James the opportunity to bring a fresh action against Bell if he chose to.[64]

---

[63] *Daily Southern Cross*, 7 June 1862, 3.
[64] *New Zealander*, 11 June 1862, 6.

Just over a week later, Henry Kemp, from the Land Purchase Department, reported to his superiors that James was again refusing to comply with the government's request to hand over his titles to certain land purchases in return for 'liberal' compensation. One of the main reasons for James shunning this offer was perfectly justifiable: the government refused to specify how much that offer would be.[65] Officials claimed more success the following month, though, and on 8 July, Bell reported to Parliament that 4,800 acres of James's land in the Bay of Islands had reverted to Crown ownership, allegedly on the payment of compensation,[66] although in fact, James received no payment at all.

Did this amount to evidence that the consequences of the alleged libel had led to James suffering damages? He was willing to test the possibility, and in December he resumed his action for libel, this time seeking damages of £7,000. The case was heard before a jury, with James arguing that the substance of his action against Bell was one of 'great public importance', and even went as far as stating that it could be 'a turning point in the misgovernment of the country'. This was vintage overstatement by James, and having thus set the tone and expectations so high, he began to outline the case. Most of the material was a reiteration of that presented in the case in June, although James seemed to stumble more around the procedures of the trial this time, and made a number of elemental mistakes for which he had to apologize.

The case took a startling unprecedented turn when Grey was called as a witness, having been subpoenaed by James. Grey had returned to New Zealand in October 1861, when he was reinstalled as Governor, and now he was appearing in court, about to be cross-examined by one of his harshest critics. The judge suggested that if Grey was there simply to produce documents, it was not absolutely necessary that he be sworn in as a witness, but James immediately signalled his intent to question the Governor, and so Grey took the oath, and James's examination got under way.

Almost immediately, Grey challenged the right of the court to subpoena a colonial governor. Arney, who was again hearing the case, pointed out that any British subject could be called before the court, and being a governor offered no right of exemption. Grey made known his view that it was 'extremely improper' for him to have to appear as a witness, but then responded to James's question, claiming practically no knowledge of the issues being raised, and obfuscating as much as he was capable of. From an evidentiary point of view, the value of Grey's appearance was negligible. However, the

---

[65] H. T. Kemp to Chief Commissioner, Land Purchase Department, 17 June 1862, in 'Report of the Land Purchase Department', in *AJHR*, Session I, C-01 (Wellington: House of Representatives, 1862), 375.

[66] F. Bell, 8 July 1862, in 'Report of the Land Claims Commissioner', in *AJHR*, Session I, D-10 (Wellington: House of Representatives, 1862), 21; *Daily Southern Cross*, 20 November 1863, 4.

fact that James had dragged a sitting governor before court and had questioned him was almost a victory in itself. For a moment, the means had become the end. Whatever the verdict, James could be satisfied in having momentarily humbled and maybe even humiliated Grey.[67] The following day, after hearing the rest of the evidence, and the judge's summing up, the jury retired to consider the verdict, and returned just seven minutes later. On all issues, they found for the defendant. James had suffered another defeat in his libel action against Bell.[68]

The Christchurch newspaper *The Press* mocked James for his efforts. 'Few of our readers in this Province know who Mr Busby is,' its editor wrote sneeringly. 'Politically, he is the last of the moas . . . one of those ante-diluvian monsters who have outlived the great overthrow of obsolete animal life.' The newspaper noted that James was an 'old land claimant' and that '[i]n the pursuit of these imaginary claims he has expended a good deal of money, a good deal more time, and nearly all the intellects with which providence entrusted him.'[69] Admittedly, much of this was written to entertain readers, but the extent to which James was freely mocked showed that he had failed to secure practically any popular support for his cause.

It is possible that the defeat in the Supreme Court was the final straw for James, as a fortnight after the verdict, he announced his resignation from the Auckland Provincial Council.[70] And two months later, his newspaper – *The Aucklander* – passed out of his ownership, having failed to secure a sufficient readership to make it sustainable.[71] At the same time, there was debate in the Provincial Council about a final payment of £50 due to James. The opposition to it was ostensibly on procedural obstacles, but it revealed a degree of antipathy to James among many of his former political colleagues.[72]

It would be difficult for a visitor to Auckland in early 1863 not to notice that war beckoned in the colony. In addition to a build-up of troops in the centre of the city, there were rumours of actual and impending attacks by Māori from the south, leading to a heightened state of nervousness that a conflagration on Auckland's doorstep was possible. Since Grey's return to the country in 1861, the government had increasingly spearheaded policies that aimed to swing the contest of land acquisition in favour of settlers, and to the detriment of Māori. Laws were one means of appropriating more land from Māori for the

---

[67] *Daily Southern Cross*, 16 December 1862, 3.
[68] *New Zealander*, 17 December 1862, 4.
[69] *Press*, 10 January 1863, 1.
[70] *New Zealander*, 2 January 1863, 3.
[71] *Nelson Examiner*, 11 March 1863, 3.
[72] *Daily Southern Cross*, 13 March 1863, 4.

pasture-based economy,[73] but increasingly, legislative weapons were laid down, and in their place, real weapons were picked up. This culminated in Grey issuing an ultimatum to Waikato Māori on 11 July 1863, which was a cynical formality designed to give a righteous complexion to his devilish scheme for his planned invasion of the region.[74]

For James, this was a period when he began to turn his back on politics and to concentrate more on his business activities. He continued to trade in kauri gum as well as horticultural products, and made frequent trips between his home at Waitangi and Auckland, which remained the colony's commercial centre. It was not a sudden disinterest that occasioned this change in priorities. He was struggling financially and could not afford the time to indulge in regional politics, and for all his years in the provincial council, he was no closer to securing title to his land purchases.

He had not, however, given up on court action. In November 1863, for example, he was the plaintiff in the Resident Magistrate's Court, seeking to recover £13 from Stanners Jones – a auctioneer who had frequently advertised in James's former newspaper, *The Aucklander*. It appeared a clear-cut case of the defendant owing the amount being claimed, but Jones's lawyer, Merriman, successfully threw up a dust-cloud of legal technicalities which obscured the issues sufficiently to lead to the case being withdrawn by the judge.[75]

Possibly because of the comparatively small sum involved, James did not seem overly perturbed by the outcome. In his mind, it was another breach of natural justice, but he had become almost inured to these after decades of being at what he saw as the wrong end of decisions by judges and officials. There was, however, one particularly bitter pill which he was still struggling to swallow: the failed libel case against Bell in December the previous year. James's contempt for the former Land Commissioner was again aroused when he read that Bell had referred to him by name during a debate in Parliament on land legislation.

In a stormy letter to the *Daily Southern Cross*, James angrily pointed out that he had not been paid anything at all by way of compensation for the thousands of acres that the government had taken from him, and likened Bell's claim to that of 'the Italian brigand to the captive whom he has carried to the mountains – pay five thousand scudi, and you will be compensated with your liberty'. The only difference, as far as James was concerned, was that Bell

---

[73] V. Wood, T. Brooking, and P. Perry, 'Pastoralism and Politics: Reinterpreting Contests for Territory in Auckland Province, New Zealand, 1853–1864', *Journal of Historical Geography* 34, no. 2 (2008): 220–41.

[74] V. O'Malley, *The Great War for New Zealand, Waikato 1800–2000* (Wellington: Bridget Williams Books, 2016), 211, 224–30, 609.

[75] *New Zealander*, 14 November 1863, 5.

was even less moral 'inasmuch as the brigand does not add breach of trust to robbery', and he expressed how he found it 'extremely painful' to have his name associated with Bell.[76]

Just over a month later, on 26 November, James took the matter further, accusing Bell publicly of delaying the settlement of the old land claims in order to maintain his 'handsome salary'.[77] James then advised the Native Affairs Minister, William Fox, that when it came to resolving the long-standing grievances of settlers in James's position, the entire matter could be reduced to one very simple axiom: that 'you should leave them in possession of what they possess, and that you should compensate them for what you have taken from them'.[78] There was some sympathy for James's circumstances at this time from one newspaper editor, who observed that the government had 'coolly appropriated' some settlers' lands, and that such an injustice had been 'perpetrated by the sanction of retrospective laws', which were founded on 'a mass of injustice'. According to James, the government had 'set an example of fraud', and had corrupted some Māori vendors in the process.[79] There was only one solution, which James suggested to Fox in December 1863: 'a total repudiation of Mr Dillon Bell and his traditions'.[80]

These arguments by James – which he ensured were printed in newspapers for maximum publicity – bore the signs that he was gearing up for another assault on the state in the fight for his land. This may have been the impression left on those following his pronouncements, but privately, his hope of ever swaying government policy had been almost completely exhausted. After battling authorities for more than two decades, all the auguries now pointed to the futility of continuing his lone campaign against a largely indifferent state.

---

[76] *New Zealander*, 20 November 1863, 4.
[77] *New Zealander*, 26 November 1863, 4.
[78] *New Zealander*, 1 December 1863, 5.
[79] *New Zealander*, 2 December 1863, 3.
[80] *New Zealander*, 8 December 1863, 3.

15

Everlasting

The injustices of the preceding two decades continued to gnaw at James, no matter how much he tried to consign them to the past. He had been repeatedly frustrated when trying to seek redress in New Zealand, and so in late 1863, he began to explore the possibility of going to England to appeal to politicians and officials there. It was a poor idea for several reasons. Firstly, it would impose a hefty financial burden on the family – not just for the cost of James's transport and accommodation, but also for the period of at least a year that he would be absent from his trading business in New Zealand. Secondly, the few contacts he had relied on in London in the 1830s were now mostly retired or dead. Then there was the towering legal and constitutional barrier: that the British government was powerless to interfere in matters to do with New Zealand land law as the colony was largely self-governing in this area. And finally, there was the physical toll that such an undertaking could take. James would shortly be sixty-two, at a time when the average life expectancy for a European male in the country was around fifty.[1] In his mind, though, it appears that doing something – however forlorn its ultimate prospects for success – was preferable to struggling with the frustration of the status quo. By the end of the year, his disgruntlement with his circumstances had reached breaking point. He now saw a journey to London as possibly his last opportunity to restore to his ownership the land he had purchased almost a quarter of a century ago.

At the end of January 1864, James sailed to Sydney on the *Otago*, arriving on 8 February, and after a fortnight's stay, he departed for London on the *Blackwall*, reaching the British capital on 24 June after a 'very comfortable' voyage.[2] He had used the months spent at sea drafting a history of New

---

[1] James W. Vaupel and Kristín G. V. Kistowski, 'Broken Limits to Life Expectancy', *Ageing Horizons* 3 (2005): 7.
[2] J. Busby to H. Carleton, 10 January 1865, in AML, MS46, box, 7, vol. 4, 10.

Zealand from 1833 to 1843,[3] and composing works which he hoped to publish in England as part of a campaign to convince the government there that his land claims should finally be confirmed. He had mapped out a general strategy for London, which would involve a combination of public lectures, garnering the support of any allies he could find, and badgering politicians for a hearing. Unrealistic he may have been, but James was no defeatist. He trusted that his persistence would yield some results, which would be crucial to justify the considerable sacrifice he had made to undertake this mission. 'I can only fight the battle with patience and perseverance to the end . . . conscious that for me the time is short,' he wrote with a tinge of foreboding.[4]

This time, though, there was to be no conference with the Secretary of State for the Colonies (Edward Cardwell, the incumbent, refused to meet him), and James found the doors of other MPs closed to him as well.[5] An opportunity of sorts did present itself when he managed to secure a slot to speak at the annual meeting of the National Association for the Promotion of Social Science, in York in September 1864. He entitled his presentation 'The Constitutional Relations of British Colonies to the Mother Country',[6] and emphasized that the system of 'responsible government' in New Zealand was lacking in responsibility, and that power in the colony was in the process of being 'monopolised by the least scrupulous traders, and made disastrous to the colonists as well as disgraceful to the mother country', which had resulted in 'the monstrous sacrifices of the public interests'.[7] James then went on to list ten aspects of New Zealand's political system that he argued were in fundamental conflict with the principles on which British government was founded.[8]

James made his points unusually concisely, and also avoided the temptation to make any reference (even obliquely) to his own circumstances. However, despite these concessions to the appearance of impartiality, and the fact that he sent copies of this address to several MPs, he still failed to get a reception from anyone in government. This was not just a show of incivility. New Zealand had been consuming an inordinate amount of time and money as a consequence of Grey's wars against Māori, and there was accordingly little will to consider what looked to be the inconsequential grievances of a lone

---

[3] Harold Rodwell research papers on James Busby and Gilbert Mair, University of Auckland, MSS & Archives, A291, folder 3.
[4] J. Busby to J. Hobbs, 24 March 1865, in Ramsden, *Busby of Waitangi*, 343.
[5] J. Busby to H. Carleton, 10 January 1865, in AML, MS46, box, 7, vol. 4, 10.
[6] J. Busby, 'The Constitutional Relations of British Colonies to the Mother Country', in *Transactions of the National Association for the Promotion of Social Science. York Meeting, 1864*, ed. G. W. Hastings (London: Longman, Green, 1865).
[7] Ibid., 608.
[8] Ibid., 610–12.

settler. Moreover, now was not the time for British authorities to add fuel to the fire by challenging the jurisdiction of the New Zealand government at the very moment when it was endeavouring to assert that authority over Māori who were defying it.

In New Zealand, James's absence did not mean he got any respite from the press. In 1865, a short work – *Remarks on the Credit of New Zealand and the Honour of Great Britain* – was published in London,[9] and although it was anonymously authored, New Zealand journalists suspected that James had written it. The volume dealt with relations between the provinces in the colony, and further tarnished James's reputation when he was least able to defend it. In the press he was depicted as a 'dirty bird', 'bilious', and someone who was attacking 'everything and everybody connected with New Zealand, except Auckland and the Aucklanders'. According to one newspaper, he '[made] up by impudence what he lacks in ability', with his publication having been conceived 'in a spirit of the narrowest selfishness'.[10] Yet the book was almost certainly not by James. The writing style is noticeably different, the structure of its argument was unlike anything James had previously written, and most importantly, its content barely touched on any of the issues James was so embroiled with.

At the beginning of 1866 another work was published in London, but this one was indisputably by James. *Our Colonial Empire and the Case of New Zealand* came out in January of that year, and at almost 200 pages, was one of the lengthiest volumes he had written. The usual elements made their appearance in it: a truncated history of New Zealand's colonization; assessments of land legislation passed in the country; an overview of the nation's political structure; and observations of the successive governors who had ruled the colony since Hobson. When he came to his account of the present time, James was clear in his view. '[I]t is not too much to say', he told his English readers, 'that a disregard of law and right has been the characteristic of legislation and administration' in New Zealand.[11] The principle of colonial trusteeship had been corrupted to such an extent that even James was at a loss when it came to suggesting a way out of the mess that the likes of Grey had been responsible for creating. On the contrary, he warned that Grey's governorship was looking like a prescription for colonial collapse.[12]

Although there was barely any interest in England in this work, in New Zealand, one newspaper suggested that the publication of *Our Colonial*

---

[9] *Remarks on the Credit of New Zealand and the Honour of Great Britain* (London: Rees and Collin, 1865).
[10] *Wellington Independent*, 3 April 1866, 4.
[11] Busby, *Our Colonial Empire and the Case of New Zealand*, ix.
[12] Ibid., 3.

Empire had occurred 'when it is most needed'. As the Crown's war with Māori – costly in lives and money – continued to be prosecuted, the book provided 'a searching investigation' into the actions of the government, and the fallacy that increased colonial self-government was somehow a panacea for the sort of crisis New Zealand was now in. On the contrary, James had argued it was the prime cause.[13]

In October 1866, James wrote to the Earl of Carnarvon, who was Secretary for State for the Colonies, expressing his disappointment that he had not been given a meeting with him, and warning that the issue he wished to raise (relating to his land claims) presented '[t]he most imminent danger to the Colonists as well as to the honour of the Crown'.[14] Again, though, James was rebuffed, and he realized that further attempts to get a hearing for his grievances would be futile. He therefore made plans to leave London and somehow seek remedies to his claims back home.

On returning to New Zealand, he was confronted with various losses. There was the financial loss he had incurred during his two years away in a failed pursuit of justice. Then he discovered that the government had snatched another 260 acres of land that he had purchased at Tutukaka, and to top it off, he was informed that one of his closest friends – Henry Williams – had died during his absence.[15] These circumstances could have dimmed any remaining optimism James had, but there was one glint of hope that was keeping the darkness of loss at bay.

It had started in July 1867 (while James was still overseas) when a petition was tabled in the Legislative Council (the colony's upper house) signed by seventeen chiefs from Whangarei. They argued strenuously that James had been wrongfully treated by the government over his claims, and reaffirmed that he was the rightful owner of the land he had purchased from them.[16] Four days later, Carleton attempted to introduce a bill into the House of Representatives 'for the relief of James Busby in respect to his titles for land in New Zealand', but failed to win sufficient support.[17] James later admitted to Carleton that he was feeling 'anxious' about the prospects of ever receiving justice over his claims,[18] but at least there were signs of activity on the matter.

On 25 August, Carleton advocated at length for a new bill to resolve James's land issues, and was supported by Donald McLean, the Member for Napier

---

[13] *Daily Southern Cross*, 30 April 1866, 4.
[14] J. Busby to A. Herbert, 20 October 1866, in AML, MS46, box, 7, vol. 4, 11.
[15] Williams died at Pakaraka on 16 July 1867.
[16] *NZPD* 1, pt 1, 26 July 1867, 197.
[17] Ibid., 30 July 1867, 243, 375.
[18] J. Busby to H. Carleton, 31 August 1867, in AML, MS46, box, 7, vol. 4, 12.

and former Chief Land Purchase Commissioner,[19] who said 'it afforded him the greatest pleasure imaginable to support the bill'.[20] One by one, politicians were revealing their positions on James and his circumstances. McLean was very much in the camp of supporters of the former Resident, but not so Charles Heaphy – the Member for Parnell and a former soldier and New Zealand Company employee – who regarded James as a persistent 'source of annoyance or irritation'.[21] Others were more positive, particularly George Graham, who declared that James had served the country during the 1830s 'almost as a missionary' who had 'exerted himself to advance civilization amongst the Native race'.[22]

Bell's position was broadly in favour of some sort of final settlement being reached. He argued that 'generous provision' should be made by the government to resolve James's grievances, but noted that one of the greatest barriers to achieving this thus far had been James himself, who was 'his own enemy', and who had made adversaries of people who were not opposed to him. This was a case of Bell rewriting his own history to make him appear far more gracious than he had been when dealing with James's land issues in the past, but the effect nonetheless was to add support for an offer of 'some measure of relief' to James.[23]

In October 1867, while James was en route to New Zealand, the House of Representatives passed the Land Claims Arbitration Act,[24] which was largely the fruit of Carleton's efforts to have James's land ownership issues resolved once and for all. Just reading the Act's preamble alone would have roused James's hopes. Was fortune finally turning in his favour? The opening lines of the legislation suggested so:

> WHEREAS James Busby of Waitangi . . . did in or about the year one thousand eight hundred and thirty-nine and at divers other times purchase from the Native chiefs of the North Island of New Zealand certain tracts of land at the Bay of Islands Ngunguru Whangarei and Waipu . . . for which said land he paid to the said Native chiefs large sums of money and gave other consideration for the same And whereas a considerable portion of the lands so purchased by the said James Busby as aforesaid have been sold by the Government to other persons whereby the said James Busby

---

[19] R. Fargher, *The Best Man Who Ever Served the Crown? A Life of Donald McLean* (Wellington: Victoria University Press, 2007), 130, 268.
[20] D. McLean, in *NZPD* 1, pt 1, 25 August 1867, 605.
[21] C. Heaphy, in ibid., 606.
[22] G. Graham, in ibid., 607.
[23] F. D. Bell, in ibid., 16 August 1867, 492.
[24] Land Claims Arbitration Act, 1867.

> has been deprived of the same And whereas certain of the lands so purchased are withheld by the Government from the said James Busby and his title to others has been impaired by the Government
>
> And whereas other complications have arisen And whereas the said James Busby has special claims against the Crown of a nature which are distinct from the claims of any other persons whomsoever ... it is expedient that provision should be made for the final settlement of the said claims of the said James Busby in manner hereinafter mentioned.[25]

As the words registered in his mind – with each 'And whereas' phrase summarizing decades of mistreatment by successive governments – James had reason to be cautiously hopeful. As he went through the Act's sections, a picture emerged of how the government proposed to deal with his long-standing and outstanding land claims. A panel of three arbitrators (one of whom would be selected by James) would be appointed to assess both the direct losses he had suffered, and the ensuing damages. Once this was completed, the government would award to him any land remaining unsold within the boundaries of James's original purchases. And to make up for the inevitable shortfall in compensation resulting from only remnants of the original purchases being returned, land scrips would be issued to James[26] to a value to be determined by the arbitrators. This would entitle him to acquire available Crown land in the Auckland province that was equal in value to the remaining amount of compensation awarded to him.[27]

James was eventually awarded a total of £36,800 in scrip,[28] which would easily have left many with the impression that he was somehow profiting from the state's compassion. Julius Vogel, the Member for the Otago electorate of Gold Fields, suggested that the amount paid to James was 'excessive',[29] and outside Parliament, there was criticism about the perceived exorbitance of the compensation James was entitled to. Among the first to condemn the deal was Benjamin Turner, a former convict, and one of the very few remaining settlers who had been in the country longer than James. Turner alleged that James had suffered no loss whatsoever, and accused him of lying and fraud.[30] One journalist, when reviewing the offer made to James, suggested that '[t]he thing is so incredible, that many don't believe in the truth of the report'.[31]

---

[25] Ibid., preamble.
[26] Under the provisions of the Land Order and Scrip Act 1856.
[27] ss. 2–8, Land Claims Arbitration Act, 1867.
[28] Arbitrators' Award in the Case of James Busby, Esq., in *AJHR*, session I, D-11, 1869, 1–3.
[29] J. Vogel, in *NZPD*, 30 September 1868, 4, 1868, 80.
[30] *New Zealand Herald*, 12 May 1868, 4.
[31] *The Press*, 25 April 1868, 2.

Such assessments ignored not only the thousands of pounds James had spent in legal challenges over the years, but also the initial sums he had spent to acquire land he was unable to use, and the ensuing three decades of income forgone as a result. And James needed the money. He had written to a friend – William Ormiston – confiding that his main hope was to be 'able to pay my debts before I die'.[32] Accordingly, he immediately began to advertise for sale some of the sections which he was about to be awarded, and invited potential buyers to meet him at his Auckland house – Providence Villa – in lower Symonds Street.[33]

However, there were some in the colony determined to deny James justice. One of those still harbouring a desire for vengeance was Williamson, who had lain in wait and was now about to pounce on his prey. At the moment when James was planning finally to settle his debts and hopefully be left with enough funds to offer some security to him and Agnes in the closing years of their lives, Williamson saw an opportunity to retaliate. In his capacity of a member of the House, he tried to frustrate James's rights to compensation under the Act by denying him access to available Crown land. Williamson warned of a 'great injury being done' to the Auckland province through James's settlement being enacted, and claimed that the former Resident could be found in Auckland's Land Office, 'looking at the maps, to see where he could find out the most valuable . . . town and suburban lots which were unsold – to see where he could secure the choicest bits that he might buy them up with his scrip'.[34] James did apply to purchase available land in the Auckland suburb of Parnell, but 'was politely informed that all provincial lands have been withdrawn from sale or selection'.[35] This was Williamson's handiwork in action.

Then, in his capacity of Superintendent of the Auckland Provincial Council, Williamson announced that it was the central government's responsibility (and not the Provincial Council's) to pay the compensation that had been awarded to James.[36] The matter of liability was thus shifted from Auckland to the capital, where it was debated in Parliament without any resolution being reached[37] before the parliamentary session closed at the end of October 1868 (with the next one not scheduled to commence until June the following year). James had travelled to Wellington to see if he could influence politicians to make a determination on his settlement, but it proved a fruitless exercise.

---

[32] J. Busby to W. Ormiston, 2 September 1867, in Ramsden, *Busby of Waitangi*, 346.
[33] *Daily Southern Cross*, 11 May 1868, 1.
[34] J. Williamson, in *NZPD* 3, 25 August 1868, 114, 262, 265.
[35] *New Zealand Herald*, 8 May 1868, 2.
[36] Ramsden, *Busby of Waitangi*, 348.
[37] As an example, see *NZPD* 4, October 1868, 251.

Carleton had considered introducing legislation to overcome the impasse, but not finding sufficient support among his colleagues, he shelved the idea.

Not wishing to appear like the villain of the piece, Williamson disingenuously offered to drop his opposition to the compensation being paid, provided that James relinquished his claim to any land in Auckland and accept land in the Bay of Islands instead. It was a means of banishing James from Auckland, and reducing his chances of being fully compensated because of the difficulty of securing sufficient land in the Bay of Islands. James rejected the suggestion outright, and Williamson happily blocked the settlement of James's claims. The spectre of a defeated James was captured by an observer at this time, who described him as looking 'very disconsolate'.[38] He departed Wellington on 22 October, with nothing to show for his efforts at lobbying politicians, and no clear idea what he ought to do next to receive that which had been promised to him. His grievance was beginning to look, as one journalist labelled it, 'everlasting'.[39]

There had been few periods in James's life where his financial circumstances were as dire as they were at the close of 1868. He was unable to obtain credit, the bank was no longer honouring his cheques, and he was faced with mounting debts that he had no means of paying. Age was also taking its toll. James's hearing had been poor for some years, but his failing eyesight was a greater concern. In discussing the state of his health at this time, he conceded to a friend that 'the machine is wearing out'.[40]

There was still some fight in James, though. Frustrated with the inertia of Parliament, which had failed to deliver the restitution that it had legislated for, he decided to pursue court action against Williamson. On 13 October, James had mentioned this plan to the Colonial Secretary, Edward Stafford, urging him to make sure the Governor did not sign any grants of land until the case was over.[41] On receiving this letter, Stafford wrote to Williamson, suggesting that James was correct, and requested that Crown grants for the lands in question be delayed until the matter was clarified.[42]

The Supreme Court case commenced on 5 December 1868. Once again, James found himself appearing before Justice Arney, but this time with the very experienced Thomas Gillies representing him. James was seeking an order from the Court requiring Williamson to cease withholding certain lands from being awarded to him. Williamson did not appear in court, and was granted five days by the judge to justify why he was delaying the settlement

---

[38] *Daily Southern Cross*, 27 October 1868, 6.
[39] *Daily Southern Cross*, 26 October 1868, 4.
[40] J. Busby to A. Berry, 19 November 1868, in Ramsden, *Busby of Waitangi*, 349.
[41] J. Busby to E. Stafford, 13 October 1868, in *New Zealand Herald*, 14 January 1869, 5.
[42] E. Stafford to J. Williamson, 11 November 1868, *New Zealand Herald*, 14 January 1869, 5.

that Parliament had required.[43] A few days later, Gillies broadened the case, adding the Waste Lands Commissioner, Edward Tole, as a defendant.[44]

The legal issues were finely balanced. The provisions of the 1867 Land Claims Arbitration Act seemed to make James's case against the defendants compelling. On the other hand, the defendants had acted within the letter of the law as far as the execution of their duties was concerned. Arney struggled with his decision, confessing that 'my own reasoning has wavered in doubt'. He was even tormented at one stage by the definition of 'such' in the phrase 'such lands' that appeared in the statute, but finally decided in James's favour, thus compelling the Land Commissioner to accept James's scrip for suburban land.[45]

Williamson immediately appealed the decision, and so any hope of a quick resolution to James's quest to have his land returned evaporated. In the meantime, James and Agnes were cast into perilous financial straits. They were practically without an income, and were relying on the support of some of their children to survive from day to day. The state's treatment of James's land claims during the previous years had been shameful, driven in the main by a small clutch of venal politicians intent on ruining him financially, and probably in other ways too.

Now more than ever, James was conscious that time was against him, and so he petitioned Parliament at the beginning of June in another effort to resolve his claim. In his submission, he noted that he had used every means available to acquire the land that he was entitled to by law, but that the Auckland Provincial Council – led by Williamson – had effectively barred him from obtaining even one acre, and was defeating the purpose of the Act that had recently been passed specifically to settle the matter. James therefore urged Parliament to intervene immediately to provide him with the relief he was due.

Carleton was James's man in the House, and emphasized that he was once again raising the matter before his colleagues because the compensation that Parliament had legislated for had been stalled by the Auckland Provincial Council. Carleton wanted James's petition sent to a select committee, but Williamson immediately opposed this, raising concerns about Parliament dealing with James's claim while the appeal over the Supreme Court decision on the issue was still in process. There were also objections from other members who felt that that Carleton ought to be disqualified from serving on any committee considering James's claim as he would be unable to act

---

[43] *New Zealand Herald*, 7 December 1868, 6.
[44] *New Zealand Herald*, 11 December 1868, 4.
[45] *New Zealand Herald*, 16 January 1869, 5.

impartially. Following a brief but bitter encounter, Carleton was forced to withdraw his motion for a committee to be formed to consider James's circumstances because of a lack of support in the House.[46]

Williamson had one further trick up his sleeve. The following month, he announced his intention to introduce a bill that would give effect to the 1867 legislation awarding James his settlement (even though he had rejected any parliamentary interference while James's case was still before the court). On the surface, this looked like an astounding reversal of his previous position, but in fact, it was a ruse – one that would allow the quantum of James's settlement to be whittled away, while at the same time delaying further the date when the matter would be finally settled.[47]

Putting his trust in his powers of advocacy and the integrity of his case, James addressed the House on 30 July for more than two hours in an effort to urge members to oppose Williamson's bill. It was largely James's stump speech on his land claims, but despite his spelling out the injustices he had faced, few politicians were swayed from their stance on the issue of his compensation.[48] He must have sensed that his prospects were slipping away, and that evening he became so ensnared by his own frustration that his judgment faltered. At the critical point when he needed the sympathy of politicians in order to get a vote in Parliament to swing in his favour, he made a tactical miscalculation that was to prove hugely damaging. On 31 July, he wrote a letter for the Premier, William Fox, and sent it, along with a covering letter (marked 'private and confidential'), to McLean. James regarded McLean as an ally,[49] and hoped that he would discuss the letter with Fox and encourage the Premier to act on its recommendation. Otherwise James warned that he would publish the letter in a Wellington newspaper, thus threatening to shame Fox publicly if his demands were not met. And probably as a gesture of goodwill which would have been interpreted very differently by the recipient, James concluded his covering letter by informing McLean that '[i]f you find yourself in a position to give me that assurance, destroy this note, if not, pray return it to me . . . Need I add that no person knows, or shall know, anything of the enclosed until it shall be necessary to publish it.'[50]

The letter itself, addressed to Fox, was anything but diplomatic in its tone. 'Sir,– you are a lawyer and ought to know something of jurisprudence', it began, '[b]ut while you give scant, if any, attention to the pleading for the

---

[46] *NZPD* 5, 3 June 1869, 10–12.
[47] *NZPD* 6, 28 July 1869, 129; 26 August 1869, 777.
[48] *Evening Post*, 31 July 1869, 2; J. Busby, *The Case of Mr Busby Stated in an Address Delivered at the Table of the House of Representatives* (Auckland: William Atkin, 1869).
[49] As an example, see W. Busby to D. McLean, 23 March 1868, MS-00320-0193, NLNZ.
[50] J. Busby to D. McLean, 31 July 1869, in *NZPD* 6, 3 August 1869, 193–4.

payment of a debt due to him by the Colony, and secured to him by an Act of . . . Parliament, you . . . listen with apparent complacency to the proposition . . . to dissolve the obligations.' James then accused Williamson of what amounted to criminal conduct, and Fox of failing to uphold the government's obligations to compensate James in the manner that had been legislated for.[51]

This was hardly going to encourage much goodwill from the Premier, but it was the attempt to use it as a threat that was James's undoing. Fox's response in Parliament to this clumsy effort to exert influence on him was scathing. Instead of yielding to James's 'threat' of making this letter public, he was happy to share its contents with Parliament. And he did so in a way that was designed to maximize the damage inflicted on James's reputation.

Fox informed the House that he was tabling a copy of James's letter that had been made by his secretary. 'I returned the original letter', he said, 'as I felt it would be an insult to let it lie on my table.' The Premier's contempt towards James could not have been plainer. Fox explained that there were various options open to him now. The first possibility was that James be called before the House to answer a charge of gross breach of privilege. Fox said he would not do that (possibly because James could use such a hearing as an opportunity to expose the corruption and underhand tactics of some politicians). Another option was to hand the matter over to the Attorney General to see if it met the threshold of a threat that would allow James to be transported from the country. Fox said that he was disinclined to do this because James was an 'aged man', and to follow this path would be too 'humiliating'. Of course, simply voicing the threat was humiliation enough for James, which was precisely Fox's intention. Finally, like some nineteenth-century Pilate, Fox announced that he would leave it to the House to take whatever measures it felt were fit. The Premier then announced that when the Bill dealing with the settlement of James's claims was returned to the House for its second reading, he would move for it to be struck off and not returned to Parliament for the remainder of the session.[52]

When the entrails of this episode were picked over in a parliamentary debate on 3 August, Carleton did his best to repair the damage. However, given the extraordinary political self-immolation that James had performed, it was a near-impossible task. All that could be done was to imply that James was no longer acting rationally: 'Mr Busby had not consulted any of his friends, who would assuredly have hindered him from taking so improper a course.' Carleton added that James's judgment 'was becoming somewhat impaired', and if that was the case, then 'those who, by a long course of persecution and

---

[51] J. Busby to W. Fox, 31 July 1869, in *NZPD* 6, 3 August 1869, 194.
[52] W. Fox, in *NZPD* 6, 3 August 1869, 194.

wrong, had brought an honourable and high-spirited man to such a pass' should feel guilty for their actions.⁵³

Ongoing debates in the House over the rival bills to deal with James's claims meant that his chances of compensation were beginning to stagnate. One newspaper wrote that when the issue was raised again in Parliament on 28 August, 'a long and wearisome discussion took place', over a topic 'which has been argued again and again until members are heartily sick and tired of it'. That evening, the speaker put an end to the debate, and as it was understood James would be taking the matter back to court, advised that it would not be dealt with in Parliament until an unspecified later date.⁵⁴

James was beginning to give up. On 3 September 1869, he wrote how it was 'sad to think that our public affairs are in the hands of men who have no sense of justice and no shame – men, in short, who 'fear not God, neither regard man!'.⁵⁵ Certainly, the press had turned against him. Typical of this was a *New Zealand Herald* editorial the following month, which alleged that the public was 'thoroughly sick' of James's claims, and that to pay the compensation he sought would 'inflict a grievous injury' on Auckland.⁵⁶

In mid-October, James's solicitor wrote to the Auckland Provincial Council, threating court action unless his client was paid what the Land Claims Arbitration Act had stipulated. When interviewed about this impending legal action, Bell 'declared in the most emphatic manner' that James's claims were 'invalid'. This was Bell at his most dishonest. He knew absolutely that he was misleading the public, but was evidently prepared to lie, and to hinder James's quest for justice, either out of spite or for popularist purposes, or some concoction of the two. The *New Zealand Herald*, for its part, sided with Bell, and did its best to undermine James and his claim: 'We fear the poor gentleman is past reason. No one has denied that Mr Busby has a claim against those who deprived him of his land. This province, however, was no party to such deprivation. No settlement, as far as the province is concerned, is possible because no liability can be admitted.'⁵⁷

At the end of October, James was back in Wellington, where Williamson and Tole were appealing their Supreme Court loss to James in the Court of Appeal. After eleven hours of hearing legal arguments, the Court was unanimous that James had a right to use his scrip in the purchase of any lands in the Auckland province that were for sale, but in a majority decision, it determined that he had no right to buy Crown land that was technically

---

⁵³ H. Carleton, in *NZPD* 6, 3 August 1869, 194.
⁵⁴ *Nelson Examiner and New Zealand Chronicle*, 1 September 1869, 3.
⁵⁵ J. Busby to A. Berry, 3 September 1869, in Ramsden, *Busby of Waitangi*, 357.
⁵⁶ *New Zealand Herald*, 12 October 1869, 4.
⁵⁷ *New Zealand Herald*, 16 October 1869, 3.

available, but not for sale. The result was that the Province's Superintendent would effectively be able to regulate what land James would be able to acquire.[58] It was the sort of decision that left all parties unsatisfied to some degree, but that at least represented for James an advance towards the day when he would hopefully receive some compensation for his losses.

Age had not mellowed James. He was as combative and resistant to compromise as ever, and if there needed to be a fight to preserve his rights and secure his entitlements, his sinews stiffened and he was once more into the fray.[59] However, he was also beginning to include his age and declining health into the calculus of his court and political battles. The prospect of death, and the practicalities of providing for a widowed Agnes, meant that at some point, it would be sensible to settle his claims, even if it involved making some concessions. James was still physically in reasonable condition, apart from his worsening deafness and the advancing cataracts that were obscuring his vision. However, if he needed any reminder that the number of days he had left were dwindling, it came to him in mid-February 1870. While visiting Pakaraka, he received the news that his brother, George, had died at Bathurst after enduring 'a long and painful illness'.[60] Conscious that his own lease on life was shortening, James was even more determined now to bring the long struggle for compensation to a close.

There was a growing acknowledgment in the Provincial Council that his grievance had to be finally laid to rest at some point. Carleton lobbied intensively throughout April 1870 for a resolution, and in the first week of May, rumours began circulating in Auckland that the Superintendent of the Auckland Province had agreed to a payment of £23,000 as a full and final settlement of James's claims.[61] Even before the rumour was confirmed, the press lambasted it as a waste of scarce funds at a time when Auckland was in urgent need of railways, roads, and harbour improvements.[62] However, if the Provincial Council procrastinated, there was a chance that Parliament would impose the terms of a settlement on them, and this ran the risk of a much higher amount having to be paid out to James.

On 11 May 1870, the rumour of a resolution was confirmed. In a single sentence published in the press, a three-decades-long struggle that had consumed so much of James's existence was finally brought to a close: 'The Busby claim is at last settled; the Provincial Government pay £23,000.'[63] Under

---

[58] *New Zealand Herald*, 1 November 1869, 3.
[59] Paraphrase of W. Shakespeare, *Henry V*, Act 3, scene 1.
[60] *Australian Town and Country Journal*, 5 February 1870, 2.
[61] *Australian Town and Country Journal*, 5 May 1870, 3.
[62] *Australian Town and Country Journal*, 6 May 1870, 3.
[63] *Evening Post*, 11 May 1870, 2.

the terms of the settlement, James had to relinquish his claims to any land (apart from his claim to land he had purchased in the Bay of Islands). And with the matter thus resolved, the Provincial Council could now put up land in its possession for sale to settlers, safe in the knowledge that James no longer had the right to claim potentially tens of thousands of acres of it as part of his compensation.[64] There was general relief that the grievance had been settled. Only the *New Zealand Herald* struck a sour note, with its editor hoping 'that we shall not again see the interests of this province wantonly sacrificed' to those who were 'self-seeking'.[65]

James's immediate response was to busy himself with a new political cause. On 24 May, he convened a meeting in the school hall in Russell, where he told the audience that the district needed to do more to let the government know how important the area was. There had been rumours that the number of political representatives from the Bay of Islands was to be reduced, which James argued forcefully was unjustified. Citing shipping activity and export revenue, he believed that the region was too important not to be represented at its current levels. It was a convincing case, but most of the local population had decided that the regatta taking place in the Bay that day was of more interest, and James's presence was not enough to draw them inside to listen to his address.[66] This political anti-climax – speaking to a half-empty rural hall on a topic of no real interest to most of the region's residents – turned out to be James's final public speech.

Meanwhile, the country's politicians were still wrestling with the issue of how to cover the cost of James's settlement, with often acrimonious debates over what became known as the 'Busby Loan'. Parliament and the Auckland Provincial Council haggled for the rest of the year in trying to determine which body was responsible for this liability, and whether there had been procedural irregularities in the payment to James.[67]

For his part, though, James had now largely drifted away from politics, and on 14 June, he and Agnes boarded the Steamship *Hero* for Sydney.[68] The purpose of the trip was twofold: James was interested in finding potential customers for a flax-exporting business he was planning, and he intended to get treatment for his failing eyesight. In both counts, he met with disappointment. The demand for flax had long since waned,[69] and his cataracts

---

[64] *Wellington Independent*, 14 May 1870, 5.
[65] *New Zealand Herald*, 23 May 1870, 4.
[66] *Daily Southern Cross*, 31 May 1870, 6.
[67] *Wellington Independent*, 4 August 1870, 3; *NZPD* 8, 2 August 1870, 219–20; 9, 6–8 September 1870, 531–4, 570–5.
[68] *Auckland Star*, 14 June 1870, 2.
[69] P. Moon, *A Savage Country* (Auckland: Penguin, 2012), 15.

required more specialized treatment than was available in Sydney. The Busbys therefore decided to go to England so that James would have the best chance of getting his sight restored. On the 27 January 1871, they boarded the *Lord Warden*, and departed for London the following day.[70]

They arrived in the British capital in May, and within a few weeks, had located a specialist who would carry out the procedure. The operation took place on 5 June in the borough of Anerley, in southeast London. It was successful, and although James was initially confined to a dark room while his eyes healed, within a few weeks he was encouraged to go outside and do some regular walking to aid his recovery. It was on one of these walks, however, that he contracted acute bronchitis. His breathing became heavy, he wheezed, and he developed a fever. The bronchitis soon led to an acute pulmonary oedema that proved fatal. James died on 15 July 1871,[71] and was buried a few days later at West Norwood Cemetery, between Anerley and Clapham.[72] The immediate reaction in New Zealand to news of James's death was surprisingly slight. Most newspapers simply reported the date, place, and cause of death. Only the *Marlborough Express* offered a sliver of commentary, churlishly referring to James in its death notice simply as 'the monster land claimant in the North'.[73]

Agnes left England as soon as she had settled whatever matters she was able to, and arrived in Auckland on 31 January 1872,[74] after what must have been a painfully lonely four-month journey. Back in Waitangi, she later lamented about her late husband, 'the longer I live, the more I miss him here . . . no one can fill his place'.[75] On 13 October 1889, during a stay with her daughter in Pakaraka, Agnes died.[76]

Epilogue

Towards the end of his life, age had only accentuated James's physical features. His was not the fleshy face and cushioned body of advancing years. Instead, his cheeks were more hollow, his jaw jutted more noticeably, and his appearance generally seemed sterner and more angular. Exasperation was etched into his expression, and to a stranger, he could have passed off as a dour parson or an aged law clerk.

---

[70] *Sydney Mail*, 4 February 1871, 12.
[71] *Wanganui Herald*, 21 September 1871, 2.
[72] South Metropolitan Cemetery Records, London, 18 July 1871, in AML, MS46, box 4, vol. 15, n.p.
[73] *Marlborough Express*, 23 September 1871, 4.
[74] *Auckland Star*, 31 January 1872, 2.
[75] A. Busby, undated, in Ramsden, *Busby of Waitangi*, 364.
[76] *New Zealand Herald*, 4 November 1889, 6.

A diary James kept in 1868 gives a glimpse into his daily life while he was living in Auckland. Mondays through to Saturdays were usually devoted almost entirely to working. He was a prolific writer of letters to officials, politicians, friends, and family, and also produced memoranda and reports for future reference. He would make time to meet people, but he kept his social circle small. He also maintained an archive of just about all the correspondence he had ever exchanged, and preserved a meticulous catalogue of these reams of yellowing papers in his head. At a moment's notice, he could cite a letter written decades earlier, and after fossicking through his files, produce the document. He frequently put this encyclopaedic recall to use when clarifying the record around his land claims, and was able to cite evidence to correct even the slightest misrepresentation of his interminable campaign for justice.

Every Sunday, James would attend St Paul's Church in Emily Place, in the centre of Auckland, often going both to morning and evening services. And if he returned to Waitangi, he would worship at the church in Paihia. It was during church services where he noticed most the deterioration in his hearing. 'At church but heard nothing of the sermon,' he wrote in August, and at various other times, he noted that he 'was unable to follow' what was said.[77]

It was not just work and piety that occupied James's life. On occasion, he and Agnes would hire a carriage and visit friends in Onehunga, or take the ferry to the North Shore. And in addition to the continuous stream of correspondence which he pored over, he managed to get some more leisurely reading in. In one of the few diary entries he made on this topic, he wrote how he had immersed himself in an autobiography of a French Protestant who had spent thirteen years as a galley slave. James felt moved to comment that it was 'a source of thankfulness that such cruelty has ceased to be practiced in the name of religion'.[78]

Costs were a constant source of watchfulness, if not anxiety for James, which was hardly surprising given both his parsimony and his perpetually strained financial situation. When he arrived in Wellington in July 1868 to lobby for his land claims to be settled, he spent the first night in the Empire Hotel. He found it 'too noisy and expensive', and so moved the next day to a room at the Princess Hotel. Likewise, even if he travelled from one part of Auckland to another, he would note the cost. Yes, he was frugal with money, but he was also very fair and generous. On a number of occasions, he would pay solicitors' staff and even government officials money that they had not sought from him simply on the basis that he was so grateful for the work they had done.[79]

---

[77] *James Busby Diary, 1868*, 9 August 1868, AML, MS46, box 6, vol. 3., n.p.
[78] Ibid., 26 July 1868, n.p.
[79] Ibid., 16, 17 July 1868 , n.p.

If the amount of detail he went into is any measure of the importance he attributed to an event, James's meeting with the new Governor, Sir George Bowen, was of great significance to him. In one of his longest entries for the year, on 26 March, James recorded:

> Attended a levee at Govt. House. After I had passed through I was followed by the Private Secty. who told me that the Govr. wished to speak to me as a very old Colonist and invited me to leave my hat and umbrella in his room and take my place amongst those who had the privilege of the Entree after all had passed through. He brought the Governor to me – who gave me his hand and addressed to me half a dozen words of little import. A Powerful man physically with a Massive countenance and great appearance of kindness.[80]

To an extent, prestige, and association with the politically powerful, still mattered to James. He never quite shook off the residue of his comparatively modest social origins, nor his desire to be adorned with a level of status that he believed befitted his natural talents. On one occasion in 1868, he excitedly noted how, when in church, '[t]he Govr. and Lady sat in the next seat but one immediately in front of us'.[81] It was not quite fawning behaviour, but it revealed a yearning to be part of the colony's social elite – something he felt he had still not achieved.

The arc of James's own status had gone through various phases during his life. From a coal-miner's son, he had ascended to budding horticulturalist, then author, colonist, school administrator, farmer, government official, and reached his peak when appointed as His Majesty's Resident to New Zealand. After being 'dethroned' in 1840, though, all that lay ahead was a tremulous descent, from struggling merchant and farmer, to provincial politician, serial litigant, and finally, in the closing years of his life, 'Old Colonist'. This label may have been innocuous and even endearing, but it signalled that he was already an anachronism, as Bowen's encounter with him at Government House had revealed.

A year before he died, James finally secured a victory in his land claims, but it had taken three tortuous decades to accomplish. When he had initially purchased the land in question, New Zealand's settler population was around one thousand. By the time his claims were settled, that number had grown to a quarter of a million – almost all of whom were 'new' colonists and their offspring. To them, James's official career, and his struggles to retain his land,

---

[80] Ibid., 26 March 1868, n.p.
[81] Ibid., 29 March 1868, n.p.

belonged to another age: to a New Zealand that was a fragile frontier settlement, not an expansive and confident colonial society. Indeed, at the time of his death, many settlers would have been unaware even who James was, apart perhaps, from the occasional disparaging references to him in the press that they might have read.

In October 1872, a tawdry serialized history of the colony was published in the *Otago Witness*. In it, James was derided as a 'pleasant man' who had been out of his depth in 1830s New Zealand. He was depicted as using 'smiles and gentle words' to enforce order, and when this inevitably failed, he was 'smitten with the covetous spirit of some pseudo-missionaries, and . . . with them and a few others, acquired some half a million acres of land from the natives'. From this falsehood, the newspaper then peddled another misrepresentation: that James had '*hocus-pocus'd* certain chiefs into a sham confederacy, and . . . succeeded in blinding the Colonial Office . . . [with] false pretences'.[82] No corrective was offered to this deeply adulterated history, and in such ways, the depiction of James as someone feeble, incompetent, and venal stuck in the popular imagination. It could not have been further from the truth. Yet in the months (and then years) that followed news of James's death reaching New Zealand, commemorations were conspicuous by their absence. There were no memorial services held, no eulogies delivered by the good and great of the colony, no tributes in Parliament, and no commemorative plaques or statues erected. One of the most important figures in nineteenth-century New Zealand, and the progenitor of the country as a nation-state, had been cast unconscionably into historical oblivion.

---

[82] *Otago Witness*, 19 October 1872, 2.

Bibliography

Manuscripts and unpublished documents

Bentham, J. University College London Manuscript Collection, 1795, box 170, 182.
Blue Book of Statistics. Auckland: Council Office, Colony of New Zealand, 1844. ref. IA 12 06, Archives New Zealand (ANZ), 122–3.
Brown, A. Ordnance Storekeeper, Sydney, Details ammunition etc., embarked on the *Nereus* (ship) for service of Busby's establishment in New Zealand, 24 July 1833, Ref R4086252, Archives New Zealand.
Busby, A. D. M. *Busby Family Records [BFR]* 1–4. Sydney, n.p. 1994.
Busby, James. Inward Records, 1832–1939, Inward Records 8156, ANZ.
Busby, James to McLean, D. 23 March 1868, MS-00320-0193, National Library of New Zealand (NLNZ).
Busby, James. 'Classified Account Book', NZMSS 168, Auckland Public Library (APL).
Busby, James. 'Despatches and Letters of James Busby, 1833–1839', qMS-0344; qMS-0345, Alexander Turnbull Library, National Library of New Zealand (ATL).
Busby, James. 'James Busby Official Letters to Various People,' Auckland Museum Library (AML), MS 46, 55–9.
Busby, James. 'Memorandum', 31 July 1833, NZMS185 (1), APL.
Busby, James. 'Official Letters to Various People, 1833–1870', qMS-0353, ATL.
Busby, James. *James Busby Diary, 1868*, 9 August 1868, AML, MS46, box 6, vol. 3., n.p.
Colenso, W. 'Day and Waste Book' MS76, AML.
Colonial Secretary Index, State Records New South Wales, 15 January 1823, (Reel 6040; 4/403).
De Thierry, C. *Historical Narrative of an Attempt to Form a Settlement in New Zealand*. APL, Ref. no. GNZMS 55, c. 1857.
Forbes Eadie Scrapbook, Ref: MSY-5842, c. 1940, NLNZ.
General Report of a Committee appointed by the Conference of 1837 to examine charges alleged against the Rev. William White, 26 February 1838 to 8 March 1838, Wesleyan Society Minutes, 1821–67, qMS-2179, ATL.
George Augustus Robinson papers, Mitchell Library, ref. A7022, State Library, New South Wales.
Harold Rodwell research papers on James Busby and Gilbert Mair, University of Auckland, MSS & Archives, A291.
Historical Environment Scotland, 'Statement of Special Interest', 41–45 (odd nos.) Thistle Street, LB43357.
James Busby records, Mitchell Library, manuscript collection, 1823, MLMSS 1668, State Library, New South Wales.

Letters and miscellaneous papers relating to James Busby and his management of the Male Orphan School Farm, 1825–1826, State Archives, New South Wales, 4/402.3.
Letters from James Busby to his Brother George Busby 1823–1830, Auckland Institute and Museum Library, MS46, boxes 1–7.
McDonnell, T. 'Chart of New Zealand. engraved by James Wyld.' Libraries Australia, Ref. 44630284.
Moriarty, W. to Kinghorne, W. 30 July 1833, Archives of Tasmania AB563/1/1, 245, 246; 31 July 1833, MB2/2/2/1.
National Records of Scotland, Old Parish Registers, Births, 685/2 120 518, St Cuthbert's.
New Zealand Gazette Extraordinary No. 1, December 30th 1840, AML, ref. 1949.16.1.
Old Parish Registers, Births 709/ 50 204, Haddington, January 1798.
Papers of the Busby and Kelman Families, 1822–1879, CY Reel 985, ref. ML MSS. 1183, State Library, New South Wales.
Plan of the City of Edinburgh, 1807, EMS.s.59A, National Library of Scotland.
South Metropolitan Cemetery Records, London, 18 July 1871, in AML, MS46, box 4, vol. 15, n.p.
State Archives, New South Wales, 2/1928; COD67.
Stephen, J. to Spring-Rice, T. 30 June 1834, National Archives (UK), CO 323/50.
Stephen, J., minute 10 October 1839, National Archives (UK), CO 209/4.
Stephen, J., minute, 3 December 1838, National Archives (UK), CO 209/3.
The Declaration of Independence, He Whakaputanga, 1835, Archives New Zealand, ref. IA9–1.
The Stranger's Guide, Being a Plan of Edinburgh & Leith Exhibiting all the Streets Principal Buildings & Late Improvements, Edinburgh, 1805, EMGB.s.25(15), National Library of Scotland.
To the Right Honourable Thomas Elder of Forneth, Lord Provost of the City of Edinburgh, this Plan of the City Including all the Latest Improvements is . . . Dedicated by . . . Thomas Brown & Jas. Watson, 1793, EMS.b.2.56, National Library of Scotland.
Turner, N., Journal 1836–1846, A 1873, Mitchell Library, SLNSW.
William Colenso papers, ATL MS Papers 4622.
Williams, P. L. B. *John Morgan of Otawhao*, Auckland War Memorial Museum Library, MS-721.

Newspapers

Auckland Chronicle and New Zealand Colonist
Auckland Examiner
Auckland Star
Auckland Times
Aucklander
Australian
Australian Town and Country Journal
Cape Town Gazette, and African Recorder
Colonial Observer

Colonial Times
Colonist
Colonist and Van Diemen's Land Commercial and Agricultural Advertiser
Daily Southern Cross
Evening Post
Geelong Advertiser and Squatters' Advocate
Hawkes Bay Herald
Hobart Town Courier
Hobart Town Gazette
Inverness Courier
Launceston Advertiser
Literary Chronicle
Lloyd's List
Maitland Mercury and Hunter River General Advertiser
Marlborough Express
Monitor
Morning Chronicle
Nelson Examiner and New Zealand Chronicle
New South Wales Government Gazette
New Zealand Gazette and Wellington Spectator
New Zealand Herald
New Zealand Herald and Auckland Gazette
New Zealand Spectator and Cook's Strait Guardian
New Zealander
Otago Witness
Press
Shipping Gazette and Sydney General Trade List
South Australian Record and Australasian Chronicle
Sydney Gazette and New South Wales Advertiser
Sydney Herald
Sydney Mail
Sydney Monitor
Sydney Monitor and Commercial Advertiser
Sydney Morning Herald
Tasmanian
Wanganui Herald
Wellington Independent

Statutes, regulations, bye-laws, bills, ordinances

A Bill to Authorize the Governor of New South Wales, with the Advice and Consent of the Legislative Council of that Colony, to Make Provision for the Prevention and Punishment of Crimes Committed by His Majesty's Subjects, in Islands Situate in the Southern Or Pacific Ocean, and Not Being Within His Majesty's Dominion, session 516, 4. London: House of Commons, 1832.

A Collection of Statutes Connected with the General Administration of the Law 6, ed. W. D. Evan. London: Thomas Blenkarm, 1836.
An Act for the More Effectual Punishment of Murders and Manslaughters Committed in Places not within His Majesty's Dominions, 1817.
The Act of Incorporation and Bye-Laws of the Belfast Academical Institution, 1810. Belfast: Royal Belfast Academical Institution, 1815.
Equitable Compensation Bill 1860.
Land Claims Arbitration Act 1867.
Land Claims Ordinance 1841.
Land Claims Settlement Act 1856.
Land Claims Settlement Extension Act 1858.
Land Order and Scrip Act 1856.
Land Titles Bill 1840.
Native Land Purchase Ordinance 1846.
Native Land Purchase Ordinance 1846
New South Wales Act, 4 Vict., No. 7, Repealed Act 1841.
New Zealand Constitution Act 1852.
Provincial Councils Ordinance 1851.
The Public General Statutes of New South Wales, 1824–1837. Sydney: T. Richards, 1861.
Waste Lands Act 1854.

Official published sources, directories, reports

Report on the Condition of the Poorer Classes of Edinburgh. Edinburgh: Edmonston and Douglas, 1868.
Arbitrators' Award in the Case of James Busby, Esq., in *Appendix to the Journals of the House of Representatives (AJHR)*, session I, D-11, 1869.
Australian Almanac for the Year of Our Lord 1831, ed. R. Mansfield. Sydney, 1831.
Bigge, J. T. *Report of the Commissioner of Inquiry into the State of the Colony of New South Wales*. London: House of Commons, 1822.
Bulletins of State Intelligence &c. London: London Gazette, 1847.
Compilation of the Reports of the Committee on Foreign Relations, United States Senate, 1789–1901, First Congress, first session to Fifty-Sixth Congress, second session. Washington, DC: United States Senate, 1901.
Copy of Correspondence Relative to a Proposal for a Grant of a Proprietary Government to the New Zealand Company. London: House of Commons, 1845.
Correspondence with the Secretary of State Relative to New Zealand. London: House of Lords, 1840.
Edinburgh and Leith Directory, from July 1804 to July 1805. Edinburgh: Denovan and Co., 1804.
Great Britain Parliamentary Papers. London: House of Commons, 1833, 1837, 1839, 1840, 1841, 1844, 1845, 1847.
Hansard. House of Commons Debates. London: House of Commons, 1832, 1845.
Historical Alumni. Edinburgh: University of Edinburgh, 2018.

Historical Records of Australia [HRA] 1, vols. 11–23, ed. F. Watson. Canberra: The Library Committee of the Commonwealth Parliament, 1917–25.
Journals of the House of Commons 100 (London: House of Commons, 1845).
Loveridge, D. M. '"A Knot of a Thousand Difficulties": Britain and New Zealand, 1769–1840.' Brief of Evidence before the Waitangi Tribunal, WAI-1040, #A18. Wellington: Waitangi Tribunal, 2009.
New Zealand Parliamentary Debates, D 1861; 1, 1867; 3, 4, 1868; 5, 6, 1869; 8, 1870; 54, 55, 56, 1886.
Papers Relating to the Recent Disturbances in New Zealand, 1859–1861. London: House of Commons, 1861.
Papers Relative to the Affairs of New Zealand. London: House of Commons, 1845.
Report from Committee on Secondary Punishments. London: House of Commons, 1831.
Report from Select Committee on Malt Drawback on Spirits: Together with the Minutes of Evidence, and Appendix of Papers. London: House of Commons, 1831.
Report from the Select Committee of the House of Lords Appointed to Inquire into the Present State of the Islands of New Zealand and the Expediency of Regulating the Settlement of British Subjects Therein: With the Minutes of Evidence Taken before the Committee and an Index thereto. London: House of Lords, 1838.
Report of the Commission to Inquire into the Supply of Water to Sydney and Suburbs. Sydney: Thomas Richards, 1869.
Report of the Land Claims Commissioner, in *AJHR*, Session I, D-10. Wellington: House of Representatives, 1862.
Report of the Land Purchase Department, in *AJHR*, Session I, C-01. Wellington: House of Representatives, 1862.
Report of the Parliamentary Select Committee on Aboriginal Tribes (British Settlements). London: House of Commons, 1837.
Reports from the Committees 7. London: House of Commons, 1831.
Reports from the Committees. Army (Colonies), vol. 6, session 19 February–10 September 1835. London: House of Commons, 1835.
Statistical Register of New South Wales for the Year 1861. Sydney: Registrar General's Office, 1862.
The Northumberland Poll Book. Alnwick: W. Davison, 1826.
The Post-Office Annual Directory. Edinburgh: Abernethy & Walker, 1810, 1818, 1820, 1822.
Votes and Proceedings of the Legislative Council 1. Sydney: Government Printer, 1852.

Journal articles

Anderson, R. D. 'School Attendance in Nineteenth-Century Scotland: A Reply', *Economic History Review* 38, no. 2, May 1985.
Arvaston, G. and Butler, T. 'Metamorphoses, Transformation and European Cities', *Ethnologia Europaea* 34, no. 2, 2004.

Ashton, J. '"So Strange a Proceeding": Murder, Justice, and Empire in 1830s Hokianga', *New Zealand Journal of History (NZJH)* 46, no. 2, 2012.
Ballantyne, T. 'Humanitarian Narratives: Knowledge and the Politics of Mission and Empire', *Social Sciences and Missions* 24, nos. 2–3, 2011.
Binney, J. 'Tuki's Universe', *NZJH* 38, no. 2, 2004.
Blyton, G. 'Rum and Corn Pipes: The Introduction of Alcohol and Tobacco into Aboriginal Populations of the Hunter Region of Central Eastern New South Wales, Australia, in the First Half of the 19th Century', *AlterNative: An International Journal of Indigenous Peoples* 9, no. 4, 2013.
Buchan, B. and Heath, M. 'Savagery and Civilization: From Terra Nullius to the "Tide of History"', *Ethnicities* 6, no. 1, 2006.
Cain, P. J. and Hopkins, A. G. 'The Political Economy of British Expansion Overseas, 1750–1914', *The Economic History Review* 33, no. 4, 1980.
Cheyne, S. 'Act of Parliament or Royal Prerogative: James Stephen and the First New Zealand Constitution Bill', *NZJH* 24, no. 2, 1990.
Cleave, P. 'Tribal and State-like Political Formations in New Zealand Maori Society, 1750–1900', *JPS* 92, no. 1, 1983.
Cumberland, K. B. 'A Land Despoiled: New Zealand About 1838', *New Zealand Geographer* 6, no. 1, 1950.
The Cyclopedia of New Zealand. Wellington: Cyclopedia Company Limited, 1897.
Darwin, C. *The Correspondence of Charles Darwin. Volume 18*. Cambridge: Cambridge University Press, 2010.
Donnachie, I. 'The Convicts of 1830: Scottish Criminals Transported to New South Wales', *The Scottish Historical Review* 65, no. 179, 1986.
Druett, J. 'The Salem Connection: American Contacts with Early Colonial New Zealand', *JNZS* 8, 2009.
Ellis, N. 'Ki to ringa ki nga rakau a te Pakeha? Drawings and Signatures of Moko by Maori in the Early 19th Century', *JPS* 123, no. 1, March 2014.
Fadiman, M. 'Kauri (Agathis Australis) Ethnobotany: Identity, Conservation and Connection in New Zealand', *The Florida Geographer* 41, 2010.
Fisher, M. H. 'Indirect Rule in the British Empire: The Foundations of the Residency System in India (1764–1858)', *Modern Asian Studies* 18, no. 3, 1984.
Fletcher, B. H. 'Administrative Reform in New South Wales Under Governor Darling', *Australian Journal of Public Administration* 38, no. 3, 1979.
Fletcher, B. H. 'Christianity and Free Society in New South Wales 1788–1840', *Journal of the Royal Australian Historical Society* 86, no. 2, 2000.
Fletcher, N. and Elias, S. 'A Collusive Suit to "Confound the Rights of Property through the Length and Breadth of the Colony"?: *Busby v White* (1859)', *Victoria University of Wellington Law Review* 41, 2010.
Ford, T. D. and Torrens H. S. 'A Farey Story: The Pioneer Geologist John Farey (1766–1826)', *Geology Today* 17, no. 2 (2001).
Foster, S. G. 'A Piece of Sharp Practice? Governor Bourke and the Office of Colonial Secretary in New South Wales', *Australian Historical Studies* 16, no. 64, 1975.
Gallagher, J. and Robinson, R. 'The Imperialism of Free Trade', *The Economic History Review* 6, no. 1, 1953.
Gray, R. Q. 'Styles of Life, the "Labour Aristocracy" and Class Relations in Later Nineteenth Century Edinburgh', *International Review of Social History* 18, no. 3, 1973.

Hamowy, R. 'Jefferson and the Scottish Enlightenment: A Critique of Garry Wills's *Inventing America: Jefferson's Declaration of Independence*', *The William and Mary Quarterly: A Magazine of Early American History* 36, no. 4, 1979.
Hargreaves, R. P. "Changing Maori Agriculture in pre-Waitangi New Zealand', *JPS* 72, no. 2, 1963.
Higman, B. W. 'The West India "Interest" in Parliament, 1807–1833', *Australian Historical Studies* 13, no. 49, 1967.
Hoeflich, M. 'The Americanization of British Legal Education in the Nineteenth Century', *The Journal of Legal History* 8, no. 3, 1987.
Houston, R. A. 'Literacy, Education and the Culture of Print in Enlightenment Edinburgh', *History: The Journal of the Historical Association* 78, no. 254, 1993.
Hudson, P. 'English Emigration to New Zealand, 1839–1850: Information Diffusion and Marketing a New World', *The Economic History Review* 54, no. 4, 2001.
Ihde, E. 'Pirates of the Pacific: The Convict Seizure of the "Wellington"', *The Great Circle* 30, no. 1, 2008.
Jackson, R. V. 'Jeremy Bentham and the New South Wales Convicts', *International Journal of Social Economics* 25, nos. 2–4, 1998.
Jardine, R. W. 'James Jardine and the Edinburgh Water Company', *Transactions of the Newcomen Society* 64, no. 1, 1992.
Jeans, D. N. 'Territorial Divisions and the Locations of Towns in New South Wales, 1826–1842', *The Australian Geographer* 10, no. 4, 1967.
Jeans, D. N. 'Town Planning in New South Wales, 1829–1842', *Journal of the Royal Australian Planning Institute* 3, no. 6, 1965.
Joseph, P. A. 'Foundations of the Constitution', *Canterbury Law Review* 4, 1989.
Kaplan, L. S. 'The Treaty of Paris, 1783: A Historiographical Challenge', *The International History Review* 5, no. 3, 1983.
Karskens, G. 'Defiance, Deference and Diligence: Three Views of Convicts in New South Wales Road Gangs', *The Australian Journal of Historical Archaeology* 4, 1986.
Kingi, T. 'Maori Landownership and Land Management in New Zealand', *Making Land Work* 2, 2008.
Leneman L. and Mitchison, R. 'Scottish Illegitimacy Ratios in the Early Modern Period', *The Economic History Review* 40, no. 1, 1987.
Leneman, L. '"No Unsuitable Match": Defining Rank in Eighteenth and Early Nineteenth-Century Scotland', *Journal of Social History* 33, no. 3, 2000.
Lockhart, D. G. "The Land Surveyor In Northern Ireland Before The Coming Of The Ordnance Survey Circa 1840', *Irish Geography* 11, no. 1. 1978.
MacIntyre, D. 'Britain's Intervention in Malaya: The Origin of Lord Kimberley's Instructions to Sir Andrew Clarke in 1873', *Journal of Southeast Asian History* 2, no. 2, 1961.
Macready, S. and Robinson, J. 'Slums and Self-Improvement: The History and Archaeology of the Mechanics Institute, Auckland, and its Chancery Street Neighbourhood. Vol. 2: The Artefacts and Faunal Material', in *Science and Research Internal Report No 91*. Wellington: Department of Conservation, 1990.
Manning, H. T. 'The Colonial Policy of the Whig Ministers, 1830–37: I', *Canadian Historical Review* 33, no. 3, 1952.

Martin, G. 'James Busby and the Treaty of Waitangi', *British Review of New Zealand Studies* 5, 1992.
Martin, G. 'Two Cheers for Lord Glenelg', *Journal of Imperial and Commonwealth History* 7, no. 2, 1979.
Matheson, A. 'Wharekahu C. M. S. Mission Station, Maketu. The Chapmans, 1845–1861', *Historical Review* 49, no. 1, 2001.
McHugh, P. 'Sovereignty This Century: Maori and the Common Law Constitution', *Victoria University of Wellington Law Review* 31, 2000.
McKeown, T. and Record, R. G. 'Reasons for the Decline of Mortality in England and Wales during the Nineteenth Century', *Population Studies* 16, no. 2, 1962.
McNab, W. 'On Preparing Large Trees Intended to be Transplanted', *The Quarterly Journal of Agriculture* 2, 1831.
Morrell, J. B. 'The University of Edinburgh in the Late Eighteenth Century: Its Scientific Eminence and Academic Structure', *Isis* 62, no. 2, 1971.
Newbury, C. W. 'Patrons, Clients, and Empire: The Subordination of Indigenous Hierarchies in Asia and Africa', *Journal of World History* 11, no. 2, 2000.
Nicolle, A. 'Ouvrard and the French Expedition in Spain in 1823', *The Journal of Modern History* 17, no. 3, September 1945.
Nix, M. 'The Australian Company of Edinburgh and Leith, Part One: A Mode of Business', *The Great Circle* 27, no. 2, 2005.
North D. C. and Weingast, B. R. 'Constitutions and Commitment: The Evolution of Institutions Governing Public Choice in Seventeenth-Century England', *The Journal of Economic History* 49, no. 4, 1989.
O'Hagan, J. E. 'Sir Thomas Brisbane, FRS, Founder of Organized Science in Australia', *Journal of the Royal Historical Society of Queensland* 6, no. 3, 1961.
O'Malley, V. 'Manufacturing Chiefly Consent? James Busby and the Role of the Rangatira in the Pre-Colonial Era', *Journal of New Zealand Studies*, 10, 2011.
Penson, L. M. 'The Origin of the Crown Agency Office', *The English Historical Review* 40, no. 158, 1925.
Priestley, S. 'Charting Some Port Phillip Myths', *Victorian Historical Journal* 87, no. 1, 2016.
Ramsden, E. 'James Busby: The Prophet of Australian Viticulture', *Journal and Proceedings of the Royal Australian Historical Society* 26, no. 5, 1940.
Ross, J. O. 'Busby and the Declaration of Independence', *NZJH* 14, no. 1, 1980.
Ross, R. 'Te Tiriti o Waitangi: Texts and Translations', *NZJH* 6, no. 2, 1972.
Rumbles, W. 'Spectre of Jurisdiction: Supreme Court of New South Wales and the British Subject in Aotearoa/New Zealand 1823–1841', *Law Text Culture* 15, 2011.
Samson, J. 'The 1834 Cruise of HMS *Alligator*: The Bible and the Flag', *The Northern Mariner/Le Marine du Nord* 3, 1993.
Sanchez-Burks, J. 'Protestant Relational Ideology and (in)Attention to Relational Cues in Work Settings', *Journal of Personality and Social Psychology* 83, no. 4, 2002.
Schaffer, S. 'Natural Philosophy and Public Spectacle in the Eighteenth Century', *History of Science* 21, no. 1, 1983.
Schaniel, W. C. 'European Technology and the New Zealand Maori Economy: 1769–1840', *The Social Science Journal* 38, no. 1, 2001.
Shawcross, K. 'Review of Narrative of a Residence in New Zealand: Journal of a Residence in Tristan da Cunha', *Journal of the Polynesian Society (JPS)* 76, no. 2, 1967.

Sheehan, C. '"I Have the Honour to Remain your Humble Servant"', *Queensland History Journal* 21, no. 12, 2013.
Stenhouse, J. 'Churches, State and the New Zealand Wars: 1860–1872', *Journal of Law and Religion* 13, no. 2, 1998.
Steven, M. 'The Changing Pattern of Commerce in New South Wales, 1810–1821', *Australian Economic History Review* 3, no. 2, 1963.
Sylvester, D. 'Governor Lachlan Macquarie, Sir James Mackintosh and the Scottish Enlightenment', *Journal of Australian Colonial History* 12, 2010.
Thompson, E. P. 'Eighteenth Century English Society: Class Struggle without Class?', *Social History* 3, no. 2, 1978.
Vaupel, J. W. and Kristín G. V. 'Broken Limits to Life Expectancy', *Ageing Horizons* 3, 2005.
Wanhalla, A. 'The "Bickerings" of the "Mangungu Brethren": Talk, Tales and Rumour in Early New Zealand', *Journal of New Zealand Studies (JNZS)* 12, 2011.
Wheeler, G. 'John Lynn: Architect/Contractor/Engineer', *Lecale Miscellany* 15, 1997.
Williams, E. T. 'The Colonial Office in the Thirties', *Australian Historical Studies* 2, no. 7, 1943.
Wolloch, N. 'The Civilizing Process, Nature, and Stadial Theory', *Eighteenth-Century Studies* 44, no. 2, 2011.
Wood, V., Brooking, T. and Perry, P. 'Pastoralism and Politics: Reinterpreting Contests for Territory in Auckland Province, New Zealand, 1853–1864', *Journal of Historical Geography* 34, no. 2, 2008.

Theses, dissertations

Bayly, N. 'James Busby: British Resident in New Zealand, 1833–40.' MA thesis, University of Auckland, 1949.
Bridges, B. J. 'The Sydney Orphan Schools, 1800–1830.' MEd thesis, University of Sydney, 1973.
Bubacz, B. 'The Female and Male Orphan Schools in New South Wales, 1801–1850.' PhD thesis, University of Sydney, 2007.
Connor, M. C. 'The Politics of Grievance: Society and Political Controversies in New South Wales, 1819–1827.' PhD thesis, University of Tasmania, 2002.
Gawith, B. 'James Reddy Clendon, 1800–1872: Trade, Entrepreneurship and Empire.' MA thesis, Massey University, 2005.
Hopa, N. K. 'The Rangatira: Chieftainship in Traditional Maori Society.' BLitt thesis, Oxford University, 1966.
Liston, C. 'New South Wales Under Governor Brisbane, 1821–1825.' PhD thesis, University of Sydney, 1980.
Neville, R. A. J. 'Printmakers in Colonial Sydney, 1800–1850.' MA thesis, University of Sydney, 1988.
Parkinson, P. 'Our Infant State: The Maori Language, the Mission Presses, the British Crown and the Maori, 1814–1838.' PhD thesis, Victoria University of Wellington, 2003.
Ritchie, J. 'Punishment and Profit: The Reports of Commissioner Bigge on the Colonies of New South Wales and Van Diemen's Land, 1822–1823; their

Origins, Nature and Significance.' PhD thesis, Australian National University, 1969.

Shawcross, K. 'Maoris of the Bay of Islands, 1769–1840.' MA thesis, University of Auckland, 1967.

Spence, C. Q. 'Ameliorating Empire: Slavery and Protection in the British Colonies, 1783–1865.' PhD thesis, Harvard University, 2014.

Miscellaneous

Durie, M. 'Keynote Address: Is there a Distinctive Māori Psychology?', in *The Proceedings of the National Māori Graduates of Psychology Symposium*. Hamilton: Waikato University, 2002.

Interview with David Rankin, Te Matarahurahu, Auckland, 21 July 2018.

Correspondence with Dr Ned Fletcher, 29 April 2019.

Correspondence with Professor Russell Stone, 24 April 2019.

Books, journals, magazines

Adams, P. *Fatal Necessity: British Intervention in New Zealand, 1830–1847*. Auckland: Auckland University Press, 1977.

Allen, D. *Early Georgian, Being Extracts from the Journal of George Allen, 1800–1877*. Sydney: Angus and Robertson, 1958.

Anderson, J. *A History of Edinburgh from the Earliest Period to the Completion of the Half Century 1850*. Edinburgh: A. Fullerton & Co., 1856.

Anderson, R. 'The History of Scottish Education pre-1980', in *Scottish Education: Post-Devolution*, eds. T. G. K. Bryce and W. M. Humes. Edinburgh: Edinburgh University Press, 2003.

Andrews, P. *No Fear of Rusting: A Biography of the Rev. Thomas Chapman*. Rotorua: Rotorua & District Historical Society, 2001.

The Annual Register, or a View of the History, Politics, and Literature of the Year 1823. London: Baldwin, Craddock, and Joy, 1824.

Armitage, D. *The Ideological Origins of the British Empire*. Cambridge: Cambridge University Press, 2001.

Arnot, H. *The History of Edinburgh from the Earliest Accounts to the Year 1780*. Edinburgh: Thomas Turnbull, 1816.

Ashton, T. S. and Sykes, J. *The Coal Industry of the Eighteenth Century*. Manchester: Manchester University Press, 1929.

The Asiatic Journal and Monthly Register for British India and its Dependencies 12, 23, 24. London: Kingsbury, Parbury, & Allen, 1821, 1826, 1827.

Attwood, B. 'Protection Claims: The British, Maori and Islands of New Zealand, 1800–1840', in *Protection and Empire: A Global History*, eds. L. Benton, A. Clulow, and B. Attwood. Cambridge: Cambridge University Press, 2018.

Balfour, J. H. *Guide to the Royal Botanic Garden, Edinburgh*. Edinburgh: Edmonston & Douglas, 1873.

Ballantyne, T. *Entanglements of Empire: Missionaries, Maori, and the Question of the Body*. Auckland: Auckland University Press, 2015.

Barcan, A. *Two Centuries of Education in New South Wales*. Sydney: New South Wales University Press, 1988.

Barrington, G. *A History of New South Wales: Including Botany Bay, Port Jackson, Parramatta, Sydney, and all its Dependencies*. London: M. Jones, 1802.

Barrington, G. *A Sequel to Barrington's Voyage to New South Wales*. London: C. Lowndes, 1800.

Beecham, J. *Remarks upon the Latest Official Documents Relating to New Zealand*. London: Hatchards, 1838.

Belgrave, M. *Historical Frictions: Maori Claims and Reinvented Histories*. Auckland: Auckland University Press, 2005.

Belich, J. *Making Peoples: A History of the New Zealanders from Polynesian Settlement to the End of the Nineteenth Century*. Auckland: Allen Lane, 1996.

Bentham, J. *A Fragment on Government*. Oxford: Clarendon Press, 1891.

Binney, J. *The Legacy of Guilt: A Life of Thomas Kendall*. Auckland: Oxford University Press, 1968.

Binney, K. R. *Horsemen of the First Frontier, 1788–1900*. Sydney: Volcanic Productions, 2005.

Blackwood's Edinburgh Magazine 14, London: William Blackwood, 1823.

Blair, D. *The History of Australasia: From the First Dawn of Discovery in the Southern Ocean to the Establishment of Self-Government in the Various Colonies*. Glasgow: McGready, Thomson Niven, 1878.

Bohan, E. *Blest Madman: Fitzgerald of Canterbury*. Christchurch: Canterbury University Press, 1998.

Briggs, A. 'The Language of "Class" in Early Nineteenth-Century England', in *Essays in Labour History*, eds. A. Briggs and J. Saville. London: Palgrave Macmillan, 1967.

Brodie, W. *Remarks on the Past and Present State of New Zealand*. London: Whittaker & Co., 1845.

Brown, A. N. *The Journals of A. N. Brown, CM.S Missionary Tauranga*. Tauranga: The Elms Trust, 1990.

Brown, W. *New Zealand and its Aborigines*. London: J. and D. A. Darling, 1851.

Bruce, D. *The Life of Sir Thomas Fowell Buxton: Extraordinary Perseverance*. Plymouth: Lexington Books, 2014.

Buick, T. L. *New Zealand's First War*. Wellington: Govt. Printer, 1926.

Buller, J. *The Maori War: A Lecture*. Auckland: Charles Williamson, 1869.

Busby, J. 'Address to the Chiefs on the Occasion of the Adoption of a Flag, 17 March 1834', in *He Whakaputanga me te Tiriti: The Declaration and the Treaty: The Report on Stage 1 of the Te Paparahi o Te Raki Inquiry*, Wai-1040. Wellington: Waitangi Tribunal, 2014.

——. 'Advice to Emigrants Newly Arrived in New South Wales', in R. Mansfield, *Australian Almanack, for the Year of Our Lord 1831*. Sydney: R. Mansfield, 1830.

——. *Authentic Information Relative to New South Wales and New Zealand*. London: Joseph Cross, 1832.

——. 'A Brief Memoir Relative to the Islands of New Zealand' [London, 1831], in Busby, *Authentic Information Relative to New South Wales*.

——. *The Case of Mr Busby Stated in an Address Delivered at the Table of the House of Representatives*. Auckland: William Atkin, 1869.

——. *Colonies and Colonization: A Lecture Delivered in the Hall of the Mechanics' Institute, At Auckland, with Especial Reference to New Zealand.* Auckland: Philip Kunst, 1857.

——. 'The Constitutional Relations of British Colonies to the Mother Country', in *Transactions of the National Association for the Promotion of Social Science. York Meeting, 1864*, ed. G. W. Hastings. London: Longman, Green, 1865.

——. *Illustrations of the System Called Responsible Government. In a Letter to His Excellency, Colonel Gore Browne.* Auckland: W. C. Wilson, 1860.——.

Journal of a Recent Visit to the Principal Vineyards of Spain and France. London: Smith, Elder & Co., 1834.

——. *Journal of a Tour through Some of the Vineyards of Spain and France.* Sydney: Stephens and Stoke, 1833.

——. 'A Letter on the Emigration of Mechanics and Labourers to New South Wales', in Busby, *Authentic Information Relative to New South Wales.*

——. *A Manual of Plain Directions for Planting and Cultivating Vineyards, and for Making Wine, in New South Wales.* Sydney: R. Mansfield, 1830.

——. 'Observations on the Alienation of Lands from the Crown in the Colony of New South Wales', Sydney, 25 October 1829, in Busby, *Authentic Information Relative to New South Wales.*

——. *Our Colonial Empire and the Case of New Zealand.* London: Williams and Norgate, 1866.

——. *The Pre-Emption Land Question: A Comprehensive View of the Proceedings of Governors FitzRoy and Grey . . . in a Letter Addressed to Governor Gore Browne.* Auckland: Richardson and Sansom, 1859.

——. *Rebellions of the Maori Traced to their True Origin.* London: Strangeways & Walden, 1865.

——. *Remarks upon a Pamphlet Entitled 'The Taranaki Question', by Sir William Martin.* Auckland: Philip Kunst, 1860.

——. *The Right of a British Colonist to the Protection of the Queen and Parliament of England against the Illegal and Unjust Acts of a Colonial Legislature or Government; A Letter to His Grace the Duke of Newcastle.* Auckland: Philip Kunst, 1860.

——. *Speech Delivered to the Provincial Council of Auckland.* Auckland: n.p., 1853.

——. *A Treatise on the Culture of the Vine, and the Art of Making Wine.* Sydney: R. Howe, 1825.

Busby, M. *The Busby Family.* Wellington: n.p., 1995.

Butlin, N. G. *Forming a Colonial Economy: Australia 1810–1850.* Cambridge: Cambridge University Press, 1994.

Callaghan, T. *Acts and Ordinances of the Governor and Council of New South Wales.* Sydney: William John Row, 1844.

Campbell, D. *Edinburgh: A Cultural And Literary History.* Oxford: Signal Books, 2003.

Carleton, H. *The Life of Henry Williams: Archdeacon of Waimate.* Auckland: Upton & Co., 1874.

Carpenter, S. D. *Te Wiremu, Te Puhipi, He Whakaputanga me Te Tiriti: Henry Williams, James Busby, A Declaration and the Treaty.* Wellington: Waitangi Tribunal, 2009.

Cayley, F. *Flag of Stars.* Adelaide: Rigby, 1966.

Chambers, W. *A Tour in Switzerland, in 1841*. Edinburgh: W. & R. Chambers, 1842.
Chaucer, G. *The Canterbury Tales*. G. J. Davis, trans. Bridgeport, CT: Insignia Publishing, 2016.
Church Missionary Record, Detailing the Proceedings of the Church Missionary Society for the Year 1832. London: Church Missionary Society, 1832.
Clark, C. M. H. *A History of Australia: New South Wales and Van Diemen's Land, 1822–1838*. Melbourne: Melbourne University Press, 1962.
Cobbett's Political Register. London: Bolt Court, 1832.
Coleman, J. N. *A Memoir of the Rev. Richard Davis*. London: James Nisbet and Co., 1865.
Colenso, W. *The Authentic and Genuine History of the Signing of the Treaty of Waitangi*. Wellington: Govt. Printer, 1890.
Collins, D. *An Account of the English Colony in New South Wales: With Remarks on the Dispositions, Customs, Manners, &c. of the Native Inhabitants of that Country*. London: T. Cadell, 1804.
Colvin, H. M. *History of the King's Works. Vol. VI: 1782–1851*. London: H.M. Stationery Office, 1973.
Cowan, M. P. and Shenton, R. W. 'The Invention of Development', in *Power of Development*, ed. J. Crush. London: Psychology Press, 1995.
A Concise History of Australian Settlement and Progress. Sydney: The Sydney Morning Herald, 1888.
Cox, A. *Men of Mark of New Zealand*. Christchurch: Whitcombe and Tombs, 1886.
Cunningham, P. M. *Two Years in New South Wales*. London: H. Colburn, 1827.
Darling, R. *Letter Addressed by Lieut.-Gen. R. Darling, Late Governor of New South Wales, to Joseph Hume, Esq. MP*. London: J. McGowan, 1832.
Darwin, C. *Journal of Researches into the Geology and Natural History of the Various Countries Visited by HMS Beagle*. London: Henry Colburn, 1839.
Davey, J. 'Atlantic Empire, European War and the Naval Expeditions to South America, 1806–1807', in *The Royal Navy and the British Atlantic World, c. 1750–1820*, eds. J. McAleer and C. Petley. London: Palgrave Macmillan, 2016.
Davidoff L. and Hall, C. *Family Fortunes: Men and Women of the English Middle Class, 1780–1850*. London: Hutchinson, 1987.
Description of a View of the Bay of Islands, New Zealand, and the Surrounding Country, ed. R. Burford. London: G. Nichols, *c.* 1838.
Dicey, A. V. *Introduction to the Study of the Law of the Constitution*. London: Macmillan, 1962.
Dickens, C. *Hard Times*. London: Bradbury and Evans, 1854.
——. *Little Dorrit*. London: Bradbury and Evans, 1857.
Documents on the Establishment of Education in New South Wales 1789–1880, ed. D. C. Griffiths. Melbourne: Australian Council for Educational Research, 1957
Downshire, A. B. S. *Letters of a Great Irish Landlord: A Selection from the Estate Correspondence of the Third Marquess of Downshire, 1809–45*. Belfast: H. M. Stationery Office, 1974.
Dunmore, J. *French Explorers in the Pacific: Volume 2, The Nineteenth Century*. Oxford: Oxford University Press, 1969.
Earle, A. *A Narrative of a Nine Months' Residence in New Zealand in 1827: Together with a Journal of a Residence in Tristan D'Acunha, an Island Situated*

between South America and the Cape of Good Hope. London: Longman, 1832.

The Edinburgh Magazine and Literary Miscellany. Edinburgh: Archibald Constable and Co., 1825.

Evison, H. C. *Te Wai Pounamu: The Greenstone Island, A History of the Southern Maori During the European Colonisation of New Zealand*. Christchurch: Aoraki Press, 1993.

Fargher, R. *The Best Man Who Ever Served the Crown? A Life of Donald McLean*. Wellington: Victoria University Press, 2007.

Ferguson, A. *An Essay on the History of Civil Society*. London: T. Cadell, 1782.

Finn, J. 'Symbol and Myth: Magna Carta in Legal and Public Discourse about Law and Rights in New Zealand, 1840–1940', in *Magna Carta and New Zealand: History, Politics and Law in Aotearoa*, eds. S. Winder and C. Jones. Cham: Palgrave Macmillan, 2017.

Fisk, W. *Discourse on Predestination and Election*. Springfield: A. G. Tannatt, 1831.

FitzRoy, R. *Narrative of the Surveying Voyages of His Majesty's Ships Adventure and Beagle*. London: Henry Colburn, 1839.

Fletcher, B. H. *Colonial Australia before 1850*. Melbourne: Nelson, 1976.

——. *Ralph Darling: A Governor Maligned*. Oxford: Oxford University Press, 1984.

Foster, J. *Members of Parliament, Scotland*, 2nd edn. London: Hazell, Watson and Viney, 1882.

Foster, S. G. *Colonial Improver: Edward Deas Thomson, 1800–1879*. Melbourne: Melbourne University Press, 1978.

Frazer, W. *Elements of Materia Medica*. Dublin: Fannin & Co., 1851.

Gann, A. J. *The New Zealand Emigration Circular for 1852*. London: Trelawney Saunders, 1852.

Geldard, R. G. *Remembering Heraclitus*. Hudson, NY: Lindisfarne Books, 2000.

The Genealogical History of Pioneer Families of Australia, ed. P. C. Mowle. Sydney: John Sands, 1939.

The General Baptist Repository and Missionary Observer 5. London: Sherwood, Gilbert, and Piper, 1843.

Gisborne, W. *New Zealand Rulers and Statesmen from 1840 to 1897*. London: Sampson, Low, and Marston, 1897.

Golder, H. *Politics, Patronage, and Public Works: The Administration of New South Wales, Volume One: 1842–1900*. Sydney: University of New South Wales Press, 2005.

Grant, J. *Cassells Old and New in Edinburgh*. London: Cassel, Petter, Galpin & Co, 1882.

Gray, T. *Waitangi: The Treaty House. The Events Surrounding its Construction and Existence*. Upper Hutt: Trish Gray, 2014.

Harris, B. and McKean, C. *The Scottish Town in the Age of Enlightenment, 1740–1820*. Edinburgh: Edinburgh University Press, 2014.

Haskell, J. *Sydney Architecture*. Sydney: UNSW Press, 1997.

Hawke, G. R. *The Making of New Zealand: An Economic History*. Cambridge: Cambridge University Press, 1985.

Haydn, J. *The Book of Dignitaries; Containing Rolls of the Official Personages of the British Empire*. London: Longman, 1851.

He Whakaputanga Me Te Tiriti: The Declaration and the Treaty. Report on Stage 1 of the Paparahi o Te Raki Inquiry, Wai 1040. Wellington: Waitangi Tribunal, 2014.
Henderson, J. *General View of the Agriculture of the County of Caithness.* London: B. McMillan, 1815.
Herbemont, N. *Pioneering American Wine: The Writings of Nicholas Herbemont, Master Viticulturist*, ed. D. S. Shields. Atlanta, GA: University of Georgia Press, 2009.
Hirst, J. B. *Freedom on the Fatal Shore: Australia's First Colony.* Melbourne: Schwartz Publishing, 2008.
Historical Records of New Zealand South Prior to 1840, ed. R. O. Carrick. Dunedin: Otago Daily Times, 1903.
Historical Records of New Zealand, 1, ed. R. McNab. Wellington: Government Printer, 1908.
Hursthouse, C. *New Zealand, or Zealandia, the Britain of the South.* London: Edward Stanford, 1857.
Jones, W. D. *'Prosperity' Robinson: The Life of Viscount Goderich, 1782–1859.* New York: St Martin's Press, 1967.
The Journal of Ensign Best, 1837–1843, ed. N. M. Taylor. Wellington: R. E. Owen, 1966.
The Journals of Captain James Cook: The Voyage of the Resolution *and* Discovery, *1776–1780* 3, ed. J. C. Beaglehole. Cambridge: Cambridge University Press, 1967.
Keith, A. *Evidence of the Truth of the Christian Religion Derived from the Literal Fulfillment of Prophecy*, Edinburgh: Waugh and Innes, 1826.
Kennedy, B. and Kennedy, B. *Sydney and Suburbs: A History and Description.* Sydney: Reed, 1982.
Kingsbury, B. 'The Treaty of Waitangi: Some International Law Aspects', in *Waitangi: Maori and Pakeha Perspectives of the Treaty of Waitangi*, ed. I. H. Kawharu. Auckland: Oxford University Press, 1989.
Laidlaw, Z. *Colonial Connections, 1815–1845: Patronage, the Information Revolution, and Colonial Government.* Manchester: Manchester University Press, 2005.
Lambourne, A. *The Treaty-Makers of New Zealand: Heralding the Birth of a Nation.* Lewes: Benton-Guy Publishing, 1988.
Landers, J. *Death and the Metropolis: Studies in the Demographic History of London, 1670–1830.* Cambridge: Cambridge University Press, 1993.
Lang, J. D. *An Historical Account of New South Wales, Both as Penal Settlement and as a British Colony.* London: A. J. Valpy, 1834.
——. *New Zealand in 1839, or Four Letters to the Right Hon. Earl Durham.* London: Smith, Elder & Co., 1839.
Legel, P. *Heritage Auckland Newspapers.* Auckland: Auckland Museum Library, 2015.
Letter to the Right Hon. the Earl of Chichester, President of the Church Missionary Society. Auckland: Williamson and Wilson, 1850.
The Letters and Journals of Samuel Marsden, 1765–1838, ed. J. R. Elder. Dunedin: Coulls Somerville Wilkie, 1932.
Liston, C. 'Sir Thomas Brisbane', in *The Governors of New South Wales, 1788–2010*, eds. D. Cline and K. Turner. Sydney: The Federation Press, 2009.
Loveridge, D. *'The Littlewood Treaty': An Appraisal of Texts and Interpretations.* Wellington: Treaty of Waitangi Research Unit, 2006.

Maclehose, J. *The Picture of Sydney: And Strangers' Guide in New South Wales for 1838.* Sydney: J. Spilsbury, 1838.
Macmillan, D. S. *Wealth and Progress: Studies in Australian Business History.* Sydney: Angus and Robertson, 1967.
Maguire, W. A. *The Downshire Estates in Ireland, 1801–1845.* Oxford: Clarendon Press, 1972.
Main, G. M. *The Newspaper Press of Auckland.* Auckland: New Zealand Herald, 1891.
Markham, E. *New Zealand or, Recollections of It.* Wellington: R. E. Owen, 1963.
Marsden's Lieutenants, ed. J. R. Elder. Dunedin: Coulls Somerville Wilkie, 1934.
Marshall, W. B. *A Personal Narrative of Two Visits to New Zealand.* London: James Nisbet, 1836.
Martin, W. *The Taranaki Question.* Auckland: Philip Kunst, 1860.
Mathew, F. *The Founding of New Zealand: The Journals of Felton Mathew,* ed. J. Rutherford. Dunedin: A. H. and A. W. Reed, 1940.
McDonnell, T. *Extracts from Mr. M'Donnell's MS Journal.* London: James Moyes, 1834.
McIntyre, J. *First Vintage: Wine in Colonial New South Wales.* Sydney: UNSW Press, 2012.
McLean, M. *'The Garden of New Zealand': A History of the Waitangi Treaty House and Grounds from Pre-European Times to the Present.* Wellington: Department of Conservation, 1990.
McNab, R. *Murihiku: A History of the South Island of New Zealand and the Islands Adjacent and Lying to the South, from 1642 to 1835.* Wellington: Whitcombe and Tombs, 1909.
———. *The Old Whaling Days: A History of Southern New Zealand from 1830 to 1840.* Wellington: Whitcombe and Tombs, 1913.
Meteorological Journal, Kept by the Assistant Secretary at the Apartments of the Royal Society. London: Royal Society, 1831, 1832.
Mill, J. S. *Considerations on Representative Government.* London: Parker, Son & Bourne, 1861.
Milliss, R. *Waterloo Creek: The Australia Day Massacre of 1838, George Gipps and the British Conquest of New South Wales.* Sydney: New South Wales Press, 1994.
Mills, R. C. *The Colonization of Australia (1829–1842): The Wakefield Experiment in Empire-Building.* London: Sidgwick & Jackson, 1915.
The Missionary Register. London: Church Missionary Society, 1833, 1834
Molloy, M. *Those Who Speak to the Heart: The Nova Scotian Scots at Waipu, 1854–1920.* Palmerston North: Dunmore Press, 1991.
Monger, G. P. *Marriage Customs of the World: From Henna to Honeymoons.* Santa Barbara: ABC-Clio, 2004.
The Monthly Supplement of the Penny Magazine of the Society for the Diffusion of Useful Knowledge. London: Charles Knight & Co., September–October 1838.
Moon, P. *FitzRoy: Governor in Crisis, 1843–1845.* Auckland: David Ling, 2000.
———. *A Savage Country: The Untold Story of New Zealand in the 1820s.* Auckland: Penguin, 2012.
———. *Te Ara Ki Te Tiriti: The Path to the Treaty of Waitangi.* Auckland: David Ling, 2002.

Mudie, J. *The Felony of New South Wales: Being a Faithful Picture of the Real Romance of Life in Botany Bay.* London: Whaley & Co., 1837.
Nechtman, T. W. *The Pretender of Pitcairn Island: Joshua W. Hill – The Man Who Would Be King Among the Bounty Mutineers.* Cambridge: Cambridge University Press, 2018.
The New Holland Journal: November 1833–October 1834. Sydney: State Library New South Wales, 1994.
The New Monthly Magazine and Universal Register 1. London: H. Colburn, 1814.
The New South Wales Magazine, 1, no. 2. September 1833.
New Zealand Parliamentary Record, 1840–1949, ed. G. Scholefield. Wellington: Govt Printer, 1950.
New Zealand Temperance Society, *Report of the Formation and Establishment of the New Zealand Temperance Society.* Paihia: Church-Mission Press, 1836.
Nicholas, J. L. *Narrative of a Voyage to New Zealand.* London: Hughes and Baynes, 1817.
Nicholson, J. *White Chief: The Colourful Life and Times of Judge F.E. Maning of the Hokianga.* Auckland: Penguin, 2006.
O'Brien, E. *The Foundation of Australia, 1786–1800.* London: Sheed & Ward, 1937.
O'Byrne, W. R. *A Naval Biographical Dictionary.* London: John Murray, 1849.
O'Malley, V. *The Great War for New Zealand, Waikato 1800–2000.* Wellington: Bridget Williams Books, 2016.
Orange, C. *The Treaty of Waitangi.* Wellington: Allen and Unwin, 1987.
The Oriental Herald, and Colonial Review 3. London: J. M. Richardson, 1824.
Oxley, J. *Journal of Two Expeditions into the Interior of New South Wales.* London: John Murray, 1820.
Parkinson, P. *Preserved in the Archives of the Colony: The English Drafts of the Treaty of Waitangi.* Wellington: New Zealand Association of Comparative Law, 2006.
Parry, W. E. *In Service of the Company: Letters of Sir Edward Parry, Commissioner to the Australian Agricultural Company.* Canberra: Australian National University, 2005.
Partridge, C. *Calumny Refuted, the Colonists Vindicated, and the Right Horse Saddled.* Auckland: Creighton and Scales, 1864.
Patterson, L. 'Schools and Schooling: 3. Mass Education 1872–Present', in *The Oxford Companion to Scottish History*, ed. M. Lynch. Oxford: Oxford University Press, 2001.
Petrie, H. *Chiefs of Industry: Maori Tribal Enterprise in Early Colonial New Zealand.* Auckland: Auckland University Press, 2013.
Plomley, N. J. B. *An Immigrant of 1824.* Hobart: Tasmanian Historical Research Centre, 1973.
Polack, J. S. *New Zealand: Being a Narrative of Travels and Adventures during a Residence in that Country between the years 1831 and 1837.* London: Richard Bentley, 1838.
Prize Essays and Transactions of the Highland Society of Scotland 6, Edinburgh: William Blackwood and Sons, 1824.
Proceedings of the Royal Society of London, 11 January 1866–23 May 1867. London: Royal Society, 1867.
Raeside, J. D. *Sovereign Chief: A Biography of Baron De Thierry.* Christchurch: Caxton Press, 1977.

Ramsden, E. *Busby of Waitangi: HM's Resident at New Zealand, 1833–40.* Wellington: A. H. & A. W. Reed, 1942.
Reeves, W. P. *The Long White Cloud: Ao Tea Roa.* London: Horace Marshall & Son, 1898.
Reid, T. *Two Voyages to New South Wales and Van Diemen's Land.* London: Longman, Hurst, Rees, Orme, and Brown, 1822.
Remarks on the Credit of New Zealand and the Honour of Great Britain. London: Rees and Collin, 1865.
Robinson, N. *To the Ends of the Earth: Norman McLeod and the Highlanders' Migration to Nova Scotia and New Zealand.* Auckland: HarperCollins, 1997.
Rusden, G. W. *History of New Zealand.* London: Chapman and Hall, 1883.
Rutherford, J. *Sir George Grey: A Study in Colonial Government.* London: Cassell, 1961.
Sachs, W. L. *The Transformation of Anglicanism: From State Church to Global Communion.* Cambridge: Cambridge University Press, 2002.
Sadler, H. *Ko Tautoro, Te Pito o Toku Ao: A Ngapuhi Narrative.* Auckland: Auckland University Press, 2014.
Schumacher, L. R. 'Greek Expectations: Britain and the Ionian Islands, 1815–1864', in *Imperial Expectations and Realities: El Dorados, Utopias and Dystopias*, ed. A. Varnava. Manchester: Manchester University Press, 2015.
The Scottish Jurist, Containing Reports of Cases. Edinburgh: n.p., 1830.
Seffern, W. H. J. *Chronicles of the Garden of New Zealand Known as Taranaki.* New Plymouth: W. H. J. Seffern, 1896.
Semmel, B. *The Rise of Free Trade Imperialism: Classical Political Economy: The Empire of Free Trade and Imperialism, 1750–1850.* Cambridge: Cambridge University Press, 1970.
Sharp, A. *The World, the Flesh and the Devil: The Life and Opinions of Samuel Marsden in England and the Antipodes, 1765–1838.* Auckland: Auckland University Press, 2016.
Sherrin, R. A. A. and Wallace, J. H. *Early History of New Zealand.* Auckland: H. Brett, 1890.
Simpson, H. M. *The Women of New Zealand.* Auckland: Paul's Book Arcade, 1962.
Sinclair, K. *A History of New Zealand.* Auckland: Penguin, 1988.
Sinclair, K. V. *Laplace in New Zealand, 1831.* Waikanae: Heritage Press, 1998.
Smith, A. *The Theory of Moral Sentiments.* London: Henry Bohn, 1853.
Stack, J. W. *Kaiapohia: The Story of a Siege.* Christchurch: Whitcombe and Tombs, 1893.
Stevenson, R. L. *Edinburgh: Picturesque Notes.* New York: Macmillan, 1896.
Stone, R. C. J. *Young Logan Campbell.* Auckland: Auckland University Press, 1982.
Swainson, W. *New Zealand and its Colonisation.* London: Smith, Elder & Co., 1859.
Symington, J. 'The Working Man's Home', in *Happy Homes for Working Men and How to Get Them*, ed. J. Begg. London: Cassel, Petter, Galpin & Co., 1866.
Taylor, R. *Te Ika a Maui, or New Zealand and its Inhabitants.* London: Wertheim and Macintosh, 1855.
Telford, T. and Rickman, J. *Life of Thomas Telford, Civil Engineer.* London: J. and L. G. Hansard and Sons, 1838.

Templeton, P. *A Sort of Conscience: The Wakefields*. Auckland: Auckland University Press, 2002.
Terry, C. *New Zealand: Its Advantages and Prospects as a British Colony*. London: T. & W. Boone, 1842.
Thomson, A. S. *The Story of New Zealand: Past and Present, Savage and Civilized*. London: John Murray, 1859.
Thomson, J. *The Seasons: A Poem*. New York: Clark, Austin & Co., [1736] 1854.
Toynbee, A. *Lectures on the Industrial Revolution in England*. London: Rivingtons, 1884.
Trubuhovich, R. V. *Governor William Hobson: His Health Problems and Final Illness*. Auckland: RVT, 2015.
Tucker, H. W. *Memoir of the Life and Episcopate of George Augustus Selwyn*. London: William Wells Gardner, 1879.
Turton, H. H. *Maori Deeds and Old Private Land Purchases in New Zealand, from the Year 1815 to 1840*. Wellington: George Didsbury, 1882.
Voices from Auckland, New Zealand. London: Alex. F. Ridgway & Sons, 1862.
Wakefield, E. G. *A Letter from Sydney, the Principal Town of Australasia*. London: Joseph Cross, 1829.
——. *A View of the Art of Colonization, with Present Reference to the British Empire*. London: Parker, 1849.
Wakefield, E. J. *Adventure in New Zealand from 1839 to 1844, with Some Account of the Beginning of the British Colonization of the Islands*. London: John Murray, 1845.
Wallace, V. *Scottish Presbyterianism and Settler Colonial Politics: Empire of Dissent*. Basingstoke: Palgrave Macmillan, 2018.
Ward, A. *A Show of Justice: Racial Amalgamation in Nineteenth-Century New Zealand*. Toronto: University of Toronto Press, 1974.
Ward, J. M. *Colonial Self-Government: The British Experience, 1759–1856*. London: Palgrave Macmillan, 1976.
Wells, W. H. *A Geographical Dictionary; or Gazetteer of the Australian Colonies*. Sydney: W. and F. Ford, 1848.
Wentworth, W. C. *A Statistical, Historical, and Political Description of the Colony of New South Wales*. London: G. and W. B. Whittaker, 1824.
West, J. *The History of Tasmania*. Launceston: Henry Dowling, 1852.
Wheaton, H. *Elements of International Law*. London: Carey, Lea and Blanchard, 1916.
Wheeler, D. *Memoirs of the Life and Gospel Labors of the Late Daniel Wheeler: A Minister of the Society of Friends*. Philadelphia, 1850.
White, H. *Tropics of Discourse: Essays in Cultural Criticism*. Baltimore: Johns Hopkins University Press, 1978.
Whyte, I. D. *Migration and Society in Britain, 1550–1830*. London: Palgrave Macmillan, 2000.
Williams, H. *The Early Journals of Henry Williams*, ed. L. M. Rogers. Christchurch: Pegasus Press, 1961.
Williams, H. *Plain Facts Relative to the Late War in the Northern District of New Zealand*. Auckland: Philip Kunst, 1847.
Wilmot-Horton, R. *An Inquiry into the Causes and Remedies of Pauperism. Containing Letters to Sir Francis Burdett, Bart. MP Upon Pauperism in Ireland*. London: E. Lloyd, 1831.

Wilson, D. *Memorials of Edinburgh in the Olden Time*. Edinburgh: A. & C. Black, 1891.
Wilson, O. *Kororareka, and Other Essays*. Dunedin: John McIndoe, 1990.
Winfield R. and Lyon, D. *The Sail and Steam Navy List: All the Ships of the Royal Navy 1815–1889*. London: Chatham, 2004.
Wolfe, R. *Hell-Hole of the Pacific*. Auckland: Penguin, 2005.
Wordsworth, W. 'Composed upon Westminster Bridge, September 3, 1802', in *The Complete Poetical Works of William Wordsworth*, ed. H. Reed. Philadelphia: Troutman & Hayes, 1848.
Wright, C. *Wellington's Men in Australia: Peninsula War Veterans and the Making of an Empire c. 1820–40*. London: Palgrave Macmillan, 2011.
Yate, W. *An Account of New Zealand, and of the Formation and Progress of the Church Missionary Society's Mission in the Northern Island*, 2nd edn. London: R. B. Seeley and W. Burnside, 1835.

Index

Adams, Peter, vii
Admiralty, 90, 130, 211
Advice to Emigrants Newly Arrived in New South Wales, James Busby, 64–5
Alligator, HMS, 124–6, 128–9, 131, 139–43
Arney, George (Chief Justice of New Zealand), 281, 285, 286, 290, 291, 297, 298, 299, 310, 311
Arthur, George, 120–1
Auckland, 235, 237–8, 242, 296–7
Auckland Chronicle and New Zealand Colonist, 239–40
The Aucklander, 294, 300, 301
Auckland Examiner, 275, 278
Auckland Provincial Council, 262–3, 279, 287–8, 300, 309, 311, 314, 315–16
  James's bids for election, 258–9, 276, 277, 292, 295–6
Australian, 92, 121–2, 123, 185
Authentic Information Relative to New South Wales and New Zealand, James Busby, 65

Bank of Australia, collapse, 1843, 238
Barnard, Edward, (Colonial Office clerk), 20, 21–2, 23–4, 25
Barrow, Sir John (Second Secretary to the Admiralty), 90, 130
Bathurst, Henry, 3rd Earl (Secretary of State for War and the Colonies, 1812–27), 17, 18, 20, 23, 26, 27, 42–3
Bay of Islands
  FitzRoy's impressions, 183–4
  population, early 1800s, 107–9
'beach rangers,' 109
Beagle, HMS, 183, 185

Beecham, Reverend John, 176
Bell, Francis Dillon (Land Commissioner), 277, 284, 287, 295, 297–8, 299–300, 301–2, 307, 314
Bentham, Jeremy, 110
Biddle, Henry, murder, 215
Bigge, John, 18, 26, 73
  Report of the Commissioner of Inquiry into the State of the Colony of New South Wales, 16–17
  Report of the Commission of Inquiry on the State of Agriculture and Trade in the Colony of New South Wales, 39–40
Blackwall, ship, 303
Board of the Commissary General and the Commissary of Accounts, 58
Bourke, Sir Richard (Governor of New South Wales, 1831–7), 86–8, 89, 95–9, 103–4, 124, 128, 130, 131, 139–40, 143–8
  alcohol ban, 163–4, 166, 175
  animosity towards James, 196, 197, 212–13
  appoints Hobson to report on NZ situation, 200–1, 210
  appoints Thomson as Colonial Secretary, 199–200
  Declaration of Independence, 170, 175
  depiction of McDonnell, 195–6
  reaction to Waikato attack, 191–2
  resigns, 200
  scheme to end Residency, 149–51
Bowen, Sir George (Governor of New Zealand, 1868–73), 319

Bragg, Gibson, 181–2
A Brief Memoir Relative to the Islands of New Zealand, James Busby, 73–9
Brisbane, Sir Thomas (Governor of New South Wales, 1821–5), 34, 35, 39, 42–3, 44
British Consul, NZ, Hobson appointed, 222–3
Broughton, Bishop William, 214
Browne, Thomas Gore (Governor of New Zealand, 1855–61), 271, 272, 276, 283, 288–9
Busby, Agnes (daughter), 251
Busby, Agnes (née Dow, wife), 65–6, 70, 93–4, 106, 151, 199, 219, 245, 316–17, 318
   arrives in NZ and house move, 118–19, 124
   births of children, 131, 161, 213, 235
   death, 1889, 317
   deaths of children, 232, 251, 286–7
   house broken into and shot fired, 133–8
   leaves NZ for NSW, over risks to safety, 192
   returns to Auckland, 1872, 317
Busby, Alexander (brother), 6, 20, 27, 51, 225, 238, 274
Busby, Catherine (sister), 6, 27, 31, 37, 51, 53, 56, 82
Busby, Daniel (uncle), 7, 8
Busby family documents, ix–x
Busby, George (brother), 5–6, 10, 51, 56, 60–1, 161, 245, 315
Busby, George (grandfather), 4
Busby, George (son), 286–7
Busby, James, *see also* land transactions and ownership; Resident
   accused of arming Māori, 252
   alcohol reforms, 63–4, 162–3
   America trips
      1844, 243–4, 247
      1845, 247
   attacks Grey in press, 253–4
   Auckland Provincial Council, 258–9, 265–3, 276, 277, 292, 295–6

Bell libel case, 297–8, 299–300
betrothal and marriage, 94–5
birth and early years, 2–3, 7, 11
births of children, 131, 161, 213, 235
character portrayals, 31–19, 100–1, 137, 185, 198, 216–17, 244, 297, 320, vii–viii
Collector of the Internal Revenue, 48–51, 54, 57, 59, 68, 69
Colonial Office, lobbies to fund family passage to NSW, 16, 17–27
death and burial, 317
deaths of children, 232, 251, 286–7
diary of daily life, 318–19
ecumenical stance, 214
education, 7, 9, 10, 11
faith, 23, 160, 318
family disagreements, 56–7, 66, 93
family leaves NZ and returns to Sydney, 1840, 232
family return to Waitangi, 1846, 249
finances, personal, 66, 82, 102–4, 121, 161, 179–80, 183, 218, 221, 234
   in 1868, 310, 311
France trip, 1831, 85
Guardian of Slaves, plans role of, 59
health, accidents and injuries, 58, 60, 61, 66–7, 219, 310, 315, 316–17, 318
House of Commons Select Committee on Secondary Punishments, 79–80
house, plans grand family, 1828, 55–6, 57, 62
jobs in Edinburgh, 10, 12, 13, 52
journey around NZ, 1836, 193–4
labourer emigration scheme, 71–3
legacy, viii
letters (*see also* correspondence, Busby family)
   of appreciation to H. Williams, 256–7
   to Prime Minister, 1854, 267–8
London, returns to, 1871, 303–6

INDEX

London trips
  1823, 19–26
  1831, 59–60, 67, 69–82
  1844, 244–7
  1864, 303–6
Male Orphan School, 40–8
Member of the Land Board, 48–51, 53, 60
partnership with Mair, 232–4, 240, 241
press attacks on him
  Australian, 92, 100, 115, 121–2, 122–4, 130–1, 185–6
  New Zealand, 239–40, 275, 276, 278–9, 284, 300, 314, 317
public lectures and speeches, 274–5, 304, 316
requests select committee investigation into Grey's land policies, 1853, 262–3
romantic relationships and lack of, 52–3, 58–9, 60, 62, 65–6
Spain trip,1831, 83–5
trading businesses, 243–4, 269, 301
Victoria, plans for city, 221–2, 223, 224, 225, 234–5
viticulture, 10–11, 31, 34, 36, 40, 41, 43, 63–4
  research in continental Europe, 70, 83–5
waste land management scheme, 67–8
Williamson libel case, 290–2
Busby, James jnr (son), 232
Busby, John (brother), 6, 22, 27, 30, 53, 185, 234
Busby, John (father), 3–9, 12–14, 32, 34, 51–2, 56, 131, 151, 155, 247
  death and funeral, 274
  Elizabeth Henrietta, salvage operation, 35–6, 37–8, 39
  finances, 34, 151, 199
  lobbies Colonial Office to fund passage to NSW, 16, 17–21, 27
Busby, John (son), 131
'Busby Loan,' 316

Busby, Margaret (grandmother), 4
Busby, Margaret (sister), 6
Busby, Sarah (daughter), 161, 266–7
Busby, Sarah (née Kennedy) (mother), 5–6, 7, 13, 27, 32, 37, 57, 155, 237
Busby, William (brother), 6, 27, 30, 37, 56, 99, 100–1, 238, 274
Busby, William (brother, 1812–1812), 6
Busby, William (son), 235, 247, 286–7
Buxton, Sir Thomas Fowell, 81, 103–4, 155

Caledonian Church, Hatton Garden, 23
Campbell, John Logan, 241, 291
Canning, George, 24
Carleton, Hugh, 290, 292–3, 306–7, 310, 311–12, 313–14, 315
Chapman, Thomas, 111, 193
Chaucer, Geoffrey, 1
Church Missionary Society, 77, 102, 105–6, 153, 256
Church of Scotland
  Busby family's shift from Church of England, 4–6
  in NSW, 42–3
Clarke, George, 173, 259, 293–4
Clendon, James, 101, 135, 173, 224
Coates, Dandeson, 77, 176
Colenso, William, 135
Collector of the Internal Revenue, 48–51, 54, 57, 59, 68, 69
Colonial Office, John and James lobby to fund passage, 17–27, 71–3
Colonial Times, 100
Colonist, 200–1
Colquhoun, John, MP, 245
Confederation of Chiefs, 190–1, 203, 208–10, 229
  James's plans for, 128, 129, 153–4, 165, 166
Consul appointed to NZ, 218, 220
convicts
  New South Wales, 15–17, 33, 43–4, 93, 198
  New Zealand, 91–2, 101, 109, 120–1, 198–9, 200
correspondence, Busby family, ix–x
  James to Alexander, 80, 106,

117–18, 131, 143–4, 150, 156, 160, 220, 221
city of Victoria, 221, 224, 225
family finances, 151
land purchases, 218, 259
position as Resident after the Declaration, 192–3, 196, 198, 201–2, 215, 219
shunning by George, 161, 183
James to George, 21, 22, 25, 28–9, 46, 50, 53, 60–1, 62, 65, 66
death of daughter Agnes, 251
deteriorating family relations, 55–7
James to John (father), 25, 141, 221
James to Kelman, 35, 39, 41, 82
James to William, 131, 203, 248
John (brother) to Catherine, 70
John (brother) to George, 58
William to Alexander, 100–1
William to George, 99
William to James, 199
Craig, James, 2

Daily Southern Cross, 253–4, 261, 263, 267, 278, 291, 296, 301
Darling, Lieutenant-General Ralph (Governor of New South Wales, 1825–31), 44, 46–8, 49, 52, 59, 60, 62, 66, 78
breakdown in relations with James, 68–9
recommends appointment of Resident, 76–7, 79
Darwin, Charles, 183, 185
Davis, Charles, 280
Davis, Reverend Richard, 115–16
Declaration of Independence, 170–8, 179–81, 183–4, 186, 209
Defoe, Daniel, 3
De Thierry, Baron Charles, 168–70, 174–5, 177, 178, 180, 181, 196, 212–13, 214
press attacks on, 185–6
Dow, Agnes, *see* Busby, Agnes
Downshire, Arthur Hill, 3rd Marquess of, 8–9
Doyle, Edward, Sydney trial, 213

Dumaresq, Lieutenant Colonel Henry, 47

Earle, Augustus, NZ journey, 107–8
Edinburgh, Busby family in, 2–3, 6, 7, 9–10, 12–13
Elizabeth, brig, 78, 79, 86
Elizabeth Henrietta, brig, salvage operation, 35–6, 37–8, 39

finances, James Busby's personal, 66, 82, 102–3, 104, 121, 161, 179–80, 183, 218, 221
borrows to fund Victoria plan, 234–5, 236–7
dealings with bank to prevent bankruptcy, 241, 242, 243–4, 248–9, 250
debt owed by Mair, 255–258
financial position, Busby family, 1828–9, 55–6
FitzRoy, Robert (Governor of New Zealand, 1843–5), 183–4, 219, 221, 223, 240, 241, 242, 245–6
Forth, barque, 69–70
Fox, Sir William (Premier of New Zealand), 302, 312–13
France, *see also* De Thierry, Baron Charles
James's trip 1831, 85
perceived threat to British interests in NZ, 88–9, 217–18
free settlers, *see* migrants

Gillies, Thomas, 310, 311
Gipps, Sir George (Governor of New South Wales, 1838–46), 178, 213, 217, 219, 220, 228, 233–4, 239
Glenelg, Lord (Secretary of State for War and the Colonies, 1835–39), 148–50, 164, 175–6, 197, 206, 211, 218, 219, 220
Goderich, Viscount (Secretary of State for War and the Colonies, 1827–1827), 78, 80, 85–8, 89–93, 98, 113, 115, 119

Goulburn, Major Frederick (Colonial Secretary of New South Wales, 1821–6), 34, 39, 40, 44, 80–1
Graham, George, 307
Grey, Sir George (Governor of New Zealand, 1845–54, re-installed 1861), 246–7, 248, 249, 252–4, 256, 258–64, 273, 283
  subpoenaed by James, 299–300
  visits Bay of Islands, 1847, 251
  wars against Māori, 300–1, 304–5, 306
Guard, John, 139, 141

Haddington, Thomas Hamilton, 9th Earl of, 5, 6, 17, 80–1, 87, 96–7, 197
Hall, William, 105–6
Harriet, barque, 139, 140, 168
Hay, Sir Robert (Under-Secretary of State for the Colonies, 1825–36), 86–7, 89–90, 91, 96, 130, 161
Hazlitt, William, 23
Heaphy Charles, 307
Heke, Hone, Te Matarahurahu chief, 121, 138, 237–8, 245, 246, 251
Herald, HMS, 227, 228, 230
Herbemont, Nicholas, 11
Hero, steamship, 316
Hill, Mrs, 52–3
Hill, Reverend Richard, 52
Hobart Town Courier, 130–1
Hobbs, Reverend John, 244
Hobson, William, Lieutenant-Governor (Consul to New Zealand), 222–3, 227–31, 235
  report on NZ, 205–7, 209–10, 211, 212
Hongi, Eruera Pare, translation of Declaration, 171, 173
Hongi Hika, chief, 167–8
House of Commons, 246
  Select Committee on Aboriginal Tribes on British Settlements, 198–9
  Select Committee on Secondary Punishments, 79–80
  'South Seas Bill,' 91–2
House of Representatives, New Zealand, 271–3, 292–3, 306–8
  James's land claims compensation, 1869, 311–14, 316
Howick, Lord (Henry Grey, 3rd Earl) (Secretary of State for War and the Colonies, 1846–52), 80–1, 91–2

immigrants, *see* migrants
Imogene, HMS, 97, 106, 111, 113
indigenous people, New Zealand, *see* Māori
indigenous population, NSW, 17
Industry, schooner, 181
influenza epidemic, 1838, 218–19
Irving, Reverend Edward, 23

Johnson, John, 261–2
Jones, Stanners, 301
Joseph Weller, ship, 139
Journal of a Tour through Some of the Vineyards of Spain and France, James Busby, 83–5, 93

Keith, Alexander, *Evidence of the Truth of the Christian Religion Derived from the Literal Fulfilment of Prophecy*, 160
Kelman, William, 35, 37, 39, 41, 51, 53, 66, 82
Kemp, Henry, 299
Kendall, Thomas, 106, 167
Kinchela, John (Attorney General), 87
Kinghorne, William, 120–21
Kingi, Wiremu, chief (earlier known as Te Rangitāke), 288–9

La Favorite, ship, 88
Lambert, Robert, 124–6, 141–2
Land Claims Arbitration Act, 1867, 307–8, 311, 314
Land Claims Ordinance, 1841, 284–6

Land Claims Settlement Act, 1856, 272–3, 276–7
Land Claims Settlement Extension Act,1858, 280, 284
Land Commission, 231, 240
   land commissioners, 235, 236, 237, 238, 240–2, 265, 277, 279–80, 284
Land Purchase Department, 299
Land Titles Bill, 1840, 234
land transactions and ownership
   De Thierry, 168–70, 174, 185–6
   Gipps's Land Titles Bill, 228, 233–4
   Henry Williams, 256
   James Busby, 228, 231, 235–6, 253, 259, 265–81, 299, 301–2, 306–15
      government confirmation of titles, 240–2, 244, 246–7, 250–1, 252, 253, 254–6, 259
      Heke land sales, 238
      Ngunguru purchase and disposal, 225, 232, 234, 249, 252, 254–5, 284, 287
      Supreme Court Actions, 268–71, 280–1, 284–6, 310–11, 314–15
      Waitangi land transfer, 105–6
      Whangarei land offered for sale by government, 260–2, 267–71, 272–3
   Lowden, 279–80, 283
   Maxwell and Mair dispute, 119–20
   McDonnell, 160, 186–9
   Waikato, 186–9
Lang, Reverend John, 42
Letter on the Emigration of Mechanics and Labourers to New South Wales, A, James Busby, 71–3
letters, Busby family, *see* correspondence, Busby family
L'Heroine, corvette, 217
Lord Warden, ship, 317
Lowden, James, 279–80, 283

Macleay, Alexander (also spelt McLeay) (Colonial Secretary of New South Wales, 1826–37), 78, 94, 95–6, 124, 154–5, 199–200
   correspondence with Busby, 50, 102–3, 150–5, 159–60, 167, 169, 180, 187, 191, 194
   alcohol ban, 162, 164–5
Macquarie, Lachlan (Governor of New South Wales, 1810–21), 16, 109
Mair, Gilbert, 119–20, 135, 173, 188, 225
   partnership with Busby, 232–4, 240, 241, 255–5, 258
Male Orphan School Farm, 39–48
Manual of Plain Directions for Planting and Cultivating Vineyards, A, James Busby, 63–4
Māori, 38–9, 73–8, 86–7, 95, 162–3, 185, 267, 301, *see also* land transactions and ownership
   approach to justice, 152–3
   chiefs' response to attack on Resident, 1834, 134–8
   community land ownership debate, 1861, 293–4
   Confederation of Chiefs, 171–2, 178, 180, 189, 190–1, 203, 208–10, 229
   Declaration of Independence, 170–8, 179–81, 183–4, 186, 209
   flag selection, 128–30
   hapū, 110
   Harriet affair and response by HMS *Alligator*, 139–43
   influence of black americans on religious beliefs, 195
   initial meeting of chiefs with James, 111–15
   Kite's trial and execution, 215–17
   land memorial to transfer land to Busby, 269–70
   loyalties, allegiances and divisions, 190
   Pōmare, 116–17, 124–6, 129–30
   presents, gifted to chiefs, 90, 98, 102, 206
   role of Resident to protect, 87, 92–3, 97–9, 109–10

settlers' concerns over perceived threat from, 135–6
status of sovereignty, 109–110
violent incidents against, 78, 86, 97
Waikato land dispute, 186–9
Wairau Massacre, 238–9
Waitangi land, 105–6
Waitangi, Treaty of, 228–31, 246, 275, 293–4
war following government sale, Pekapeka land, 288–9
Yates's petition, 88–9, 98, 102
Margaret, schooner, 260
Markham, Edward, 137
Marlborough Express, 317
Marsden, Mary, 60–1, 65
Marsden, Reverend Samuel, 60, 65, 75–6, 77, 81, 90, 105, 108, 109, 206
   war in Northland, 200, 201
Marshall, William, 124, 126, 129–30, 140
Martin, Sir William, 293
Maxwell, Thomas, 119–20
Mayhew, William, 242, 243
McDonnell, Thomas, Additional Resident, 146–7, 154–5, 159–60, 161
   alcohol ban, 163, 164
   Busby's attack on, 180–1
   correspondence with Bourke, 163, 165, 181–2, 212
   correspondence with Busby, 165–7, 183
   forms committee of chiefs, 182
   Gibson Bragg murder, 181–2
   resigns, 195–6
   Waikato, land dispute, 186–9, 191
   William White trial, 182, 194–5
McKenzie, Duncan, 265–6, 267, 268–70, 272, 284–5
McLean, Donald, 306–7, 312
McLeay, Alexander, *see* Macleay, Alexander
McLeod, Norman, 260
Merriman, Frederick, 255, 258, 280–1, 290, 291, 301
middle classes, emerging, C18th-19th, 1–2, 3, 12

migrants
   to New South Wales, 15–17, 260
   to New Zealand, 260, 262
missionaries, in New Zealand, 89, 92, 98, 101–2, 105–6, 108, 112, 115
   alcohol ban, 162, 163
   efforts with Māori to maintain peace, 117, 126, 153
   letter to support armed response, 1836, 192
   Select Committee report, 1837, 198, 199
Missionary Register, The, 112
Mitchell, Thomas, 16
Moore, William, 78
Morgan, Reverend John, 115
Murray, Sir George (Secretary of State for War and the Colonies, 1828–30), 60, 68, 69

National Association for the Promotion of Social Science, James's speech, 304
Native Land Purchase Ordinance, 1846, 255
Nene, Tamati Waka, chief, 138
Nereus, barque, 118–19
New South Wales colony, 1820's, 15–17
New South Wales Magazine, 41
New Zealand Banking Company, 237, 242, 243, 244, 248–9, 250
New Zealand Company, Wakefield's, 222, 223, 225, 238, 240, 245–6, 256, 260, 266, 273
New Zealand Constitution Act, 1852, 260
New Zealander, newspaper, 249, 258, 276, 278, 291, 293
New Zealander, ship, 106, 116, 127–8
New Zealand Government Gazette, 267
New Zealand Herald, 314, 316
New Zealand Temperance Society, 162
Nias, Joseph, 230–1
Nicholas, J. L., 110

Normanby, Lord (Secretary of State for War and the Colonies, 1839–39), 222, 223
Northland, wars, 200–3, 207, 248, 249

Orange, Claudia, vii
orphan school farm, 39–48
Otago, ship, 303
Otago Witness, 320
Our Colonial Empire and the Case of New Zealand, James Busby, 305–6

Parliament, New Zealand, James's land claims compensation,1869, 311–14, 316
Parry, Sir Edward, 81, 106
Pekapeka land, acquired by Browne, 288–9
penal settlements, New South Wales, 15–17, 33, 198, *see also* convicts: New South Wales
Piper, Captain, 34
Planter, barque, 93
Polack, Joel, 133, 135, 136, 174–5, 201–2
Pōmare, chief, 124–6, 200, 203
Pompallier, Bishop Jean Baptiste, 214, 217–18
postal services, Bay of Islands, 252
Poukoura, junior chief, 261
Presbyterian community, New South Wales, 42–3
The Press, 300
Prince of Denmark, schooner, 115
Provincial Councils Ordinance, 1851, 258

Ramsden, Eric, ix
Rattlesnake, HMS, 205–7
Reddall, Reverend Thomas, 40, 44, 104
Reeves, William Pember, vii
Remarks on the Credit of New Zealand and the Honour of Great Britain, anon., 305
Remarks Upon a Pamphlet Entitled 'The Taranaki Question,'
by Sir William Martin, James Busby, 293–4
Report from the Select Committee of the House of Lords, Appointed to Inquire into the Present State of the Islands of New Zealand, 218
Resident
 Additional Resident, 146–7, 154–5, 159–60, 161
 attitude towards missionaries, 202, 214–5, 223–4
 authority and security, 91, 98–100, 101–2, 117–18, 120–2, 127–31, 164–5
 asks for armed support, 153, 189–90, 191
 Bourke calls for naval protection, 1834, 139–40
 Glenelg's attempts to address, 164
 house burglary and shots fired, 133–8, 143
 issues with Pōmare, 124–6
 success in dealings with Māori, 190
 Bourke, plan to have fired, 196–7
 Cabinet Office proposal and decision, 76–9, 85–93
 comments on Māori culture, 195
 confederation of chiefs, plans, 128, 129, 153–4, 165, 166
 decision to appoint, 85–8, 89–93
 decline of Residency and dismissal, 206, 218, 220–25
 duties and functions, 89–90, 97–9
 finances, 121, 197, 206, 220
 Glenelg's assessment and review, 148–50
 handover of authority to Consul, 227–8
 initial speech to Māori, 113
 James's expectations of role, 90–1
 as Judge at Kite's trial, 215–17
 landing in NZ and initial meeting with Māori chiefs, 1833, 111–15
 proposes new British role in NZ,1837, 207–10

INDEX 349

role in Treaty of Waitangi, 75, 76, 165, 194, 208, 228–31
snubs Māori chief, 116–17
status of Māori sovereignty, 109–11
Resident Magistrate's Court, 301
Resident's residence, Waitangi, 90, 91, 94–6, 102, 115, 116, 121, 124, 128, 183
    garden, 197–8
Rete, chief, 136, 138, 151–3
Ripon Regulations, 68
Robinson, George Augustus, 28, 30
Rochfort, Singleton, 170, 269, 285
Ross, Dr Adolphus James, 119, 138
Royal Belfast Academical Institution, 9

Scott, Archdeacon Thomas Hobbes, 42–3, 45, 48
Selwyn, Bishop George, 237, 245
settlers, NZ, 185, 228, 256, 319
    alcohol ban, 162, 163–4
    disputes with Māori, 184
    land purchases, 228
    petition for military support, 202
ships, made in NZ, registration of, 127–31
Shortland, Willoughby (Colonial Secretary of New Zealand, 1841–3), 235–6
Sinclair, Andrew (Colonial Secretary of New Zealand, 1844–56), 260–1
Sinclair, Keith, vii
Sinclair, Sir John, 9
Sir George Murray, ship, 127
Smith, Adam, 1–2
Smithson, Esther, 283–4
Snowden, Henry, 268–9
social classes
    Britain, 18th-19thc
    New South Wales, 33–4, 65
social status, Busby family, 55, 65
South Seas Bill, 91–2, 96
Spring Rice, Thomas (Secretary of State for War and the Colonies, 1834–1834), 148, 155
Stafford, Edward (Colonial Secretary of New Zealand, 1856–61), 310

Stanley, Lord (Secretary of State for War and the Colonies, 1833–4), 130, 147, 241, 246, 247
State Library, New South Wales, ix
St Cuthbert's Church, Edinburgh, 2
Stephen, James (Under-Secretary of State for War and the Colonies, 1836–47), 210, 222
    Stephen Doctrine, 210–11
Stephen, John, solicitor-general, 46
Stevenson, Robert Louis, 14
Stewart, Captain John, 78
Story, Joseph, 244, 247
St Paul's Church, Auckland, 318
Supreme Court, New Zealand, James's actions, 268–71, 280–1, 284–6, 310–11, 314–15
Swainson, William, 235
Sydney, Busby family's arrival, 33–5
Sydney Gazette and New South Wales Advertiser, 37–8, 64, 185–6, 213, 222
Sydney Monitor, 52, 92, 100
Sydney Morning Herald, 239

Taranaki, attack and rescue mission, 139–43
Tareha, chief, 187, 191
Tasmanian, 186
Te Rauparaha, Ngati Toa chief, 78
Thomson, Anna, 155
Thomson, Sir Edward Deas (Colonial Secretary of New South Wales, 1837–56), 155, 199, 206, 207, 220, 227–8, 235
Titore, chief, 135, 138, 187, 191, 200, 203
Tole, Edward, 311, 314
trade, between New Zealand and New South Wales, 73–4, 75, 77, 99, 114, 117, 130, 145, 165
training farm, 39–48
Treatise on the Culture of the Vine, and the Art of Making Wine, James Busby, 10
Triton, Busby family voyage to New South Wales, 27–32
Turner, Benjamin, 308

Turner, Nathaniel, 195
Tyninghame Parish Church, ix

Vaile, George, 276
Verge, John, 94–5
Victoria, 221–5, 228, 234–5, 242, 248, 249, 250, 253, 255
Vindication of the Character and Proceedings of Archdeacon Henry Williams, A, James Busby, 257
Vogel, Julius, 308

Waikato, Ngapuhi chief, 186–9
Wairau Massacre, 238–9
Waitangi, Treaty of, 228–31, 246, 275, 293–4
    James's role in, 75, 76, 165, 194, 208, 228–31
Wakefield, Edward Gibbon, 67–8, 71, 221, 222, 233–4, 245, 260
    A Letter from Sydney, the Principal Town of Australasia, 67
    New Zealand Company, 222, 223, 225, 238, 240, 245–6, 256, 260, 266, 273
Waterton, Edward, 123
Wellington, brig, x
Wentworth, William, 233–4
Wheeler, Daniel, 198
Whitaker, Frederick (Attorney General), 254–5, 276–7, 280–1, 290, 297
White, John, 285
Whitekirk, 5
White, Reverend William, 163, 182, 194–5

White, Titus, 284–6
Williams, Henry, 105, 122, 124, 186, 256–7, 267, 287, 306
    burglary and attack on Resident, 134–6, 138, 143
    Declaration of Independence, 170–1, 173–4
    designs for flag, 128–9
    dismissal, 256–7
    falling out with Busby, 214–5, 223
    HMS *Alligator*, 141–3
    HMS *Rattlesnake*, 136, 138
    James's arrival in NZ, 111–15
    peacekeeping efforts, 117, 124, 200, 245
    war in Northland, 200, 201
Williams, John, 266–7
Williams, Marianne, 131
Williamson, John, 276, 289–92, 296, 309–15, 314
Williams, William, 125, 129–30, 188
Wilmot-Horton, Robert (Under-Secretary of State for War and the Colonies, 1821–8), 18, 20, 26, 70–2, 168
    An Inquiry into the Causes and Remedies of Pauperism, 71
Wilson, Dr, 83–4
Wilson, John Cracroft, 292
Woore, Lieutenant Thomas, 142
Wynyard, Colonel Robert (Acting Governor of New Zealand, 1854–1855), 266

Yate, William, 63, 88–9, 95, 98, 101–2, 118, 125–6, 130

www.ingramcontent.com/pod-product-compliance
Lightning Source LLC
Chambersburg PA
CBHW060939230426
43665CB00015B/2001